Monetary Policy in a World of Knowledge-Based Growth, Quality Change and Uncertain Measurement

Monetary Policy in a World of Knowledge-Based Growth, Quality Change and Uncertain Measurement

Edited by

Kunio Okina
Director of the Institute for Monetary and Economic Studies
Bank of Japan

and

Tetsuya Inoue
Manager in the Policy Board Secretariat
Bank of Japan

First published 2001 by
PALGRAVE
Houndmills, Basingstoke, Hampshire RG21 6XS and
175 Fifth Avenue, New York, N. Y. 10010
Companies and representatives throughout the world

PALGRAVE is the new global academic imprint of
St. Martin's Press LLC Scholarly and Reference Division and
Palgrave Publishers Ltd (formerly Macmillan Press Ltd).

ISBN 0–333–74031–9

This book is printed on paper suitable for recycling and made from fully managed and sustained forest sources.

A catalogue record for this book is available from the British Library.

Library of Congress Cataloging-in-Publication Data
Monetary policy in a world of knowledge-based growth, quality change and uncertain measurement / edited by Kunio Okina and Tetsuya Inoue.
    p. cm.
Papers presented at the eighth international conference on the theme 'Monetary policy in a world of knowledge-based growth, quality change, and uncertain measurement' on 18–19 June 1998, held by the Institute for Monetary and Economic Studies, the Bank of Japan.
Includes bibliographical references and index.
ISBN 0–333–74031–9
    1. Monetary policy—Congresses. 2. Technological innovations—
—Economic aspects—Congresses. 3. Information technology—Economic aspects—Congresses. I. Okina, Kunio, 1951– II. Inoue, Tetsuya, 1961–
III. Nihon Ginko. Kin'yu Kenkyujo. IV. Title.

HG230.3 .M6374 2001
332.4'6—dc21
                                                        00–062708

10   9   8   7   6   5   4   3   2   1
10   09   08   07   06   05   04   03   02   01

Printed in Great Britain by Antony Rowe Ltd, Chippenham, Wiltshire

Contents

PART VI   CONCLUDING COMMENTS

PART VII   BACKGROUND PAPER

List of Tables

List of Figures

Preface

The world economy is currently confronting an irreversible trend toward an increasingly conceptual and intangible form of output, and at the same time the fundamental structure of our economy is being subjected to drastic changes. The ever-growing fraction of overall value-added may reflect intellectual components such as computer software, patent rights and so on, which are difficult to measure statistically compared with physical products. These developments have made the conduct of monetary policy more difficult. Not only has the decomposition of output into price and quantitative components become much more difficult than before, but also, in some countries there is considerable uncertainty about the unemployment rate at which the price level begins to accelerate. Because of these difficulties, central banks have come to face growing uncertainty with respect to their policy goals: namely, price stability.

In order to discuss these issues and exchange views with central bankers and academia, the Institute for Monetary and Economic Studies of the Bank of Japan, held its Eighth International Conference on the theme 'Monetary Policy in a World of Knowledge-based Growth, Quality Change, and Uncertain Measurement' on 18–19 June 1998. The publication contains chapters produced from keynote speeches, presentation papers and discussants' comments as well as a background paper.

At the organizing stage of the conference, I was very grateful to Professor Allan H. Meltzer and Professor John B. Taylor, both Honorary Advisers to our Institute, for their helpful advice. I would also like to thank all conference participants for contributing to the discussion on these difficult but timely and important issues. In addition to the participants, many in the Institute also contributed. I would especially like to thank Kazuhiko Ishida, Tetsuya Inoue and Tooru Ohmori for organizing the conference, and Junko Miyoshi, Noriko Furuya and Aki Ino for their secretarial support.

KUNIO OKINA
Director
Institute for Monetary and Economic Studies
Bank of Japan

List of Participants

Halim Alamsyah
Manager, Macroeconomic Studies Division, Bank Indonesia

Palle S. Andersen
Senior Economist, Bank for International Settlements

Kazumi Asako
Professor, Hitotsubashi University

Gan Wee Beng
Advisor, Economics Department, Monetary Authority of Singapore

Paul A. David
William Robertson Coe Professor of American Economic History, Stanford University

William G. Dewald
Senior Vice President and Director of Research, Federal Reserve Bank of St. Louis

W. E. Diewert
University of British Colombia

Frieda Donkers
Advisor with the Research Department, National Bank of Belgium

Jorgen Elmeskov
Counsellor for Structural Policy, Economics Department, Organisation for Economic Co-operation and Development

Roger W. Ferguson, Jr
Member, Board of Governors of the Federal Reserve System

Kevin J. Fox
Senior Lecturer, University of New South Wales

Shin-ichi Fukuda
Assistant Professor, University of Tokyo

Peter M. Garber
Professor, Brown University

Robert J. Gordon
Stanley G. Harris Professor in the Social Sciences, Northwestern University

David W. Gruen
Chief Economist, Economic Analysis Department, Reserve Bank of Australia

Masaru Hayami
Governor, Bank of Japan

Thomas M. Hoenig
President, Federal Reserve Bank of Kansas City

Lex Hoogduin
Co-ordinator of the Counsel to the Executive Board, European Central Bank
Professor of Money and Banking, Groningen University

Kokwang Huh
Senior Advisor, Research Department, Bank of Korea

Tetsuya Inoue
Manager and Senior Economist, Institute for Monetary and Economic Studies, Bank of Japan

Kazuhiko Ishida
Manager and Senior Economist, Institute for Monetary and Economic Studies, Bank of Japan

Takatoshi Ito
Professor, Hitotsubashi University

Nigel Jenkinson
Head, Structural Economic Analysis Division, Bank of England

Charles I. Jones
Assistant Professor, Stanford University

Dale W. Jorgenson
Professor of Economics, Harvard University

Keimei Kaizuka
Professor, Chuo University

Reiner König
Head of Economics Department, Deutsche Bundesbank

Gerard Korteweg
Assistant Manager, Monetary and Economic Policy Department, De Nederlandsche Bank N.V.

Marvin H. Kosters
Resident Scholar and Director, Economic Policy Studies, American Enterprise Institute

Masahiro Kuroda
Professor, Keio University

Hans Lindberg
Deputy Director, Sveriges Riksbank

Robert D. McTeer, Jr
President and Chief Executive Officer, Federal Reserve Bank of Dallas

Allan H. Meltzer
The Allan H. Meltzer University Professor of Political Economy, Carnegie Mellon University

Michael H. Moskow
President, Federal Reserve Bank of Chicago

John D. Murray
Chief, International Department, Bank of Canada

Nobuyuki Nakahara
Member of the Policy Board, Bank of Japan

Kiyohiko G. Nishimura
Professor, University of Tokyo

Koji Nomura
Keio University

Kunio Okina
Director, Institute for Monetary and Economic Studies, Bank of Japan

Masahiro Okuno-Fujiwara
Professor, University of Tokyo

Adrian B. Orr
Chief Manager, Economics Department, Reserve Bank of New Zealand

Robert T. Parry
President and Chief Executive Officer, Federal Reserve Bank of San Francisco

Guido Pellegrini
Economist, Head, Sectoral and Regional Analysis Unit, Research Department, Bank of Italy

Christian Pfister
Deputy Director, Monetary Research and Statistics Division, Banque de France

Hooi Eng Phang
Senior Manager, Economics Department, Bank Negara Malaysia

Georg Rich
Director, Head of Economic Division, Swiss National Bank

Charles Steindel
Senior Vice-President, Federal Reserve Bank of New York

James H. Stock
Professor of Political Economy, Harvard University

Susumu Taketomi
Member of the Policy Board, Bank of Japan

John B. Taylor
Professor of Economics, Stanford University

Mahito Uchida
Chief Manager, Institute for Monetary and Economic Studies, Bank of Japan

Kazuo Ueda
Member of the Policy Board, Bank of Japan

Hal R. Varian
Dean, School of Information Management and Systems, University of California, Berkeley

Jim H. Y. Wong
Senior Manager, Hong Kong Monetary Authority

Duo Xie
Deputy Chief, Open Market Operation Division, The People's Bank of China

Yutaka Yamaguchi
Deputy Governor, Bank of Japan

Eric Yip
Harvard University

Opening Remarks

Masaru Hayami

The Bank of Japan offers special thanks to Honorary Advisers to the Institute for Monetary and Economic Studies, Professor Allan Meltzer and Professor John Taylor, for their valuable advice in preparing the international conference which formed the basis for this revision, and for their kind acceptance of our request to provide the keynote speeches.

Achieving and maintaining price stability has always been our most important task as central bankers. Article 2 of the new Bank of Japan Law, which took effect on April 1 1998, clearly states our mission: 'Currency and monetary control shall be aimed at, through the pursuit of price stability, contributing to the sound development of the national economy'. However, depending on the changing structure of our economy, price measures which central banks should stabilize are not the same. In fact, the current wave of innovation in information technology may be affecting the concept of price stability and the indicators of inflation.

For example, it has been said that an ongoing fall in computer prices can only be compared to those of the railway and electricity in their formative years. At the same time, all types of equipment embodied with information technology have been introduced rapidly into almost all industries. In addition, the chain of intermediate inputs or the existence of externalities will spread the effects to other industries as well. You may have noticed that the current wave of innovation is not temporary in nature.

Thus, the broadness and duration of the wave of innovation in information technology has led us not only to issues of price stability but also to many more questions: whether this wave has become a driving force for changes in the macroeconomic structure; whether the correlation among major economic indicators is still stable; and whether our current system of economic statistics can still convey accurate macroeconomic information.

These are the most important reasons why the organizers of the Eighth International Conference chose its theme to be, 'Monetary Policy in a World of Knowledge-based Growth, Quality Change, and Uncertain Measurement'. Now, I hope our task and goal for this conference is clear: theoretically and empirically investigating the mechanisms for overall effects of the wave of innovation of our times, reviewing problems with the current system of economic statistics, and discussing how we can more efficiently conduct monetary policy in such an evolving world of economy.

Although our task may appear to be very challenging, we certainly recognize that the participants of this conference have the strongest background to discuss the issues related to this theme. Our new law establishes the Bank of Japan's framework on the principles of 'Independence' and 'Transparency'. With the principle of transparency in mind, we welcome this opportunity to exchange our views with both domestic and foreign economists. We hope this conference will serve as a cornerstone for future academic innovation in this area, and will lead to more efficient policy through exciting discussion with fellow central bankers and academic economists.

Reader's Guide

Tetsuya Inoue

Before we proceed to the main text of the book, I will summarize it briefly. For further details of the theme of the conference upon which it is based, please refer to the background paper at the end of the book, Chapter 14 (a summary is included in this Reader's Guide).

Keynote Presentation

Both of the keynote speeches given by the honorary advisers of the Institute address the main theme of the conference: that is, the conduct of monetary policy under the irreversible trend of knowledge-based economy.

Professor Allan H. Meltzer confirms that, because of the impact of Information Technology (IT), it is becoming harder to measure accurately economic statistics that are indispensable for optimal monetary policy. He also shows empirically that there exist some stable long-term relationships between nominal macroeconomic indicators and base-money in Japan, the United States of America and Germany. Based on these findings, he asserts that central banks can achieve the goal of monetary policy by utilizing such stable relationships.

Professor John B. Taylor points out that it has conflicting implications for the conduct of monetary policy. While increasing uncertainty about policy goals and tools hampers efficient monetary policy, central banks are able to tackle such uncertainty by analyzing a variety of economic models and the effects of different kinds of shock with the help of fast-processing computers. He claims that the latter can be dominant. He also adds that, under such uncertainty, it is more important to maintain some robust policy rules in achieving the ultimate policy goal.

Part I

The first part, entitled 'The Overview and Case Study of the Development of a Knowledge-based Economy', mainly compares the impact of current IT innovation with major innovations in past industrial revolutions. Discussion covers implications obtained from historical analysis of past industrial revolutions, and characteristics of the information goods that are central to current innovation.

The principal message of Professor Paul A. David's chapter is that, in order to understand the impact of current IT innovation, we should examine in detail the impact of the advent of electrification at the beginning of the twentieth century. He points out three common characteristics concerning 'general purpose technology' (GPT). First, in the early years after its introduction, it is not possible to evaluate the effect on aggregate production. Second, it is not until the spread of a new GPT that the increase in 'total factor productivity' (TFP) can be identified. Third, in order for a new GPT to have a strong impact, complementary innovations and overall changes in industrial organization are indispensable. In addition, he insists that educating unskilled labour is an important role for the public sector. Governor Roger W. Ferguson, Jr suggests that we may have grasped the effects of IT as an increase in TFP, since the cost of switching to computers is much smaller than that of switching to electricity. He also agrees with Professor David about the role of the public sector.

Hal R. Varian deals with the characteristics of information goods and their implications for the actual market economy. He recognizes that information goods pose serious difficulties for neoclassical economic models, since they have such characteristics as experience goods, increasing returns to scale, and public goods. He shows, however, market mechanism so far deals with such goods rather well; for example, monitoring, browsing, reviewing, monopolistic competition, and patents are the devices for transactions. But he adds that we will have to seek creative solutions for information overload problems. Professor Masahiro Okuno-Fujiwara claims that we should limit patent term and content, and promote the development of substitutes. He also believes that the reduction in communication costs has helped the activities of NGOs and NPOs.

Professor Kiyohiko G. Nishimura, Dr Toshiaki Watanabe, and Dr Kentaro Iwatsubo discuss theoretically the impact of IT innovation on asset price movements, and through his empirical study examines its magnitude. They show the conflicting effects of IT innovation on asset markets: first, asset prices may be stable because of reduced transaction costs; second, all participants may be able to obtain information easily; and third, asset prices may be unstable because of the entry of uninformed investors. Then, using a theoretical model with the assumption of asymmetric information, they show that the sensitivity of prices increases as a result of more diverse expectations on the part of buyers, and that sellers may be able to control such expectations. They also show empirically that the expectations of Tokyo Stock Exchange participants have diverged increasingly in recent years. Hans Lindberg suggests that Professor Nishimura should seek a clearer indicator of IT innovation and analyze the relationship between market participants' heterogeneity and transaction volume.

Part II

The title of this part is 'The Productivity Paradox and Mismeasurement Problems', in which explanatory hypotheses and countermeasures to 'the productivity paradox' discussed. Analyses of the effects of introducing new goods and services, and those of quality change, are presented. We discuss how to improve the estimation of TFP and output of service industries.

Professor Masahiro Kuroda and Dr Koji Nomura offer an explanatory hypothesis for 'the productivity paradox' by introducing new concepts of TFP (static-unit-TFP and dynamic-unit-TFP). First, they outline the paradoxical movements of TFP in both Japan and the USA, and put forward a variety of explanatory hypotheses. They then explain the estimation of these new TFPs. Static-unit-TFP is estimated by considering the contribution from other industries along with capital and labour inputs, whereas dynamic-unit-TFP is estimated from static-unit-TFP plus other historical inputs to form the capital. Finally, they show, from his estimate of dynamic-unit-TFP, that innovation in Japan has had no paradoxical effect. Jorgen Elmeskov claims the existence of 'the productivity paradox' based on his estimates of OECD countries, and takes up the empirical problem of how to deal with the speed at which computer capital becomes obsolete. Professor Kazumi Asako suggests that Professor Kuroda should consider other propagation channels for innovation than the capital coefficient.

Professor W. Erwin Diewert and Dr Kevin J. Fox discuss the cause of 'the productivity paradox' from the viewpoint of mismeasurement in economic statistics. They point out drawbacks to the explanatory hypotheses such as the lag in propagation of a new GPT, or the relatively small share of computer stock in aggregate capital. They, then explain the quality change bias as a representative example of mismeasurement, and examine such errors in some service industries. They suggest that more resources should be devoted to improving the quality of economic statistics, and draw attention to the possibility that regulatory and tax systems may distort the price mechanisms of goods and services. Dr Charles Steindel questions why so much importance should be attached to mismeasurement problems, since the quality of economic statistics has been greatly improved. He also believes that the problem may not be so serious for the conduct of monetary policy although it may be important for considering medium-term economic growth.

Part III

In Part III, entitled 'Implication of a Knowledge-based Economy on Economic Growth and Labour Market', the macroeconomic impact of IT innovation is discussed in detail, using economic growth models and aggregate data. This part saves as an introduction to Part IV, which discusses the conduct of monetary policy.

Professor Dale W. Jorgenson and Dr Eric Yip review the cause of the long-term economic growth from the viewpoint of changes in investment and productivity. First, they explain the methodology for allocating the sources of economic growth between investment and productivity. Using their empirical study based on the historical data of the G-7 countries, they show that, while the contribution of investment has been overwhelming, that of productivity has fallen dramatically since 1973. They also test the hypothesis of neoclassical theory that relative levels of output per capita must converge in the long run. Finally, they provide alternative approaches to endogenous growth by introducing the concept of human capital. Dr Reiner König asserts that the public sector should be more active in promoting investment, including knowledge-based capital and retraining older workers. As for empirical studies, he points out that human capital should be treated more carefully, since its aggregate data may contain mismeasurements.

Dr Charles I. Jones examines the effect of the diffusion of new ideas using the 'new growth theory' model. He points out that the characteristics of information, such as non-rivalry and difficulty in exclusion, are sources of increasing returns to scale and monopolistic competition in a knowledge-based economy. Then, using the economic growth model and assuming increasing returns to scale, he illustrates the importance of R & D activity for economic growth by simulating the impact of Japanese R & D on global economic growth. He also emphasizes the importance of intellectual property rights for promoting such activities. Dr Lex Hoogduin points out that calibration should be performed more carefully and R & D modelled as an endogenous activity. Dr Shin-ichi Fukuda suggests extending the model, such as simulating the effects of the global diffusion of a new idea, and analyzing the effects of both increasing returns to scale in R & D activities as well as the accumulation of human capital.

Dr Marvin H. Kosters deals with the effects of IT innovation on the labour market by studying USA. He shows empirically that wage inequality has been widening to an unusual degree, but adds that its adverse social and political consequences have been limited by the absence of pronounced cleavages between groups of workers. He also points out that, in the skilled labour market, supply has been outstripped by a strong growth in demand. Although it is argued that the average worker's wage has declined, and that layoffs have heightened vulnerability to losing jobs, he insists that such arguments have been based on partial and incomplete measures. At the same time, he admits that the mechanism for the favourable combination of employment and inflation has not been well understood. Palle S. Andersen suggests that both the change in the international division of manufacturing and the fall in capital costs have contributed to low unemployment in the USA. As for the relationship between IT innovation and the labour market, he agrees with Dr Kosters, since development of the non-accelerating inflation rate of unemployment (NAIRU) is so divergent in European countries. He also insists that we should consider the trade-off between fairness and efficiency in evaluating the welfare effect of IT innovation on the labour market.

Part IV

The last part is entitled 'Monetary Policy under the Irreversible Trend of a Knowledge-based Economy', which examines the mechanism through which IT innovation changes the macroeconomy, and discusses the conduct of monetary policy under such unstable circumstances.

Professor Robert J. Gordon examines the concern of central bankers regarding the changes caused by IT innovation, and takes up explanatory hypotheses for 'the productivity paradox'. He shows that IT innovation has acted as a beneficial supply shock that has improved the inflation–unemployment trade-off, particularly in the 1990s. But he questions the existence and importance of 'the productivity paradox' itself. He insists that little evidence has been found that productivity growth has slowed down more than the average in sectors where their activities are hard to measure. He adds that the most dramatic productivity improvement has been limited to the computer manufacturing industry.

Professor James H. Stock considers the effects of the trend towards knowledge-based production on indicators for conducting monetary policy, and its resulting implications for policy rules. He shows empirically that the relationship between such a trend and the development of NAIRU is not clear at the present time. However, he recognizes that NAIRU and other key macroeconomic relations have shifted, which introduces important uncertainties for policy-makers. Through his study of a small macroeconomic model of the USA which assumes stochastic parameters, he suggests that a central bank facing uncertainty about the structure of the economy should consider policies that are more aggressive than have been suggested by most theoretical models.

Michael H. Moskow shows that the characteristics of our economy – such as falls in productivity growth and in prices of new capital goods – can be identified in the Industrial Revolution, and supports the 'time-lag' hypothesis for 'the productivity paradox'. He also suggests that policy-makers should consider seriously the effects of market participants' unstable expectations because of substantial changes in interest rates. At the same time, he recognizes that policy-makers should seek the stability of the final goal rather than that of the operational goal. Professor Takatoshi Ito points out that the underdevelopment of software industries and their particular characteristics in labour markets as the reasons why NAIRU in Japan has not fallen so far. He also suggests that, with the development of IT innovation, 'Lucas Critique' may be more relevant, since it might be easier for market participants to expect a policy action by a central bank. Dr George Rich points out the importance of introducing a structural relationship in the macroeconomy for estimating NAIRU. He also points out that the simulation model has specification problems, such as the lag of monetary policy to inflation and the lasting nature of shocks. Finally, he emphasizes that money supply control is effective in Switzerland, since the relation between money supply and nominal aggregate indicators is stable.

Part VI

Professor Peter M. Garber, in Concluding Comments, suggests some future extensions to this research project. He believes that the conference has some useful implications for studies of the impact of IT innovation on the industrial sector, and recognizes that discussion of the mismeasurement of economic statistics is fruitful. However, he argues that further comprehensive study and discussion of the impact of IT innovation on macroeconomic structure such as NAIRU, economic growth and inflation is necessary. Also, as another goal of this research project, he suggests that the impact of IT innovation on the financial market and the central bank itself should be examined. He points out that, because of IT innovation, financial market transactions have changed drastically and prices become more unstable. He also emphasizes that it may be necessary for a central bank to consider how to make speedier policy judgements to prevent systemic risk, and to examine the effects of introducing electronic money on its balance sheet.

Part VII

In the final part of the book, Chapter 14, I offer a background to the International Conference, outlining the issues discussed and surveying studies and analyses in fields related to the theme. The chapter is in two halves: the first covers discussions on the propagation mechanisms of IT innovation, and the impact on the economy. Here is insisted that switching costs from existing technologies and network externalities may play important roles at the microeconomic level. In addition to aggregation effects, the possibility that the cost of reallocating capital and retraining labour may hamper macro-economic performance is discussed. It is also argued that mismeasurement in economic statistics may prevent us from making optimal decisions. In the second half of the chapter, discussion covers the conduct of monetary policy, focusing on price mechanisms. It is suggested that policy-makers should be careful as to whether to accommodate the supply shock caused by IT innovation, or not, considering the possibility of nominal rigidities or change in the relationship between relative prices and general price level. It is also claimed that mismeasurement in price indexes may damage the credibility of a central bank by making it difficult to observe the achievement of a policy commitment.

Part I
Keynote Speeches

1
Monetary Policy and the Quality of Information*

Allan H. Meltzer

The personal computer and the development of websites permit everyone to have rapid access to enormous quantities of data. If it were ever true that policy analysis in developed countries was hindered by availability of timely information, that restriction has now all but disappeared. Data in developed countries become available to all interested parties everywhere almost as soon as they are put out.

The organizers of the Bank of Japan's eight international conference ask us to consider an important question: has the quality of information increased commensurately? Do we now know substantially more about what is happening in the world or in our own countries? Or, has the increase in information lagged far behind the increase in data that central bankers and financial markets receive?

One important issue of this kind is the measurement of productivity and economic growth. In developed countries, especially, and in many developing countries to a lesser degree, service sector output has grown relative to agricultural output. In developing countries, the share of agricultural and manufacturing output in total output and employment peaked some time ago. A significant share of employment is now in government, financial services, health care, education and other services, where output is difficult to measure with precision or, often, to measure at all.

If one cannot measure output reliably, one cannot know what is happening to the price level. Recent, extensive discussion of the several biases affecting the US consumer price index suggests that the bias in the index may be as much as 1.5 per cent. A central bank seeking to maintain price stability has difficulties enough without adding uncertainty about the level that it seeks to maintain.

The problem is not limited to the price level and output. In the USA, and no doubt elsewhere, there is considerable uncertainty about the unemployment rate at which the price level begins to accelerate, or NAIRU, and a sizable shift

* My thanks to Randolph Stempski for his assistance.

3

in mainstream beliefs. A standard range for NAIRU of 6 to 6.5 per cent a few years ago has been adjusted down to 5 per cent or below.[1]

These examples are not meant to be exhaustive. Others could be added without changing the point. The main issues for monetary policy-makers and economists lies not in the number of examples but in their consequences for effective policy. Two issues are critical: whether the quality of information has worsened and, if so, whether the reduced quality significantly changes the opportunities for monetary policy or requires a shift in the way monetary policy is conducted.

I reach a mixed conclusion. The following section looks at changes in data for US gross domestic product (GDP) over time. I find that short-term movements are now much less variable, and there is evidence of a change in the trend rate of growth. Next I consider whether there is sufficient stability over time in nominal magnitudes and their relation to money growth to be useful for policy in Germany, Japan and the USA. I conclude that there is sufficient stability in monetary relations to support a policy of monetary control if policy-makers take a long-term view.

The changing quality of data

Most measures of output, employment or productivity on which we rely are of recent origin. Pioneering work in the measurement of gross national product (GNP) was done in the 1930s by Kuznets and others. Much of what is reported for the years before the Second World War was constructed long after the event. Often data for GNP are based on relatively few underlying series.

Data for real GNP growth show a major change in the postwar years. Measured variability declines sharply. There is nothing comparable to the depressions of 1920–2 or 1929–33. And reported quarterly values are also much less variable. Figure 1.1 shows the Balke and Gordon (1986) data for the USA. Data for prices and rates of price change would show a persistent trend rate of inflation but substantially lower variability around the trend after the Second World War. Recent research suggests that part of the increased variability in earlier years is spurious, a result of building GNP from the few series that are available (see Watson, 1994). Nevertheless, some of the underlying series were the data available to policy-makers when they made their decisions.

Answering the questions that central bankers now ask was harder, not easier, in the 1920s and 1930s. The much greater variance would have made it relatively more difficult to separate temporary from permanent changes in GNP, if these data had been available. The risk of over-or under-response to short-term changes would have been greater and, with it, the prospect of increasing variability.

Since GNP or GDP was not available, central bankers used substitutes – generally less comprehensive measures of economic activity and prices than

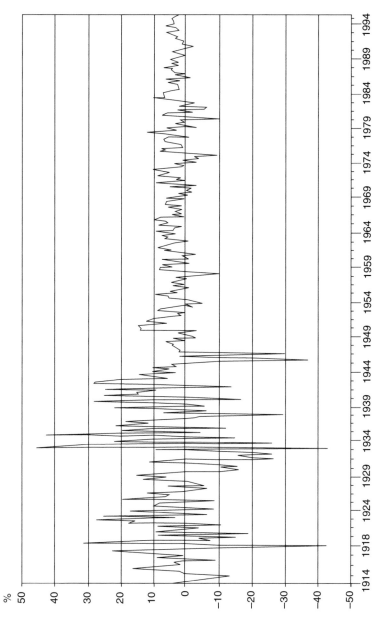

Figure 1.1 United States, annualized quarterly real GNP growth

are available now. Central banks often took the lead in developing or improving measures of industrial production, prices, department store sales and other measures of activity. However, in the 1920s and after, central bankers relied heavily on proxy measures of activity such as the growth of credit or changes in member bank borrowing from the central bank. Excess reserves of member banks had a similar role in the mid-1930s (see Friedman and Schwartz, 1963).[2]

Imprecise data did not prevent the Federal Reserve from maintaining low inflation and steady growth interrupted only by brief recessions in 1923–4 and 1926–7. Nor did it prevent Federal Reserve officials from recognizing recessions when they occurred. This period is generally judged to have been one of the most successful in Federal Reserve history. Friedman and Schwartz (1963) call it the system's 'high tide'.

As is well known, the period of relative stability ended in the great depression. The main causes of the depression were policy mistakes, not imprecise data. The Federal Reserve, and much of the world, believed in the real bills doctrine, so they regarded the use of credit in the stock market as evidence of inflation. And while there was widespread agreement about the stabilizing properties of the gold standard, neither France nor the USA was willing to follow gold standard rules when they called for domestic inflation (see Meltzer, 1997).

Again, the quality of data had no role in the great inflation from 1965 to 1980. After 1971, inflation in developed countries differed markedly in ways that depend very much on the theories or beliefs guiding central banks, or the goals they pursued, and very little on differences in the quantity or quality of information. Freed from the restraints imposed by the Bretton Woods system, Japan, Germany and Switzerland adopted policies leading to low inflation. The USA, the UK and France chose very different policies and produced very different results.

The major welfare losses resulting from the great depression or the great inflation owed little to lack of information. Can a better case be made for more normal periods?

US real GDP is often approximated by a random walk along a growth trend. The assumption of a constant trend within each of the two periods, 1951–73 and 1973–97, is well supported by the data. Differences between the two periods are relatively small; the main difference is the estimated trend. As is well known, trend growth of GDP was lower in the second period. The first two rows of Table 1.1 show estimates for

$$y_t = a + b y_{t-1} + u_t$$

where y_t is quarterly US GDP growth at annual rates.

To reduce some of the noise, the last two rows of Table 1.1 repeat the comparison for the two periods with y_t measured as a four-quarter moving

Table 1.1 GDP growth as a random walk (standard errors below the coefficients)

Period	a	b	s.e.	DW
1951/1–1973/1	0.025	0.34	.041	1.96
	0.006	0.10		
1973/2–1997/4	0.018	0.29	.034	2.01
	0.004	0.09		
1951/1–1973/1	0.008	0.78	.016	1.03
	0.003	0.06		
1973/2–1997/4	0.004	0.83	.012	1.29
	0.002	0.05		

average. The smoothed data show a much larger response to their lagged value and, as expected, serial correlation increases markedly.[3]

The data in Table 1.1 show no evidence of substantial change in the process underlying US GDP growth. Of course, a relatively small recent change in trend may be hidden within the range covered by the standard error. To check on this possibility, I used a unit dummy variable for the expansion beginning in second quarter, 1991. The results show no evidence of a shift in trend growth. The coefficient of the dummy variable using quarterly data from 1973 to 1997 is 0.002 ± 0.008. Similar results are found using a four-quarter moving average. These findings provide no evidence of an important shift in trend. The point estimate, though not significant, suggests that the trend could be 2/10 of 1 per cent higher in the 1990s.[4] A change of this magnitude is well within the control error for monetary policy and has no significance for policy.

One solution for central banks and governments is to invest heavily in measurement and data gathering. Another is to develop procedures that are less subject to measurement errors. Although some improvements in data quality would be cost-effective, conceptual problems limit possibilities for improving measures of service sector output.

Unless the size of measurement errors changes frequently, difficulties in measuring prices and output do not carry over fully to output growth and inflation. By basing decisions on rates of change, central banks can avoid some of the measurement problems. They would not know the 'true' growth rate or rate of inflation, but they would have useful information about acceleration and deceleration of prices and output. This information could be used with a policy of controlling nominal GDP.

Velocity and interest rates

Monetary measures and nominal interest rates are much less influenced by problems arising in the measurement of prices or the productivity of capital and labour. The long-term interest rate reflects the expected productivity of capital, expected inflation, and any risk premium that the market demands for holding non-monetary assets. The long-term interest rate would change with a change in perceived productivity or its rate of change. Monetary velocity is the ratio of nominal GDP (GNP) to nominal money, so the division between productivity and price changes has no effect on velocity.

Innovation and productivity changes also affect financial instruments. The preferred definition of money is the one least subject to major change. The monetary base, consisting mainly of currency on the uses side, is less subject to change through innovation than other monetary aggregates. It is not free of all influences of this kind. Credit cards are substitutes for currency. Electronic payments may become important in the future.

This section looks at the relationship of base velocity to interest rates in Germany, Japan and the USA. Base velocity is the ratio of nominal GNP or GDP to the monetary base. Nominal GDP is unaffected by biases in the measurement of prices and output, although it may be subject to change arising from increases in market activity relative to non-market activity, leisure or unreported transactions.

If base velocity has a relatively stable relationship to an interest rate, a central bank can influence nominal GNP by changing the monetary base. Moreover, stability of the relationship over time would suggest that the velocity relationship is independent of productivity change. Evidence of this kind would suggest that the relationship is robust, and hence useful for policy operations.

United States of America

Figure 1.2 shows the relationship of monetary base velocity to a long-term interest rate in the USA, quarterly, for 306 quarters from the beginning of 1919 to the middle of 1995. All observations are included: depressions and recessions, wars, inflations and deflations, periods of price control, and periods with very different rates of productivity change.

The points in the figure cover a wide range: interest rates from 2 per cent to 14 per cent, velocity from about 5 to 20. Two periods show persistent deviations from what appears to be almost a textbook drawing of the relationship between velocity and an interest rate. From 1919 to 1923, and from 1931 to 1934, the data lie above the curve. Relative to the long-term relationship, velocity is lower than expected for the prevailing interest rates. Both periods include sizeable deflations; periods when the return to holding money was positive. Both are also periods of heightened uncertainty. Allowing for these influences removes at least part of the discrepancy.

The deflation following the First World War caused many bankruptcies. The gold standard was not restored until later in the decade. This was a fact of great importance to many businesses and bankers at the time; one that altered their anticipations. A new institution, the Federal Reserve, faced its first major recession.

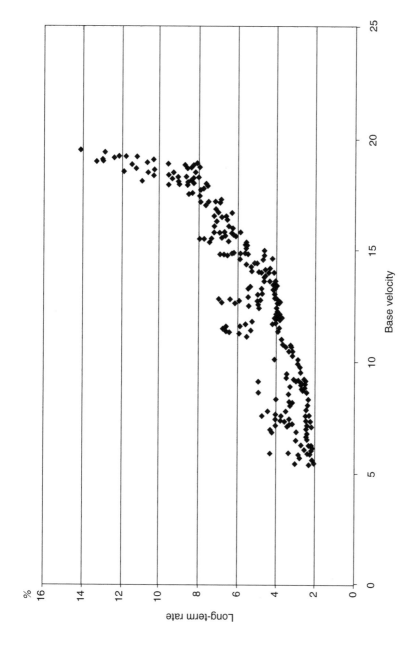

Figure 1.2 United States, base velocity versus long-term Treasury Bond rate, 1919:I–1995:II

The period 1931–3 raised doubts about the survival of the financial system and capitalism. Uncertainty, deflation, or both together, encouraged increased money holdings relative to output, so velocity is smaller than expected from the relationship. In both periods, therefore, money-holding should rise relative to GNP, thus reducing velocity. And the shift in demand for money, resulting from the higher pecuniary and non-pecuniary return to money-holding, raised the interest rate.

The data in figure 1.2 help to answer the question about the importance of measurement bias for monetary policy. Data points for the 1950s and 1960s lie on top of points for the 1920s. When the long-term rate returned to the level reached in the late 1920s, velocity also returned to that level. Further, when the long-term rate and velocity declined with falling inflation in the 1980s and 1990s, the points descended along the path followed during the period of rising inflation in the 1970s.

There is no evidence of a significant shift in the velocity relationship, or instability, during the almost eighty years covered by these data. Because the points in Figure 1.2 overlap in several periods, Figure 1.3 shows the same data smoothed using an eight-quarter moving average. I chose eight quarters to represent the medium-term over which many central bankers claim to operate.

Some comment on the use of a long-term interest rate is in order. This is the rate I have used in previous work on the demand for money. Aside from consistency, the use of the long-term rate reflects the Brunner and Meltzer (1972) general equilibrium model of assets, output and price level. In that model, short-term rates depend principally on activity in banking or credit markets, while the long-term rate more fully reflects the expected return to real capital, expected inflation, and the effects of productivity change. If these disrupt or alter the relationships with velocity, because of changes in the quality of monetary or output data, the data will show the problem. Use of a long-term rate also reflects the hypothesis that, even in periods of high inflation, a central bank can reduce a short-term rate temporarily, both absolutely as well as relative to the long rate. Unless expectations of persistent inflation change, the long-term rate will change much less than the short-rate, and the demand for money (and velocity) will continue to be dominated by the anticipation of long-term inflation or deflation. For these reasons, I continue to treat the long-term rate as being relevant for velocity, but I do not exclude additional, or supplemental, effects from a short-term rate.

Germany

Hyperinflation and political division limit the availability of data for Germany. For part of the period after the Second World War there is no long-term debt. I have used quarterly data for twenty-five years, 1972 to 1997 (101 observations in all). Data for the (long-term) interest rate on the public debt range from 5 to 11, data for velocity from about 11 to 18.

11

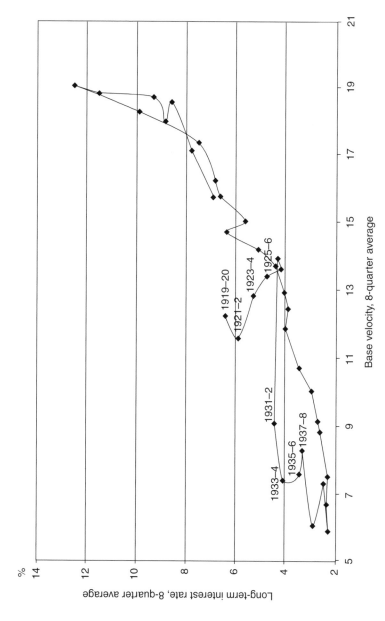

Figure 1.3   United States, base velocity versus long-term interest rate, 8-quarter averages

12

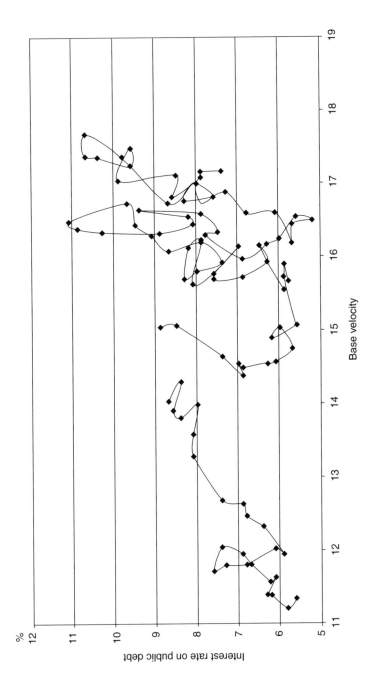

Figure 1.4 Germany, base velocity versus interest rate on public debt, 1972:I–1997:I
The left side of the chart shows the data after unification.

The slope and position of the relationship appears to change at the time of reunification. Nevertheless, in both periods, points with different dates lie above one another. These data again suggest that, for the period examined, there is little evidence that measurement errors, changes in intermediation or other changes in financial structure that would mislead a central bank attempting to follow a medium-term strategy of controlling inflation using the monetary base (or central bank money) as its instrument. This conclusion is supported partly by the experience of the Federal Republic where control of money, using a broader monetary aggregate, is the means of implementing the central bank's medium-term strategy (see Issuing, 1997).

Japan

Japanese data offer some challenge, but they do not contradict the conclusion about problems associated with productivity measurement error. After the early 1970s, Japan's average real growth rate fell from about 7–10 per cent to 4–5 per cent. In the 1990s, the average growth rate declined again. The first decline, coming at the time of the oil shock and the first postwar revaluation of the yen following the so-called Nixon shock, heightened uncertainty about future growth. The steep increase in oil prices was mitigated by a 15–20 per cent appreciation of the yen against the dollar, but the combined effect was a steep increase in the imported price of oil and the dollar price of Japanese exports.

The second large shock came at the end of the boom in the 1980s. Again, there was a large appreciation of the yen after the internationally co-ordinated attempt to manage exchange rates failed. And again there was substantial uncertainty about future growth, as suggested by the decline in the index of common stock prices from almost 40 000 to about 15 000.

A striking feature of Figure 1.5 is the similarity of the movement in velocity relative to the interest rate in the years 1972–6 and 1987–92. The two periods – one following the oil shock; the other following the so-called 'bubble' economy–are clearly visible in Figure 1.5. In both cases, base velocity declines at first; and money-holders increase cash balances relative to GDP. This behaviour in the face of rapid change and heightened uncertainty has an effect on velocity similar in direction but larger in magnitude to the effect of the 1920s and 1930s deflations in the USA and reunification in Germany. In each of these cases, velocity is lower for a given interest rate during the period of heightened uncertainty. Again, the data suggest that in these periods of uncertainty and/or deflation, the return to holding money rose, and the demand for base money increased.

In Japan, as in the USA, velocity returned to a stable path relating base velocity to a long-term interest rate. For Japan, the path is much clearer, using annual rather than quarterly data, but the number of Japanese data points is therefore limited. Opportunity to extend the annual data is restricted by the absence of long-term government debt in the early postwar decades.

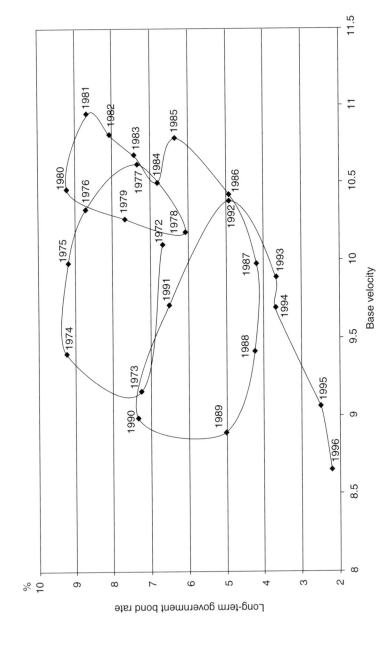

Figure 1.5 Japan, base velocity versus long-term Government Bond rate

The two periods pose a challenge to economic analysis. The data suggest that similar processes were at work – that whatever happened to the relationship of money to output during the so-called 'bubble years' had happened before. The challenge is to go behind the bubble to see if systematic forces are at work.

Figure 1.6 suggests some similarity in the way in which the rise in velocity occurred in the two periods. At the start of both periods, the monetary base rose absolutely and relative to nominal GDP. Then the base decelerated sharply, preceded by deceleration of output in one case, and followed by deceleration of output in the other. In both periods, short-term interest rates rose at first, then declined. The decline in interest rates followed deceleration of the monetary base. Judged by the deceleration of the monetary base, monetary policy was contractive in both 1974–5 and 1990–2. Judged by the decline in short-term interest rates, monetary policy was expansive after both 1973 and 1989. In both periods, growth of nominal GDP either declined or remained low, as suggested by monetary base growth.

A second similarity is that both periods are preceded by large changes in the nominal exchange rate. From 1971 to 1986, the yen/dollar exchange appreciated more than 50 per cent, from 360 to 168.[5] Much of this movement occurred in two periods: in 1971–2 and 1985–6, the years before the two puzzling sequences. The Louvre agreement to fix exchange rates within a band slowed the appreciation after 1986, but required the Bank of Japan to accelerate the monetary base. Growth of the base rose from 6 per cent per year to 14 per cent. Base growth remained above a 10 per cent annual rate until the spring of 1990. In the 12–18 months following April 1990, base growth declined from 10 per cent or more to 2 per cent or less. The deflationary impulse continued with modest change until 1996. Figure 1.7 shows the magnitude and sharpness of these changes in the 12-month moving average.

Preliminary Conclusion

Three preliminary conclusions about central bank control of a nominal aggregate can be drawn from these charts. First, a central bank that relies on the stability of the velocity relationship would have problems following a medium-term strategy only when there are very large changes in the economy. For Japan, periods of heightened uncertainty accompanied by large currency revaluations disrupted the velocity relationship for a time. In the following section I show that, with a modest addition, the bivariate relationship remains useful even in these years. For the USA, severe deflation interfered temporarily with the bivariate relationship in the past, but it was restored and remains useful. For Germany, uncertainties associated with reunification, and reunification itself, produced one off changes in the relationship that appear to have persisted. Second, many of these changes had their origin in public policy – deflation in the USA, monetary aspects of German reunification and substantial acceleration or deceleration of the monetary base in Japan.[6] Third,

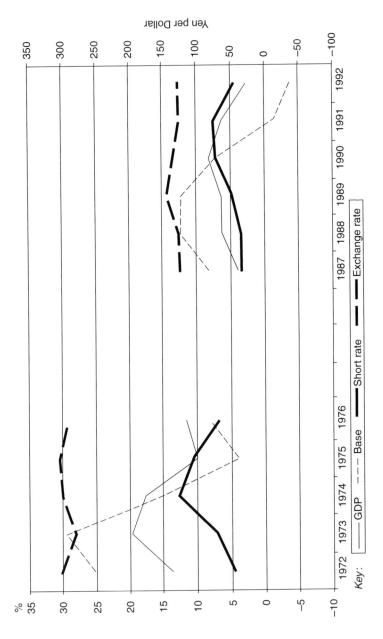

Figure 1.6 Japan, nominal GDP growth, money market rate, exchange rate and monetary base growth, 1972–6 and 1987–92

Key: GDP —— Base – – – Short rate ▬▬ Exchange rate ▬ ▬

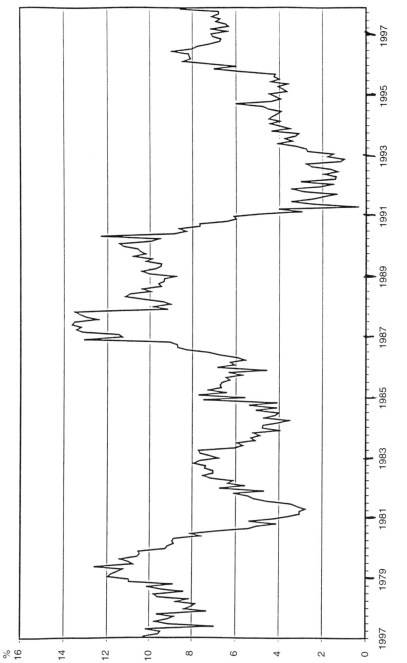

Figure 1.7 Japan, monetary base growth, 12-month moving average

there is no evidence of drift or disturbance resulting from changes in productivity and financial innovation, or from changes in the quality of information.

Some econometric evidence

An important research finding of the past twenty years is that many economic time series are reasonably well described as random walks at quarterly, or shorter, frequencies. This section investigates whether monetary policy, acting through its effects on anticipated inflation and the expected return to capital, has a statistically significant effect on monetary velocity after allowing for a random walk.

United States of America

Table 1.2 shows two different sets of regressions using logarithms of annual data for the USA in two periods, 1920–94 and 1960–96. The first data set uses high-powered money (the monetary base) from Friedman and Schwartz (1963). These data do not adjust for changes in reserve requirement ratios. The interest rate is a long-term bond rate; its maturity changes with debt management practice. The second data set removes these problems by using the St. Louis monetary base and a 10-year bond rate. This measure of the base adjusts for changes in reserve requirement ratios by removing or adding the reserve equivalent of changes in reserve requirement ratios.[7]

The equations that use an AR1 correction to adjust for serial correlation show a significant effect of interest rates on velocity in both periods. The different point estimates for the two periods are economically, but not statistically, significant.

Table 1.3 repeats these estimates using first differences of the logarithms. The estimated interest elasticities are about the same for levels and first differences. The significant effect of lagged changes in velocity in the 1964–96

Table 1.2 Annual regressions for velocity

Period	i_t	V_{t-1}	c	AR1	R^2	DW
1920–94	0.03	0.94	0.11		0.94	1.33
	(0.67)	(14.24)	(1.11)			
1921–94	0.27	0.56	0.67	0.65	0.96	1.75
	(3.33)	(3.80)	(2.40)	(4.37)		
1960–96	0.11	0.68	0.69		0.96	1.29
	(4.09)	(10.42)	(4.93)			
1961–96	0.11	0.66	0.77	0.37	0.97	1.96
	(4.00)	(8.44)	(4.22)	(2.06)		

Notes: All data are logarithms; t-statistics in parentheses; interest rate is long-term rate. The table is reproduced from Meltzer (1998).

Table 1.3 Annual regressions for velocity growth

Period	Δi_t	ΔV_{t-1}	c	AR1	R^2	DW
1921–94	0.19	0.26	0.003		0.14	1.71
	(2.25)	(2.42)	(0.32)			
1922–94	0.24	0.05	0.002	0.32	0.16	1.85
	(2.84)	(0.16)	(0.13)	(1.04)		
1963–96	0.09	0.36	0.002		0.32	2.24
	(3.20)	(2.54)	(0.42)			
1964–96	0.09	0.48	0.001	–0.23	0.32	2.05
	(3.18)	(2.83)	(0.34)	(1.02)		

Notes: See notes to Table 1.2.

period suggests that, at annual frequency, velocity does not follow a simple random walk. This evidence suggests persistent effects of changes in payments arrangements and other technological changes affecting the payments system. Innovations such as credit cards, automated teller machines, and other changes in financial arrangements, permanently increase the velocity level. They do not appear to make the velocity relationship unstable.[8] There is no evidence of instability that would stop the Federal Reserve from achieving its medium-term goal for nominal GDP or its growth rate.

Japan

Row 1 of Table 1.4 shows annual estimates for Japan using the same specification as for the USA. The coefficients for Japan are similar to postwar estimates for the USA, using the comparable specification. Both estimates for Japan show significant effects of anticipated inflation and productivity growth operating on velocity via the long-term interest rate.

Table 1.4 Regressions for Japan

Period	i_t	V_{t-1}	V_{t-2}	P_t	var_t ($\times 10000$)	AR1	R^2 DW
1973–96	0.09	0.69				0.50	0.80
	(1.78)	(2.24)				(1.06)	1.90
1972–96	0.06	1.11	–0.59				0.84
	(4.37)	(8.56)	(4.87)				2.09
1972–96	0.14			–0.79	1.17		0.46
	(4.01)			(2.80)	(1.34)		(1.00)
1972–96	0.13			–0.67	0.66	0.47	0.57
	(3.07)			(2.08)	(0.83)	(2.51)	(1.16)
1972–96	0.11	0.55		–0.41			0.71
	(3.62)	(4.01)		(1.69)			1.05

Notes: V_t and i_t are logarithms of fourth-quarter values; p_t is the current inflation rate; and var_t is the variance of monthly exchange rates; p_t and var_t are decimals.

As expected from Figure 1.5 (see page 14), the equation for Japan fits less well than comparable equations for the USA or Germany. In discussing Figure 1.5, I suggested that deflation provides a positive return to holding money. The demand for money or velocity should reflect this return, in addition to the opportunity cost of holding money. Similarly, inflation may impose a cost of holding money that is not fully reflected in a single market interest rate. To test this suggestion and the effect of uncertainty, rows 3 and 4 of Table 1.4 introduce the measured rate of inflation (p_t) and the average monthly variance of the nominal exchange rate (var$_t$).

The data give better support to the additional effect of inflation, given the interest rate, than to the measure of uncertainty used in this test. The results are suggestive only. I have used actual inflation instead of expected inflation, and have not tried other measures of uncertainty. A measure such as the spread between yields on risky bonds and government bonds may do better.

Row 5 shows that the effect of inflation remains after reintroducing $\ln V_{t-1}$ in the regression. An AR1 correction did not converge after twenty iterations and was not significant when convergence was achieved after more than forty iterations.

Figure 1.8 shows that, including the effects of inflation and uncertainty, (as in row 4 of Table 1.4) improves the fit. The large deviations from 1973 to 1975 are substantially reduced. The same is true of 1988 and 1991, two years with large deviations in Figure 1.5. Errors in 1989 and 1990 are reduced but remain relatively large.[9]

Previous estimates of the demand for base money in Japan has an estimated income elasticity slightly above unity, based on quarterly data (see Bank of Japan, 1997). They suggest that making base velocity independent of real income does not introduce major error for the sample period. The bank's study also shows that the fit of the base velocity equation could be improved.[10] As suggested, better measures of uncertainty and expected inflation are candidates.

Germany

Data for Germany (see Figure 1.4 on page 12) suggest that the slope and level of the velocity relationship changed around 1991. I have used dummy variables in the regressions shown in Table 1.5. Both dummy variables have a value of zero until 1991 and a value of 1 for 1991–6. The coefficient for the change in the slope (*DS*) suggests that the slope declined modestly from 0.14 to 0.12; the intercept declined also, for reasons discussed earlier.

The annual regressions suggest that the interest elasticity of the velocity relationship is approximately the same in the three countries – 0.09 to 0.12 – using the estimate for Germany after reunification. The elasticity with respect to lagged velocity also lies in a narrow range – 0.66 to 0.77. The principal difference between the countries is in goodness of fit. The German data fit less

21

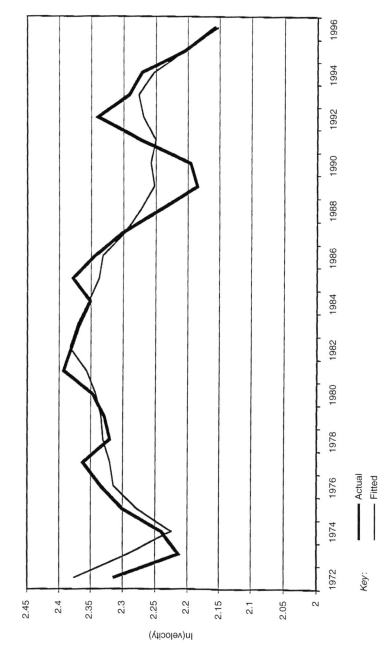

Figure 1.8 Japan, regression of ln (base velocity) on ln (long-term interest rate), inflation, and ln (base velocity −1)

Table 1.5   Regressions for Germany

Period	i_t	V_{t-1}	D	DS	AR1	R^2/DW
1973–96	0.14	0.77	–0.05	–0.02		0.75
	(2.68)	(6.35)	(1.81)	(1.90)		2.38
1973–96	0.14	0.79	–0.47	–0.19	–0.04	0.75
	(2.67)	(4.70)	(1.70)	(1.78)	(0.14)	2.35
1972/3–	0.02	0.92	–0.03		–0.27	0.99
1997/1	(3.03)	(36.16)	(4.05)		(2.67)	2.03

Note: Logarithms of annual data are for the fourth quarter.

well than the others. The last row of Table 1.5 shows that the fit for Germany improves using quarterly data.

Conclusion

A stable velocity function is a necessary condition for a predictable effect of money on nominal GDP. The evidence for the three countries suggests that, if the central bank chooses to control or respond to growth of the monetary base, it could keep growth of nominal GDP at a rate consistent with low inflation. This does not require the central bank to use the base as its instrument. It could continue to carry out policy actions by changing a short-term interest rate.

Of all monetary aggregates, the monetary base is perhaps least influenced by changes in the quality of information resulting from financial innovation, changes in intermediation, or financial regulation. It is often said that the base consists mainly of currency. It is no less true that the base consists of the principal assets the central bank acquires through its operations in domestic credit markets and the foreign exchange market.

It may be said that evidence of the ability to affect nominal GDP bypasses the issue of measuring and separating nominal and real magnitudes. If so, the evidence here does not address the measurement problem for an economy where productivity growth cannot be measured reliably because of a large service sector or increasing reliance on information technology. There is some truth in that criticism but, for monetary policy, the criticism is overstated.

There are two reasons. First, precise measurement, though desirable, is not necessary for effective policy. Measurement of productivity or its growth rate may have become more difficult in principle, but measurement of real GDP or output has improved considerably in practice. This is shown by the comparison of recent data with the highly variable data reported for the 1920s and 1930s. Arguably, the years 1922–8 were one of the best periods for monetary policy in the USA. Available data were rudimentary when compared to current data. Yet, the Federal Reserve at that time was more successful in keeping inflation close to zero than in any period of comparable length.[11]

Second, many central banks now claim that their principal goal is medium-term stability. A few have adopted medium-term strategies – for example, rules or quasi-rules to achieve price stability or zero inflation. Some have implemented such rules successfully since 1990 or 1995. By using adaptive rules, these central banks have been able to conduct policy effectively, despite problems arising from mismeasurement of productivity growth and other causes. McCallum (1993) shows that an adaptive rule using the monetary base worked reliably in Japan and elsewhere.

Concern for the measurement problem is perhaps most acute in countries such as the USA, where market practitioners and policy-makers seem most concerned about the ebb and flow of monthly and quarterly data. Here, too, errors in measuring prices and productivity growth seem small compared to the difficulties of estimating seasonal factors, sorting the systematic from the large random component in these data, or separating persistent and transitory changes. Recent work by Shiratsuka (1997) and Cecchetti (1996), using trimmed means, suggest that large transitory changes in a small number of commodity prices often have effects on reported rates of inflation that are likely to be large relative to the effects of mismeasurement of productivity growth. Typically, these effects do not persist. A central bank that follows a medium strategy does not respond to such short-term changes.

I draw the following conclusions: first, a central bank that tries to make frequent, small adjustments faces many problems. Errors of measurement in separating real and nominal values is one of those problems, though probably not the most serious one. Second, there are many reasons for a central bank to follow a medium-term strategy to control inflation or nominal GDP. Measurement error, or quality of information, is one of the reasons, but probably not the most important one. Third, the effects of major policy changes aside, the evidence suggests that the relationship between monetary base and nominal GDP has remained stable through many years of financial innovation and economic change.

Economics has never been the science that delivers highly accurate quarterly or annual forecasts, or precise measures of most variables. There is no such science. Policy-makers have learned to use procedures that do not depend on precisely measured data or very accurate forecasts. Robust relationship will generally be more useful for planning and implementing medium-term strategies. The data suggest that, with some qualifications, some robust relationships relating money to nominal GDP are available and useful for policy decisions.

Notes

1. Econometric work by King and Watson (1994) suggests considerable variability in NAIRU and a relatively unstable trade-off between inflation and unemployment. There is no reason why NAIRU should be constant or invariant to changes in tax rates, regulation and demographic changes.
2. Prewar errors in monetary policy were not caused principally by faulty data. To cite just two examples, central bankers could not, and did not, fail to notice the rise in unemployment after 1929, nor did the Reichsbank fail to notice that inflation was rising rapidly prior to 1924.
3. Efforts to estimate Equation (1.1) for Germany and Japan did not produce useful results, perhaps because fewer data points were available in the two sub-samples.
4. Reporting error may make such estimates unreliable. Zvi Griliches (1994) concluded, after decades of work, that we can not expect to measure productivity growth accurately, or satisfactorily explain why it changed around 1970.
5. There is a period of relative stability, even slight reversal, from 1980 to 1985, the years of the strong dollar. The yen/dollar rate rose from 226 to 238. There is a local peak at 249 in 1982.
6. All data for the base are taken from the Bank of Japan's web page.
7. The Federal Reserve used an interest target over most of the period. If the interest target remained unchanged, the effect of reserve requirement changes was offset on the monetary base.
8. This conclusion is the opposite of the conclusion reached by Benjamin Friedman (1997 and elsewhere). One reason is that Friedman considers only quarterly data where the random walk properties are strong.
9. Using the regression in row 5 with $\ln V_{t-1}$ produces nearly identical errors.
10. The bank's study finds that base money and GDP are cointegrated. There is also evidence of variable lags, not surprising in the light of Figure 1.5.
11. The Federal Reserve took the lead in developing many statistical series, so US data at the time were better than data for many other countries.

References

Balke, N. S. and Gordon, R. J. (1986) 'Appendix B. Historical Data' in R. J. Gordon (ed.), *The American Business Cycle: Continuity and Change* (Chicago: University of Chicago Press for the National Bureau of Economic Research).

Bank of Japan (1997) 'On the Relationship between Monetary Aggregates in Japan: A Study Focusing on Long-term Equilibrium Relationships', *Bank of Japan Quarterly Bulletin* (November), pp. 103–24.

Brunner, K. and Meltzer, A. H. (1976) 'An Aggregative Theory for a Closed Economy', in J. Stein (ed.), *Monetarism* (Amsterdam: North-Holland), pp. 69–103.

Cecchetti, S. G. (1996) 'Measuring Short-Run Inflation for Central Bankers', NBER Working Paper No. 6183.

Friedman, B. (1997) 'The Rise and Fall of Money Growth Targets as Guidelines for U.S. Monetary Policy', in I. Kuroda (ed.), *Towards More Effective Monetary Policy* (London: Macmillan, in association with the Bank of Japan), pp. 137–64.

Friedman, M. and Schwartz, A. J. (1963) *A Monetary History of the United States 1867–1960* (Princeton, NJ: Princeton University Press for the National Bureau of Economic Research).

Griliches, Z. (1994) 'Productivity, R&D, and the Data Constraint', *American Economic Review*, Vol. 84 (March), pp. 1–23.

Issing, O. (1997) 'Monetary Targeting in Germany: the Stability of Monetary Policy and of the Monetary System', *Journal of Monetary Economics*, vol. 39 (June), pp. 67–79.

King, R. G. and Watson, M. W. (1994) 'The Postwar U.S. Phillips Curve: A Revisionist Econometric History', *Carnegie Rochester Conference Series on Public Policy*, vol. 41, (December), pp. 157–219.

McCallum, B. T. (1993) 'Specification and Analysis of a Monetary Policy Rule for Japan', *Bank of Japan Monetary and Economic Studies*, Institute of Monetary and Economic Studies, vol. 11 (November), pp. 1–46.

Meltzer, A. H. (1997), *A History of the Federal Reserve* (unpublished), ch. 4 (Pittsburgh: Carnegie Mellon University).

Meltzer, A. H. (1998) 'Monetarism: The Issues and the Outcome'. Invited Address, *International Atlantic Economic Journal*, vol. 26 (March), pp. 1–31.

Shiratsuka, S. (1997) 'Inflation Measures for Monetary Policy: Measuring the Underlying Inflation Trend and Its implications for Monetary Policy Implementation', *Monetary and Economic Studies*, Bank of Japan, vol. 15 (December), pp. 1–26.

Watson, M. (1994) 'Business Cycles Durations and Postwar Stabilization of the U.S. Economy', *American Economic Review*, vol. 84 (March), pp. 24–46.

2
Information Technology and Monetary Policy

John B. Taylor

The purpose of the conference at the Bank of Japan was to examine the trend towards a world economy based on knowledge or information technology. In my view, information technology has two countervailing effects on monetary policy.

First, it makes monetary policy decision-making more difficult by increasing uncertainty about the targets and the instruments of this policy. The targets of monetary policy – low inflation and stable output, for example – are harder to define and to measure when information goods and services are a large or growing part of the economy. The instruments of monetary policy – in particular the monetary aggregates – also become harder to define and measure when information technology causes the payments system to undergo rapid transformation. Moreover, information technology increases uncertainty about the relationship between the instruments and the targets, through the development of new financial products or new ways in which goods are traded or prices formed.

Second, information technology makes monetary policy decision-making easier by improving the processing of information and by permitting greater quantification and handling of uncertainty. Faster computers and computer algorithms allow policy-makers to analyze different policies in more realistic settings. Information technology enables the use of modern methods of decision theory and control theory in the formulation of monetary policy.

The first effect is a cost of information technology, while the second is a benefit. Both the costs and the benefits are growing as information technology. improves. In my view, the benefits are growing faster than the costs. To support this, I shall first describe how better information technology has improved research on monetary policy. I shall then show how this improved research can help policy-makers to deal with the uncertainties caused by information technology itself.

The impact of information technology on monetary policy research

I focus on the impact that information technology – defined as the development of computers, software or networks – has had on the evaluation of alternative strategies, plans or rules for setting the instruments of monetary policy. In its broadest sense, monetary policy research aims at finding ways to improve the design and implementation of monetary policy in order better to achieve the goals of policy. In this sense, monetary policy research is much like any other type of applied economic research that aims to improve decision-making, whether by business firms, by investors, or by consumers.

Much of monetary policy research is historical and empirical; researchers look for correlations – primarily between in the instruments of policy and the outcomes for inflation or employment – that might suggest how the instruments should be set in order to achieve certain goals for the target variables. But good policy research is also theoretical; it uses monetary theory to determine how different policies would work. The monetary policy research of Milton Friedman (1960), for example, which resulted in the proposal that monetary policy keeps the growth rate of money constant, was based on both empirical and theoretical considerations.

The formal way to combine monetary theory and empirical observations is through a quantitative model of the economy; because monetary theory involves changes over time, such models are likely to be both dynamic and stochastic. The idea of applying optimal decision theory to monetary policy decisions using a dynamic or stochastic model of the economy goes back to the work of Phillips (1954), Theil (1957), Howrey (1967) and Brainard (1967). Phillips (1954) used dynamic deterministic models to study the effects of different policy rules that described how the instruments of policy reacted to the economy. In looking for a plausible class of policy rules, he borrowed the concepts of proportional, derivative and integral control from the engineering literature. Theil (1957) added stochastic shocks to the models. Howrey (1967) examined policy rules in models that were both dynamic and stochastic, and Brainard (1967) explicitly considered multiplicative uncertainty.

These policy studies focused on the instruments of policy. (Fiscal policy instruments were as often the focus of this earlier literature as monetary policy instruments.) A loss function for the deviations of the target variables from some desired levels was specified. The decision about the instrument was cast as an optimal decision problem in which instruments were set so as to minimize the expected value of the loss function. The expectations were taken across the distribution of the stochastic disturbances, and perhaps also the parameters of the model, as suggested by the optimal statistical decision theory available at the time (see, for example, Raiffa and Schlaifer (1961). For the most part this research could be done without computers: the models were small, linear, and simple.[1] Poole's (1970) important analytical research on the choice of an interest rate or money supply instrument was conducted within this framework.

The advent of rational expectations in macroeconomics in the 1970s had a radical effect on this decision theory approach to monetary policy. Of course, it placed more emphasis on credibility and therefore on policy rules or contingency plans for policy; but policy rules were already the focus of the earlier work of Phillips, Howrey and others. More important for this discussion, rational expectations placed a much greater demand on computers and computer software. The same optimal decision problems that could be performed analytically on the back of an envelope now required super-computers. In order to deal with the Lucas (1976) critique, the models had to be forward-looking. Leads as well as lags of the variables entered the models, either because this was implied by the decision rules, as in Taylor (1979), or because it was implied by the first-order conditions of individual agent's optimization problems, as in Hansen and Sargent (1980). In sum, rational expectations greatly increased computational complexity. This was true even after algorithms were developed to solve non-linear rational expectations models. For example, solving a non-linear rational expectations model using the extended path method required many hundreds of times the computing speed of the pre-rational expectations models. Rational expectations made monetary policy research much more difficult. Few had the time or resources to conduct formal econometric policy evaluation studies.

Fortunately, information technology came to the rescue of monetary policy evaluation research. The same types of computer hardware and software innovations that led to productivity increases and quality improvements throughout the economy, also led to productivity and quality improvements in monetary policy research. What was impossible in the early 1980s is routine at the start of the twenty-first century.

Looking back over the years since the rational expectations revolution, the progress that has been made in computation speed and computer algorithms is striking. Evaluating monetary policy rules in which the instruments of policy react to macroeconomics variables is now routine in the most complex forward-looking model. Econometric policy evaluation methods of the type advocated by Lucas are now used with models consisting of hundreds of equations with estimated numerical parameter values. The models that took many hours to solve when first developed now take only a few minutes.

The technological breakthrough in research on policy rules is clearly demonstrated in the book by Bryant *et al.* (1993). This project brought many researchers together, using very large multicountry stochastic systems to evaluate different monetary policy rules. While no obvious single policy rule emerged from the simulations of many different models, there were some common characteristics. Rules with the interest rate as the instrument performed better than rules with the money supply as the instrument. Rules that reacted strongly to *both* inflation deviations from a target inflation rate and real output deviations from potential output worked best. Rules that reacted to the exchange rate did not work as well as those that placed little or no emphasis on the exchange rate. These results showed that it is important for policy-makers to have a target inflation rate; the task of policy is to keep small the fluctuations in inflation around this target, recognizing that fluctuations in real output around potential output can be affected by monetary policy.

In examining this research, I noted (see Taylor, 1993) that there is a simple rule that possesses key characteristics of more complicated rules and that would therefore be expected to work well as a guideline for setting the policy instruments. The simple rule has the short-term interest rate adjusting both to inflation and to real GDP. The target inflation rate is 2 per cent and the implied real interest rate is 2 per cent. The weight on inflation is 1.5 and the weight on real output is 0.5.

Historical analysis supports the findings about the interest rate response to inflation and output found in model simulations as well as in the simple rule. The response of interest rates to inflation and real output in the 1980s and 1990s in the USA is very similar to the simple rule that emerged from the model simulations. Moreover, these responses are much larger than they were during the late 1960s and 1970s. The estimated inflation response coefficient is about 0.8 for the 1960s and 1970s, compared to about 1.5 for the 1980s and 1990s. Because the inflation rate and real output were more stable in the 1980s and 1990s than in the late 1960s and 1970s, this historical comparison provides some evidence that the proposed response coefficients are about right (see Taylor, 1998b).

In sum, information technology has made modern econometric policy evaluation research possible. And even though the rules for monetary policy that have emerged from this research are simpler than would be implied by the more complex models, it is unlikely that the simple rules would have appeared without the computer-intensive research with complex models.

Dealing with monetary policy uncertainties

As I stated in the introduction, information technology is likely to add uncertainty to the instruments of monetary policy, to the target variables of monetary policy, and to the relationship between the instruments and the targets. Dealing with the implications of information uncertainty is therefore much like dealing with uncertainty in general. I shall now consider several ways in which modern computer-intensive monetary policy research can deal with this uncertainty.

Robustness to uncertainty about model specification

How robust are policy rules to model uncertainty? Monetary models can be specified in different ways. Some of these differences may reflect different information assumptions on the part of agents and thus might be affected by improvements in information technology. For example, if the Internet is used widely to buy, sell and price goods and services, then the resulting faster flow of information could cause prices to adjust more quickly. Because some monetary models assume a greater degree of price flexibility than others, the differences between the models could capture this potential effect of information technology. More generally, comparing the performance of policy rules in different models is useful if the differences in the models reflect some of the uncertainty in the real world.

There are a number of ways to test for robustness of policy rules across models. Here I report briefly a recent robustness study (see Taylor, 1998a) which is illustrative of what can be done. Nine models were used in this exercise, developed by Laurence Ball; Andrew Haldane and Nicoletta Batini; Ben McCallum and Edward Nelson; Glenn Rudebusch and Lars Svensson; Julio Rotemberg and Michael Woodford; and Jeffrey Fuhrer and George Moore. Two of the nine are models used at the Federal Reserve Board (a small model and a large model), and one of them is a multicountry model I developed at Stanford several years ago (TMCM). The models represent a wide variety of approaches. Most are rational expectations models, but others are purely backward-looking. Most of the models are small, but a few are large. Some specify explicit optimization problems for agents, while others assume decision rules. Some are open economy models, but most are closed. All the models are dynamic, stochastic and economy-wide.

A number of different policy rules were part of this robustness study, but a brief description of two of these will be sufficient to illustrate the benefits of this type of approach. I focus on two rules in which the central bank's interest-rate decisions respond to both inflation and real GDP. In both rules the response to the inflation rate is 1.5: when the inflation rate rises by 100 basis points, the short-term interest rate rises by 150 basis points. The rules differ in the response to real GDP, which equals 0.5 for the less output-responsive rule and 1.0 for the more output-responsive rule.[2] The rule with the output response coefficient of 0.5 is the rule proposed in Taylor (1993). The other rule has an output response coefficient of 1.0 rather than 0.5 on real output, reflecting the recent views of some researchers that the interest rate should respond more aggressively to output than the 0.5 response coefficient in the simple rule. Of course, there are many other policy rules besides these two, including money supply rules, and rules that react to the exchange rate or to inflation forecasts. But these two rules serve as an example of how one can look at different models to assess the robustness of monetary policy rules to certain types of uncertainty.

Assessing the robustness to uncertainty by looking at different models is less straightforward than it might at first seem, because some models show that all rules work much better than other models show. Absolute performance measures across models are arbitrary, because certain modelling decisions – such as which variables are exogenous – are arbitrary. This arbitrariness also

Table 2.1 Robustness results from nine models

	Standard deviation of:	
	Inflation	Output
Rule with lower output response		
Ball	1.85	1.62
Haldane–Batini	1.38	1.05
McCallum–Nelson	1.96	1.12
Rudebusch–Svensson	3.46	2.25
Rotemberg–Woodford	2.71	1.97
Fuhrer–Moore	2.63	2.68
Small Fed Model	0.70	0.99
Large Fed Model	1.86	2.92
TMCM	2.58	2.89
Average	2.13	1.94
Rule with higher output response		
Ball	2.01	1.36
Haldane–Batini	1.46	0.92
McCallum–Nelson	1.93	1.10
Rudebusch–Svensson	3.52	1.98
Rotemberg–Woodford	2.60	1.34
Furher–Moore	2.84	2.32
Small Fed Model	0.73	0.87
Large Fed Model	2.02	2.21
TMCM	2.36	2.55
Average	2.16	1.63

makes comparing estimated variances with historical variances difficult. One can get around this problem by considering rankings between rules. For example, Table 2.1 shows the standard deviations of the inflation rate and real output for the two rules. Despite the conjectures that the more aggressive of the two rules would work better, neither rule dominates the other across the models. For all models, the more output-responsive rule gives a lower variance of output. However, for six of the nine models, this higher output response rule also gives a higher variance of inflation.

The change in the average standard deviations across all the models shows a trade off between inflation variability and output variability.

The comparison across models indicates a degree of robustness for both rules in the sense that neither rule results in terrible performance in any model. For none of the models would these rules be likely to lead to another great inflation or a great depression with double-digit inflation or double-digit percentage decline in real GDP below potential. This is not true of all policy rules, as I shall consider next.

Another type of policy rule that has frequently been suggested has the interest rate responding to the lagged interest rate, in addition to output and inflation. Comparing such rules with the two rules that do not respond to the lagged interest rate shows that neither type of rule dominates across all models. However, for a number of models, the rules with lagged interest rates have very poor performance, with extraordinarily large variances. These could be great depression or great inflation scenarios in some models. It turns out, however, that the models that predict very poor performance for the lagged interest rate rules are those without rational expectations, or in which forward-looking effects are not strong in the model. Why? Interest rate rules that respond with a lag exploit people's forward-looking behaviour; these rules assume that people will expect later increases in interest rates if such increases are needed to reduce inflation. Models without forward-looking terms clearly cannot describe such forward looking. A rule proposed in recent research by Rotemberg and Woodford (1998) has a lagged interest rate coefficient greater than one; it is even less robust than the other rules because it performs badly when evaluated with models without strong forward-looking behaviour.

Although only recently becoming a regular part of research on monetary policy rules, robustness studies like this seem very promising as a means of dealing with the effects of uncertainty on monetary policy. I hope that my brief example hints at what can now be done. I would hope in the future to see many more robustness studies of many more policy rules.

Robustness to uncertainty about the persistence of shocks

It is possible to pinpoint more precisely the form of uncertainty to which one would like a policy rule to be robust. This may be very useful for dealing with uncertainties caused by information technology. For example, uncertainty about the trend in potential GDP, or in longer-term movements in the real interest rate, could be caused by a shift in productivity in services or some other non-tangible output that is not measured properly. Such uncertainties raise serious problems for policy rules that set the interest rate.

In a recent study, Sargent (1998) developed a procedure to calculate policy rules that are robust to this form of uncertainty. In particular, he calculated the parameters of a policy rule that is robust to changes in the serial correlation structure of the model. In other words, the policy-maker assumes that there is no serial correlation, while in reality there is some serial correlation of a general variety. This situation could occur if potential GDP or the real interest rate started to drift away from the policy-maker's estimate. Sargent focuses on simple interest rate rules such as the ones discussed earlier. He finds that the robust rule responds more aggressively than either of the simple policy rules. His results depend on the form of the serial correlation, but one calculation is that the interest rate should be increased by 300 basis points for every rise in the inflation rate by 100 basis points, compared with 150 basis points for the simple rule mentioned earlier. For example, if the inflation rate rose in the USA from 2 per cent to 4 per cent next year, then the Fed would increase the interest rate from about 5.5 per cent to 11.5 per cent, holding the real output gap constant. Sargent (1988) also found that the interest rate should be much more responsive to real output fluctuations. The response coefficient on real output is 1.6 rather than the 0.5 or 1.0 in the other two rules.

It may seem surprising that the robust rule is more aggressive in the face of uncertainty. The reason is that, with the chance of a shock being persistent, the policy-maker must guard against the shock having long-lasting effects by reacting to it more aggressively. For example, if there is an inflation shock, then the response will have to be more aggressive if the shock is expected to persist than if it is temporary. The robustness methods applied by Sargent are computationally intensive and, at least when applied to larger models, require the advances in information technology we have seen since the 1980s.

Robustness to uncertainty about key elasticities

Another specific form of uncertainty that might arise because of information technology concerns the effect of the policy instruments on the target variables. In another study, Stock (1998) calculate a policy rule that is robust to this type of uncertainty. In particular, the policy rule calculated by Stock is robust to different values of the slope of the IS curve (the impact of the interest rate on real output) and the speed of adjustment of inflation in a price adjustment equation (the impact of real output on inflation), rather than to different serial correlation assumptions, as in Sargent's (1988) robust policy rule. Stock's robust rule is a minimax policy with respect to this parameter uncertainty. In other words, within the class of policies in which the interest rate responds to real output and inflation, he finds a policy rule that minimizes the expected loss (a weighted average of inflation and output variance) for the worst-case scenario (set of parameters). Stock also finds that the optimal policy should be more aggressive in responding to inflation and output than the two simple rules I mentioned earlier. For example, the interest rate responds by 390 basis points when the inflation rate changes by 100 basis points; if the inflation rate rise from 2 per cent to 4 per cent next year in the USA, the Fed would raise the Federal Funds rate to 13.3 per cent. This aggressive response is the implication of the minimax strategy because the worst case scenario has very small coefficients on the interest rate in the IS equation and on output in the inflation equation. In such adverse circumstances, not reacting enough to inflation could cause the inflation rate to fluctuate by a huge amount, in turn leading to large output fluctuations.

Uncertainty and the effects of learning over time

Uncertainty raises another type of policy strategy question. In the face of uncertainty about the structure of the model, should the central bank adjust its instruments so as to obtain more information that might reduce the uncertainty? This is the learning and control problem studied in some special cases by Prescott (1972) and Taylor (1974). This problem could simply not have been handled in the type of models needed for monetary policy without the improvements in information technology. Wieland (1998) has calculated the optimal learning strategy when the uncertainty results from imprecise estimates of the natural rate of unemployment. Wieland finds that the optimal learning policy – which balances the gains from learning and the costs of deviating from the optimal choice in the current period – is more aggressive than the policy that uses caution in the face of uncertainty (as in Brainard, 1967), but is less aggressive (except in some unusual cases) than the certainty equivalent policy. The certainty equivalent policy is assumed in the two simple rules I mentioned earlier. In other words, while learning, along with robustness, may be a reason for greater aggressiveness, it could be offset by the caution caused by the parameter uncertainty itself.

Simple monetary policy rules versus complex monetary policy rules

Another recent paper by Levin *et al.* (1998) shows that simple rules are more robust to model uncertainty than more complex optimal rules. They find that optimal rules from one model perform worse than simple rules when simulated in other models. The reason for this finding is apparently that the optimal rule exploits certain properties of a model that are specific to that model. If the optimal rule is simulated in another model with different properties, then by exploiting the wrong properties the optimal rule fails.

Robustness to information lags

Yet another policy question relating to uncertainty is the effect of information lags on monetary decisions and performance. Suppose that policy cannot respond to current quarter values. Would the estimated performance deteriorate? According to simulations in the nine models mentioned earlier, if policy reacted to lagged inflation and lagged output ($i_t = g_\pi \pi_{t-1} + g_y \, y_{t-1}$) there would be little effect on economic performance. The variances of inflation and output increase by only a small amount when policy must react to lags in this way. Hence, information lags of about one quarter in length do not cause major difficulties for policy rules.

Concluding remarks: the importance of translational economics

While improvements in monetary policy *research* resulting from faster computers and better software are impressive, I think it is important to ask whether the improved information technology has infact helped in achieving the goals of monetary policy. Has the research improved actual monetary policy? I think the answer is yes, but this answer may pertain more to the USA, with which I am more familiar and on which much of the modelling has focused, than to other countries at this time. Central bankers in the USA have used monetary policy rules as a guide to their decisions; and they discuss specific policy guidelines in speeches. Financial market economists use policy rules to help predict monetary policy decisions. As with the remarkable improvements in information technology, I think it is striking to see how far the practical application of policy rules has come.

However, I think economists need to focus more on the process by which economic research is applied to solve real world problems. I hope my remarks demonstrate the power of the economic research, such as described in the remaining chapters of this book. But if this research is to be useful we need also to focus more in the future on *translational economics*, the process of translating economic research into practical policy decisions.

Notes

1. An exception was the type of optimization problems considered by Prescott (1972) and Taylor (1974), which tried to deal with the fact that the choice of instrument would affect the flow of information about the parameters. These problems required much greater computing speed and better algorithms; as a consequence, only the most elementary problems could be handled.
2. Ignoring the constant term, the mathematical form of the two rules is $i_t = g_\pi \pi_t + g_y Y_t$, where i is the nominal interest rate, π is the inflation rate, y is real GDP measured as a deviation from potential GDP, and where $g_\pi = 1.5$ and $g_y = 0.5$ or 1.0.

References

Brainard, W. (1967) 'Uncertainty and the Effectiveness of Policy', *American Economic Review, Proceedings*, vol. 57, pp. 411–25.

Bryant, R., Hooper, P. and Mann, C. (1993) *Evaluating Policy Regimes: New Research in Empirical Macroeconomics* (Washington, DC: Brookings Institution).

Friedman, M. (1960) *A program for Monetary Stability* (New York: Fordam University Press).

Hansen, L. P. and Sargent, T. (1980) 'Formulating and Estimating Dynamic Linear Rational Expectations Models', *Journal of Economic Dynamics and Control*, vol. 2, pp. 7–46.

Howrey, E. P. (1967) 'Stabilization Policy in Linear Stochastic Models', *Review of Economics and Statistics*, vol. 49, pp. 404–11.

Levin, A., Wieland, V. and Williams J. C. (1998)'Robustness of Simple Monetary Policy Rules under Model Uncertainty', in J. B. Taylor (ed.), *Monetary Policy Rules* (University of Chicago Press).

Lucas, R. E. (1976) 'Econometric Policy Evaluation: A Critique', *Carnegie Rochester Conference Series on Public Policy*, vol. 1, pp. 19–46.

Phillips, A. W. (1954) 'Stabilization Policy in a Closed Economy', *Economic Journal*, vol. 64, pp. 290–323.

Poole, W. (1970) 'Optimal Choice of Monetary Policy Instruments in a Simple Stochastic Macro Model', *Quarterly Journal of Economics*, vol. 84, pp. 197–216.

Prescott, E. C. (1972) 'The Multiperiod Control Problem Under Uncertainty', *Econometrica*, vol. 40, pp. 1043–57.

Raiffa, H. and Schlaifer, R. (1961) *Applied Statistical Decision Theory* (Cambridge, Mass: MIT Press).

Rotemberg, J. and Woodford, M. (1998) 'Interest Rate Rules in an Estimated Sticky Price Model', in J. B. Taylor (ed.), *Monetary Policy Rules* (University of Chicago Press).

Sargent, T. (1998) 'Discussion of "Policy Rules in an Open Economy" by Laurence Ball', in J. B. Taylor (ed.), *Monetary Policy Rules* (University of Chicago Press).

Stock, J. (1998) 'Making Policies Robust to Model Uncertainty: Commént on "Policy Rules for Inflation Targeting" by Glenn Rudebusch and Lars Svensson', in J. B. Taylor (ed.), *Monetary Policy Rules* (University of Chicago Press).

Taylor, J. B. (1974) 'Asymptotic Properties of Multiperiod Control Rules in the Linear Regression Model', *International Economic Review*, vol. 15, pp. 472–84.

Taylor, J. B. (1979) 'Estimation and Control of a Macroeconomic Model with Rational Expectations', *Econometrica*, vol. 47, pp. 1267–86.

Taylor, J. B. (1993) 'Discretion versus Policy Rules in Practice', *Carnegie – Rochester Conference Series on Public Policy*, vol. 39, pp. 195–214.

Taylor, J. B. (1998a) 'Introductory Remarks', in J. B. Taylor (ed.), *Monetary Policy Rules* (University of Chicago Press).

Taylor, J. B. (1998b) 'An Historical Analysis of Monetary Policy Rules', in J. B. Taylor (ed.), *Monetary Policy Rules* (University of Chicago Press).

Theil, H. (1957) 'A Note on Certainty Equivalence in Dynamic Planning', *Econometrica*, vol. 25. pp. 346–9.

Part II

An Overview and Case Study of the Development of a Knowledge-based Economy

3
Waiting for the Information Technology Revolution?

Paul A. David

Introduction: computer and dynamo revisited

In the USA and other developed economies, the idea of a 'productivity paradox' continues to be kept alive by the conjunction of this persisting productivity slowdown puzzle with ongoing rapid innovation and increasing deployment of new information and communication technologies. There is now a stronger consensus among economic analysts that real output growth is being underestimated substantially, as a consequence of the difficulty of measuring nominal product for some sectors, and systematic upward biases in many of the available output price deflators. This newly gained understanding, however, goes further towards dispelling the sense of 'paradox' than it does towards explaining the productivity slowdown. Although a wide assortment of other hypotheses have been advanced, we remain without a compelling explanation for the collapse of the total factor productivity residual and the sustained slowdown of measured labour productivity growth into the 1980s and beyond – long after the effects of the oil embargo and inflation shocks of the 1973–9 period had presumably faded.

This chapter revisits the suggestion made some time ago by David (1990, 1991), that in several of its salient features the present situation has precedents in previous extended episodes of *techno-economic regime transition*, involving the elaboration and diffusion of 'general-purpose engines'. The particular historical parallel that can be drawn between the electrical dynamo revolution and the microprocessor-based computer revolution still seems to provide useful general illumination of the current scene. It does so by reference to both of the conditions contributing to the 1890–1914 'productivity pause', and the key technological developments underlying the subsequent post-1918 surge of labour productivity and total factor productivity growth in the US economy.

Nevertheless, several of its key messages have been misconstrued in some quarters. Rather than ignoring the problem of measurement errors, the suggestion was that underestimation of output quality improvements is likely

39

to be especially serious in the early phases of a general-purpose technology's application. Far from discerning the inevitable coming of a 'computer-productivity surge' after an historically predictable period of gestation, the analysis indicated reasons why such major measurable productivity effects as might emerge would tend to be deferred until productive assets embodying the new technology were diffused very extensively throughout the economy.

Historical analogies are primarily metaphorical in purpose, and so, in telling the 'computer and dynamo' stories side by side, no strict correspondence between the two was implied, nor could any literal equation of electricity with information be warranted. The parallels are suggestive none the less. Computer and dynamo each form the nodal elements of physically distributed (transmission) networks. Both occupy key positions in a web of strongly complementary technical relationships that give rise to 'network externality effects' of various kinds, and so make issues of compatibility standardization important for business strategy and public policy. In both instances we can recognize the emergence of an extended trajectory of incremental technical improvements, the gradual and protracted process of diffusion into wide-spread use, and the confluence with other streams of technological innova-tion, all of which are interdependent features of the dynamic process through which a general purpose engine acquires a broad domain of specific applications (see Bresnahan and Trajtenberg, 1995). Successful exploitation of the new technology's evolving productivity potential will be found, in each epoch, to entail the production and financing of investment projects whose novelty – in terms of scale, technical requirements, or other characteristics – posed significant challenges for the existing agencies supplying capital goods and the established capital market institutions.

When used properly, close reference to analogous historical experiences can serve temporarily to liberate economic analysis from the confining effects of being too close to the specific details of the current problem to be able to perceive it 'in the round'. In that way one may uncover different angles along which inquiry may proceed fruitfully. Reflexively, the present perceptions inform and re-inform our approach to understanding the past. Thus, rather significantly, recent research on the 1909–29 era of factory electrification has highlighted the role of new information systems in facilitating management and control for 'high-throughput' assembly operations, as well as in batch- and continuous-process production. A second, and perhaps still more important, set of germane findings concern the expansion of public secondary schooling in the USA. Getting under way in the 1890s, this eventually provided a flow of high-school graduates sufficient to match the intensified demands from the technologically most progressive branches of industry for new kinds of skill among their blue-collar workforce, as well as the increasing requirements for white-collar employees.

These historical findings further reinforce the central theme that the mutual adaptation and eventual convergence of complementary institutional, organizational and technological changes have been critical in bringing about economic transformations profound enough to deserve being labelled 'revolutionary'. There is enough micro-level evidence today to support the view that the economic potentialities of the innovations taking place in information and communications technologies are not illusory, even if much uncertainty still surrounds the precise manner in which they can best be realized. What is delusory is to await passively their delivery by the automatic forces of the market, alternating between states of expectancy and frustrated disillusionment – like the characters Estragon and Vladimir in Samuel Beckett's (1956) play, *Waiting for Godot*. To make the ICT revolution happen, more active strategies of *finding Godot* will be called for.

An indicated array of strategies involving joint actions from the private and public sectors has been taking clearer shape since the early 1990s. Macroeconomic stability and financial market regulation alone will not suffice to mobilize the necessary tangible and intangible infrastructure resources, because existing financial market institutions are not adequate to serve growing requirements for intangible investment. Furthermore, some governmental initiatives are likely to be critical in supporting experimentation with new modes of formal education, training and retraining that would be more closely congruent with emerging technologies and the changing nature of work. Beyond this lies the setting of public policies affecting security and privacy of enhanced electronic communications, expediting the formation of open standards for interoperability of digital systems, and protecting new forms of intellectual property rights, without creating monopolistic inhibitions on the widespread application of innovations or unduly restricting access to the knowledge-base upon which further technological advances can be built.

Persisting puzzles: the slowdown and the productivity paradox

A generation of economists who were brought up to identify increases in total factor productivity indexes with 'technical progress' has found it quite paradoxical for the growth accountants' residual measure of 'the advance of knowledge' to have vanished at the very time that a wave of major innovations was appearing – in microelectronics; in communications technologies based on lasers and fibre-optics; in composite materials; and in biotechnology. Disappointments with 'the computer revolution' and the newly-dawned 'information age' in this regard have been felt especially keenly in the USA, which had been supposed to be an early leader in R&D and the commercial introduction of electronics. Indeed, the notion that there is something anomalous about the prevailing state of affairs drew much of its initial appeal from the apparent failure of the wave of innovations based on the microprocessor and the memory chip to elicit a surge of growth in productivity from those very sectors of the US service economy that were investing so heavily in computers and office equipment.[1]

That same generation of economists had been told by Abramovitz (1956) that they ought to regard the total factor productivity residual as 'a measure of our ignorance', and some had followed the lead of Griliches and Jorgenson (1967) in attempting to account for the growth of real output as completely as possible by reference to costly inputs of resources, leaving no embarrassing residual. Yet there was much consternation, rather than celebration, when the measure of 'our ignorance' shrank to the meagre dimensions that appear in the data (see Table 3.1, p. 52) for the US private domestic economy (PDE) during the trend period 1966–89. Indeed, on a still more comprehensive accounting (see Table 3.2, p. 54) in which intangible inputs are considered, the 1.35 percentage points per annum contraction of the residual between its level for the long trend interval 1929–66 and 1966–89 is sufficient to push the latter estimate well into the negative zone (specifically –0.25 per cent per annum). This state of affairs is not entirely without precedent in the history of the American economy but, as Table 3.1 testifies, nothing resembling it has been experienced since the era of the Civil War (1855–71).

The economics profession's reactions to these anomalous and perplexing developments have tended to be expressed in one of three canonical forms. First there are the sceptics, who take the position that there must surely be a positive multifactor productivity residual, in view of all the ongoing innovations, and therefore maintain that the mismeasurement of output and hence of productivity is hiding it from us. Second, one hears from the pessimists, or 'realists', who contend that the post-Second World War sized residual is a thing of the past, and productivity growth at a pace even approaching that is not coming back soon, because old technologies have been exhausted while information and communications technology (ICT) has turned out to be more nightmare than dream. Furthermore, it is pointed out, other much-hyped sources of commercial innovation, such as advances in biotechnology, high-temperature superconductivity and new materials remain at best rather far off in the future as major generators of conventional productivity improvement.

Lastly, there are cautious optimists: there may well be a rebound in the measured residual to which further advances in ICT will contribute importantly, but they insist that this will also require the concurrent addressing many difficult non-technological organizational problems. While the foregoing caricature certainly is rather overdrawn – too much so to warrant attaching names to these positions – it serves well enough to capture the spirit of much of the recent debate. But rather than constructing the matter in terms of alternative hypotheses among which one is obliged to choose, it is perhaps better to acknowledge from the outset that they each reflect some part of the reality. So the course pursued here is that of trying to see how the ensemble may fit together to form an instructively holistic picture of the current situation.

Towards better measures for mismeasures

The mismeasurement explanations have focused on hard-to-measure outputs, and relatedly on deficiencies in construction of output price deflators, and they create a case for the existence of downward bias in measured output growth. This helps to resolve the 'paradox' but not the Slowdown Puzzle.

One might point out in this connection that the data in Table 3.2 are implausible in suggesting a negative residual for the period 1966–89; it is just too paradoxical and so strengthens the idea of some measurement error. Yet, to apply even a correction as large as the 1.1 per cent per annum suggested by the Boskin Commission (Boskin *et al.*, 1996) on the measurement errors in the CPI, only suffices to pull the 're-measured' refined total factor productivity growth estimate for the 1966–89 period (in Table 3.2) back up to 0.82–0.86 percentage points per annum. The implication of a slowdown of approximately 0.3 percentage points per annum would still be forced upon us even were it supposed, improbably, that the measurement bias had been nil in the preceding 1929–66 period.

Robert J. Gordon (see, for example, 1999) and others who have looked into the matter carefully, however, have failed to produce conclusive indications that the problem of upward-biased deflators has been growing worse. What we need are better measures of the changing seriousness of measurement biases over time. What is available is at best fragmentary and suggests that no dramatic alterations occurred within the twentieth century.

Zvi Griliches' (1994) point that there has been a relative growth of output and employment in the 'hard-to-measure' sectors of the economy is undisputable. But, given the observed differences in the productivity growth rates between the 'hard-to-measure' and the 'well measured' sectors, one may calculate that the effect of the increased weight of the 'unmeasurable' sector in total manhours in the PDE remains too small (at 0.22 percentage points per annum) to account for much of the (1.25 percentage point) drop in the annual labour productivity growth rate between the periods 1948–73 and 1979–96. Furthermore, Gordon (1999) has shown that the slowdown in average labour productivity, at least, is pervasive and not significantly more frequent in industries that are hard to measure than among the others.

Two hypotheses warranting closer examination suggest that the problem of unmeasured quality improvement has become more pronounced, and this may be in some part traceable to the effects of the emerging ICT regime. First, we might consider the distinct possibility that new Computer-aided design/ Computer-aided engineering (CAD/CAE) technologies, along with flexible modern manufacturing and closer communications between design, production engineering and marketing teams are enabling faster, less costly product innovation, and corresponding shorter product life cycles. In indirect support of this conjecture, we may draw upon Diewert and Fox's (1999) presentation of evidence from Nakamura (1997) on the fourfold acceleration of the rate of introduction of new products in US supermarkets during 1975–92 compared to 1964–75. By combining this with data from Baily and Gordon (1988) on the rising number of products stocked by the average US grocery supermarket, it is possible to gauge roughly the movement in the ratio between these flow and stock measures, thereby getting a better idea of the movement in the new product turnover rate.

What this reveals is that, in contrast with the essential stability prevailing between the mid-1960s and the mid-1970s, there was in fact a marked rise in the new product fraction of the stock between 1975 and 1992: if only a half of the new products on offer were stocked by the average supermarket, the share they represented in the stock would have increased from about 0.09 to 0.46. With such an elevation of the relative entry rate of new products, the potential is raised for underestimation of average output growth because of the delayed linkage of new to old price series.

There is a further implication worth noticing. The broadening of the product line by competitors may be likened to a common-pool/overfishing problem, causing crowding of the product space, with the result that even the reduced fixed costs of research and product development must be spread over fewer units of sales. Moreover, to the extent that congestion in the product space raises the expected failure rate in new product launches, this reinforces the implication that initial margins are likely to be high when these products first appear and will be found to have fallen rapidly in the cases of the fortunate few that succeed in becoming a standard item.

A second hypothesis along the same general lines is simply that in the early phase of the deployment of a new, general-purpose technology, it is likely that many applications will embody novel qualitative improvements over existing goods and services. The cases of the dynamo's application in electric lighting and tramcars illustrate this point. A further instance is found in the application of DC electric motors in passenger and freight lifts, permitting the development of multistorey offices and emporiums. Compared to climbing stairs, the passenger lift was a decided convenience for shoppers in department stores. And in their maintenance, reliability of operation and ease of control, the electric freight lift greatly outstripped the performance characteristics of steam-powered 'winding engines'.

In a sense, the problem just indicated is less one of improper deflation and has more to do with the deficiencies of the conventional productivity measures, which are especially problematic in treating the new kinds of products and process applications that tend to be found for an emergent general-purpose technology during the initial phases of its development. Here too, the story of the dynamo revolution holds noteworthy precedents for some of the problems frequently mentioned nowadays in connection with the suspected impact of the computer (see, for example, Baily and Gordon, 1988): (i) unmeasured quality changes associated with the introduction of novel commodities; and (ii) the particular bias of the new technology towards expanding production of categories of goods and services that previously were not being recorded in the national income accounts.

In the case of the dynamo, initial commercial applications during the 1890–1914 era were concentrated in the fields of lighting equipment and urban transit systems. Notice that qualitative characteristics such as brightness, ease of maintenance and fire safety were especially important attributes of incandescent lighting for stores and factories, as well as for homes – the early electric lighting systems were designed to be closely competitive with illuminating gas on a cost basis. Similarly, the contributions to the improvement in economic welfare in the form of faster trip speeds and shorter passenger waiting times afforded by electric tramcars, and later by subways – not to mention the greater residential amenities enjoyed by urban workers who were then able to commute to the central business district from more salubrious residential neighbourhoods – all remained largely uncaptured by the conventional indexes of real product and productivity (see, for example, Byatt, 1979, pp. 29–45).

Measurement biases of this kind persisted in the later period of factory electrification, most notably with regard to some of the indirect benefits of implementing the 'unit drive' system. One of these was the improvement in machine control achieved by eliminating the problem of belt slippage and installing variable speed DC motors. This yielded better-quality, more standardized output without commensurately increased costs (see Devine, 1983, pp. 363ff). Factory designs adapted to the unit drive system also brought improvements in working conditions and safety. Lighter, cleaner workshops were made possible by the introduction of skylights where formerly overhead transmission apparatus had been mounted; and by the elimination of the myriad strands of rotating belting that previously swirled dust and grease through the factory atmosphere, and which, unenclosed by safety screening, threatened to maim or kill workers who became caught up in them.

Regime transition: the pace of the dynamo revolution in theory and practice

The history of electrification after 1900 (see, for example, Byatt, 1979; Hughes, 1983; Minami, 1987) lends considerable plausibility to the 'regime transition thesis' of Freeman and Perez (1988). They suggest that productivity growth was sluggish in the latter years of the twentieth century, and very well might remain so, because the emergence and elaboration of a new techno-economic regime based on computer and communications innovations – supplanting the mature, ossified Fordist regime of mass production – will more than likely be a protracted and historically contingent affair. In much the same fashion as the present-day enthusiasts of the information age have heralded the revolutions to be wrought by the advent of universal access (via miniaturization and high-speed transmission networks) to massive amounts of computing power, when the twentieth century was new there were farsighted electrical engineers who had already envisaged many of the profound transformations that the dynamo revolution would bring to factories, stores and homes. But the materialization of these presbyopic visions was less imminent than it appeared to be to many at the time.

It is true that the diffusion of electric street railways in America took place almost overnight, following the widely publicized successful operation of the electric trolley car system designed by F. J. Sprague for the city of Richmond, Virginia in 1887. By 1890 there were 154 such systems in operation, accounting for almost 16 percent of street railways' total track mileage, and 9 per cent of their rolling stock (tramcars). Within scarcely more than another decade, by 1902, 97 per cent of the country's total street railway trackage, and 85 per cent of the tram cars, belonged to electric traction systems (see Passer, 1972, pp. 341–2, tables 35–6). Elsewhere, however, the dynamo's progress was comparatively halting and piecemeal. Accordingly, the sphere of the new technology's diffusion remained more circumscribed in 1899: electric lighting was being used in a mere 3 per cent of all US residences (and in only 8 per cent of urban dwelling units); the horsepower capacity of all (primary and secondary) electric motors installed in manufacturing establishments in the country represented less than 5 per cent of factory mechanical drives. In contrast with the explosive growth that had made electrification virtually co-extensive with the relatively new field of urban mass transit by 1900, another two decades, roughly speaking, would be required before the aggregate measures of the extent of domestic and factory electrification attained even the 50 per cent diffusion level (see David, 1989, table 3, for estimates and sources).

A useful perspective on the situation at the start of the twenty first century may be gained from the foregoing figures by noticing that in 1900 an observer of the progress of the 'electric age' stood about as far distant in time from the introduction of the carbon filament incandescent lamp by Edison, and Swann (1879), and of the Edison central generating station in New York and London (1881), as we now stand from comparable 'breakthrough' events in the computer revolution: the introduction of the 1043 byte memory chip (1969) and the silicon microprocessor (1970) by Intel. Although the pace of the computer's diffusion in the business and public sectors of the industrialized societies since the early 1980s has been rather faster than that recorded for the dynamo during its comparable early phase of adoption, an IBM executive recently estimated that only 10 per cent of the world's 50 million business enterprises today are using computers, and only 2 per cent of the world's business information has been digitized (see Lewis, 1989).

Certainly, the transformation of industrial processes by the new electric power technology was a long-delayed and far from automatic business. It did not acquire real momentum in the USA until after 1914–17, when the rates charged to consumers of electricity by state-regulated regional utilities fell substantially in relation to the general price level, and central power station generating capacity came to predominate over generating capacity in *isolated* industrial plant. Particularly rapid gains in the efficiency of electricity generation during the power 1910–20 underlay these developments (see David, 1989; table 4 and figure 14). The sharp acceleration that appears in Kendrick's (1961, table H–VI) estimates of total factor productivity (TFP) growth for the electric utility industry during this decade closely reflected the fact that the number of kilowatt-hours of power per dollar of central power station generating costs (in constant prices) was increasing at the average rate of 9.4 per cent per year, whereas over the two preceding decades (1890–1910) it had been rising at 5.0 per cent per annum.

To realize the economies of scale that were attainable with immense central power plants that used high-speed steam turbines to drive massive alternating current generators required more than the very substantial direct investments represented by such facilities: it necessitated the integration and extension of power transmission networks over an expanded territory. Within a larger service area, the greater diversity of electricity users contributed to mitigating the peak-load problem; and load-balancing improved the utilization of fixed capacity, to which the cost structure of the industry was extremely sensitive.

But this was not simply a matter of technology; it required adaptations in other dimensions affecting business practice. In the American setting, two 'social innovations', pioneered by Samuel Insull (at the Chicago-based Commonwealth Edison Co.) greatly facilitated the channelling of investment into the formation of regional electric utilities during the second decade of the twentieth century. One was an adjustment of the political environment, advantageously affecting the terms on which long-term monopoly franchises could be secured, and the transactions costs entailed in obtaining franchises to operate in many contiguous communities (see MacDonald 1962, pp. 82–9, 114–17, 177–8). This change was largely accomplished during the period 1907–14, through a campaign (on the part of the National Electric Light Association) to transfer regulatory authority over the electricity supply business from municipal and town governments to specially created state public utility commissions. The second 'innovation' was the application (first by Insull, in creating the Middle West Utilities Co. in 1912) of the holding company form of corporate organization to the problem of financing both the acquisition and the incremental investment needed to physically integrate numerous small, local utility operations within an extensive, centrally-managed regional network (see MacDonald, 1962, Ch. 5).

Factory electrification did not reach full fruition in its technical development and in its impact on productivity growth in manufacturing before the early 1920s, at which time only slightly more than half of factory mechanical drive capacity had been electrified. This was four decades after the first central power station opened for business. The proximate source of the delay in the exploitation of the productivity improvement potential incipient in the dynamo revolution was, in large part, the slow pace of factory electrification.

The latter, in turn, was attributable to the unprofitability of replacing still-serviceable manufacturing plants embodying production technologies adapted to the old regime of mechanical power derived from water and steam. Thus, it was the American industries that were enjoying the most rapid expansion in the early twentieth century – tobacco, fabricated metals, transportation equipment, and electrical machinery itself – that afforded the greatest immediate scope for the construction of new, electrified plants along the lines recommended by progressive industrial engineers (see DuBoff, 1979, p. 142; Minami, 1987, pp. 138–41). More widespread opportunities to embody best-practice manufacturing applications of electric power awaited the further physical depreciation of durable factory structures, the locational obsolescence of older-vintage industrial plants sited in urban core areas, and, ultimately, the development of a general fixed-capital formation boom in the expansionary macroeconomic climate of the 1920s.

The persistence of durable industrial facilities embodying older power generation and transmission equipment had further consequences that are worth noting. During the phase of the US factory electrification movement extending from the mid-1890s to the eve of the 1920s, the 'group drive' system of power transmission remained in vogue (see DuBoff, 1979, p. 144; Devine, 1983, pp. 351, 354). With this system – in which electric motors turned separate shafting sections, so that each motor drove related groups of machines – the retrofitting of steam- or water-powered plants typically entailed adding primary electric motors to the original stock of equipment. While factory owners rationally could ignore the sunk costs of the existing power transmission apparatus, and simply calculate whether the benefits in the form of reduced power requirements and improved machine speed control justified the marginal capital expenditures required to install the group drive system, productivity accountants would have to reckon that the original belt and shaft equipment, and the primary engines that powered them, remained in place as available capacity. The effect would be to raise the capital-output ratio in manufacturing, which militated against rapid gains in TFP (especially if the energy input savings, and the quality improvements from better machine control were left out of the productivity calculation).

This sort of overlaying of one technical system on a pre-existing stratum is not unusual during historical transitions from one technological paradigm to the next. Examples could be cited from the experience of the steam revolution (von Tunzelmann, 1978, pp. 142–3, 172–3). Indeed, the same phenomenon has been remarked upon in the case of the computer's application in numerous data-processing and recording functions, where old paper-based procedures are being retained alongside the new, microelectronic-based methods – sometimes to the detriment of each system's performance (see, for example, Baily and Gordon, 1988, pp. 401–2).

Finally, it would be a mistake to suppose that large potential gains from factory electrification were obtainable from the beginning of the century onwards, just because there were farsighted electrical engineers who at the time were able to envisage many sources of cost-savings that would result from exploiting the flexibility of a power transmission system based on electric wires, and the efficiency of replacing the system of shafting and belts with the so-called 'unit drive' system. In the latter arrangement, individual electric motors were used to run machines of all sizes (see Devine, 1983, pp. 362ff). The advantages of the unit drive for factory design turned out to extend well beyond the savings in inputs of fuel derived from eliminating the need to keep all the line shafts turning, and the greater energy efficiency achieved by reducing friction losses in transmission. Factory structures could be redesigned radically once the need for bracing, to support the heavy shafting and belt-housings for the transmission apparatus that typically was mounted overhead, had been dispensed with. This afforded (i) savings in fixed capital through lighter factory construction; and (ii) further capital-savings from the shift to building single-storey factories, whereas formerly the aim of reducing power-losses in turning very long line shafts had dictated the erection of more costly multi-storey structures. Single-storey, linear factory layouts, in turn, permitted (iii) closer attention to optimizing materials handling, and flexible reconfiguration of machine placement and handling equipment to accommodate subsequent changes in product and process designs within the new structures. Related to this, (iv) the modularity of the unit drive system and the flexibility of wiring curtailed losses of production incurred during maintenance, rearrangement of production lines, and plant retrofitting; the entire power system no longer had to be shut down in order to make changes in one department or section of the mill.

   Although all this was clear enough in principle, the relevant point is that its implementation on a wide scale required working out the details in the context of many kinds of new industrial facilities, in many different locales, thereby building up a cadre of experienced factory architects and electrical engineers familiar with the new approach to manufacturing. The decentralized sort of learning process this entailed was dependent upon the volume of demand for new industrial facilities at sites that favoured reliance upon purchased electricity for power. It was, moreover, inherently uncertain and slow to gain momentum, owing in part to the structure of the industry responsible for supplying the capital that embodied the new, evolving technology, because the business of constructing factories and shops remained extremely unconcentrated and was characterized by a high rate of turnover of firms and skilled personnel. Difficulties in internalizing and appropriating the benefits of the technical knowledge acquired in such circumstances is likely to slow experience-based learning. A theoretical analysis of an interdependent dynamic process involving diffusion and incremental innovations based on learning-by-doing (see David and Olsen, 1986) demonstrates that where the capital goods embodying the new technology are competitively supplied and there are significant knowledge spillovers among the firms in the supplying industry, the resulting pace of technology adoption will be slower than is socially optimal.

The more qualitative indirect benefits of the replacement of shafts and belting with wires as a means of power transmission within the factory came as part of a package containing other gains that, as has been seen, took the form of more readily quantifiable resource-savings. Consequently, a significantly positive cross-section association can be found between the rise in the industry's TFP growth rate (adjusted for purchased energy inputs) during the 1920s, *vis-à-vis* the 1910s, and the proportionate increase of its installed secondary electric motor capacity between 1919 and 1929. Making use of this cross-section relationship, approximately half of the 5 percentage point acceleration recorded in the aggregate TFP growth rate of the US manufacturing sector during 1919–29 (compared with 1909–19) is accounted for statistically simply by the growth in manufacturing secondary electric-motor capacity during that decade (see Table 3.5, p. 57, and Figure 3.1, p. 64).

But even that did not exhaust the full productivity ramifications of the dynamo revolution in the industrial sector during the 1920s. An important source of measured productivity gains during this era has been found to be the capital-saving effects of the technological and organizational innovations that underlay the growth of continuous process manufacturing and the spread of continuous shift work, most notably in the petroleum products, paper and chemical industries (see Lorant, 1966, chs 3, 4 and 5). Although these developments did not involve the replacement of shafts by wires, they were bound up indirectly with the new technological regime that buil up around the dynamo. Advances in automatic process control engineering were dependent on the use of electrical instrumentation and electro-mechanical relays. More fundamentally, electrification was a key complementary element in the foregoing innovations, because pulp and paper-making, chemical production and petroleum refining – like the primary metals, and the stone, clay and glass industries, where there were similar movements towards electrical instrumentation for process control, and greater intensity in the utilization of fixed facilities – were the branches of manufacture that made particularly heavy use of electricity for process heat.[2]

From electricity to information: qualifications and conclusions

Closer study of parts of the economic history of technology, and familiarity with the story of the dynamo revolution in particular, should help us to avoid both the pitfall of undue sanguinity and that of unrealistic impatience, into which discussions of the productivity paradox seem to plunge all too frequently. Some closing words of caution are warranted, however, to guard against the dangers of embracing the historical analogy too literally.

Computers are not dynamos. The nature of man-machine interactions and the technical problems of designing efficient interfaces for humans and computers are enormously more subtle and complex than those that arose in the implementation of electric lighting and power technology. Moreover, information as an economic commodity is not like electric current. It has special attributes (lack of super-additivity and negligible marginal costs of transfer) that make direct measurement of its production and allocation very difficult and reliance on conventional market processes very problematic. Information is different too, in that it can give rise to 'overload', a special form of congestion effect arising from inhibitions on the exercise of the option of free disposal usually presumed to characterize standard economic commodities. Negligible costs of distribution are one cause of 'overload'; information transmitters are encouraged to be indiscriminate in broadcasting their output. At the user end, free disposal may be an unjustified assumption in the economic analysis of information systems, because our cultural inheritance assigns high value to (previously scarce) information, predisposing us to try screening whatever becomes available. Yet, screening is costly; while it can contribute to a risk-averse information recipient's personal welfare, the growing duplicative allocation of human resources to coping with information overload may displace activities producing commodities that are better recorded by the national income accounts.

In defence of the historical analogy drawn here, the information structures of firms (that is, the types of data they collect and generate, and the way they distribute and process it for interpretation) may be seen as direct counterparts of the physical layouts and materials flow patterns of production and transportation systems. In one sense they are, because they constitute a form of sunk costs, and the variable cost of utilizing such a structure does not rise significantly as they age. Unlike conventional structures and equipment stocks, however, information structures *per se* do not automatically undergo significant physical depreciation. While they may become economically obsolete and be scrapped on that account, one cannot depend on the mere passage of time to create occasions leading to a radical redesign of a firm's information structures and operating modes. Consequently, there is likely to be a very strong inertial component in the evolution of information-intensive production organizations.

But even these cautionary qualifications serve only to further reinforce one of the main thrusts of the dynamo analogy. They suggest the existence of special difficulties in the commercialization of novel (information) technologies that need to be overcome before the mass of information-users can benefit in their roles as producers, and do so in ways reflected by our traditional, market-orientated indicators of productivity.

Notes

1. See, for example, Roach (1987, 1988), Baily and Gordon (1988).
2. See DuBoff (1979) pp. 179–81.

Table 3.1 Sources of labour productivity growth, US private domestic economy, 1800–1989

| | Measures across long-swing intervals | | | | | | | | | |
| | I Nineteenth Century | | | | | II Twentieth Century | | | | |
	1800–55	1855–71	1871–90	1890–05	1905–27	1890–05	1905–27	1929–48	1948–66	1966–89
1. Output per manhour	0.39	0.14	1.84	1.36	2.45	1.93	2.05	1.96	3.11	1.23
Sources										
2. Capital stock per manhour	0.19	0.53	0.84	0.45	0.73	0.55	0.48	0.07	0.81	0.57
3. Crude total factor productivity	0.20	–0.39	1.00	0.91	1.72	1.38	1.57	1.89	2.30	0.66
4. Labour quality	–	–	–	0.10	0.19	0.10	0.19	0.38	0.43	0.31
5. Capital quality	–	–	–	–	–	–	–	0.08	0.40	0.31
6. Refined total factor productivity	0.20	–0.39	1.00	0.81	1.53	1.28	1.38	1.43	1.47	0.04
Addenda										
7. Vintage effect	–	–	–	–	–	–	–	–0.11	0.16	0.00
8. Age-neutral refined total factor productivity	–	–	–	–	–	–	–	1.54	1.31	0.04

Notes:

Frame I, Nineteenth Century

Gross output per manhour: see Abramovitz and David, tables II and IIA. Abramovitz (1993), Appendix provides descriptions of scope and underlying data sources

Manhours: See Abramovitz and David, tables II and IIA.

Capital: See Abramovitz (1993), Appendix.

Labour quality, 1890–1927: based on figures for the contributions of age, sex and education in the National Economy in 1909–29, from Denison (1962). The figures are adjusted for the difference between Denison's share weights for labour in National Income and the share weights for labour in Gross National Income in the Private Domestic Economy. There are further adjustments to conform to Denison's later procedures and to allow for the slower growth of workers' education between 1890 and 1909. Factor share, see Abramovitz (1993), Appendix.

Frame II, Twentieth century
1890–1929

Gross output and manhours: from Kendrick (1961), table A–XXII.

Capital stock per manhour: net capial stock in the Private Domestic Economy from Kendrick (1961), TableA–XV. Manhours: *ibid.*, Table A–XXII.

Labour quality: see the description under Frame I, above.

Factor shares: Capital's gross factor share is capital's net share in Kendrick (1961), Table A–10 plus an estimated depreciation rate of 9 percentage points. The allowance for depreciation is the difference between capital's gross compensation as a fraction of gross national income and its net compensation as a fraction of net national income, as shown in Kendrick (1973), Table A–v. Labour's shared is calculated as total (–1) minus capital's share.

Table 3.1 (continued)

1929–1966

Gross output per manhour: from National Income and Product Accounts, of the US (NIPA). Abramovitz (1993) and Kendrick (1961) provide descriptions of data.

Capital stock per manhour: capital stock growth rates calculated from the sums of fixed private, reproducible, gross non-residential capital stock and private residential capital stock from Bureau of Economic Analysis (1993), tables A-6 and A-9. Manhours growth rates, Kendrick (1961) provides descriptions of data. Labour quality: 1929–66 from Dension's figures for the contributions of age, sex and education in the Non-residential Business Economy (1985), table 7-1). The figures are adjusted for the difference between Dension's net share weights and the gross share weights used in this table.

Capital quality: calculated from Jorgenson (1973), table 15.

Factor shares: Capital's gross income shares were calculated as the quotients of Private Gross Capital Compensation in the Private Domestic Economy divided by the Gross National Income. Private capital compensation was obtained as the sum of total capital consumption plus proprietor's net income (less the imputed labour compensation of self-employed persons) plus net rental income plus net corporate profits plus net interest income. Underlying figures from Bureau of Economic Analysis, *NIPA*, op. cit. Labour share is calculated as total (=1) minus capital's share above.

1966–89

Output per manhour and capital stock per manhour: as in 1929–66 above.

Labour quality: based on figures for the growth rates of 'Labour Composition', which represents the effects of sex, experience and education, as given by Bureau of Labour Statistics (BLS) computer printouts underlying BLS Bulletin 2426 (Dec. 1993). The resulting growth rates were raised by the ratio of the growth-rate level of the Denison figures to that of the BLS figures in the overlapping period 1948 to 1966. The original BLS figures are:

	1948–66	1966–89
Labour quality	0.22	0.16
Refined TFP	1.68	0.19
Vintage effect	0.17	0.01
Age neutral refund TFP	1.51	0.18

Capital quality: from the BLS figures for 'Capital Composition' in the BLS computer printout referred to above. The resulting growth rate was virtually identical with that of the Jorgenson figure used above in the overlapping period 1948–66, so no adjustment was made.

Factor shares: see the description for 1929–66.

Addenda on the Vintage Effect and age-netural refined TFP, 1929–89, see Appendix note on the Vintage Effect, below.

Source: Abramovitz, M. and P. David (2000) 'American Macroeconomic Growth in the Era of Knowledge-Based Progress: The Long-Run Perspective', in S. L. Engerman and R. E. Gallman (eds) *The Cambridge Economic History of the United States*, vol. 3., Cambridge University Press.

Table 3.2 The twentieth-century decline in the growth rate of total input efficiency (E*); second calculation

| | Augmented Solow model | | | | | Standard model | | | |
	E*	Capital quality (1)	Capital quality (2)	E* refined (1)	E* refined (2)	Crude TFP	Labour quality	Capital quality	Refined TFP
Frame I									
1890–1927	1.10	0.0	0.0	1.10	1.10	1.39	0.15	0.0	1.24
Frame II									
1890–1927	1.30	0.0	0.0	1.30	1.30	1.49	0.15	0.0	1.34
1929–66	1.25	0.184	0.149	1.07	1.10	2.09	0.40	0.24	1.45
1966–89	–0.05	0.235	0.189	–0.28	–0.24	0.66	0.31	0.32	0.04

Source: Abramovitz and David (2000).

Augmented Solow Model: E* from Table I. Capital quality (1) from the capital quality input figures behind Part I, Table IV multiplied by the Table IV share weight for capital θ_{KT} as modified by α_{KT}. Capital quality (2), the same input growth rate multiplied by the ratio of θ_K/θ_{KT} from source notes for Table II.3.3.

Standard Model: 1890–1927 – crude TFP from Part One Table IV. The contributions of Labour quality and Capital quality are both included (as in Part One, Table IV) on the grounds that in the absence of the Human Capital contribution, both sources of quality growth are relevant. Refined TFP = crude TFP minus (Labour quality + Capital quality).

Table 3.3 Sources of labour productivity growth in US PDE: estimates allowing for (intangible capital) augmented factor inputs, 1890–1989

	Labour productivity	Contributions of factor inputs (percentage points)		Augmented TFP residual (Crude)
	$Y^*_A - L_A$	$\theta^*_{KT}(K^*_T - L^*)$	$\theta_H(H^8 - I^*)$	
Frame I				
1890–1905	1.37	0.55	0.18	0.64
1905–27	2.81	0.73	0.67	1.41
Frame II				
1890–1905	1.94	0.51	0.19	1.24
1905–27	2.40	0.47	0.59	1.34
1929–66	2.71	0.36	1.10	1.25
1966–89	1.06	0.39	0.72	−0.05

Notes: Real Gross Product augmented by forgone earnings component of Human Capital function through education and training, and intangible investment in the form of R&D. The contributions of the factors are the products of their growth rates times their gross factor share weights adjusted to allow for intangible capital. The augmented TFP residual is the growth rate of Labour Productivity minus the contributions of the factors. The factor growth rates are from Table IA; the factor share weights are from Table IB.
Source: Abramovitz and David (2000).

Table 3.4 Output and factor input growth rates, US, PDE: 1890–1989

	Y^*	Y^*_A	L^*	K^*_T	H^*	$Y^*_A - L^*$	$K^*_T - L$	$H^* - L^*$
Part One, Frame I								
1890–1905	3.80	3.81	2.41	3.64	4.40	1.37	1.20	1.94
1905–27	3.30	3.66	0.83	2.43	4.40	2.81	1.59	3.54
Part One, Frame II								
1890–1905	4.25	4.26	2.28	3.49	4.40	1.94	1.16	2.07
1905–27	3.31	3.67	1.24	2.43	4.40	2.40	1.18	3.12
1929–66	3.05	3.24	0.52	1.85	3.88	2.71	1.32	3.34
1966–89	2.86	2.69	1.61	3.11	3.82	1.06	1.48	2.17

Source: Abramovitz and David (2000)

Part One, Frame I: Y^*, L^*; see Statistical Appendix for Part One, Tables IA, and IIA (Frame I) and description of sources for these tables in Section 2. K^*_T from figures underlying Table IVA and source description for that table in Statistical Appendix, Section 2. H^* from Part Two, Table II.3.1. Y^*_A obtained by augmenting Y^* as shown above by the difference between David's estimate of Y^*_A from Part Two, Table II.3.1.

Part One, Frame II: 1890–1905 and 1905–27 Y^* and L^* from Statistical Appendix for Part One, Tables IA and IIA (Frame II). Original source: Kendrick, 1961, table A-xxii. K^*_T from figures underlying Table IV. Original source: Kendrick, 1961, table xv. H^* from Part II, Table II.3.1. Y^*_A obtained by the same procedure as in Frame I.

1929–66 and 1966–89: Y^* and L^* from Statistical Appendix for Part One, Tables IA and IIA. Original source NIPA, (1992) and (1993). See source description in Part One Statistical Appendix; Section 2. K^*_T from figures underlying Part One, Table IVA. Original source: BEA, tables A6 and A9. Y^*_A obtained by the same procedure as in Frame I.

Table 3.5 Gross factor share weights for standard and augmented factor input, 1890–1989

	Weights for standard input		Adjustment ratios		Weights for augmented inputs		
	θ_L	θ_{KT}	α_L	α_{KT}	θ'_L	θ'_{KT}	θ_H
Frame I							
1890–1905	0.54	0.46	0.092	0.00	0.448	0.46	0.092
1905–27	0.54	0.46	0.185	0.003	0.355	0.457	0.188
Frame II							
1890–1905	0.56	0.44	0.092	0.00	0.468	0.44	0.092
1905–27	0.60	0.40	0.185	0.003	0.415	0.397	0.188
1929–66	0.64	0.36	0.244	0.084	0.396	0.276	0.328
1966–89	0.65	0.35	0.246	0.084	0.404	0.266	0.330

Source: Abramovitz and David (2000).

Frame I: Standard weights: see Statistical Appendix for Part One, Section 2, Sources for figures from 19th century. Adjustment ratios from Part Two, Table 11.3.1A. Weights for augmented inputs are the standard ratios minus α_L or α_K. $\theta_H = \alpha_L + \alpha_K$.

Frame II: 1879–1905 and 1905–27: standard weights; Kendrick (1961), table A X. The Kendrick figures for net share weight of capital are raised by 9 percentage points, an estimate of the weight of capital consumption. Adjustment ratios and weights for augmented inputs from the same sources and procedures as in Frame I.

Table 3.6 US manufacturing sector average labour productivity and total factor productivity growth rates, 1869–1948 (per cent per annum)

| Periods | Estimates using Kendrick's (1961) measures for output and inputs | | | | Estimates using alternative measures for output and labour inputs | | |
| | Labour productivity | | TFP | | Labor productivity | | TFP |
	(V^*-H^*)	(V^*-L^*)	(A_a^*)	(A_g^*)	$(V^*)-(H^*)$	$(V^*)-(L^*)$	(A_g^*)
1869–89	1.67	1.60	1.41	0.77	3.97	3.96	2.99
1869–79	0.95	0.96	0.87	0.31	3.23	3.24	2.61
1879–89	2.40	2.24	1.96	1.23	4.71	4.69	3.37
1889–1909	1.37	1.44	0.09	0.68	1.39	1.31	0.70
1889–99	1.43	1.43	1.12	0.86	1.14	1.15	0.65
1899–1909	1.31	1.46	0.72	0.50	1.64	1.47	0.74
1909–29	3.34	3.18	2.77	2.70			
1909–19	1.15	0.82	0.29	0.17			
1919–29	5.59	5.59	5.31	5.29			
1919–48	1.76	1.61	1.76	1.73			
1929–37	1.97	1.82	1.95	1.96			
1937–48	1.56	1.39	1.56	1.56			

Notes: Asterisked variables denote growth rates for real gross product originating per manhour $(V^* - H^*)$ and per relative wage-weighted manhour $(V^* - L^*)$; growth rates for total factor productivity from arithmetic factor share weighting of inputs (A_a^*), and from geometric factor share weighting of inputs (A_g^*).

Source: Paul A. David (1991) 'Computer and Dynamo: The Modern Productivity Paradox in a Not-Too Distant Mirror', *Technology and Productivity: The Challenge for Economic Policy*, (Paris: Organization for Economic Co-operation and Development).

Sources: Kendrick-based estimates: calculated from labour productivity and capital productivity data in Kendrick (1961), table D-1, cols. 5, 7, 11; table D-14 for decadal factor share weights, 1919–48. For 1869–1919, the 1919–29 weights were used throughout.

Alternative estimates: calculated from Gallman (1960), p. 43 constant (1879) dollar value added for (V); manhours (H) from sectoral data underlying aggregate manhours in David (1977); (L) from adjustment of H by ratio of relative wage weighted labour inputs to manhours given by Kendrick (1961), Table D-1, cols. 6 and 4, respectively. The capital input estimates from Kendrick (1961), D-1, col. 8, and the alternative labour input estimates were geometrically weighted, using the invariant (1919–29 Kendrick (1961), Table D-14) weights .232 and .768, respectively.

Table 3.7 ICT diffusion in the US manufacturing sector, 1988, percentage of establishments reporting use

Technology	All US manufacturing, 1988 Sizes of establishments		All computer-intensive industries SICs 34-38	Low usage industries (SIC)	High usage industries (SIC)
	20–499	500+			
Design and Engineering					
Computer-aided design (CAD)	36.3	82.6	58.8	46.5 (34)	65.8 (38)
CAD-controlled machines	–	–	25.6	18.5 (38)	34.8 (35)
Digital CAD	–	–	11.3	7.0 (34)	16.1 (36.38)
Fabrication/Machining Systems					
Flexible manufacturing systems	9.1	35.9	12.7	9.5 (34)	17.0 (36)
NC/CNC machines	39.6	69.8	46.9	34.5 (36)	61.9 (35)
Lasers	n.a.	n.a.	5.0	3.4 (34)	7.8 (36)
Pick-place robots	5.5	43.3	8.6	5.4 (35)	15.2 (36)
Other robots (assembly)	3.9	35.0	4.8	3.6 (35)	11.7 (37)
Automated Material Handling					
Automatic storage/retrieval	1.9	24.4	2.6	1.2 (34)	4.8 (38)
Guided vehicle systems	0.8	13.1	1.1	0.3 (34)	2.2 (37)
Automated Sensor-based Inspection					
Materials sensors	–	–	9.9	8.1 (34.35)	15.6 (37)
Output sensors	–	–	12.5	9.6 (34)	17.5 (36)

Table 3.7 (continued)

All US manufacturing, 1988 Sizes of establishments 20–499 500+	Technology	All computer-intensive industries SICs 34–38	Low usage industries (SIC)	High usage industries (SIC)
Communication and Control				
– – –	LAN for technical data	29.3	20.1 (34)	40.7 (38)
– – –	Factory LAN	22.1	14.5 (34)	30.5 (36)
– – –	Intercompany computer network	17.9	15.3 (38)	23.4 (37)
– – –	Programmable controllers	30.4	29.0 (35)	30.7 (36.37)
– – –	Computers used on factory floor	26.9	20.2 (34)	29.0 (38)

Key: The two-digit industry codes used here are 34 = Fabricated metal products, except machinery and transportation equipment; 35 = Industrial and commercial machinery and computer equipment; 36 = Electronic and other electrical equipment and components, except computers; 37 = Transportation equipment; 38 = Measuring, analyzing and controlling instruments.

Sources: All US Manufacturing, 1988: from 'Diffusion of Microelectronics and Advanced Manufacturing Technology: A Review of National Surveys', in Graham Vickery and Jim Northcott (1995), *Economics of Innovation and New Technology*, vol. 3, table 7, p. 263.
Technology, All Computer Intensive Industries, Industry Usage: from The Conference Board (1997), *Perspectives on a Global Economy: Technology, Productivity and Growth: U.S. and German Issues*, Report no. 1206-07-RR, Winter, table 2, p. 8.

Table 3.8 The growth of secondary electric motor (horse power) capacity and the acceleration of multifactor productivity in US manufacturing, 1909–29

Industry	[1] Percentage points of change in multifactor productivity growth rate, 1909–19 to 1919–29	[2] Ratio of secondary electric motor HP capacity, in 1919	[3] Proportion of primary HP capacity electrified in 1919
Paper products	4.40	3.34	0.34
Leather products	4.30	1.02	0.74
Stone, clay, glass;4.10	2.42	0.54	0.19
Lumber products	3.42	2.83	0.65
Chemicals	3.80	1.78	0.57
Petroleum and coal products	3.20	2.91	0.96
Machinery, electrical	2.27	1.03	0.37
Iron and steel	1.60	1.99	0.47
Food products	1.60	1.45	0.76
Machinery, non-electrical	1.56	1.29	0.85
Non-ferrous metals	0.60	1.14	0.79
Rubber	0.50	1.49	0.93
Printing and publishing	0.30	1.16	0.86
Transportation equipment	−0.60	1.45	

Sources:

1. From Woolf (1984), table 2, estimates adjusted for energy inputs. Estimates in column (1) for Electrical and Non-electrical machinery were obtained by combining Kendrick's figures using (value added) weights of 0.333 and 0.667, respectively, and finding Woolf's estimate for machinery to be 0.71 of the combined figure. The latter multiplier was used to scale down the column estimates.
2 and 3. From DuBoff (1979), table E-12C, D; table 26, respectively.

Table 3.9   Education–skill premia by occupation, 1895, 1926 and 1939

| | Clerk/production worker wage | | |
	1895	*1926*	*1939*
Males			
Bookkeepers	2.278	1.604	1.268
Typists, stenographers	1.638	1.319	1.100
Clerks	1.388	1.084	1.088
Machine operators	–	0.816	0.960
Females			
Typists, stenographers	2.099	1.641	1.652
Bookkeepers	2.001	2.205	1.613
Clerks	1.798	1.177	1.499
Machine operators	–	1.404	1.492

Notes: The weekly wage for clerks in 1939 has been adjusted for consistency with the other years by calculating the implied figure for clerks other than those in the 'other' category (e.g., mail and filing clerks). The figures are $30.16 for males and $22.77 for females. In all years the annual figures for production workers have been divided by 52 to obtain the weekly wage.

Source: Goldin, C. and L. Katz (1995) 'The Decline of Non-Competing Groups: Changes in the Premium to Education, 1890 to 1950', National Bureau of Economic Research Working Paper No. 5202 (Cambridge, Mass., table 6).

References

Abramovitz, M. (1956) 'Resources and Output Trends in the United States since 1870', *American Economic Review*, vol. 46, no.2, pp. 5–23.

Abramovitz, M. (1993) 'The Search for the Sources of Growth: Areas of Ignorance, Old and New', *Journal of Economic History*, vol. 53, no.2, pp. 217–43.

Abramovitz, M. and P. David (2000) 'American Macroeconomic Growth in the Era of Knowledge-based Progress: The Long-Run Perspective', in Engerman S. L. and R. E. Gallman (eds), *The Cambridge Economic History of the United States*, vol. 3, Cambridge, United Kingdom: Cambridge University Press.

Baily, M. and R. Gordon (1988) 'The Productivity Slowdown, Measurement Issues, and the Explosion of Computer Power', *Brookings Paper on Economic Activity*, (2), pp. 347–431.

Boskin, M. *et al.* (1996) 'Toward a More Accurate Measure of the Cost of Living: Final Report to the Senate Finance Committee from the Advisory Commission to Study the Consumer Price Index', Washington DC.

Bresnahan, T. and M. Trajtenberg (1995) 'General Purpose Technologies 'Engines of Growth?', *Journal of Econometrics*, 65, pp. 83–108.

Brynjolfsson, E. (1996) 'The Contribution of Information Technology to Consumer Welfare', Information Systems Research 7, September.

Byatt, I. C. R. (1979) *The British Electrical Industry 1875–1914: The Economic returns to a new Technology*, Oxford: Clarendon Press.

Conference Board (1997) *Perspectives on a Global Economy: Technology, Productivity and growth: U.S. and German Issues*, Report No. 1206–07–RR, Winter, p. 8.

David, P. (1977) 'Invention and Accumulation in America's Economic Growth', in Brunner, K. and A. H. Meltzer (eds), *International Organization, National Policies and Economic Development*, Amsterdam: North-Holland Publishing.

Table 3.10   Pace of increase in average school years of US population and labour force, 1910–65

Average decadal percentage rates of growth in average number of school years completed

| Decades | (1) All males, 25+ | Years | Civilian labour force | | |
			(2) Males	(3) Females	(4) Total
1910–20	6.4				
1920–30	7.6				
1930–40	8.9				
1940–50	10.4				
1950–60	7.6	1948–59	9.0	6.6	8.3
		1952–62	8.5	7.1	8.0
		1957–62	11.8	7.5	10.4
		1957–65	11.1	7.0	9.7

Source: Abramovitz and David (2000), table 2.
Notes:
Col. (1): the changes from 1940–50 and 1950–60 are based on Census data. Those for 1910–40 are based on Denison's (1962) estimates by the cohort method subject to an upward adjustment of 0.2 percentage points per annum to allow for a suspected reporting error. See E. F. Denison (1962) *The Sources of Economic Growth in the United States and the Alternatives Before Us* (New York: Committee for Economic Development), table 4, col. (2).
Cols (2) and (3): Based on data from Current Population Reports as summarized in E. F. Denison (1964) 'Measuring the Contribution of Education (and the Residual)' ch. 1 in *The Residual Factor and Economic Growth* (Paris: OECD), table F-9.
Col. (4): Cols. (2) and (3), above, estimates of the average number of school years completed by males, were combined with those for females with weights of $\frac{1}{3}$ and $\frac{1}{3}$ respectively, the weights representing the approximate proportions of men and women in the labour force. Percentage changes per decade were then derived from the resulting average numbers of school years completed.

David, P. (1989) 'Computer and Dynamo: The Modern Productivity Paradox in a Not-Too Distant Mirror', Center for Economic Policy Research, No.172, Stanford University, CA.

David, P. (1990) 'The Dynamo and the Computer: An Historical Perspective on the Modern Productivity Paradox', *AEA Papers and Proceedings*, 80 (2), pp. 355–61

David, P. (1991) 'Computer and Dynamo: The Modern Productivity Paradox in a Not-Too Distant Mirror', in *Technology and Productivity: The Challenge for Economic Policy*, Paris: Organization for Economic Cooperation and Development.

David, P. and T. Olsen (1986) 'Equilibrium Dynamics of Diffusion when Incremental Technological Innovations are Foreseen', *Ricerche Economiche*, October–December, vol. 40, pp. 738–70.

Denison, E. (1962) *The Sources of Economic Growth in the United States and the Alternatives Before Us*, New York: Committee for Economic Development.

Denison E. (1964) 'Measuring the Contribution of Education', in *The Residual Factor and Economic Growth*, Paris; Organization for Economic Cooperation and Development.

Devine W. (1983) 'From Shafts to Wires: Historical Perspective on Electrification', *Journal of Economic History*, 43 (2), pp. 347–72.

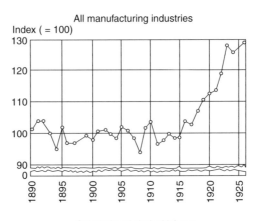

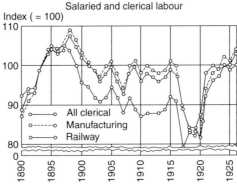

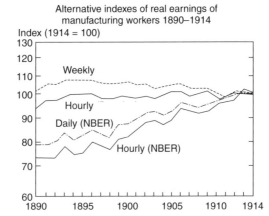

Figure 3.1   US real wages and real annual earnings movements, 1890–1926

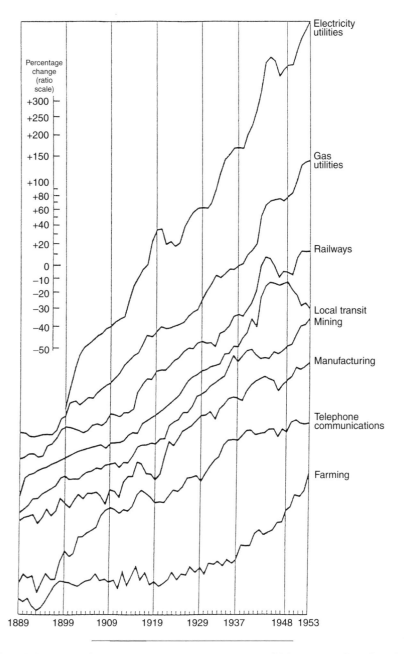

Figure 3.2 Private domestic economy; output per unit of labour input by selected industry group, 1889–1953 (1929 = 100)
Source: Kendrick (1961), p. 176.

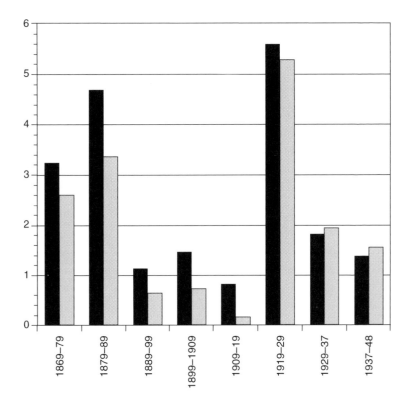

Figure 3.3 Average annual growth rates of US manufacturing sector's labour productivity (black columns) and total factor productivity (grey columns)
Sources: Kendrick (1961), David (1977).

Diewert, E. and K. Fox (1999) 'Can measurement Error Explain the Productivity Paradox?', *Canadian Journal of Economics*, vol. 32, no. 2, pp. 251–80.

DuBoff, R. (1979) *Electrical Power in American Manufacturing 1889–1958*, New York: Arno Press.

Freeman, C. and C. Perez (1997) 'Structural Crises of Adjustment: Business Cycles and Investment Behavior', in Dosi, G., Freeman, C., Nelson, R., Silverberg, G. and Soete, L., (eds), '*Technological Change and Economic Theory*, London: Pinter.

Goldin, C. and L. Katz (1995) 'The Decline of Non-Competing Groups: Changes in the Premium to Education 1890–1950', NBER Working Paper No. 5202.

Gordon, R. (1999) 'Monetary Policy in the Age of Information Technology', *IMES Discussion Paper Series 99–E–12*, Bank of Japan.

Griliches, Z. (1994) 'Productivity, R&D and Data Constraint', *American Economic Review*, vol. 84, pp. 1–23.

Griliches Z. and D. Jorgenson (1967) 'The Explanation of Productivity Change', *Review of Economic Studies*, vol. 34, no. 99, pp. 249–80.

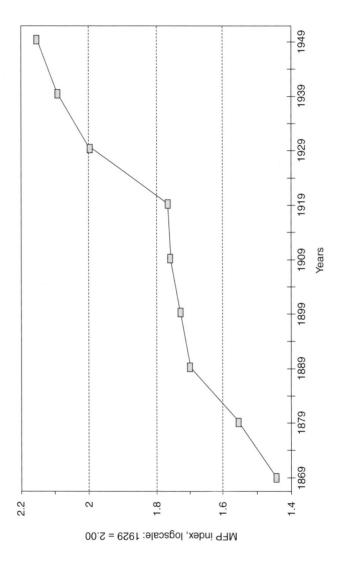

Figure 3.4 US manufacturing, 1869–1949, multifactor productivity trend
Source: David (1991).

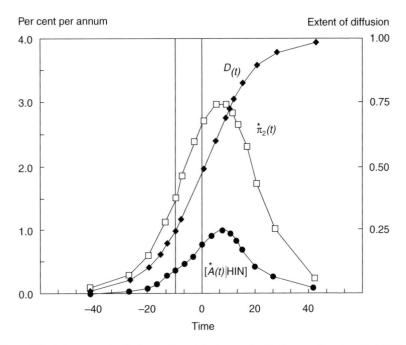

Figure 3.5 Labour productivity and total factor productivity growth rates along the diffusion path

Source: Paul A. David (1991).

Hughes, T. (1983) *Networks of Power: Electrification in Western Society, 1880–1930*, Baltimore: Johns Hopkins University Press.

Irwin, D. A. and P. J. Klenow (1996) 'High-tech R&D subsidies: estimating the effects of Sematech', *Journal of International Economics*, 40, pp. 323–44.

Jorgenson, D. and K. Stiroh (1995) 'Computers and Growth', *Economics of Innovation and New Technology*, vol. 3., Economia e Produzione, Milan.

Kendrick, J. (1961) *Productivity Trends in the United States*, Princeton: Princeton University Press for the National Bureau of Economic Research.

Lewis, P. (1989) 'The Executive Computer: Can There Be Too Much Power?', *The New York Times*, December 31, p. 9.

Lorant, J. (1966) *The role of Capital-Improving Innovations in American Manufacturing during the 1920's*, New York: Arno Press.

Minami, R. (1987) *Power Revolution in the Industrialization of Japan: 1885–1940*, Tokyo: Kinokuniya Shoten.

Nakamura, L. (1997) 'Is the U.S. Economy Really Growing Too Slowly? Maybe We're Measuring Growth Wrong', *Business Review*, Federal Reserve Bank of Philadelphia, March/April, pp. 3–14.

Roach, S. (1987) 'America's Technology Dilemma: A Profile of the Information Society', *Morgan Stanley Dean Witter Special Economic Study*, September 22, New York.

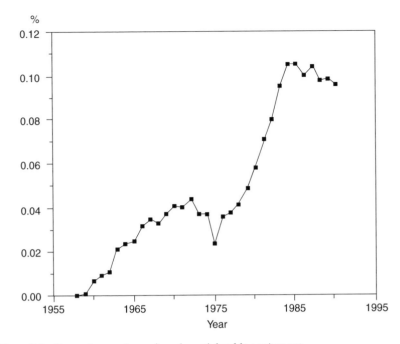

Figure 3.6   Computers as share of producers' durable equipment
Source: Brynjolfsson (1996), based on data from BEA, National Income and Wealth Division (1990 data is prepublication).

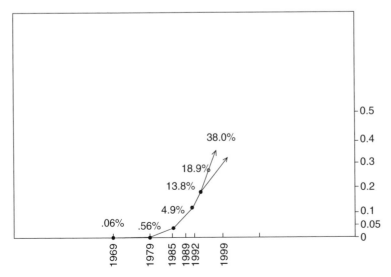

Figure 3.7   Computer equipment services as a fraction of (non-residential) PDE services, 1987 prices
Source: D. Jorgenson and K. Stiroh (1995) 'Computers and Growth,' *Economics of Innovation and New Technology*, vol. 3, no. 3–4, table 1.

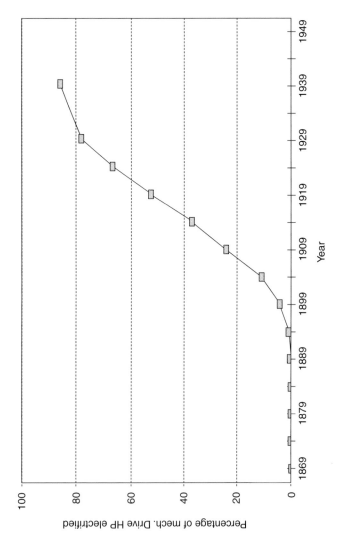

Figure 3.8 US manufacturing sector, 1869–1939, factory electrification
Source: David (1991).

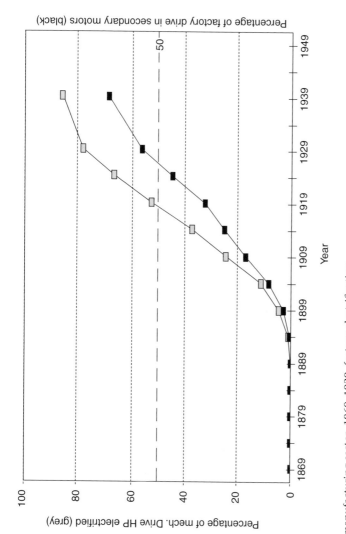

Figure 3.9 US manufacturing sector, 1869–1939, factory electrification
Source: David (1991).

Roach, S. (1988) 'White Collar Productivity: A Glimmer of Hope?', *Morgan Stanley Dean Witter Special Economic Study*, September 16, New York.

Vickery, G. and J. Northcott (1995) 'Diffusion of Microelectronics and Advanced Manufacturing Technology: A Review of National Surveys', *Economics of Innovation and New Technology*, vol. 3, Economia e Produzione, Milan.

von Tunzelmann, G. N. (1978) *Steam Power and British Industrialization to 1860*, Oxford: Clarendon Press.

Woolf, Arthur G. (1984) 'Electricity, Productivity, and Labor Saving: American Manufacturing, 1900–1929', *Explorations in Economic History*, 21(2), April, pp. 176–91.

Comments

Roger W. Ferguson, Jr*

Introduction

I would like to focus my comments on three areas. First, I would like to put forward some facts – or at least some published data – by presenting the recent evidence on productivity growth for the USA. As I shall show, the performance of US productivity has improved noticeably during the 1990s, leading some observers to assert that the long-awaited productivity benefits from the high-tech revolution are finally showing up in the statistics. However, there are reasons to question this interpretation of recent data, and, in my view, the bottom line is by no means clear.

Second, I would like to offer some specific comments on Professor David's very thoughtful and interesting chapter on the historical precedents to the computer revolution. I find the approach of bringing specific events in economic history to bear on current economic issues to be quite appealing, and Professor David points out many striking similarities between the time-lines of the diffusion of electricity and the diffusion of computing technology. However, there are also important differences between these two episodes, and it is important to consider the extent to which these differences might influence our assessment of whether, as Professor David suggests, a substantial productivity payoff from computers is still on the cards, or whether, as has been argued by others, we have already enjoyed whatever payoff might be expected.

Finally, I want to spend some time on the role of monetary policy in a world of knowledge-based growth. That is, what if computers, or some other set of factors, have raised – or are about to raise – the trend rate of productivity growth? What are the implications for the economy? And, perhaps more relevant for this book, what is the appropriate monetary policy response to such an improvement in economic growth?

---

* I wish to acknowledge the assistance of Dan Sichel, Bill Wascher and John Williams. The views expressed in this comment are my own and do not necessarily reflect those of the Board of Governors of the Federal System or its staff.

Weighing the evidence for a higher productivity trend

Turning first to recent data, Figure C3.1 shows the US data on labour productivity in the non-farm business sector from 1960 to the end of the first quarter of 1998. The solid line shows the actual path of productivity over this period, while the dashed line represents longer-run trends; the numbers in the inset table report these trends, which are measured as the average annual growth rates over these periods. The well-known – albeit still not fully understood – slowdown in productivity growth beginning in the 1970s can be seen in the Figure, as can an acceleration in productivity in recent years – if one looks closely enough. In particular, as is also shown in the inset table, productivity growth has picked up from roughly 0.8 per cent per year over the period 1990–95 to almost 2 per cent per year from 1996–8.[1]

A key question, of course, is how to interpret this pick-up in measured labour productivity growth. That is, does the recent growth spurt represent a permanent increase in the trend rate of growth? Or is it a temporary phenomenon reflecting the short-run increasing returns to labour typically found in cyclical models that relate output to productivity.

One relatively straightforward way to address this question is to see if the recent behaviour of productivity is above what would be predicted by a simple short-run model of labour demand, assuming no recent increase in trend growth. Although I have relegated the details of the model to an appendix (see page 84), the simulation of this model is shown in Figure C3.2. This is a dynamic simulation beginning in 1973 and running to the end of the first quarter of 1998. Generally, the model appears to fit relatively well and tends to pick up the cyclical movements in productivity. What is especially striking, though, is the comparison of the simulated and published values of productivity since 1990. In particular, productivity growth was considerably stronger than predicted by the model in the economic recovery of 1991 and 1992 (recall that this period was referred to in the USA as the 'jobless recovery' at that time), but considerably weaker in the subsequent two years. Since mid-1995, productivity growth was again somewhat stronger than predicted by the model. But even so, the larger increases in productivity in recent years have only now returned measured productivity to the simulated value from the model. Thus the level of productivity as of 1998 is not much different from what a simple model with a constant trend says it should be, given the strong recent output growth. Of course, this simplistic model does not take into account other information that might influence our view of whether this strength in productivity growth is more permanent in nature. In particular, one could imagine a similar model with a somewhat lower trend rate of growth in the early 1990s and a somewhat higher trend rate in the later 1990s. Not surprisingly, given the short time-period involved, formal statistical tests have difficulty in picking up significantly different trends in these two sub-periods, although the coefficient estimates do point in that direction. But knowing that

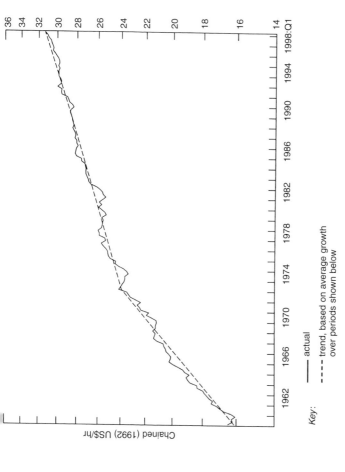

75

Figure C3.1 Productivity growth, non-farm business: US$ 1992/hr average annual percentage change)

Notes: 1960–Q2 to 1973–Q13.1 per cent
1973–Q2 to 1990–Q21.1 per cent
1990–Q3 to 1998–Q11.2 per cent
1990–Q3 to 1995–Q20.8 per cent
1995–Q3 to 1998–Q11.8 per cent

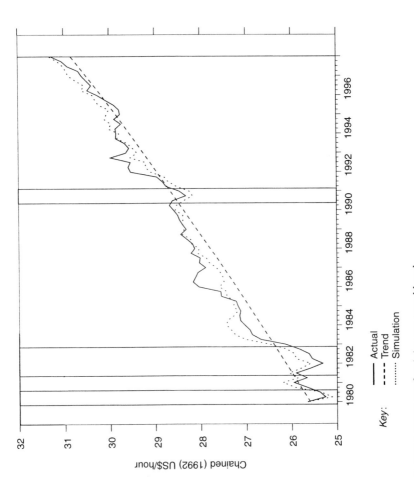

Figure C3.2 Non farm business sector productivity, no trend break
Note: Vertical lines mark dates of NBER recessions.

such tests will have a hard time distinguishing between these alternatives, it is worth considering whether there might be plausible explanations for such a break, and whether other information supports this story.

One such explanation relates to the rapid pace of investment in the later 1990s and the corresponding expansion of the US, capital stock. As can be seen from Figure C3.3, the growth rate of capital services has picked up smartly, from roughly 2.25 per cent per year over the first half of the 1990s to around 3.75 per cent by 1996. Given capital's share of nominal output (around 0.3) and an increase in hours 1996 of about 1.5 per cent, this increased rate of capital deepening – according to the Bureau of Labor Statistics (BLS) calculations – contributed 0.7 percentage point to labour productivity growth in 1996, up from an average contribution of 0.4 percentage points per year during 1990–95. Another explanation relates to multifactor productivity (MFP) which, over long periods, can be thought of as a measure of technical progress. As shown in the lower panel of Figure C3.3, multifactor productivity growth has also picked up in the most recent data shown, from 0.1 per cent per year over the first half of the 1990s to around 1 per cent in 1996.

Both of these developments are possibly related to the strides in knowledge-based technology and are causes for optimism. We know that business purchases of computers and other information-based technology have been a significant component of the recent investment boom and are one source of the faster growth in capital services. Moreover, it has been hypothesized – and there is some anecdotal evidence supporting this hypothesis – that synergies between high-tech investment and other factors of production – notably labour – might be a source of faster MFP growth.

However, it is also true that neither the increase in the pace of capital deepening nor the pick-up in MFP growth are necessarily permanent features of a new era. Both these components of labour productivity growth also exhibit fairly clear cyclical tendencies and, as with labour productivity, it is often difficult to disentangle the trend from the cycle. Thus in the end, the only thing that we can say definitively is that time will tell. In the interim, however, it is useful to reconsider the productivity paradox, as Paul David has done.

Comments on the dynamo–computer analogy

Professor David's work has performed an important service by drawing economists' attention back in time as a means of better understanding this paradox. We have much to learn from historical analysis, and I found his chapter to be quite interesting and provocative. Here, as in other papers that have preceded it, Professor David suggests that the big productivity gains to be made from computerization still lie ahead. He argues that radically new technologies – such as computers – take a long time to diffuse through the economy, both because companies must learn how to use the new resources

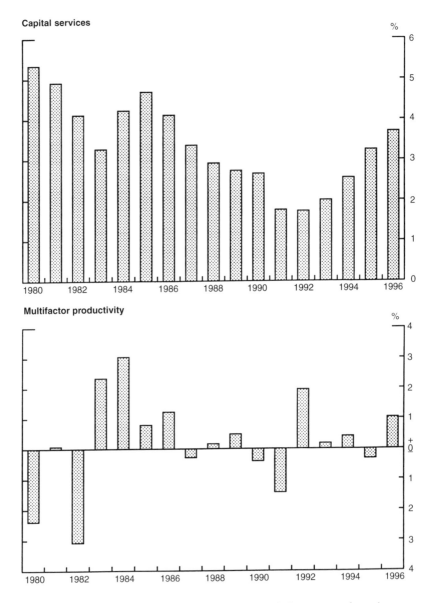

Figure C3.3   Factors affecting labour productivity growth (percentage change)

effectively and because it may not be possible or profitable to integrate new technologies quickly and redesign core processes.

Professor David makes this argument vivid by drawing an analogy to the development and diffusion of electric motors. The fundamental scientific discoveries needed for the commercial application of electricity had taken place by 1880, but many years passed before electric power was used throughout the economy. For many factories, the switch from steam to electric power was complicated, entailing significant adjustment costs and requiring the scrapping of machinery that was still working perfectly well. Moreover, early applications of electric technology – such as the replacement of a large steam-powered unit by a large electric-powered unit without redesigning the production process – generated only modest savings from reduced power costs. Thus in many cases, the returns to the new technology were not viewed as being high enough to justify the large adjustment costs or the risk associated with implementing it.

Nonetheless, over time, the use of electric power diffused through the economy, and by 1919, electricity accounted for 50 per cent of the mechanical drive power used in manufacturing. Perhaps more importantly, the way in which the new technology was applied changed as well. Rather than just replacing large steam-powered units with large electric dynamos, companies began to distribute many smaller electric motors throughout factories, and this allowed a transition from old-style factories with a single large power shaft linked by belts to individual machines. In the older arrangement, turning on a single machine tool on the shop floor required the powering up of the drive shaft for the entire factory. In the new paradigm of distributed power, production and materials handling could be arranged far more efficiently. In addition, the new unit electric drives did away with the noise, dirt and danger associated with large belts running through the factory. By the 1920s, these more fundamental changes were well under way, and productivity growth picked up.

At first glance, this story would seem to apply to computers as well. Computers are a relatively new and seemingly revolutionary technology. The initial applications of computers were limited to tasks already being done with existing technologies, but over time information technology has been applied to ever wider sets of tasks. Indeed, the list of things that can be done, given the rapid developments in information technology, is incredible: electronic commerce on the Internet; the rise of entirely new industries (such as express package delivery); an explosion in the variety of financial products; just-in-time inventory control in manufacturing and retailing; and telecommuting and 'virtual' workplaces. Some observers have suggested that these developments could radically reduce the need for office buildings, highways and other physical infrastructure. Other revolutionary applications of information technology remain to be discovered. And, as Professor David points out, many years may pass before businesses learn to exploit information technology fully, and before the full productivity benefits are realized.

On the other hand, the spread of electric power and desktop computers also differ in important ways. For one thing, there are variety of reasons to think that the transition to computers might be faster and less costly than was the transition to electric power. Retooling a manufacturing plant to use electric rather than steam power required huge expenditure to reconfigure the physical plant and, as I mentioned earlier, such large transition costs were one reason that the transition proceeded at such a modest pace. In contrast, the transition from older office equipment to computers, and from mainframe computers to desktop machines, probably entails smaller adjustment costs. If so, we could expect computers to diffuse more rapidly through the economy, and therefore companies would realize the gains from computers more rapidly.[2] In addition, computers have already been around for a considerable length of time, having been used in commercial applications by businesses since the mid-1950s. Contemporary press accounts suggest that, even then, companies were thinking hard about how business structures should be reorganized to use the new, so-called 'electronic brain', most effectively, suggesting that the transition to computers has proceeded relatively rapidly.[3]

Finally, there is a sense in which computers can be viewed as an evolutionary extension of earlier office automation technologies, such as typewriters, adding and calculating machines, automated tabulating equipment, printing and duplicating machines, telegraphs, and telephones. These earlier tools of office automation also underwent rapid innovation over the years, and the companies producing this equipment were large and important players in the economy.[4] For example, in the 1840s, sending a one-page message from New York City to Chicago took about ten days. After the telegraph became available in the 1850s, sending the same message took about five minutes. Even though the cost went up significantly, the price–speed ratio increased by a factor of 100. As another example, the US National Census was compiled with automated tabulating equipment for the first time in 1890. By the time of the next Census in 1900, the price per unit of speed of tabulating equipment had fallen by a factor of four. To the extent that the development of computers has been more evolutionary than revolutionary, we may not see a sudden step up in productivity growth, but rather a continuation of the productivity gains achieved through the adoption of other technologies in earlier decades.

I do not want to push this counter-argument too far. I find the capabilities and possibilities of modern computing equipment to be remarkable, and I find much to like in Professor David's argument. Rather, my point is to highlight the uncertainty about what the future holds. Professor David could well be correct, and we central bankers might find ourselves in the desirable position of responding to improved long-term prospects for the economy. On the other hand, information technology is just one driver of change in a very large and complex world economy, and computers still represent quite a small share of the capital stock in the USA. While I am hopeful about the future prospects for information technology and for productivity growth, I still judge it too soon to know with certainty that we have turned the corner.

What if trend productivity has picked up?

It should be clear by now that I am relatively agnostic on the question of whether the seemingly omnipresent advances in computer technology we have seen since the early 1980s have engendered an increase in the trend rate of productivity growth. But let us assume for the moment that the productivity trend – and here I am referring to multifactor productivity – has increased in recent years from its sluggish pace of the 1980s and early 1990s. What would be the implications of such a pickup for the US economy – and for monetary policy in particular? The answer differs somewhat between long-run and short-run.

Long-run implications

Increases in labour productivity are the ultimate source of increases in real wages and living standards. Thus, if productivity growth has truly picked up, then we can expect a more rapid pace of advance in living standards than has been realized in the period since 1975 or so. Faster growth of real wages and living standards could have vast social and economic consequences, easing the financing challenges facing public pensions and other pressures faced by fiscal authorities, helping to alleviate poverty, and providing a welcome economic boost and new opportunities for all our citizens. Such developments would be extremely favourable for all our economies, although they are not much related to the conduct of monetary policy.

As for monetary policy and the implications of a faster productivity trend, let me start by using the simple theoretical growth model originated by Robert Solow.[5] On the simplistic assumption of a constant saving rate, the primary long-run implication of an increase in trend productivity (MFP) growth in this model is an increase in the equilibrium real interest rate – that is, the rate consistent with maintaining a balanced growth equilibrium for the economy. This occurs because a permanent increase in the growth rate of productivity raises the amount of capital investment that would be needed to maintain a given capital–output ratio. For a given saving rate, capital becomes more scarce (the capital–output ratio falls), and its price, the real interest rate, rises.

Of course, assuming that the saving rate is invariant to changes in the rate of growth is a very strong assumption, and in reality, the saving rate may shift following a pick-up in trend growth, depending, for example, on the responses of the fiscal and foreign sectors, and on the interest-sensitivity of personal saving. For this reason, the predictions of the simple Solow growth model may be off, but this model none the less points to a potentially important influence in the long run.

Short-run implications

In the short run, the policy implications of faster productivity growth depend on the dynamic responses of real spending and prices to an increase in trend productivity. Figure C3.4 shows some simulations using the Board's quarterly model, assuming a permanent increase in the rate of trend productivity growth arising from a faster pace of MFP growth. As in the computation of the long-run implications, these results are sensitive to the particular assumptions made, particularly those influencing the way that consumers and business form expectations, and those governing the responses of the fiscal and foreign sectors.

The basic story is as follows. An increase in productivity growth raises aggregate supply directly, and indirectly boosts aggregate demand through

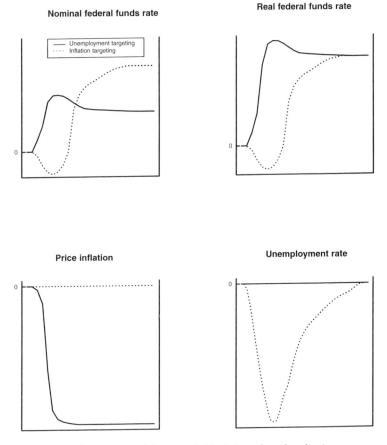

Figure C3.4   Shocks to productivity growth (deviations from baseline)

firms' estimates of desired capital stocks and consumers' expectations of permanent income. Because of accelerator effects, the initial impulse to aggregate demand exceeds that of supply. At the same time, the fall in labour costs reduces inflationary pressures. This is a pleasant situation for the policy-maker: either the existing inflation target can be retained and the unemployment rate allowed to fall below the NAIRU for a time, or resource utilization can be maintained at its normal level, in which case the inflation rate will fall permanently. In either case, the faster productivity growth will ultimately feed through to more rapid growth in real wages. However, the choice of policy response will determine how much of the additional real wage growth will reflect faster nominal wage growth, and how much will reflect a lower rate of price inflation.

If the policy-makers wish to reap the benefits of faster productivity growth in the form of lower inflation – which is referred to as 'unemployment targeting' in Figure C3.4 and shown by the solid line – they must raise interest rates to check demand. In this scenario, both the nominal and real federal funds rate rise at the onset of faster trend growth. Because of the combination of higher productivity growth and the tightening of policy, the inflation rate falls and stays down. Under the alternative response – which is referred to as 'inflation targeting' and is shown by the dotted lines in Figure C3.4 – downward pressure on inflation can be checked by lowering both the nominal and real funds rates initially. Because policy does not act immediately to choke off all excess demand, investment booms, real GDP rises above potential, and the unemployment rate falls. Over time, inflation and the unemployment rate return to their previous levels. But under either policy response, the real funds rate eventually must adjust to its new long-run equilibrium level, which may well be higher than before.

Conclusions

To conclude, allow me briefly to reiterate my main comments:

1. There is little hard evidence in the data of an increase in the trend rate of labour productivity growth, once we control for the standard cyclical properties of productivity. We should recognize, however, that such statistical procedures will only capture an acceleration in the trend with a lag, and thus we should remain open to the possibility of a faster trend. In this sense, the increased rate of capital deepening in recent years is a positive sign, as is the evidence of a more rapid pace of multifactor productivity growth.
2. As for the productivity paradox, Professor David's analogy to the spread of electrification gives us reason to hope for greater productivity benefits from investments in information technology. On the other hand, the historical analogy is not exact, and there may be reasons why computers will not lead

to a large pick-up in productivity growth. I am hopeful, but I still think it is too soon to know for sure.

3. Finally, I have provided an illustration of how the economy might be influenced by an increase in the productivity trend. The only thing one can say for certain is that real wages – and living standards – will rise more rapidly than before. The actual path that the economy will take – lower inflation or higher nominal wage growth – will depend on the reaction of the monetary authority to the favourable productivity shock.

Appendix

The stock adjustment model for aggregate hours is of the form:

$$\Delta h_t = \beta(h_t^* - h_{t-1}) \tag{C3.2}$$

where h_t is the log of hours in period t and h^* is the desired stock of (log) hours. The desired stock of hours is, in turn, given by:

$$h_t^* = qt - \pi_t \tag{C3.3}$$

where q_t is the log level of output and π is the log level of trend productivity. This simple model was estimated with quarterly data from 1960 to 1997, using a linear spline – broken in 1973 – for trend productivity. The estimated adjustment parameter in the model is well below 1.0 (about 0.4), and the estimate of trend productivity growth since 1973 is about 1 per cent per year.

Notes

1. A small portion of the increase in measured productivity growth in recent years reflects changes implemented by the Bureau of Labor Statistics to reduce the overstatement of inflation.
2. Although not quite on point, some data assembled by the Consumer Electronics Manufacturers Association suggests that personal computers spread to 25 per cent of the population considerably faster than did household electricity.
3. See Daniel E. Sichel (1997) *The Computer Revolution* (Washington DC: Brookings Institution) for a discussion of contemporary press accounts of computers.
4. See Sichel, ch. 5, for a more complete discussion; the two examples used here are discussed on pp. 125–7.
5. In this model, the relationship between a change in the long-run equilibrium real interest rate, RR^*, and a change in the trend rate of growth, G, is given by:

$$\Delta RR^* \quad \Delta G = \alpha/s \tag{C3.1}$$

where α denotes the capital share of income, and s the gross saving rate.

4
Markets for Information Goods

Hal R. Varian

Much has been written about the difficulties that 'information' poses for neoclassical economics. How ironic that ICE – information, communication and entertainment – now comprises the largest sector in the American economy. If information poses problems for economic theory, so much the worse for economic theory: real markets seem to deal with information rather well.

This paradox is the central theme of this chapter: information, that slippery and strange economic good, is, in fact, handled very well by market institutions. The reason is that real markets are much more creative than those simple competitive markets studied in first year economics. The fact that real-life markets can handle a good as problematic as information is a testament to the flexibility and robustness of market institutions.

Definition of information good

Let us first seek a general characterization of the ICE economy. The basic unit transacted is what I call 'information goods'. I take this to be anything that can be digitized – a book, a film, a record, a telephone conversation. Note carefully that the definition states anything that *can* be digitized; I do not require that the information *actually be* digitized. Analogue representations of information goods, such as video tapes, are common, though they will probably become less so in the future.

In this chapter I shall not be very concerned with asymmetric information. This topic has been dealt with extensively in the literature and I have little to add to the standard treatments. Instead, I want to focus on information as a good – as an object of economic transactions.

Information as an economic good

Information has three main properties that would seem to cause difficulties for market transactions.

(i) *Experience good*   You must experience an information good before you know what it is.
(ii) *Returns to scale*   Information typically has a high fixed cost of production but a low marginal cost of reproduction.
(iii) *Public goods*   Information goods are typically non-rival and sometimes non-excludable.

We shall deal with these topics one at a time.

Information as an experience good

You can only tell if you want to buy some information once you know what it is – but by then it is too late. How can one transact in goods that one has to give away in order to show people what they are? There are several social and economic institutions that are used to overcome this problem.

Previewing and browsing

Information producers typically offer opportunities for browsing their products: Hollywood offers previews, the music industry offers radio broadcasts, and the publishing industry offers bookstores, nowadays complete with easy chairs and cappucinos. One of the great difficulties faced by sellers of information on the Internet is figuring out ways to browse the products. Video and previews work well, but it appears that previewing textual information would be quite difficult.

However, things are not quite as bad as they seem. The National Academy of Sciences Press found that when they posted the full text of books on the Web, the sales of those books went up by a factor of three. Posting the material on the Web allowed potential customers to preview the material, but anyone who really wanted to *read* the book would download it. MIT Press had a similar experience with monographs and online journals.

Reviews

Another way to overcome the experience good problem is for some economic agents to specialize in reviewing products and providing these evaluations to other potential consumers. This is especially common in the entertainment industry: film reviews, book reviews and music reviews are ubiquitous.

But reviews are also found in the purer sort of information goods. The most academic popular papers (as measured by citation) are typically surveys, since the specialization required for frontier work in the sciences has created a demand for such overviews.

Peer review is the standard technique used in the sciences for evaluating the merit of papers submitted for publication, while most humanities use academic presses to provide a similar function. This institution survives because it meets an important need: evaluating information.

Reputation

The third way that producers of information goods overcome the experience good problem is via reputation. I am willing to purchase the *Wall Street Journal* today because I have read it in the past and found it to be worthwhile. The *Journal* invests heavily to establish and maintain its brand identity. For example, when it started an online edition, it went to great lengths to create the same 'look' and 'feel' as the print edition. The intent was to carry over the reputation from the off-line edition to the online version.

Investing in brand and reputation is standard practice in the information business, from the MGM lion to the *Time* magazine logo. This investment is warranted because of the experience good problem of information.

Returns to scale

Information is costly to produce but cheap to reproduce. It can easily cost over a hundred million dollars to produce the first CD of a Hollywood film, but the second CD can cost well under a dollar. This cost structure – high fixed costs and low marginal costs – cause great difficulties for competitive markets.

It's even worse than that. The fixed costs for information goods are not just fixed – they are also sunk. That is, they typically must be incurred prior to production and are usually not recoverable in case of failure. If the movie bombs, there isn't much of a market for its script, no matter how much it cost to produce.

Competitive markets tend to push price to marginal cost, which, in the case of information goods, is close to zero. But this leaves no margin to recover those huge fixed costs. How is it that information can be sold at all?

The obvious answer is that information is rarely traded on competitive markets. Instead, information goods are highly differentiated. Each pop CD is different from the others (or so the listeners think), and each movie is unique. But not completely unique. There is still an advantage in encouraging some similarities, because of the reputation effect described earlier.

The market structure for most information goods is one of monopolistic competition. Because of product differentiation, producers have some market power, but the lack of entry restrictions tends to force profits to zero over time.

The fact that information goods generally have some degree of market power also allows producers to recover fixed costs through more creative pricing and marketing arrangements. Price discrimination for information is common: different groups of consumers pay different prices, and quality discrimination is commonplace.

Publishers first issue a book in hardback and then, some time later, in paperback. Films come out first for cinemas, then, a few months later, on video. Investors pay one price for real time stock prices and another, much lower, price for delayed prices. In each of these examples, the sellers use delay to segment in the market by willingness to pay.

There are many other dimensions along which one can 'version' information goods. Shapiro and Varian (1998) describe several of these dimensions, including delay, user interface, convenience, image resolution, format, capability, features, comprehensiveness, annoyance and support.

Information as a public good

A pure public good is both non-rival and non-excludable. Non-rival means that one person's consumption does not diminish the amount available to other people, while non-excludable means that one person cannot exclude another person from consuming the good in question. Classic examples of pure public goods are goods such as national defence, lighthouses, TV broadcasts and so on.

The two properties of a public good are quite different. Non-rivalness is a property of the good itself: the same amount of defence, lighthouse services and TV broadcasts are available to everyone in the region served, by the very nature of the good. Excludability is a bit different, since it depends, at least in part, on the legal regime. For example, TV broadcasts in Britain are supported by a tax on owing a television set; those who do not pay the tax are *legally* (but not technologically) excluded from watching the broadcasts. Similarly, in the USA, cable TV broadcasts may be encrypted and special devices are required to decode them.

For that matter, it is 'merely' a legal convention that ordinarily private goods are excludable. If I want others to be prevented from consuming my car, for example, I either have to use technology (such as locks) or legal authority (such as the police) to prevent them.

Even such classic examples as street lights *could* be made excludable if one really wanted to do so. For example, suppose that the lights produce only the infrared wavelength, and special goggles are required to take advantage of their services. Or, if this seems like too much trouble, cities could offer 'street light licences', the purchase of which would be required to use street light services. Those who don't go out after dark, don't need to buy.

This is not as farfetched as it seems. Coase (1988) describes how the British authorities collected payment for lighthouse services based on the routes followed by ocean-going vessels.

Exclusion is not an inherent property of goods, public or private, but is rather a social choice. In many cases it is *cheaper* to make a good such as street lights universally available rather than make them excludable, either via technology or by law.

These observations have a bearing on information goods. Information goods are inherently non-rival, because of the tiny cost of reproduction. However, whether they are excludable or not depends on the legal regime. Most countries recognize intellectual property (IP) laws that allow information goods to be excludable. The US Constitution explicitly grants Congress the duty 'to promote the progress of science and useful arts, by securing, for limited times, to authors and inventors, the exclusive right to their respective writings and discoveries'.

Economics of intellectual property

The key phrase in the quotation from the US Constitution is 'for a limited time'. Intellectual property law recognizes that no exclusion would create poor incentives for the creation of IP. But at the same time, *permanent* intellectual property rights would lead to the standard, deadweight losses of monopoly.[1]

Length is only one of the parameters of intellectual property protection. The others are 'height', in the sense of the standard required for novelty; and the 'breadth', in the sense of how broadly the IP rights are interpreted. Different forms of IP have different combinations of these characteristics; for example, copyright protects the expression of ideas for quite long periods (up to seventy-five years), with a low standard for novelty, but a narrow scope.

There has been much economic analysis of intellectual property protection for patents. Nordhaus (1969) examined the optimal length of a patent, finding that twenty years was not unreasonable. Scotchmer (1991) noted that invention is often cumulative, and that shorter patent lives could lead to reduced incentives to invent, but more invention because of the ability to build on to earlier inventions.

Several authors, such as Dasgupta and Stiglitz (1980), and Gilbert and Newbery (1982), have recognized that the 'prize' nature of patents leads to socially wasteful duplication of effort. The patent system sets up a race, which can cause firms to devote more resources to speeding up their discoveries than would be justified by a benefit/cost test. Suppose, for example, that a number of research teams were on the verge of making an important discovery, perhaps one that was the next logical step along a well-known research path. Granting the winning team long-term exclusive rights merely because they were slightly faster than others to make the discovery could well create more monopoly power than was necessary to elicit the innovative effort, and slow down future invention as well.

There has been much less investigation of the economics of copyright. The first problem is that existing copyright terms appear to be much too long from an economic point of view. At conventional interest economic transactions, thirty or forty years in the future are of negligible value, so copyright terms of fifty to seventy five years seem much too long to be based on economic calculation.

In fact, as recently as the late 1960s copyrights lasted for, only for twenty-eight years in the USA. Each subsequent reform of copyright law increased the term. The difficulty has been that each term extension 'grandfathered in' the existing copyrights; even though no one would be willing to bargain seriously over possible cash flows fifty years down the road, the owners of about-to-expire and still valuable copyrights had significant economic incentive to extend them.

Software patents

Up until recently, the US Patent and Trademark Office and the courts interpreted algorithms as 'mathematical formulas' which could not be patented. However, in the mid-1980s they reversed this policy and began to issue patents for software algorithms. Subsequently, the patent office has issued many thousands of software patents.

There are several policy issues raised by software patents. First, until the mid-1990s, the patent office did not have adequate expertise to evaluate the novelty of submitted patents. This has resulted in ludicrous examples such as the Compton patent on multimedia; the UCSF (University of California, San Francisco) patent on downloading executable code; and the Software Advertising Corporation's patent on incorporating advertising into software programs.[2]

Second, there is the problem of 'submarine patents': patents that are not available publicly because they are under consideration by the Patent Office. In some cases, applicants have allegedly purposely delayed their applications in order to wait for the market to 'mature', to maximize the value of their patents, and to make improvements before others are apprized of their basic patent. These tactics can distort the returns to patent holders, frustrate the disclosure of patented inventions, which is a basic *quid pro quo* for patent protection under the US patent system, and lead to unnecessary duplication of effort and lawsuits. A recent change in patent lifetime to twenty years after filing has gone a long way towards reducers the problem of submarine patents.

Many of these problems are especially severe for software patents. Innovations that are embodied in physical goods can be bought and sold for a listed price on the open market, so there is no uncertainty about the cost of incorporating an innovation into a product.[3] However, the market for software components is still primitive, so much software is created in house. Thus, one software developer can easily infringe upon another developer's algorithm, and after years, find itself in a very vulnerable position if the algorithm is eventually patented.

All these reasons suggest that patents on algorithms should be interpreted narrowly, and be subject to high standards of novelty. Davis *et al.* (1994) also argue that software patents should have a shorter lifespan than other types of patent. Each of these policies should be considered carefully. As a practical matter, it would be far easier for the PTO to set high novelty standards and grant narrow software patents than for Congress to alter patent lifetimes selectively for software patents. Furthermore, in many cases the patent lifetime is unimportant, because the pace of progress is great enough that the patent has lost all its value by its expiry date.

Other ways to deal with exclusion

Assigning of property rights are not the only way to deal with intellectual property issues. A second way is to bundle the content with a good that *is* excludable. Indeed, traditional media for transmitting information goods, such as books, records, videotapes, CDs and so on are a type of bundling. Only one person can read a book at a time, so exclusion is not much of a problem.

This does not work for purely digital information goods, since the medium itself does not have much significance, but recent technologies such as cryptographic envelopes play a similar role by bundling the information good with an 'excludable' authentication mechanism.

A third technique for dealing with the exclusion problem is by using auditing or statistical tracking. The American Society of Composers, Authors, and Publishers (ASCAP) and Broadcast Music, Inc. (BMI) perform this task for the music industry while the Copyright Clearance Center deals with print media by auditing photocopying practices over a period of time and basing a yearly fee on this sample.

A fourth technique for dealing with exclusion is to embrace it, and bundle the information good with information that sellers *want* to be widely disseminated, such as advertising.

Terms and conditions

Intellectual property law assigns default property rights to users, but licenses and other forms of contract can specify other terms and conditions. This contacting choice poses an interesting trade-off: more liberal terms and conditions will generally increase the value a particular information good to its potential users, but it will also decrease the quantity sold. That is, a license to an information good that can be shared, resold, archived and so on will be worth more than one that cannot; however, sharing, resale and archiving all potentially reduce the final demand for the information goods.

Roughly speaking, more liberal terms and conditions increase the value of the information good, shifting the demand curve *up*. However, liberal terms and conditions also reduce the sales of the good, shifting the demand curve *in*. The profit-maximizing choice of licensing terms balances these two effects.

Piracy

Simply specifying terms and conditions or intellectual property laws does not ensure that they will be enforced. Illicit copying is a perennial problem.

Luckily, as with most contraband, there is a mitigating factor. In order to sell illicit copies to consumers, sellers must know where to find the copies. The larger the scale of operation of an IP pirate, the more probable it will be detected by the authorities. This means that, in equilibrium, reasonable efforts to enforce the law lead to relatively small scales of operation. Varian (1998) offers a model of this phenomenon.

International concerns

According to estimates from the Software Publishers Association, there are many countries where software piracy is rampant. Figure 4.1 shows the relationship between per capita income and the fraction of illegal software in use in various countries.

Figure 4.1 shows that the lower the per capita income, the higher the incidence of illegal copies. This should not be surprising. Less developed countries have little to lose if they pirate software, and have neither the resources nor the inclination to invest in enforcement.

The same effect shows up in environmental practices. In general, the lower the per capita income, the less environmentally aware a country is. As per capita income grows, so does the desire for a cleaner environment. Once a country passes US$5000 or so of per capita income, environmentally-aware policies, begin to be instituted, (see Coursey, 1992, and Grossman and Krueger, 1991).

We expect that the same effect will occur with intellectual property piracy. As countries become richer, their desire for local content increases. But as more and more local content is produced, the necessity for intellectual property protection becomes more and more apparent. As enforcement of intellectual property laws increase, both domestic *and* foreign producers benefit.

Taiwan is a prime example. Its government refused to sign the International Copyright Agreement (ICA) until recently. Prior to this, Taiwan was notorious for intellectual property violations. However, once the country became

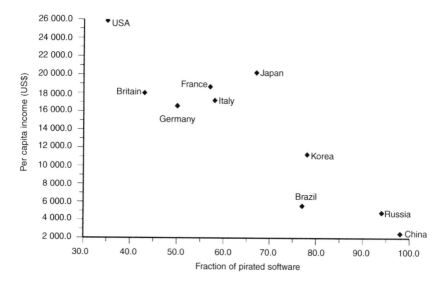

Figure 4.1   Per capita income versus fraction of software pirated, various countries
Source: Software Publishers Association and author's calculations.

prosperous and developed a large publishing industry, they joined the ICA in order to assure a market for their own publishing and printing industry.

USA as copyright pirate

The history of international copyright policy in the USA is an instructive example of what to expect from today's underdeveloped countries.

The US Constitution gave Congress the authority to create laws regulating the treatment intellectual property. The first national copyright law, passed in 1790, provided for a fourteen-year copyright – but only for authors who were citizens or residents of the USA. The USA extended the copyright term to twenty eight years in 1831, but again restricted copyright protection only to citizens and residents.

This policy was unique among developed nations. Denmark, Prussia, the United Kingdom, France, and Belgium all had laws respecting the rights of foreign authors. By 1850, only the USA, Russia and the Ottoman Empire refused to recognize international copyright.

The advantages of this policy to the USA were quite significant: they had a public hungry for books, and a publishing industry happy to publish them. And a ready supply was available from the UK. Publishing in the USA was virtually a no-risk enterprise: whatever sold well in Britain was likely also to do well in the USA.

American publishers paid agents in Britain to acquire popular works, which were then rushed to the USA and set in type. Competition was intense, and the first to publish had an advantage of only days before they themselves were subject to copying. Intense competition leads to low prices. In 1843, Charles Dickens' *Christmas Carol* sold for 6 cents in the USA and the equivalent of $2.50 in the UK.

Throughout the nineteenth century, proponents of international copyright protection lobbied Congress. They advanced five arguments for their position: (i) it was the moral thing to do; (ii) it would help to create domestic authors; (iii) it would prevent British publishers from pirating American authors; (iv) it would eliminate ruthless domestic competition; and (v) it would result in better-quality books.

Dickens toured the USA in 1842 and on dozens of occasions pleaded for international copyright. American authors supported his position, but their pleading had little impact on the public at large, or on Congress.

It was not until 1891 that Congress passed an international copyright act. The arguments advanced for the act were virtually the same as those advanced in 1837. But this time, although the arguments were the same, the outcome was different. In 1837 the US had little to lose from copyright piracy. By 1891 they had a lot to gain from international copyright – the reciprocal rights granted by the British. On top of this was the growing pride in the purely American literary culture and the recognition that American literature could only thrive if it competed with British literature on an equal footing.

The only special interest group that was firmly opposed to international copyright was the typesetters' union. The ingenious solution to this problem was to buy them off: the Copyright Act of 1891 extended protection only to those foreign works that were typeset in the USA![4]

There is no question that it was in the economic self-interest of the USA to pirate British literature in the early days of nationhood, just as it is clearly in the economic self-interest of China and other Countries to pirate American music and videos now. But as these countries grow and develop a longing for domestic content, they will probably follow a similar path as the USA and restrict foreign competition to stimulate the domestic industry.

Overload

Herbert Simon once said that a 'wealth of information creates a poverty of attention'. This has become painfully obvious with the advent of the World Wide Web.

Despite the hype, the Web is not all that impressive as an information resource. The static, publicly accessible Hypertext Markup Language (HTML) text on the Web is roughly equivalent in size to a million books. The University of California, Berkeley library has eight million volumes, and the average quality of the Berkeley library content is far higher! If 10 per cent of the material on the Web is 'useful', that means there are about 100 000 useful book-equivalents on the Web, the size of good public library. The real figure for 'useful' is probably more like 1 per cent, which is 10 000 books, or half the size of an average mall bookstore.

The value of the Web lies not in the quantity of information but rather in its *accessibility*. Digital information can be indexed, organized and hyperlinked relatively easily compared to textual information. A text is just a click away rather than a drive across town and an hour in the library.

But, of course, it isn't that simple. Hundreds of millions of dollars has been invested in catalogues and cataloguing textual information, while cataloguing online information is in its infancy. The information on the Web is highly accessible – once you know where to look.

The publishing industry has developed a variety of institutions to deal with this problem: reviewers, referees, editors, bookstores, libraries and so on. There are whole set of institutions to help us find useful information. But where are the Better Bit Bureaus for the Internet?

The problem is getting worse. I would like to coin a 'Malthus's law' of information. Recall that Malthus noted that the number of stomachs grew geometrically, but the amount of food grew linearly. Pool (1984) noted that the supply of information (in virtually every medium) grows exponentionally, whereas the amount that is consumed grows *at best* linearly. This is ultimately because our mental powers and time available to process information is constrained. This has the uncomfortable consequence that the fraction of the information produced that is actually consumed is asymptoting towards zero.

Along with Malthus's law of information, I may as well coin a Gresham's law of information. Gresham said that bad money drives out good. Well, bad information crowds out good, and cheap, low-quality information on the Internet can cause problems for providers of high-quality information.

The *Encyclopedia Britannica* offered an Internet edition to libraries with a site licence subscription price of several thousand dollars. Microsoft's *Encarta* retails at US$49 for a CD ROM. *Encarta*'s doing fine; but *Britannica* is in serious trouble. *Britannica* is now offering a home subscription for US$150 per year, and a home CD version for US$70, but even this may be too high.

So perhaps low-quality information really can drive out good. Maybe – but Gresham's law really should be restated – it is not that bad money crowds out good, but rather that bad money sells at a discount. So bad information should sell at a discount. Good information – relevant, timely, high-quality, focused and useful information – such as that provided by *Britannica* – should sell at a premium. And this brings me back to the Better Bit Bureaus. The critical problem for the commercial providers of content is to find a way to convince the user that they actually have timely, accurate, relevant and high-quality information to sell.

When publishing was expensive, it made sense to have lots of filters to determine what was published and what was not: agents, editors, reviewers, bookstores and so on. Now publishing is cheap: anyone can put up a homepage on the Web. The scarce factor is *attention*. The 0–1 decision of 'publish-or-not' no longer makes sense – what we need are new *institutional* and *technological* tools to determine where it is worthwhile to focus our attention.

They are not here yet, but some interesting things are happening in this area.

One interesting approach involves *recommender systems* such as FireFly, GroupLens and so on. FireFly present a list of old film titles and the viewer indicates which ones he/she likes or dislikes. The computer then finds people who have similar tastes to the viewer and shows *recent* film titles that *they* liked – with the implication that the viewer might like them too.

In GroupLens, participants rate news items that they read. When the viewer is presented with a list of items to examine, he/she sees a weighted average of the ratings of previous readers. The gimmick is that the weight each person receives in this average depend on how often they have agreed with that person in the past.

Systems such as FireFly and GroupLens – what we are calling 'recommender systems tems' or 'collaborative filtering systems' – allow a person to 'collaborate' with others who have common interests, and thus reduce his/her own search costs.

Business models

How are recommender systems paid for? What is the economic model? There are several problems.

First, there is the issue of incentives. How is it ensured that people contribute honestly to the system? First, observe that if it is possible get them to contribute, it is in their interest to do it honestly. If a user of FireFly just clicks at random, then he/she messes up the correlations on which the system depends.

The big problem is getting people to contribute at all. Once a person has seeded the system with his/her preferences, what is the incentive to continue to rate new films? If a person go to a film that no one has rated, then I may see a bad film. But if everyone only goes to films that someone else has rated, who rate the unrated ones?

There are two solutions to this problem: people can be paid to do the ratings, or people who refuse to do their fair share of ratings can be excluded. The first solution is the way Siskel and Ebert make their living: they specialize in recommendations and get paid by people who find their recommendations useful. The second way makes more sense in a community rating system: either an appropriate share of the ratings to provided or a person is excluded from the system.

Getting people to contribute to knowledge bases – recommendations or any other sort of information – can be quite difficult. One of the major consulting firms has spent millions of dollars setting up a knowledge base. When the consultants finish a project they are supposed to file a report of useful material. I asked one of the consultants how this worked. His somewhat sheepish reply was that he was six months behind in filing his reports. The reason was, he said, that every time he posted something useful, he got fifteen e-mails the next day asking him for more information! The system had *negative* incentives! The consulting firm had spent millions to set up the technology, but had not throught through the incentive problem. Oh well, they can always hire a consultant...

The production of knowledge is a tricky thing. By its nature it is easy to copy and share. And since it costs nothing to share, it is socially efficient to do so. But how then do we compensate the people who produce knowledge in the first place?

Conventional methods for protecting intellectual property do not apply: ideas cannot be patented, and copyright only protects the expression of ideas, not the ideas themselves.

Let me suggest that one place firms might look for ways to provide incentives for knowledge production is by looking to the industry whose entire economic base is knowledge – and by that I mean academia. The academic system has a lot of peculiar features: publish or perish, tenure, plagiarism taboos, peer review, citation and so on. When one looks at these features it can be seen that most of them are designed to provide incentives to produce good ideas.

Take tenure, for example. As Carmichael (1988) points out, one role of tenure is to encourage experts to evaluate truthfully people who are close substitutes for themselves. It is hard to get people to hire their own replacements – unless a tenure guarantee is offered that says they will not be replaced.

Institutions

Another approach to the filtering problem is the institutional approach: creating the equivalents of the editors, publishers and reviewers for online content. This is the strategy of AOL, Compuserve and Microsoft. They hope to become the intermediaries that filter and organize online information for the masses.

I have my doubts about this strategy. I think that the 'mass market' is going to be less significant in the future than it has in the past.

One of the most striking features of the print media since the early 1980s has been the demise of the newspaper and the rise of the magazine. Most major cities have only one newspaper; and in those few cities with two newspapers, it is pretty clear that one is going to go.

But you can now get magazines for just about every possible interest group, from butterfly collectors to body-builders – and there is probably one for those who do both!

The same thing has happened with television. Since 1990, the 'Big-3' TV networks have seen their market share drop while dozens of new channels have sprung up to serve niche markets. The Science Fiction Channel, the Discovery Channel and the History Channel are all offering content targeted to those with very specific interests.

I think that the Internet will accelerate this trend. People will be able to coalesce around their particular interest, be it butterfly collecting or body-building. Everybody who wants to will be a publisher. Editors will filter with regard to topic and quality – but there will be many different editors to choose from, so the search problem for individual users will be just as severe, if not more so, than it is now.

There is no getting away from the fact that information management is going to be an increasingly large part of our lives. We shall need to have better tools to do this task ourselves, and to utilize information management specialists when necessary. Whether we are producers or consumers of information we shall need additional expertise to help us locate, organize, filter, retrieve and use the information we need.

This expertise is what we have set out to produce at Berkeley. We have created a School of Information Management and Systems whose mission is twofold: our research mission is to produce more powerful tools to manage information, and our teaching missing is to train the information management specialists of the future. We are giving our students a core curriculum with computer science, library science, law and management. After these core courses, the students will take electives in areas of specialization such as electronic documents, archiving, databases, information retrieval, human – computer interfaces and so on.

Our students will be skilled in building and using information management tools. We think this expertise will be attractive to anybody who needs to manage information – which means just about everybody, these days. Whether you are a producer or a consumer, a professional or a dilettante, you have some information to manage – and our students will be there to help you do it.

So take heart – help is on the way!

Notes

1. In fact, this is not so obvious. If monopoly owners of information goods engage in price discrimination, as they commonly do, the deadweight losses may be much less less than those generated under a single-price regime. This point definitely requires further investigation.
2. Indeed, Bruce Lehman, the former Commissioner of the Patent and Trademark Office (PTO), has conceded that a number of software patents were granted in error.
3. Also, under the first-sale doctrine of patent law, a patent holder (or applicant) who sells an item containing the patented technology loses the right to further restrict the use of that item in commerce.
4. This provision remained in effect until the mid 1960s! Our source for this discussion is Clark (1960).

References

Carmichael, L. (1988) 'Incentives in Academics: Why is there Tenure?', *Journal of Political Economy*, vol. 96, no. 3 pp. 453–72.

Clark, A. J. (1960) *The Movement for International Copyright in Nineteenth Century America* (Washington DC: Catholic University of American Press).

Coase, R. (1988) *The Firm, the Market, and the Law* (University of Chicago Press).

Coursey, D. (1992) *The Demand for Environmental Quality*, Technical report, (University of Chicago, Public Policy School).

Dasgupta, P. and Stiglitz, J. (1980) Uncertainty, Market Structure and the Speed of R&D, *Bell Journal of Economics*, pp. 1–28.

Davis, R. Kapor, M. Reichman, J. H. and Samuelson, P. (1994) 'A Manifesto Concerning the Legal Protection of Computer Programs, *Columbia Law Review*, vol. 94.

Gilbert, R. J. and Newbery, D. M. (1982) 'Preemptive Patenting and the Persistence of Monopoly', *American Economic Review*, vol. 72: pp. 514–26.

Grossman, G. M. and Krueger, A. B. (1991) *Environmental Impacts of NorthAmerican Free Trade Agreement*, Technical report, Princeton University. Department of Economics.

Nordhaus, W. (1969) *Invention, Growth, and Welfare* (Cambridge, Mass.: MIT Press).

Pool I. De S. (1984) *Communication Flows: A Census in the United States and Japan* (New York: Elsevier Science).

Scotchmer, S. (1991) 'Standing on Shoulders of Giants: Cumulative Innovation and Patent Law', *Journal of Economic Perspectives*, pp. 29–42.

Shapiro, C. and Varian, H. R. (1998) *Information Rules: A Strategic Guide for the Network Economy* (Cambridge, Mass.: Harvard Business School Press).

Simon, H. (1971) 'Designing Organizations for an Information–Rich World', in M. Greenberger (ed.) *Computers, Communications, and the Public Interest*, Baltimore: Johns Hopkins University Press, 37–53.

Varian, H. R. (1998) *Intellectual Property Piracy*, Technical Report, SIMS, UC Berkeley, Calif.

Comments

Masahiro Okuno-Fujiwara

I enjoyed reading Professor Varian's chapter. It is a very nice piece of applied microeconomics. I also agree with his basic message, where he insists that real-life markets are much more creative than the markets described in textbooks. But I would like to go a bit further than that; I would rather say that the real-life markets are much more creative than what governments try to do, or even the central banks sometimes try to do. I think the real world is quite complex. And sometimes human design cannot solve things, but the evolutionary pressures and profit-seeking motivations provide much stronger incentives to solve complex problems that characterize the information goods and knowledge-based economy.

I would like to make two basic comments: first that, while Professor Varian emphasizes the real-life market economy, I would like to draw the attention of readers not only to such market activities but also to non-market activities. In other words, we have recently observed an emergence of the the non-government organizations (NGOs) and the the non-profit organizations (NPOs). I think the reason for this emergence is partly due to the decline in 'search costs', a typical phenomenon associated with the decline in the cost of information processing. The NGOs and the NPOs typically are organized by voluntary participants. With the decline of the cost of information processing and 'search costs', people from all over the world can join one particular organization such as on ecology organization, or an NPO for peace. Because participation is voluntary, the members of the NGO or the NPO tend to have a common interest, and with members having a similar or common interest, there is less need to check for moral hazard problems. Using the jargon of economics members do not play 'games' but instead become team players acting towards their common objective. While, in the game theory, people have diversified interests, in the team theory, people have a common interest. In this sense, the organization does not have to deal too much with the problem of incentives. I think that the reduction in the cost of information processing seems to make the advantages of the NGO and the NPO work better, because they can attract many similar members. Perhaps there is a possibility that these non-market activities might become an important sector in the economy, and might even affect the discussion about monetary policy.

As my second point, I agree with Professor Varian that the market economy tends to solve the problem of information very well. But still there are some problems, and these sometimes call for government intervention. Let me discuss some of these. The first is about intellectual property rights. As Professor Varian writes, while intellectual property laws exist in many countries, in some countries they are not enforced very well. Figure 4.1 on page 92 shows downward trend, meaning that the piracy of software decreases as per capita income increases. Japan seems to be a kind of outlier; I agree that, intellectual property rights are not enforced properly in Japan. I think the legal system must be designed so as to function well. On the other hand, the US patent system has many structural problems. One of the problems, 'submarine patents', is that a patent application is not disclosed immediately after the application is filed, which is why some patents remain unknown even after they have been filed, and when it is announced that the patents have been granted, the ideas have become well-known to be public and many manufacturers have started to use them without knowing that patents have been granted. One other important point is that the USA is the only country in the world which uses the first-to-invent principle; whoever invent something first is granted the patent, while almost all other countries operate under a first-to-file principle – whoever files the idea first is granted the patent. I think it is important to harmonize the legal system concerning intellectual property rights to enable it to function well.

I agree with Professor Varian in the sense that most informational problems can be solved by the market economy. Professor Varian suggested that the problems of information goods come from the experienced goods property, the returns to scale property, and the public goods property, and suggested that all of these can be solved by the market economy. But, in particular when these properties exist simultaneously, serious problems might occur which may not be able to be solved by markets alone. Particular examples I am thinking about are central processing units for computers, for example, Intel's Pentium; or the operating system for desktop computers – for example, Microsoft's Windows. In these cases, we see the huge market power commanded by Intel and Microsoft. Basically, I think the problem is as follows: in the case of information goods, because of the public goods property, we have to protect intellectual property rights. And because inventors' rights are protected, they are interested in producing inventions. But, as Professor Varian explains in his paper, it also creates an *ex-post* monopoly problem; after something is invented, especially with regard to intellectual property rights, the inventor has monopoly rights, and distorts the market allocation. Most of the time this does not create any problems, because the distortion is created by a temporary monopoly power, or what we call quasi-rent, which attracts further inventions to provide close substitutes, and the temporary monopoly profit or quasi-rent would disappear eventually. If this temporary monopoly power comes with other characteristics such as huge returns to scale, or what we call network externalities, meaning that the more people who start to purchase the good, the larger the value of the good, a natural monopoly will be created. A natural monopoly makes the production of a close substitute very difficult, and so temporary monopoly power becomes permanent. That is why Microsoft and Intel have enjoyed huge and long-lasting monopoly power. Of course, others may disagree, and I myself sometimes think that, in this sort of economy, it may be possible to topple the market monopoly, especially when a drastic change occurs in the product itself. But still, there is some risk; what I am trying to say is that the nature of public goods, together with other characteristics that can solidify the market power of the product, might jeopardize the market resource allocation. I think we have many historical precedents for this. In the area of telecommunications, there were some similar cases with network externalities, which were finally resolved by providing interconnections that guaranteed fair access to the main local network for any new entrants and/or outsiders. During the Industrial Revolution, around the early 1900s are, major problem was monopoly in the oil industry, which was finally resolved by the enforcement of anti-monopoly rights and the division of large firms. We may need some means of market intervention such as the application of monopoly law in order to enforce fair and public access to the intellectual property, even if that property right was owned by a monopolist, in order to improve the resource allocation of the economy.

Let me repeat my comment: I agree with Professor Varian that we should trust the market economy and perhaps the non-market economy as well. But at the same time, it may be that there are some areas where public interventions might be called for.

5

Effects of the Developments of a Knowledge-based Economy on Asset Price Movements: Theory and Evidence in the Japanese Stock Market

Kiyohiko G. Nishimura, Toshiaki Watanabe and Kentaro Iwatsubo *

Introduction

Since the mid-1980s, East and South East Asian countries have experienced turbulent asset prices that have resulted in subsequent severe economic recessions. Japan enjoyed renewed vigour in economic activities in the late 1980s because of the upsurge of stock and real estate prices that peaked in 1990, but since then the precipitous fall in princes has created loan problems that have dragged down the country's growth for almost a decade. Booming economies of the early 1990s in Thailand and other South East Asian countries also suffered from severe covering of their asset markets in 1997, and the resulting financial crisis has slowed their growth considerably.

This period of turbulent asset prices has also been characterized as an era of transition to a 'knowledge-based economy', in which innovation in information technology has transformed the world economy, and the industrial structure has changed through its advent. Moreover, the way people use information has also changed because of the availability of sophisticated information processing and transmitting devices. East and South East Asian economies are no exception. A natural question arises: has the recent development of a knowledge-based economy influenced the turbulent behaviour of asset prices experienced at the north-western edge of the Pacific?

To examine this problem, textbook finance theory is not suitable, since it pre-supposes supposes well-developed asset markets, implicitly assuming fully-fledged information technology. The hallmark of modern finance theory is the no-unexploited-arbitrage-opportunity condition, meaning smooth

* We are grateful to the participants of the conference at the Bank of Japan for valuable comments and suggestions. The section has been rewritten since the conference to incorporate points made at that time.

transactions and fast information diffusion. This may be a good description of the US financial markets, but may not be an appropriate characterization of other markets, especially those in Asia.

The purpose of this chapter is twofold. First, we develop a model of less-developed asset markets, taking explicit account of high transaction and information costs, and examine the effect of the knowledge-based economy on the magnitude of asset price sensitivity. We characterize less-developed asset markets as an asset market of atomistic price-posting, and examine whether prices in such a market exhibit excessive sensitivity to changes in the underlying factors. Second, we examine the validity of this model in the Japanese stock market, and gauge the impact of the knowledge-based economy there.

The plan of this chapter is as follows: in the next section, we develop a theory of less-developed asset markets with transactionally and information-ally separated trading posts, and examine excess sensitivity of asset prices. The third section examines the Japanese stock market data, and tests the validity of the theory, and concluding remarks are found in the fourth section.

Asset markets with atomistic price-posting

A model of less-developed asset markets

Let us consider an asset market of 'developing' economies,[1] where there are substantial transaction costs making arbitrage insufficient, and information costs making market participants under-informed about the market. Some investors are well-informed, but others are not. Investors' opinions vary about the intrinsic value of particular stocks. Sellers and buyers post their offers atomistically and transaction takes place if an offer is accepted by other investors. Thus, *there is no Walrasian auctioneer nor market-maker who might act as a stand-in for the Walrasian auctioneer.*[2]

In such a market, both sellers and buyers are price-makers rather than price-takers. Moreover, because of insufficient arbitrage and diverse opinion, the seller who offers a high asking price still has a chance to sell stock, although the chance is smaller than when the seller offers a low asking price. This implies that sellers have some market power: by changing their asking price, they can influence the *probability* of the successful sale of their stock. The same is true for the buyer. The buyer bidding a low price still has a chance to buy the stock, though his/her chance is smaller than that of the buyer who bids a high price. Thus the market can be characterized as one of monopolistic competition rather than perfect competition. This deviation from perfect competition is the hallmark of this market.

Let us consider price determination in such a market. Below we offer a simplified version of Nishimura (1999).[3] A large number of stocks are traded individual trading posts, and we consider one stock, called *i*, to be a representative stock. A few investors are well-informed of the true intrinsic value of the stock, while other investors are uninformed. To make the analysis simple, we assume that one investor is well-informed and offers the price (that is, places a limit order), while the other investors are uninformed and decide whether to accept it or not that is to place a market order or not). All investors are assumed to be risk neutral. Because of transaction costs, information costs, and/or the limited ability of investors, not all uninformed buyers show up in all trading posts of stocks. For analytical simplicity, we assume that only one buyer shows up at this particular trading post. Finally, we assume a once-and-for-all market in which, if the trade between them fails there is no further trade on this particular stock.

Let us consider the case that the informed investor is the seller, while the uninformed investor is the buyer. (A symmetrical argument applies and the result is the same in the opposite case, where the informed investor is the buyer while the uninformed investor is the seller.) The informed investor's pricing problem is as follows. Let x_i be the unexpected change in the intrinsic value of this stock i that is the value of holding this stock. We have assumed that only the seller (informed investor) knows x_i.

The buyer (uniformed investor) j has his own subjective expectations about x_i, denoted by $E^j(x_i)$. The seller does not know the expectations $E^j(x_i)$ of the particular buyer he/she encounters, but he/she is assumed to know the distribution of the expectations among uniformed investors:

$$Pr(E^j(x_i) < y) = F(y) \tag{5.1}$$

(For example, an investor survey may be conducted and the result may be made public.) The seller determines his the price change p_i corresponding to x_i based on this information.

Since the buyer j is risk-neutral, he/she buys the stock if the price change p_i is no more than his/her expected intrinsic-value change x_i, or equivalently, $p_i \leq E^j(x_i)$. Thus the probability of a successful sale, $\phi(p_i)$ is a function of p_i such that

$$\phi(p_i) = 1 - F(p_i) \tag{5.2}$$

Keeping this in mind, the risk-neutral seller determines p_i to maximize his/her expected profit:

$$Max_{pi} \; Expected \; Profit_i = \phi(p_i)(p_i) + (1 - \phi(p_i))(x_i) \tag{5.3}$$

It is evident that the optimal price change in Equation (5.3) satisfies the following equation;

$$p_i = \left(1 + \frac{\phi(p_i)}{\phi'(p_i)(p_i)}\right)^{-1} x_i = \frac{1}{1 - (1/\eta_\phi)} x_i \tag{5.4}$$

where

$$\eta_\phi = -\frac{p_i}{\phi} \phi'(p_i)$$

is the price elasticity of the sale probability. If the trade is completed, this is the market price change of the stock.

Equation (5.4) shows that the price change p_i is a mark-up of the unexpected intrinsic-value change x_i. Moreover, the mark-up rate depends on the inverse of the price elasticity η_ϕ of the sale probability $\phi(p_i)$. The smaller the elasticity, the more sensitive the price. In addition, so long as η_ϕ is positive and greater than unity, the coefficient of x_i in Equation (5.4) is always greater than unity. Thus, in this case, we have excess price sensitivity.

Equation (5.2) implies that the sale probability depends on F, the distribution of buyers' expectations. Thus Equation (5.4) shows that the price effect of the unexpected change in the intrinsic value depends crucially on the shape of the distribution of uninformed investors' expectations.

To illustrate this point, let us note that the price elasticity of $\phi(p_i) = 1 - F(p_i)$ is small if, for given p_i [> 0] and ϕ, the absolute value of $\phi'(p_i)$ small. Since $-\phi'(p_i) = F'(p_i) = f(p_i)$, where f is the density function, this means that smaller $f(p_i)$ or, in other words, the more dispersed expectations around the optimal price, implies higher price sensitivity. Thus, foregoing analysis suggests that in some cases an increase in the variance of the distribution of expectations may induce excessive price response to unexpected changes in the intrinsic value of stock.

In this subsection, we *ignore* the effect of the uninformed investors' rational expectation formation on price. Thus uninformed buyers' behaviour in this sub-section is described as unsophisticated, compared with rational (Bayesian) behaviour under imperfect information. Rational expectations will be considered in the next sub-section.

Information technology and variable price sensitivity

The advancement of information technology, which underlies the emergence of the knowledge-based economy, means that economic agents become sophisticated in their decision-making. It also implies that more information about the market becomes available. In this sub-section, we explore implications of this sophistication in information gathering and processing on price behaviour in the non-Walrasian asset market. We summarize the result obtained by Nishimura (1999), which incorporates rational expectations into the model given in the previous sub-section.[4]

Sophistication in information processing: rational expectation formation

One immediate consequence of rational expectations is that the buyer will learn about the fundamental value x_i from the price offer p_i of the seller. One may argue that the excess sensitivity result in the previous sub-section is caused by non-rational expectations. Bayesian buyers learn the intrinsic value through sellers' offers, which diminishes the *ex-post* heterogeneity considerably so as to reduce the price sensitivity. However, this is not generally true.

The intuitive reason is as follows. Although buyers' learning about the value x_i reduces their *ex-post* heterogeneity and thus price sensitivity, there is a new source of excess sensitivity inherent in the case of rational expectations. Since the buyer tries to get information from the seller's offer, the seller can influence the buyer's perception of the stock by changing his/her offer. In general, the buyer thinks, quite rightly, that a high price is a (noisy) signal of a high intrinsic value, and vice versa. Thus, on the one hand, the optimistic seller's optimal price increases further than it would otherwise have done since his/her higher price may lead the buyer to think the stock's value is higher, thus making room for a further price rise.

On the other hand, the pessimistic seller's optimal price decreases further than it would otherwise have done, since his/her price may be taken as a signal of a low stock value, so that he/she to lower his/her price further in order to ensure a successful sale. Thus, even under fully rational expectation formation, we still have excessive sensitivity. This expectation-influencing mechanism makes prices more sensitive.

Advancement of information technology

The advent of information technology makes increasing amounts of market information accessible to market participants with a lower cost. Such an advancement of information technology is likely to reduce price sensitivity in the long run. First, it may increase the accuracy of individual prior information about the market and thus reduce expectation heterogeneity. Second, faster information diffusion because of advanced technology may enable various contemporaneous information about the market to reach investors. Such additional information is valuable for investors in improving forecast accuracy, and thus reducing expectation heterogeneity. In the short run, however, learning about new technology and new sources of information may produce errors, which may counteract the positive effect of information technology advancement.

In sum, sophistication of information processing and advancement of information technology do not alter the basic picture of less-developed asset markets. Their prices may be excessively sensitive to unexpected changes in underlying market fundamentals. However, sensitivity is likely to be reduced in the long run as more and more information is available at a lower cost.

Expectation heterogeneity and the sensitivity of Japanese stock prices

Methodology

The model developed in the previous section can be incorporated into the framework of the arbitrage pricing theory (APT). In this theory, the innovation of an asset price is determined by the innovation of k factors $f_{j,t}$ $(j = 1, \ldots, k)$, that is:

$$p_t = \alpha_t + \sum_{j=1}^{k} \beta_{j,t} f_{j,t} + u_t \tag{5.5}$$

where $\beta_{j,t}$ $(j = 1, \ldots, k)$ are the factor loadings which measure the sensitivity of the asset return to the factors. For simplicity, assuming that $k = 1$, we use the following one-factor model:

$$p_t = \alpha_t + \beta_t f_t + u_t \tag{5.6}$$

In the conventional framework, β_t is a constant parameter. However, our model (Equation (5.4)) suggests that it depends on the dispersion of expectation and the state of information technology. Consequently, we assume that:

$$\beta_t = g(\sigma_t) + h(t) \tag{5.7}$$

where σ_t is a variable which measures the dispersion of investors' expectations, and that time t represents the effect of increasing usage of sophisticated information technology over time. Then, we have

$$p_t = \beta_t f_t + u_t = \{g(\sigma_t) + h(t)\} f_t + u_t \tag{5.8}$$

Since p_t and f_t are innovation, we have $E(f_t \mathbf{I}_{t-1}) = 0$ and $E(\mu_t \mathbf{I}_{t-1}) = 0$, where $\mathbf{I}_{t-1}$ is the information set available up to time $t - 1$. For identification, we assume that $E(f_t^2 \mathbf{I}_{t-1}) = 1$. We further assume that μ_t is homoskedastic, that is, $\sigma_\mu^2 \equiv E(\mu_t^2 | \mathbf{I}_{t-1})$ does not depend on time t. This is an augmented APT model, in which factor loading depends on the expectation diversity σ_t and time t. The data used for σ_t will be discussed in the next sub-section.

The theory does not impose any restriction on the functions $g(\sigma_t)$ and $h(t)$. In the following analysis, we consider the following three specifications:[5]

$$g(\sigma_t) = \begin{cases} g_0 + g_1 \sigma_t, & \text{1. Linear} \\ g_0 + g_1 \exp[-\sigma_t / \Phi_1], & \text{2. Negative exponential} \\ g_0 + g_1 \exp[\sigma_t / \Phi_1], & \text{3. Positive exponential} \end{cases} \tag{5.9}$$

$$h(t) = \begin{cases} h_0 + h_1 t, & \text{1. Linear} \\ h_0 + h_1 \exp[-t / \Phi_2], & \text{2. Negative exponential} \\ h_0 + h_1 \exp[t / \Phi_2], & \text{3. Positive exponential} \end{cases} \tag{5.10}$$

where g_0, g_1, h_0 and h_1 are parameters to be estimated, and Φ_1 and Φ_2 are scale parameters. In the following analysis, we assume that Φ_1 is the sample mean of σ_t and Φ_2 is the sample size. We have checked the sensitivity of the results to several different values of Φ_1 and Φ_2, but the results are not very sensitive to the particular choice of Φ_1 and Φ_2.

To estimate the parameters in the model that consists of Equations (5.7)–(5.10), we take the following approach.[6] First, we extract the innovations of economic variables and asset return by fitting the vector autoregressive (VAR) model to the vector that consists of the economic variables and the asset price. The VAR model is estimated by using ordinary least squares (OLS). Given the OLS estimates, we take the residual as being innovations of the economic variables and the asset price. Second, we assume that the innovations of the economic variables, ϵ_t, are determined by the same factor f_t that determines the asset price, that is:

$$\epsilon_t = C f_t + w_t \tag{5.11}$$

where C is a $(M \times 1)$ vector of factor sensitivities for the economic variables, and w_t is a $(M \times 1)$ vector of idiosyncratic error terms. We assume that $E(w_t | I_{t-1}) = 0$, $E(f_t \, w_t | I_{t-1}) = 0$, $E(u_t \, w_t | I_{t-1}) = 0$, and $E(w_t \, w'_t | I_{t-1}) = \Gamma$, a positive semi-definite diagonal matrix. For simplicity, we assume that w_t are also homoskedastic. Third, given the residuals obtained from the VAR, we estimate simultaneously the parameters in the following system that consists of equations (5.7)–(5.11) by the maximum likelihood method:

$$\zeta_t = B_t f_t + v_t \tag{5.12}$$

where

$$\zeta_t = \begin{bmatrix} p_t \\ \epsilon_t \end{bmatrix} \tag{5.13}$$

$$B_t = \begin{bmatrix} \beta_t \\ C \end{bmatrix} \tag{5.14}$$

$$v_t = \begin{bmatrix} v_t \\ w_t \end{bmatrix} \tag{5.15}$$

in which the log-likelihood may be written as:

$$\ln L = -(M+1)T \ln(2\pi)/2 - (1/2) \sum_{t=1}^{T} \ln | \Sigma_t | -(1/2) \sum_{t=1}^{T} \zeta'_t \Sigma_t^{-1} \zeta_t \tag{5.16}$$

where

$$\Sigma_t = B_t B'_t + \begin{bmatrix} \sigma_u^2 & 0 \\ 0 & \Gamma \end{bmatrix} \tag{5.17}$$

Given the parameter estimates, we can estimate the factor by using:

$$E(f_t \mid I_t) = B'_t \Sigma_t^{-1} \zeta_t \tag{5.18}$$

Estimation results

The Japanese stock market

The stock price we use is the closing figure for the Tokyo Stock Price Index (TOPIX) on the last trading day of each month. The TOPIX is the value-weighted average of prices of all stocks traded in the First Section in Japan. The sample period is 1985:5 to 1997:12.

To measure the dispersion of investors' expectations, we use the survey data collected by the Japan Center for International Finance (JCIF) in Tokyo.[7] The JCIF has conducted telephone surveys on Wednesday's twice a month, in the middle and at the end, since May 1985. Point forecasts of the yen/dollar exchange rate for one-, three-, and six-month horizons are obtained from foreign exchange experts in forty four companies.[8] The JCIF calculates the average, the standard deviation, the maximum and the minimum of the fourty-four responses. Among them, we use the standard deviation calculated based on the survey at the end of each month as a proxy for the dispersion of investors' expectations.[9] Similar survey data on the stock market, if it existed, would be more desirable, but unfortunately we do not have such data. Figure 5.1 plots the standard deviation series, which appear to have a negative time trend. This might be the effect of increased sophistication in information usage because of advancements in information technology. The augmented Dicky–Fuller (ADF) test rejects the null hypothesis of the presence of a unit root in this series, while a statistically significant time trend is detected. We remove the time trend by regressing the log of the standard deviation on a constant and on time $t = 1, 2, \ldots, T$. The exponential function of the residual of this regression is used for σ_t. The secular effect which might measure the effect of increased information is represented in the time trend.

To extract factors, we use monthly data on the eight macroeconomic variables that may be expected to affect stock returns in Japan:[10] (i) short-term interest rates measured by the collateralized call rate; (ii) long-term interest rates measured by the yield on 10-year government bonds; (iii) the dollar – yen exchange rate; (iv) industrial production; (v) consumer price index; (vi) trade balance; (vii) money supply measured by M1 plus quasi-money currency; and (viii) Saudi Arabian light oil spot price per barrel in Japanese yen. Details of the definitions and sources of these index variables may be found in the Appendix on page 000. In the following analyses, we take a logarithm of all the variables except the trade balance. The ADF tests do not reject the null hypothesis of the presence of a unit root in all eight macroeconomic variables, so that the VAR model is fitted to the vector which consists of the stock price change and the first-order differences in all macroeconomic variables. The fitted VAR model also includes monthly dummies. Both the Akaike (1973) information criterion (AIC) and the Schwarz (1978) information criterion (SIC) lead to a lag length of one. However, when the lag length is set a one or two, Ljung and Box (1978) tests strongly reject the null hypothesis of no autocorrelation in the obtained residuals for some variables. Table 5.1 presents the conventional Ljung – Box statistics up to twelfth-order autocorrelation and the one corrected for heteroskedasticity following Diebold (1986) when the lag length is set at three. No matter which Ljung–Box statistic is used, the null hypothesis of no autocorrelation is not rejected at any standard level in the residuals of all

111

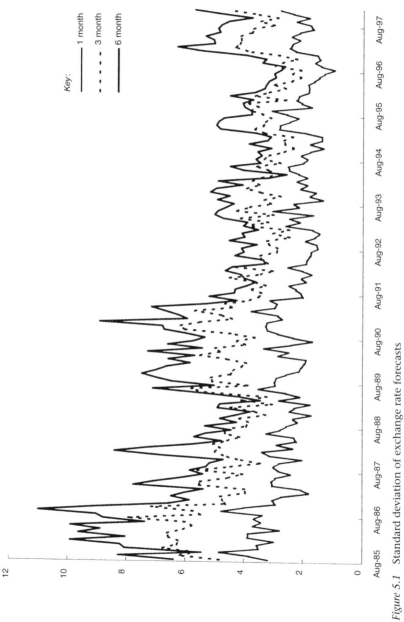

Figure 5.1 Standard deviation of exchange rate forecasts
Source: Survey of Exchange Rate Forecasts by Japan Center for International Finance.

Table 5.1 Ljung–Box test for innovations in macroeconomic variables

Variable (innovations in)	LB (12)	LB* (12)
Stock price	10.47	11.04
Short interest rate	18.82	14.48
Long interest rate	12.61	9.26
Dollar/Yen exchange rate	17.11	16.59
Industrial production	6.32	6.06
Consumer price	7.70	8.32
Trade balance	5.31	4.81
Money supply	23.66	20.68
Oil price	5.91	5.91

Notes: LB (12) is the Ljung–Box statistic for up to twelfth-order autocorrelation. LB* (12) is the heteroskedasticity-corrected Ljung–Box statistic (e.g., Diebold, 1988). The asymptotic distributions of LB (12) and LB* (12) are χ^2 with twelve degrees of freedom. χ^2 (12) critical values: 18.55 (10%), 21.03 (5%), 26.22 (1%).

variables except the money supply. Even for the money supply, the conventional Ljung – Box statistic does not reject the null hypothesis at 1 per cent significance level, and neither does the heteroskedasticity-corrected one at 5 per cent. We therefore set the lag length as being equal to three.

Results

Now we estimate the parameters in the model in Equation (5.12) by maximizing the log-likelihood given by Equation (5.16). As a frame of reference, let us first make the conventional assumption that g (σ_t and h (t) are constant and independent of σ and t (constant β). Table 5.2 presents the estimate of β jointly with the estimate of factor loading C for each of the

Table 5.2 Estimates of factor loadings β and C when β is constant

		Estimate	Standard error
β		−1.103	0.618
C			
	Short interest rate	0.227	0.132
	Long interest rate	0.368	0.146
	Exchange rate	0.498	0.190
	Industrial production	0.042	0.116
	Consumer price	−0.171	0.171
	Trade balance	−0.103	0.130
	Money supply	0.110	0.152
	Oil price	0.604	0.231

Note: Estimates of C in Equation (5.11): $\epsilon_t = Cf_t + \omega_t$.

Table 5.3 Factor score weights (regression coefficients)

Variable (innovations in)	Weights
Short interest rate	0.105
Long interest rate	0.197
Exchange rate	0.309
Industrial production	0.020
Consumer price	−0.081
Trade balance	−0.041
Money supply	0.035
Oil price	0.445

Note: Based on OLS regression of factor estimates calculated using Equation (5.18) on innovations in economic variables.

economic variables described above. Their standard errors are calculated using the Hessian of the log-likelihood at the optimum. Although not so strong, we find evidence that the factor affects the stock price. Specifically, a standard two-sided t test rejects the null hypothesis of $\beta = 0$ at the 10 per cent significance level. Table 5.3 shows the factor score weights, obtained by regressing the factor estimates calculated using Equation (5.18) on the innovations in our economic variables. The factor has relatively large weights on the innovation in the oil price and the yen–dollar exchange rate. Hence, the negative value for the estimate of β is intuitive, when one takes account of the heavy dependence of the Japanese economy on oil imports. Moreover, the close relationship between the factor on the one hand and the exchange rate and the oil price on the other justifies our usage of the standard deviation of exchange-rate forecasts as the relevant expectation diversity.

Next, let us examine whether β_t has a time trend. This is an indirect test of whether advancement of information technology has a significant effect on the stock market's sensitivity to innovations in macroeconomic variables. Here, we neglect the possibility for the dependence on σ_t and postulate that $\beta_t = h(t)$, where three specifications are given by Equation (5.10). Table 5.4 presents the estimates of the parameters in each specification. No matter which specification is used, we do not find evidence for a significant time trend in β_t. Thus we fail to detect any significant effect of information technology advancement on stock price sensitivity.

Finally, let us turn to the effect of expectation diversity on price sensitivity; that is, the relationship between σ_t and β_t. Since β_t does not significant time trend, we assume that $\beta_t = g(\sigma_t)$. Table 5.5 presents the estimate parameters in Equation (5.9). A significant negative relationship between β_t and σ_t is detected when the standard deviation of three-months-ahead forecasts is used for σ_t. In all three specifications of the three-months-ahead forecast case, both the t test and the likelihood ratio test reject the null hypothesis of $g_1 = 0$ at the

Table 5.4 Estimates of time trend in β_t

Specification	h_0	h_1	Log-likelihood	LR
1. Linear	−1.485	0.006	−2134.32	0.136
	(1.079)	(0.013)		
2. Negative	−1.103	0.000	−2134.15	0.000
exponential	(0.615)	(0.106)		
3. Positive	−2.546	0.871	−2134.15	0.458
exponential	(2.082)	(1.195)		

Notes: Standard errors in parentheses. LR denotes the likelihood ratio statistic to test the null hypothesis of no time trend, i.e. H_0: $h_1 = 0$. The asymptotic distribution of this statistic is Ξ^2 with one degree of freedom. χ^2 (1) critical values: 2.71 (10%), 3.84 (5%), 6.63 (1%).

Table 5.5 Estimates of the relationship between the expectation heterogeneity σ_t and β

Panel A One-month-ahead forecasting

Specification	g_0	g_1	Log-likelihood	LR	Max.	Min.
1. Linear	3.479	−4.233	−2133.34	2.08	1.25	−3.405
	(4.508)	(4.212)				
2. Negative	−5.382	12.053	−2133.36	2.05	1.83	−2.914
exponential	(3.056)	(8.368)				
3. Positive	3.008	−1.401	−2133.46	1.85	0.667	−3.831
exponential	(3.137)	(1.078)				

Panel B Three-months-ahead forecasting

Specification	g_0	g_1	Log-likelihood	LR	Max.	Min.
1. Linear	7.215	−7.516	−2130.57	7.63	2.009	−5.337
	(2.918)	(2.635)				
2. Negative	−8.521	20.784	−2131.30	6.17	2.231	−4.279
exponential	(2.957)	(8.262)				
3. Positive	7.131	−2.809	−2129.87	9.02	1.702	−6.631
exponential	(2.896)	(0.953)				

Panel C Six-months-ahead forecasting

Specification	g_0	g_1	Log-likelihood	LR	Max.	Min.
1. Linear	2.554	−3.583	−2133.33	2.10	0.426	−3.624
	(2.641)	(2.540)				
2. Negative	−5.415	11.314	−2133.07	2.63	0.928	−3.307
exponential	(2.777)	(7.053)				
3. Positive	1.819	−1.045	−2133.65	1.47	−0.045	−3.790
exponential	(2.215)	(0.785)				

Notes: Standard errors in parentheses. *Max.* and *Min.* denote the maximum value and the minimum value of the estimated β_t respectively. LR denotes the likelihood ratio statistic to test the null hypothesis of no relation between σ_t and β_t, i.e. H_0: $g_1 = 0$. The asymptotic distribution of this statistic is χ^2 with one degree of freedom. χ^2 (1) critical values: 2.71 (10%), 3.84 (5%), 6.63 (1%).

Table 5.6 Estimates of g (σ_t) and $g(\bar{\sigma}_t)$

Three-months-ahead forecasting

Specification	g (σ_t)	$g(\bar{\sigma}_t)$
1. Linear	2.009	–5.337
	(1.360)	(1.588)
2. Negative	2.231	–4.279
exponential	(1.522)	(1.329)
3. Positive	1.702	–6,632
exponential	(1.150)	(1.904)

Notes: Standard errors in parentheses. σ_t and $\bar{\sigma}_t$ denote the minimum value and the maximum value of σ_t in the sample, respectively.

5 per cent significance level. This is consistent with the theory of the previous section. However, we need to carry out one more step before coming to any conclusion. The theory predicts that the sign β_t does not depend on σ_t and the absolute value of β_t is increasing in σ_t. (For example, an oil price increase must have a negative effect on a stock price index such as TOPIX no matter whether the increase is large or small, with the negative effect being larger when the increase is larger). We should examine whether this is true in our empirical analysis. Table 5.5 also presents the maximum and minimum values for the estimates of β_t. In all three specifications, the maximum value is positive, while the minimum value is negative. If the sign of β_t changes depending on the value of σ_t, it is inconsistent with our theory. Table 5.6 presents the estimates of g (σ_t) and $g(\bar{\sigma}_t)$ with their standard errors, where σ_t and $\bar{\sigma}_t$ denote the minimum value and maximum value of σ_t in the sample. A standard one-sided t test does not reject the null hypothesis of $g(\sigma_t) \leq 0$ at any standard level, while the null hypothesis of $g(\bar{\sigma}_t) \geq 0$ is strongly rejected. Therefore, we can conclude that β_t is not significantly different from zero when σ_t is sufficiently small, while it is significantly below zero and decreasing in σ_t when σ_t is sufficiently large. This result is consistent with our theory.

Thus far we have assumed that Φ_1 is equal to the sample mean of σ_t. We also estimate the model that consists of Equations (5.12) with (5.9) setting $\Phi_1 = \frac{1}{10}, \frac{1}{5}, \frac{1}{2}, 1, 2, 5$, and 10. We find that the likelihood value is the largest when Φ is set $\frac{1}{5}$ in Specification 3. The estimation results of Specification 3 with $\Phi_1 = \frac{1}{5}$ are shown in Tables 5.7, where the maximum and minimum values both decrease, to 0.415 and –14.32 respectively.

Concluding remarks

In this chapter, we have developed a model of less-developed asset markets, and have shown that the sensitivity of asset prices to unexpected changes in their fundamental value depends on the heterogeneity of investors' expecta-

Table 5.7   Estimates of the relationship between the expectation heterogeneity and β, when $\Phi_1 = \frac{1}{5}$

Three months ahead forecasting

Specification	g_0	g_1	Log-likelihood	Max.	Min.
3. Positive Exponential	0.545 (0.857)	−0.005 (0.0013)	−2128.57	0.415	−14.322

Notes: Standard errors in parentheses. *Max.* and *Min.* denote the maximum value and the minimum value of the estimated β_t respectively.

tions. The more dispersed investors' expectations, the more sensitive asset prices are with respect to unexpected changes in the fundamental value. It has also been argued that advancement of information technology is likely to reduce price sensitivity, since increasing amounts information is available to improve investors' forecasting.

We tested the validity of these implications for the Japanese stock market. Using the data on exchange-rate expectations, we found strong evidence that the sensitivity of Japanese stock price innovation to intrinsic-value factor innovation (which is closely related to the yen–dollar exchange rate and the oil price) depends on the standard deviation of investors three-months-ahead exchange-rate forecasts. This suggests strongly that the Japanese stock market might be explained by the model developed here. However, we have failed to detect any statistically significant downward trend in the price sensitivity over the sample period. Thus, whether the advancement of information technology reduces the price sensitivity or not is still inconclusive.

The results of this chapter's empirical analysis thus suggest the importance of heterogeneity on investors' expectations in understanding asset price behaviour. However, there are several problems and possible extensions of the model and empirical analysis. First, in our empirical result, diversity in one-month-ahead and six-months-ahead forecasts apparently do not matter, although it does in three-months-ahead forecasts. It is interesting to consider why there is a difference between the three-months-ahead forecasts and the others.

Second, the stock market is not the only asset market. For example, the real-estate market may be closer to the postulated model of less-developed asset markets than the stock market, since transaction and information costs are higher in the real-estate market than the stock market. To examine whether real-estate prices are excessively sensitive to innovations in their market fundamental is an important topic, and we are now doing preliminary research on this subject.

Third, our specification of the advancement of information technology; that is, time trends in the price sensitivity function, may not be appropriate to measure its real effect. The failure to detect its effect may be caused by this possible misspecification. Although it is generally hard to find data on the advancement of information technology, more direct testing is desirable and will be a subject of future research.

Appendix: data source

The definition of variables used in this chapter, and the source of the data, are as follows.

Stock prices: TOPIX, end of period, *Tokyo Stock Exchange Statistics Report*, various issues.

Short-term interest rate: Call-market interest rate, monthly average, taken from *Nomura Research Institute* database.

Long-term interest rate: Yield on 10-year Kokusai, end of period, taken from *Datastream* database.

Exchange rate: Japanese yen per US dollar, end of period, taken from *Datastream* database.

Index of industrial production: Taken from *Datastream* database.

Consumer price index: All items seasonally adjusted, taken from *Datastream* database.

Trade balance: Taken from *Datastream* database.

Money supply: M1 plus quasi-money currency, end of period, taken from *Datastream* database.

Oil price: Saudi Arabian light oil spot price per barrel, end of period, taken from *Datastream* database.

Notes

1. Here the adjective 'developing' may not be appropriate, since developed economies may also have this type of under-developed asset market. See Note 2 below.
2. This description fits well to *the zaraba* price formation in the Tokyo Stock Exchange. Between the opening of the market and its closing, the market price is determined by the *zaraba* pricing scheme. In the *zaraba* scheme, limit orders are accumulated *as* buyers and sellers make them before a market order is made. Then at a given point in time, if a buyer (seller) makes a market order, then the lowest (highest) limit order is executed and the lowest (highest) limit order price becomes the market price. If the quantity of the particular buyer's market order is more than the lowest-price limit selling order, then the second-lowest price limit selling order is executed, and so on. If a buyer (seller) makes a limit order and this price is matched by the existing lowest selling (buying) order, then that order is executed. If the buyer's limit order does not match existing limit orders, the buyer's order is simply posted as other unexecuted limit orders. Here, both buyers and sellers make prices, and transactions take place if their offer are accepted by other investors.
3. Nishimura specifies the structure of the non-Walrasian asset market and distribution of investors' expectations in detail, and derives rational expectations (Bayesian Nash) equilibrium. Since it is rather complicated, we adopt a simpler approach here.
4. Nishimura (1998) contrasts the effect of imperfect information between asset and product markets under a rational expectations framework.
5. Some researchers have used the second specification in order to examine the relationship between volatility and autocorrelation in stock returns (see, for example, LeBaron (1992); Bollerslev *et al.*, (1995); and Watanabe (2001)).
6. In this chapter, we follow recent empirical studies on asset pricing (see Engle *et al.* (1990); Ng *et al.* (1992); and King *et al.* (1994)) except for one point. These empirical studies applying factor analysis to asset pricing assume that the sensitivity is

constant, but they explicitly take into account the heteroskedasticity in both of asset returns and factors. Here we allow that the sensitivity is variable but assume homoskedasticity. To allow both variable sensitivity and heteroskedasticity is more desirable, but estimation procedure becomes complicated and expensive (see Aguilar and West, 1998).

7. For the details of this data, see Ito (1990).
8. These companies consist of 15 banks and brokers, 4 securities companies, 6 trading companies, 9 export-orientated companies, 5 life insurance companies, and 5 import-orientated companies.
9. We also used the standard deviation divided by the sample mean; that is the coefficient of variation, but the results are unaltered.
10. Our choice of economic variables follows King *et al.* (1994).

References

Aguilar, O., and West, M. (1998) 'Bayesian Dynamic Factor Models and Variance Matrix Discounting for Portfolio Allocation', Technical Report 98–03, ISDS (North Carolina: Duke University).

Akaike, H. (1973) 'Information Theory and Extension of the Maximum Likelihood Principle', in B. N. Petrov and F. Csaki (eds), *Second International Symposium on Information Theory* (Budapest: Akademiai Kiado).

Bollerslev, T., Engle, R. F. and Nelson, D. B. (1995) 'ARCH Models', in R. F. Engle and D. McFadden (eds), *The Handbook of Econometrics*, vol. 4, (Amsterdam: North-Holland).

Diebold, F. X. (1988) *Empirical Modeling of Exchange Rate Dynamics* (New York: Springer-Verlag).

Engle, R. F., Ng, V. M. and Rothchild, M. (1990) 'Asset Pricing with a Factor-ARCH Structure: Empirical Estimates for Treasury Bills', *Journal of Econometrics*, vol. 45, pp. 213–37.

Ito, T. (1990) 'Foreign Exchange Rate Expectations: Micro Survey Data', *American Economic Review*, vol. 80, pp. 434–49.

King, M., Sentana, E. and Wadhwani, S. (1994) 'Volatility and Links between National Stock Markets', *Econometrica*, vol. 62, pp. 901–33.

LeBaron, B. (1992) 'Some Relations between Volatility and Serial Correlations in Stock Market Returns', *Journal of Business*, vol. 65, pp. 199–219.

Ljung, G. M., and Box, G. E. P. (1978) 'On a Measure of Lag of Fit in Time Series Models', *Biometrika*, vol. 67, pp. 297–303.

Nishimura, K. G. (1998) 'Expectation Heterogeneity and Price Sensitivity', *European Economic Review*, vol. 42, pp. 619–29.

Nishimura, K. G. (1999) 'Expectation Heterogeneity and Excessive Price Sensitivity in the Land Market', *Japanese Economic Review*, 50, 27–44.

Ng, V. M., Engle, R. F. and Rothchild, M. (1992) 'A Multi-Dynamic Factor Model for Excess Returns', *Journal of Econometrics*, vol. 52, pp. 245–66.

Ross, S. A. (1976) 'The Arbitrage Theory of Capital Asset Pricing', *Journal of Economic Theory*, vol. 13, pp. 341–60.

Schwarz, G. (1978) 'Estimating the Dimension of a Model', *Annals of Statistics*, vol. 6, pp. 461–4.

Watanabe, T. (2001) 'Margin Requirements, Positive Feedback Trading, and Stock Return Autocorrelations: The Case of Japan', *Applied Financial Economics*, forthcoming.

White, H. (1980) 'A Heteroskedasticity-Consistent Covariance Matrix Estimator and a Direct Test for Heteroskedasticity', *Econometrica*, vol. 48, pp. 817–38.

Comments

Hans Lindberg

The Chapter by Nishimura, Watanabe and Iwatusbo examines the effects of the development of a knowledge-based economy on the magnitude of asset price sensitivity. The authors develop a highly stylized model of an asset market characterized by high transaction and information costs, in which we effectively have monopolistic competition.

Financial economics tends to focus exclusively on price effects. However, this model also has implications for the volume of trade, since a decrease in trader heterogeneity leads to a lower probability of completing a trade. Thus a decrease in heterogeneity leads to a lower trading volume. This is something the authors do not discuss explicitly, but it is an additional implication of the model that could be tested in the framework of some empirical trading volume model. This would add another dimension to the chapter, which is usually lacking in financial analysis. With the notable exceptions of the research by Sanford Grossman, Hal Varian and a few others, finance models typically do not have anything to say about trading volume, for the simple reason that agents do not trade in these models.[1] This is also true in the limit for this model: as heterogeneity goes to zero the probability of completing a trade successfully goes to zero.

There is a methodological difficulty when the authors move on to test the model. They state that the model they have developed 'can be incorporated into the framework of the arbitrage pricing theory', but the APT, of course, is derived using the no arbitrage condition, while an important characteristic of the model developed in the paper is the presence of 'transaction costs making arbitrage insufficient'. This might make the use of the APT framework somewhat problematic for the analysis conducted in the chapter.

In examining empirically the effect of the knowledge-based economy on asset price sensitivity, two specific questions are addressed:

(i) Do prices exhibit excessive sensitivity to changes in the underlying factors?

(ii) Does this sensitivity decrease over time, as a result of increased sophistication in information gathering and processing, as well as the fact that more information becomes available?

The parameterization of the factor loadings, using a measure of the dispersion of investors' expectations and a time trend, seems to be a novel and interesting way of trying to capture the effect of the development of information technology on the sensitivity of asset prices to the underlying factors. But, rather than a time trend, I would have preferred the use of some more direct measure of the increased flow of information – for example, the number of analysts employed, the number of newsletters in circulation, or the number of Reuters terminals in use. I think it would be worthwhile to spend some time trying to come up with some types of direct measures of information technology and the flow of information. These should after all be the crucial variables in the analysis.

I also think it is overly restrictive to include only one factor in the APT, especially as an attempt is made to relate the factor to macroeconomic variables. The authors find that the factor is related to the price of oil and the yen–dollar exchange rate. This contrasts with the famous study by Chen *et al.* (1986) for the USA. These authors found that the oil price risk was not separately rewarded in the US stock market. Hence, it seems that Japan is different in this respect, but there are other factors that could be important as well. I would expect that a second factor would have picked up the interest rates (an interest-rate factor), since the term spread has proved to be important in predicting stock returns in a number of studies. A third factor would probably turn out to be closely related to the monthly growth rate of industrial production. I would therefore allow for at least three factors in an arbitrage pricing model, to give these macroeconomic variables a chance to be picked up by the factors used in the model.

My last point concerns the measure of heterogeneity. While the authors are using a model of a less-developed asset market, their measure of heterogeneity comes from the foreign exchange market, which cannot be said to be characterized by 'transaction costs making arbitrage insufficient' nor by 'information costs making market participants underinformed about the market'. On the contrary, according to MacDonald and Marsh (1996), currency forecasters seem to have similar information, but they interpret it differently. Hence, it is because they use different models that they develop different beliefs about the fundamental value of a currency. This is the source of the heterogeneity among currency forecasts. Using the insight of the MacDonald and Marsh study, technological development in information gathering and processing could reduce heterogeneity among forecasters if it facilitated the evaluation of which models work well and which models work less well, so that, over time, more weight is given to the 'good' models and less to the 'bad' models. We should also expect to see the development of more sophisticated and computationally demanding models taking advantage of the technological progress. It could be this type of evolution that explains the downward trend in the heterogeneity in exchange-rate forecasts documented in this chapter.

Note

1. See, for example, Grossman (1976, 1978) and Varian (1989).

References

Chen, N.-F., Roll, R. and Ross, S. A. (1986) 'Economic Forces and the Stock Market', *Journal of Business*, vol. 59, pp. 383–403.

Grossman, S. (1976) 'On the Efficiency of Competitive Stock Markets Where Traders Have Diverse Information', *Journal of Finance*, vol. 31, pp. 573–85.

Grossman, S. (1978) 'Further Results on the Informational Efficiency of Competitive Stock Markets', *Journal of Economic Theory*, vol. 18, pp. 81–101.

MacDonald, R. and Marsh, I. W. (1996) 'Currency Forecasters Are Heterogeneous: Confirmation and Consequences', *Journal of International Money and Finance*, vol. 15, pp. 665–85.

Varian, H. R. (1989) 'Differences of Opinion in Financial Markets', in C. C. Stone (ed.), *Financial Risk: Theory, Evidence and Implications* (Boston: Kluwer).

Part III

The Productivity Paradox and Mismeasurement Problems

6
An Explanation of the Productivity Paradox: TFP Spillover through Capital Accumulation

Masahiro Kuroda and Koji Nomura

Introduction

Recent statistics released by Organization for Economic Cooperation and Development (OECD) countries suggest that productivity growth at the macro level has not seen a rapid recovery since the great shock of the first oil crisis. In fact, as we can see in Table 6.1, the annual growth rate of total factor productivity (TFP) in Japan during the early 1980s was still less than 1 per cent, while in the USA it was less than 0.3 per cent, after the economic downturn of the early 1970s. In both countries we can observe sizeable increases in real investment. The recent growth of investment in the USA reached a high level of more than 3 per cent per annum. Also, in Japan, real investment, especially in electrical machinery (including computer and information facilities) increased rapidly during the 1980s. We should also note from the table that partial productivity of labour has been increasing gradually since 1960, while the partial productivity of capital has declined during the same period. It seems that increases in labour productivity have been achieved at the cost of decreases in capital productivity.

Table 6.1 shows that there has been a sort of paradoxical shift in the relationship between the trend of real investment and total factor productivity growth during the periods of recent Japanese and US economic recovery. It is our intuitive belief that this situation means productivity growth has not been achieved in spite of sizeable increases in real investment, along with new developments in technology, including information technology and high-tech instruments. This is called a 'conceptualization problem', or 'Solow's paradox in productivity'. It seems that these problems originate from the above questions.[1] Although these are, initially, hypothetical questions, they also, include various important issues which should be clarified from the viewpoint of new technologies, as well as the measurement of productivity

Table 6.1   Aggregated Productivity in Japan and the USA (annual growth rate)

	1960–65	1965–70	1970–75	1975–80	1980–85	1985–90
Total factor productivity						
Japan	2.62	4.58	–2.08	–0.02	0.69	0.91
USA	1.23	0.52	0.26	0.04	0.23	0.18
Labour productivity						
Japan	6.78	8.13	3.70	1.40	1.95	2.40
USA	2.21	1.49	1.67	0.64	0.67	0.19
Capital productivity						
Japan	–2.40	0.69	–9.45	–2.31	–1.27	–1.23
USA	1.61	–1.19	–1.84	0.09	–1.31	–0.59
Capital input						
Japan	12.52	11.10	14.46	6.58	5.06	5.86
USA	2.95	4.30	4.29	3.51	3.54	3.07

Asset Share of Capital Stock in Japan

	1960	1965	1970	1975	1980	1985	1990
Construction	91.00	85.23	80.42	75.35	76.33	74.84	70.86
Machinery	4.25	7.31	9.81	11.86	10.83	11.02	11.89
Electric machinery	0.74	1.52	2.42	4.68	5.92	7.78	10.64
Motor vehicles	0.45	1.17	1.82	2.90	2.89	2.45	2.77
Other transport machinery	2.25	3.05	3.04	2.88	1.99	1.74	1.56
Precision machinery	0.11	0.21	0.28	0.36	0.44	0.54	0.65

growth. Broadly speaking, there might be several alternative ways of explaining these paradoxical phenomena in productivity trends:

(i) Measurement errors. There are two possible explanations for the errors in productivity measurement. It is often argued that TFP growth measures have a number of possible measurement errors because of their definitions, whereby they are defined by differences between observed growth rates of input and output. From this perspective, qualitative changes in output and input might be highly important ways of generating measurement errors of productivity. Experiments to revise the price and quantity index numbers of including a hedonic approach suggested that considerations regarding qualitative measures of input and output could be expected to produce sizeable changes in the results of TFP growth measures. A second source of measurement errors in TFP growth measures comes from an aggregation bias. Measures of input and output in the estimation of TFP growth are defined by an aggregate measure of various heterogeneous types of inputs and outputs, even at the industry level, as well as at the macro level. We can observe changes in the composition of the inputs and outputs in our historical statistics. In the simple aggregate procedures, which ignored qualitative differences of components and changes in their allocation among sectors, these might create a sort of aggregation bias.

(ii) There have been many developments in new technologies since the time of the Industrial Revolution. In addition, there have been occasions in history when it took a considerable amount of time for these developments to diffuse themselves into society after their theoretcial conception and contribute to improved efficiency in production Information technologies might have similar features. It might take some time to apply the knowledge that develops in this field and, as a result, achieve gains in productivity.

(iii) Substitutability between labour and capital. New technologies such as information technology require sizeable real investment to enable them to be integrated into the production process. It might increases labour productivity by substituting labour input with capital input, while capital productivity might decline. Since increases in labour productivity would be cancelled out by decreases in capital productivity, total factor productivity could not be improved as much as might be expected by the new technologies.

(iv) Externality. Externality is one of the important characteristics of new information technology. Since the external effects of the new technologies could not be evaluated endogeneously in terms of market prices, it might be difficult to measure their contributions to productivity by the growth-accounting framework.

(v) The spillover effect of technology. Recently-developed technologies have contributed to improved efficiency in high-tech machinery sectors. Also, new technologies (including computers and information technologies) have brought about a big change in the composition of investment goods in almost all industrial sectors, where the share of general and electrical machinery in investments would increase dramatically. As a consequence, the productivity gains in machinery sectors could have a spillover effect on the improvement of productivity in all industrial sectors. The productivity gains in machinery sectors could not only spill over among sectors through the static framework of interdependence of the technology among sectors, but also have a dynamic effect among sectors through capital accumulation. This spill-over effect must be distinguished from the external effects of technology. It should be evaluated as a pecuniary impact of the efficiency gains in new technology.

As indicated above, we can provide several alternative explanations for these recent paradoxical and puzzling trends in productivity. Within the previous five alternative explanations, we do not consider the second possibility – 'the time lag hypothesis' here. It seems to us to be difficult to identify the validity of the hypothesis by using short-term data over just three decades. With regard to the third explanation, we cannot deny the possibility of a substitution between labour and capital during the process of installing new technology. As shown in Table 6.1, however, the phenomenon of substitution in order to improve productivity is not necessarily a recent characteristics of new technology. We can observe the same phenomenon occuring in productivity trends since 1960. Therefore, it is important to explain the implications of installing new technology where it would be implemented even at the cost of productivity improvement of capital. As for the externality issues in the fourth explanation, we also cannot deny the effect of externality on new technology. We wonder, however, if there could be some kinds of non-pecuniary effects caused by the installation of new technology. If so, it should be included in the growth rate of the TFP, and be measured in the residuals where all pecuniary effects are excluded.

In this chapter, we would like to focus on two alternative possibilities in order to explain these puzzling problems. One is an explanation of measurement errors, and the other is an explanation related to spill-over effects within the pecuniary framework. In the second section, we would like to focus on the explanation of measurement errors from the viewpoints of qualitative evaluation of inputs and aggregation biases at the macro level. We try to break down the sources of economic growth in Japan into changes of quantities of factor inputs, changes of qualities of factor inputs, and changes of allocation of resources of output and input among sectors. This should provide definite verification of the measurement error hypothesis in order to explain the recent puzzling trend of productivity. When it comes to evaluating the effects of qualitative change on capital input, we can observe that there were fairly dominant qualitative changes on capital input recently. This was because of a strict relationship with the increasing shares of machinery (especially electrical machinery) in the composition of assets in new investment and capital stock in all industrial sectors. In the third section we try to summarize our observations concerning the changes in the composition of assets in capital formation and stock. The development of new technologies is assumed to be realized by the changes in composition among capital goods in capital formation and observed by the changes of the capital coefficients in capital stock by assets. We begin with the development of the measures of capital input in current and constant prices for each of the forty-three industrial sectors in Japan for the period 1955–92. We have estimated capital matrices in terms of flow and stock in order to evaluate the impact of the structural changes in capital coefficients on the economy, where new technology has been expected to be embodied. Furthermore, when we try to consider the impact on productivity growth of structural changes in the capital composition, we have to propose a theoretical framework in productivity measurement in order to evaluate these.

In the fourth section we try to evaluate quantitatively the implications of the spill-over effect of TFP growth for structural changes in the Japanese economy. The concept of spill-over discussed in this chapter should be distinguished from that of externality. Our concerns are related to the structural changes of input coefficients of intermediate inputs and factor inputs (such as labour and capital), which are brought about by the installation of new technology. Structural changes that are implemented by new technologies might have a sizeable impact on the framework of linkage among various economic sectors, which is the second implication of the spill-over effect. We can see that the structural changes brought about by new technologies could produce an extension of the spill-over effect of TFP growth, and contribute to an increase in efficiency within the economy, while the ordinary measure of TFP growth in each industrial sector is relatively lower. Our analytical framework is based upon an input–output analysis approach. In our framework, the spill-over effect of the structural changes on productivity can be measured not only by the static interdependent relationship among sectors through the transactions of their intermediate goods, but also by the dynamic interrelationship among sectors through the capital accumulation process. We assume here that the development of new technologies could be embodied in changes of capital stock through new investment, and that this would have a spill-over effect on the whole economy through productivity growth. These approaches to the static and dynamic measures of the spill-over effect provide us with extended concepts of the measurement of total factor productivity. Our concept of the measurement of total factor productivity is an extension of the concept of the ordinary TFP measures by sectoral analysis, from the viewpoints of technological properties of commodity production and the spill-over effect of the technology as a system.

Measurement problems in TFP

The TFP measurements shown in Table 6.1 represent figures in both Japan and the USA, and we have tried carefully to remove the possibility of any measurement errors. By this definition, the growth rate of TFP could be observed only as the difference between the growth rates of outputs and inputs. Therefore results depend entirely upon the measurement of quantities of output and input, as well as those of prices of output and input. In particular, they should be carefully adjusted to measure changes of quality of output and input in the measurements of quantities and prices. If we assume all outputs and inputs to be homogeneous in their qualities, we can define the aggregated quantities of outputs and inputs as a simple sum of each quantity of outputs and inputs respectively. If this is not the case, however, the aggregated quantities of outputs and inputs defined as a simple sum might include some measurement errors. It is because there are, presumably, overlooked qualitative changes in outputs and inputs. Then, the growth rate of TFP, defined as the difference between the growth rates of the aggregated output and input, might also include some measurement errors.

One way of explaining the recent paradoxical trends of productivity is to attribute this to the measurement errors of TFP. Furthermore, the measurement errors in the aggregated level can impute to the qualitative changes in outputs and inputs by the following two sources. One is the error that arises from neglect of qualitative changes of output and input in specific industrial sectors, and the other is bias, which comes from a disregard for allocational changes of output and input among industrial sectors. We try to distinguish the former qualitative changed in one sector from the latter allocational biases in the distribution of resources. Concerning the former qualitative changes in output by sector, it should be noted that qualitative changes in output have already taken into account measurements of output deflators in Wholesale Price Index (WPI). In particular, recent changes of quality in high-tech commodities, such as computers, have been measured in WPI of commodities by using the hedonic approach method. Here, we focus only on qualitative changes of inputs at the aggregate level of the economy.

Our first objective is to measure value added for the economy as a whole. Our measurements of the sectoral gross output are based on the input–output accounting framework. Both our input–output accounting framework and the sectoral price functions give aggregate measures of value-added price and factor input prices. These prices create the quantity of aggregate value added and factor inputs as a dual index, in which nominal accounting balances in each sector and the economy as a whole are maintained. It should be emphasized that we do not necessarily assume the existence of an aggregate production function or an aggregte price function. The assumption of the existence of an aggregate function imposes stringent restrictions on sectoral models of production. All sectoral price functions must be identical to the aggregate price function; and all sectoral value-added prices, capital service prices and labour service prices must be equal to each aggregate price, respectively. Unless these assumptions of the aggregate production model are met, the analysis of sources of economic growth creates differences between sectoral and aggregate models of production and technical change. Contributions of reallocations of value-added and primary factor inputs among sectors can be identified by the rate of aggregate technical change.

We begin with estimates of aggregate value added, based on our input–output accounting framework. Next, we allocate the growth of value added among its components: the contributions of capital and labour inputs in the economy as a whole, and the rate of aggregate technical change. We can further break down the contribution of capital and labour inputs at the aggregate level into the aggregates of the quality changes by sectoral level and the allocational bias of capital and labour inputs among sectors. Third, we present the methodological framework in order to allocate the rate of aggregate technical change among a weighted sum of rates of sectoral technical change and reallocations of value added, and the primary factor inputs among sectors. Finally, we present the results of the breakdowns of the rate of aggregate technical change in the Japanese economy, and give some indication of a measurement error hypothesis as a way of explaining the recent puzzling trend in productivity.

Aggregate output

Our measurement of the sectoral gross output is based on the input–output accounting framework. The quantity of aggregate output is defined as the sum of the quantities of value added over all sectors.

Accounting balance in the j-th industrial sector is represented as follows:

$$
\begin{aligned}
p_v^j V^j &= p_L^j L^j + p_K^j K^j \\
&= p_I^j Z_I^j - \sum_{i=1} p_i X_i^j
\end{aligned}
\tag{6.1}
$$

where p_0^j and V_i are, respectively, the value-added deflator and quantity of the value-added of the j-th sector, p_L^j, L^j and p_K^j, K^j represent price and quantity of labour and capital service inputs of j-th sector. p_I^j, Z_I^j and p_i, X_i^j stand for price and quantity of output of j-th sector and price and quantity of i-th intermediate inputs in j-th sector. Differentiating Equation (6.1) logarithmically with respect to times, we have:

$$
\begin{aligned}
\frac{p_v^j}{p_v^j} + \frac{V^j}{V^j} &= \left\{ \frac{p^{j*} Z_I^j}{p_v^j V^j} \left(\frac{p_I^j}{p_I^j} \right) - \sum_{i=1} \left(\frac{p_i X_i^j}{p_v^j Vj} \right) \left(\frac{p_i}{p_i} \right) \right\} \\
&+ \left\{ \frac{p_I^j Z_I^j}{p_v^j V^j} \left(\frac{Z_I^j}{Z_I^j} \right) - \sum_{i=1} \left(\frac{p_i X_i^j}{p_v^j V^j} \right) \left(\frac{X_i^j}{X_i^j} \right) \right\}
\end{aligned}
\tag{6.2}
$$

In Equation (6.2), the term of the first parenthesis on the right-hand side of the equation corresponds to the definition of the growth rate of the divisia price index for the value-added deflator. The growth rate of the divisia price index is then subtracted from the rate of growth of net output values in current prices in order to obtain a measure of the growth rate of real value-added.

Next, we define gross domestic products (GDP) – the nationwide aggregate measure of net output – as the sum of sectoral value added as follows:

$$
\begin{aligned}
p_v V &= \sum_{j=1}^n p_v^j V^j \\
&= \sum_{j=1}^n (p_L^j L^j) + p_K^j K^j)
\end{aligned}
\tag{6.3}
$$

where p_v and V are GDP deflator and real GDP respectively. Differentiating (6.3) logarithmically with respect to time, we have:

$$
\frac{p_v}{p_v} + \frac{V}{V} = \sum_{j=1}^v \frac{p_v^j V^j}{p_v V} \left(\frac{p_v^j}{p_v V} \right) + \sum_{j=1}^n \frac{p_v^j V^j}{p_v V} \left(\frac{V^j}{v^j} \right)
\tag{6.4}
$$

The growth rate of the divisia price index, p_v, which is represented by the first term on the right-hand side of Equation (6.4), is then subtracted from the rate of growth of the nominal gross domestic product in order to obtain a measure of the growth rate of the real GDP defined by the second term of the right-hand side of the equation. The last term of the right-hand side of Equation (6.4) gives us the growth rate of the divisia quantity index of the real GDP, V.

The sum of value added in all sectors $p_v V^j$ is equal to the sum of capital compensation and labour compensation for the economy as a whole. Value added for the economy as a whole is equal to the sum of the value added at current price over all sectors:

$$p_v V = \sum_{j=1}^{n} p_v^j V^j = \tilde{p}_v \sum_{j=1}^{n} V^j \tag{6.5}$$

where $\tilde{p}_v$ is an aggregate price index on average which is defined as corresponding to the sum of the quantities of real value-added in all sectors in Equation (6.5). The divisia price index p_v is not necessarily equal to the aggregate price index on average, $\tilde{p}_v$. They are equal if, and only if, prices of value-added in all sectors are identically equal to p_v and value shares ω^j in all sectors are constant. On the other hand, we can define the growth rate of the simple summation of the sectoral real value-added as follows:

$$\frac{V^*}{V^*} = \sum_j \left(\frac{V^j}{V^*}\right)\left(\frac{V^j}{V^j}\right) = \frac{\sum V^j}{V^*} \tag{6.6}$$

We can then define a measurement of rates of changes of the allocation of real value added among setors, $\frac{\dot{A}_v}{A_v}$ as a difference between growth rate of divisia aggregate index of real value-added, $\frac{\dot{V}}{V}$ and that of a simple summation of real value-added, $\frac{\dot{V}^*}{V^*}$ as follows. We call it a measure of the allocational bias of the value-added.

$$\frac{\dot{A}^v}{A^v} = \frac{\dot{V}}{V} - \frac{\dot{V}^*}{V^*} = \sum_j \frac{p_v^j V^j}{p_v V}\left(\frac{\dot{V}^j}{V_j}\right) - \sum_j \frac{V^j}{V^*}\left(\frac{\dot{V}^j}{V_j}\right)$$

$$= \sum_j \left(\frac{p_v^j V^j - \tilde{p}_v V^j v}{p_v V}\right)\left(\frac{\dot{V}^j}{V^j}\right) \tag{6.7}$$

The second part of Equation (6.7) implies that the allocational bias of the value added is defined by a shift of the allocation of value-added among sectors. If the changes of allocational bias, $\frac{\dot{A}_v}{A_v}$ is positive (negative), resources would be allocated to the sectors which are characterized by the higher (lower) value-added ratio rather than that the average.

Aggregate labour and capital input

According to our accounting identities, aggregate labor and capital compensations are equal to the sum of compensations paid for each type of labor and capital over all sectors respectively. Let us denote the number of types of labor[2] as the subscript l and the number of types of capital as the subscript, k. p^j_{Ll} and L^j_l stands for the price and quantity of the l-th labour service input, while p^j_{Kk} and K^j_k stand for price and quantity of the k-th capital service input.

We can define the aggregate compensation of labour and capital as follows respectively:

$$p_L L = \sum_j B^j_L = \sum_j \sum_l p^j_{Ll} L^j_l \qquad (6.8)$$

$$p_k K = \sum_j B^j_K = \sum_j \sum_k p^j_{Kk} K^j_k \qquad (6.9)$$

where B^j_L and B^j_K stand for the total compensation of labour and capital in the j-th sector, which are defined as the sum of the compensation for all types of labour and capital in the sector.

Let us begin with the definition of the measurement of qualitative change of labour and capital in the j-th sector. Growth rates of divisia aggregate index for labour and capital in j-th sector are defined as follows:

$$\frac{\dot{L}^j}{L^j} = \sum_l \left(\frac{p^j_{Ll} L^j_l}{p^j_L L^j}\right)\left(\frac{\dot{L}^j_l}{L^j_l}\right) \qquad (6.10)$$

where

$$p^j_L L^j = \sum_l p^j_{Ll} L^j_l = B^j_L$$

and

$$\frac{\dot{K}^j}{K^j} = \sum_l \left(\frac{p^j_{Kk} K^j_k}{p^j_K K^j}\right)\left(\frac{\dot{K}^j_k}{K^j_k}\right) \qquad (6.11)$$

where

$$p^j_K K^j = \sum_k p^j_{Kk} K^j_k = B^j_K$$

On the other hand, we can define growth rates of a simple summation of labour and capital service inputs in the j-th sector as follows. A simple summation suggests that there are assumed to be no differences of quality among the various types of service input:

$$\frac{\dot{L}^{*j}}{L^{*j}} = \sum_l \left(\frac{L^j_l}{L^{*j}}\right)\left(\frac{\dot{L}^j_l}{L^j_l}\right) = \frac{\Sigma_l \dot{L}^j_l}{L^{*j}} \qquad (6.12)$$

$$\frac{\dot{K}^{*j}}{K^{*j}} = \sum_k \left(\frac{K^j_k}{K^{*j}}\right)\left(\frac{\dot{K}^j_k}{K^j_k}\right) = \frac{\Sigma_k \dot{K}^j_k}{K^{*j}} \qquad (6.13)$$

Next, we can define the growth rate of qualitative change of labour and capital inputs in the *j*-th sector as a difference of the growth rate between divisia aggregate and simple sum indexes of each input:

$$\frac{\dot{Q}_L^j}{Q_L^j} = \frac{\dot{L}^j}{L_j} - \frac{\dot{L}^{*j}}{L^{*j}}$$

$$= \sum_l \left(\frac{p_{Ll}^j L_l^j}{p_L^j L^j} - \frac{L_l^j}{L_l^j} \right)$$

$$= \sum_l \left(\frac{p_{Ll}^j L_l^j}{p_L^j L^j} - \frac{p_L^j L_l^j}{p_L^j L^j} \right) \left(\frac{\dot{L}_l^j}{L_l^j} \right) \tag{6.14}$$

where

$$\tilde{p}_L^j = \frac{p_L^j L^j}{L^{*j}} = \frac{B_L^j}{L^{*j}}.$$

$$\frac{\dot{Q}_K^j}{Q_K^j} = \frac{\dot{K}^j}{K^j} - \frac{\dot{K}^{*j}}{K^{*j}}$$

$$= \sum_k \left(\frac{p_{Kk}^j K_k^j}{p_K^j K_j} - \frac{K_k^j}{K^{*j}} \right) \left(\frac{\dot{K}_k^j}{K_k^j} \right)$$

$$= \sum_k \left(\frac{p_{Kk}^j K_k^j}{p_K^j K^j} - \frac{p_K^j K_k^j}{p_K^j K^j} \right) \left(\frac{\dot{K}_k^j}{K_k^j} \right) \tag{6.15}$$

where

$$p_K^{-j} = \frac{p_K^j k^i}{K^{*j}} = \frac{B_k^j}{K^{*j}}$$

$\frac{\dot{Q}_L^j}{Q_L^j}$ and $\frac{\dot{Q}_K^j}{Q_K^j}$ represent the growth rates of quality change in labour and capital service inputs by sector. According to the definitions in Equations (6.14) and (6.15), if weights of inputs among various types of labour and capital services were to shift to inputs where the prices are relatively higher than the average input prices $\tilde{p}_l^j$ and p_k^j, qualitative changes of inputs should be evaluated as positive. In our theoretical framework, each input price corresponds to marginal productivity. Then the positive (or negative) change in the quality in labour and capital services implies that the total aggregates of the marginal productivity of these inputs in the sector should be increased (or decreased) by the changes of the qualities of the inputs. Now let us turn to the nation wide aggregate of inputs. With regard to inputs such as labour and capital, we defined the measure of quality in each sector by the changes of composition among various types of input, which have different rates of marginal productivity. At the aggregate level, we can also observe changes of allocation in the factors among sectors.

This should be distinguished from the quality measures within these sectors. We shall call it a measure of allocational bias of factor. First, let us begin with the definition of growth rate of divisia input quantity indexes of the nationwide aggregate concerning labour and capital:

$$\frac{\dot{L}}{L} = \sum_j \sum_l \frac{p^j_{Ll} I^j_l}{p_L L} \left(\frac{\dot{L}^j_l}{L^j_l}\right)$$

$$= \sum_j \frac{p^j_L L^j}{p_L L} \left(\frac{\dot{L}^j}{L^j}\right) \tag{6.16}$$

where L and L^j stand for the divisia aggregate quantity index of the nationwide and sectoral aggregates for labour service and p_L and p^j_L *correspond to their price indexes, respectively.*

Similarly, we can define the divisia quantity index of capital of the nationwide aggregate as follows:

$$\frac{\dot{K}}{K} = \sum_j \sum_k \frac{p^j_{Kk} K^j_k}{p_K K} \left(\frac{\dot{K}^j_k}{K^j_k}\right)$$

$$= \sum_j \frac{p^j_K K^j}{p_K K} \left(\frac{\dot{K}_j}{K_j}\right) \tag{6.17}$$

where K and K^j stand for the divisia aggregate quantity index of the nationwide and sectoral aggregates for capital service, and p_k and p^j_k correspond to their price indexes, respectively.

On the other hand, we can define the following two types of growth rate of input quantity index as a simple summation of factor inputs. One is defined by the simple summation of the sectoral divisia quantity of input defined by Equations. (6.10) and (6.11):

$$\frac{\dot{L}^{**}}{L^{**}} = \sum_j \frac{L^j}{L^{**}} \left(\frac{\dot{L}^j}{L^j}\right) = \frac{\sum_j \dot{L}^j}{L^{**}} \tag{6.18}$$

$$\frac{\dot{K}^{**}}{K^{**}} = \sum_j \frac{K^j}{K^{**}} \left(\frac{\dot{K}^j}{K_j}\right) = \frac{\sum_j \dot{K}_j}{K^{**}} \tag{6.19}$$

where L^{**} and K^{**} represent simple summations of sectoral divisia quantities of labour and capital for the nationwide aggregates. These indexes suggest that inputs by sector which are adjusted changes of the quality within each sector are homogeneous among sectors, and they can be aggregated by a simple summation. Alternatively, if we could assume that there are no differences of quality of inputs among inputs types and sectors, we could define the growth rate of the aggregate quantity of inputs by the following simple summation:

$$\frac{\dot{L}^*}{L^*} = \sum_j \sum_l \frac{\dot{L}^j_l}{L^*} \left(\frac{\dot{L}^j}{L^j_l}\right) = \frac{\Sigma_j \dot{\Sigma}_l I^j_l}{L^*} \tag{6.20}$$

$$\frac{\dot{K}^*}{K^*} = \sum_j \sum_k \frac{\dot{K}^j_k}{K^*} \left(\frac{\dot{K}^j_k}{K^j_k}\right) = \frac{\Sigma_j \dot{\Sigma}_k K^j_k}{K^*} \tag{6.21}$$

where L^* and K^* represent indexes defined by the simple summation of all types of labour and capital inputs among types and sectors for the nationwide aggregate. It implies that all inputs among types and sectors are homogeneous with regard to labour and capital, respectively; and then it can be aggregated nationwide by the simple summation.

We can define a measure by which we can evaluate the changes of the resource allocation among sectors at the nationwide level. It is defined by the differences between growth rate of the nationwide divisia aggregate defined by Equation (6.16) and (6.17) and the growth rate of the simple summation of the sectoral divisia quantities as defined by Equation (6.18) and (6.19) concerning labour and capital, respectively. As for the difference between Equation (6.16) and (6.18), the allocational bias of labour input is formulated as follows:

$$\frac{\dot{A}_L}{A_L} = \frac{\dot{L}}{L} - \frac{\dot{L}^{**}}{L^{**}}$$

$$= \sum_j \frac{p^j_L L^j}{p_L L} \left(\frac{\dot{L}^j}{L^j}\right) - \sum_j \frac{L^j}{L^{**}} \left(\frac{\dot{L}^j}{L^j}\right)$$

$$= \sum_j \left(\frac{p^j_L L^j - \tilde{p}_L L^j}{p_L L}\right) \left(\frac{\dot{L}^j}{L^j}\right) \tag{6.22}$$

where

$$\tilde{p}_L = \frac{p_L L}{L^{**}}$$

Similarly, as for the difference between Equations (6.17) and (6.19), the allocational bias of capital input is formulated as follows:

$$\frac{\dot{A}_K}{A_K} = \frac{\dot{K}}{K} - \frac{\dot{K}^{**}}{K^{**}}$$

$$= \sum_j \frac{p^j_K K^j}{p_K K} \left(\frac{\dot{K}^j}{K^j}\right) - \sum_j \frac{K^j}{K^{**}} \left(\frac{\dot{K}^j}{K^j}\right)$$

$$= \sum_j \left(\frac{p^j_K K^j - \tilde{p}_K K^j}{p_K K}\right) \left(\frac{\dot{K}^j}{K^j}\right), \tag{6.23}$$

where

$$\tilde{p}_K = \frac{p_K K}{K^{**}}$$

$\frac{\dot{A}_L}{A_L}$ and $\frac{\dot{A}_K}{A_K}$ represent takes of changes of allocation of the factors among sectors. We call them allocational biases of labour and capital inputs. As shown in the above formulations, $\tilde{p}_l$ and $\tilde{p}_k$ stand for average prices at the nationwide level of labour and capital services. Then the index of the allocational biases implies that if it is positive (or negative), resources such as labour and capital services would be allocated to sectors where the price of the factor seems to be more expensive (less expensive) than the average. From the perspective of cost efficiency on the resource allocation, positive (or negative) value of the allocational biases implies that resources are allocated less (or more) efficiently by the shift among sectors.

Finally, by rearranging the difference between the growth rate of the nationwide divisia aggregate index of input defined by Equation by (6.10) or (6.11) and the growth rate of the nationwide simple summation index of the corresponding input defined by equation by (6.20) or (6.21) respectively, we can decompose, sources of change of quality of inputs at the nationwide aggregate level. By subtracting Equations (6.20) from Equation (6.10), or Equation (6.21), from Equation (6.11), we can deduce the following formulations:

$$
\begin{aligned}
\frac{\dot{L}}{L} - \frac{\dot{L}^*}{L^*} &= \sum_j \sum_l \frac{p_L^j L_l^j}{p_L L} \left(\frac{\dot{L}_l^j}{L_l^j}\right) - \sum_j \sum_l \frac{L_l^j}{L^*} \left(\frac{\dot{L}_l^j}{L_l^j}\right) \\
&= \sum_j \frac{L^j}{\Sigma L^j} \sum_l \left\{\frac{p_{Ll}^j}{p_L^j} - \frac{L_l^j}{L^{*j}}\right\} \left(\frac{\dot{L}_L^j}{L_l^j}\right) \\
&\quad + \sum_j \left\{\frac{p_L^j L^j}{p_L L} - \frac{L^j}{\Sigma L^j}\right\} \left(\frac{\dot{L}^j}{L^j}\right) \\
&\quad + \sum_j \sum_l \left\{\frac{L^j L_l^j}{L^{*j} \Sigma L^j} - \frac{L_l^j}{L^*}\right\} \left(\frac{\dot{L}_l^j}{L_l^j}\right) \quad (6.24)
\end{aligned}
$$

$$
\begin{aligned}
\frac{\dot{K}}{K} - \frac{\dot{K}^*}{K^*} &= \sum_j \sum_k \frac{p_{Kk}^j K_k^j}{p_K K} \left(\frac{\dot{K}_l^j}{K_l^j}\right) - \sum_j \sum_k \frac{K_k^j}{K^*} \left(\frac{\dot{K}_k^j}{K_k^j}\right) \\
&= \sum_j \frac{K^j}{\Sigma K^j} \sum_k \left\{\frac{p_{Kk}^j}{p_k^j} - \frac{K_k^j}{K^{*j}}\right\} \left(\frac{\dot{K}_k^j}{K_k^j}\right) \\
&\quad + \sum_j \left\{\frac{p_k^j K^j}{p_K K} - \frac{k^j}{\Sigma K^j}\right\} \left(\frac{\dot{K}^j}{K^j}\right) \\
&\quad + \sum_j \sum_k \left\{\frac{K^j K_k^j}{K^{*j} \Sigma K^j} - \frac{K_k^j}{K^*}\right\} \left(\frac{\dot{K}_k^j}{K_k^j}\right) \quad (6.25)
\end{aligned}
$$

The formulations in Equations (6.24) or (6.25) suggest to us that the growth rate of quality of input in the nationwide aggregate as the differences between Equations (6.10) and (6.20) or (6.11) and (6.21) could be broken down into three components, respectively. The first is represented by the first term on the right-hand side of the second equation, which is an aggregate measure of qualitative changes among various categories of the factor. The second term of the right-hand side of the second Equation represents a measure of the allocational biases defined by Equations (6.22) or (6.23). Finally, the third term of the right-hand side of the second equation is a sort of the interactive effect of the above two components.

Aggregate productivity index

We have presented indices of output and input for the economy as a whole. Our next objective is to formulate an index of TFP change for the economy as a whole. We have already presented an index of productivity at the sectoral level as follows:

$$
\upsilon^j_T = \frac{\dot{Z}^j_I}{Z^j_I} - \sum_{i=1} \frac{p_i X^j_I}{p^j_I Z^j_I} \left(\frac{\dot{X}^j_I}{X^j_I} \right)
$$
$$
\sum_l \frac{p^j_{Ll} L^j_l}{p^j_I Z^j_I} \left(\frac{\dot{L}^j_l}{L^j_l} \right) - \sum_k \frac{p^j_{Kk} K^j_k}{p^j_I Z^j_I} \left(\dot{K}^j_k j_k \right) \tag{6.26}
$$

Alternatively, using the definitions of the value added in the *j*-th sector as shown in Equation (6.2), we can write the index of the rate of TFP change υ^i_T:

$$
\upsilon^j_T = \left(\frac{p^j_\upsilon V^j}{p^j_I Z^j_I} \right) \left(\frac{\dot{V}^i}{V^i} \right)
$$
$$
- \sum \left(\frac{p^j_{Ll} L^j_l}{p^j_I Z^j_I} \right) \left(\frac{\dot{L}^j}{L^j_l} \right) - \sum_k \left(\frac{p^i_{Kk} K^j_k}{p^j_I Z^j} \right) \left(\frac{\dot{K}^j_k}{K^j_k} \right) \tag{6.27}
$$

As a nationwide accounting balance we can define GDP or a nationwide aggregate measure of net output in Equation (6.3), and can rewrite it as follows.

$$
p_\upsilon V = p_L L + p_K K \tag{6.28}
$$

where V, L and K stand for divisia aggregate quantity indexes of value-added, labour and capital inputs, while p_υ, p_L and p_K correspond to the respective price at the aggregate level. The growth rate of each divisia quantity index for net outputs and inputs at the aggregate level has already been formulated in the previous sections.

With regard to the growth rate of net output at the aggregate level, we defined it in Equation (6.4) as follows:

$$
\frac{\dot{V}}{V} = \sum_j \frac{p^j_\upsilon V^j}{p_\upsilon V} \left(\frac{\dot{V}^j}{V^j} \right) = \frac{\dot{V}^*}{V^*} + \frac{\dot{A}_\upsilon}{A_\upsilon} \tag{6.29}
$$

The right-hand side of the second equation represents the decomposition of the growth rate of net output at the aggregate level, which is shown in Equation in (6.7).

On the other hand, we defined the growth rate of labour and capital inputs at the aggregate level in Equations (6.16) and (6.17). Moreover, we can formulate the breakdown of the sources of the growth of labour and capital in Equations (6.22) or (6.24), and (6.23) or (6.25). We can rearrange these as follows:

$$\frac{\dot{L}}{L} = \sum_j \sum_l \frac{p_{Ll}^j L_l^j}{p_L L} \left(\frac{\dot{L}_l^j}{L_l^j}\right)$$

$$= \frac{\dot{L}^{**}}{L^{**}} + \frac{\dot{A}_L}{A_L}$$

$$= \frac{\dot{L}^*}{L^*} + \frac{\dot{Q}_L}{Q_L} + \frac{\dot{A}_L}{A_L} + \frac{\dot{I}_{LQA}}{I_{LQA}} \tag{6.30}$$

$$\frac{\dot{K}}{K} = \sum_j \sum_k \frac{p_{Kk}^j K_k^j}{p_K K} \left(\frac{\dot{K}_k^j}{K_k^j}\right)$$

$$= \frac{\dot{K}^{**}}{K^{**}} + \frac{\dot{A}_K}{A_K}$$

$$= \frac{\dot{K}^*}{K^*} + \frac{\dot{Q}_K}{Q_K} + \frac{\dot{A}_K}{A_K} + \frac{\dot{I}_{KQA}}{I_{KQA}} \tag{6.31}$$

In Equations (6.30) and (6.31), $\frac{\dot{I}_{LQA}}{I_{LQA}}$ and $\frac{\dot{I}_{KQA}}{I_{KQA}}$ represent the contribution of the interactive effect of allocational bias and quality change on the growth rate of quantities of labour and capital inputs respectively, which are defined in Equation (6.24) and (6.25).

We can define an index of productivity change at the aggregate level by using the aggregate accounting balance, Equation (6.28):

$$v_T = \frac{\dot{V}}{V} - s_L \frac{\dot{L}}{L} - s_K \frac{\dot{K}}{K} = \sum_j \frac{p_l^j Z_l^j}{p_v V} v_l^j \tag{6.32}$$

where

$$s_L = \frac{\Sigma_j \Sigma_l p_{Ll}^j L_l^j}{p_v V}, \quad s_K = \frac{\Sigma_j \Sigma_k p_{Kk}^j K_k^j}{p_v V}$$

The right-hand side of the second equation in Equation (6.32) indicates that the growth rate of productivity at the aggregate level is consistent with the weighted sum of the sectoral productivity change, v_t^i defined by Equation (6.26), where p^j are utilized as weight.

Finally, we can provide the implications of the breakdown of the sources of the economic growth at the aggregate level by rearranging all of the above formulations. Rearranging the following equation by Equation (6.29), (6.30) and (6.31),

$$\frac{\dot{V}}{V} = s_L \frac{\dot{L}}{L} + s_K \frac{\dot{K}}{K} + \upsilon_T$$

we can obtain the following expression.

$$\frac{\dot{V^*}}{V^*} + \frac{\dot{A}_\upsilon}{A_\upsilon} = s_L \left(\frac{\dot{L^*}}{L^*} + \frac{\dot{Q}_L}{Q_L} + \frac{\dot{A}_L}{A_L} + \frac{\dot{I}_{LQA}}{I_{LQA}} \right)$$

$$+ s_K \left(\frac{\dot{K^*}}{K^*} + \frac{\dot{Q}_K}{Q_K} + \frac{\dot{A}_K}{A_K} + \frac{\dot{I}_{KQA}}{I_{KQA}} \right) + \upsilon_T \qquad (6.33)$$

The final formulation represents an interesting breakdown of the sources of economic growth at the aggregated level. The growth of the net output at the aggregated level was broken down into the contribution of the growth of the factor input, such as labour and capital, and the growth of productivity. The contribution of the growth of the factors is broken down into four sources. The first is the contribution of the growth measure as defined by the growth rate of the simple summation of input quantity formulated as $\frac{\dot{L^*}}{L^*}$ or $\frac{\dot{K^*}}{K^*}$. The second is the contribution of the growth measure defined by the change of the quality of input formulated as $\frac{\dot{Q}_L}{Q_L}$ or $\frac{\dot{Q}_K}{Q_K}$. The third is the contribution of the growth measure as defined by the change of the allocational bias formulated by $\frac{\dot{A}_L}{A_L}$ or $\frac{\dot{A}_K}{A_K}$, and the fourth is the contribution of the interactive effect of changes of quality and allocational bias formulated as $\frac{\dot{I}_{LQA}}{I_{LQA}}$ or $\frac{\dot{I}_{KQA}}{I_{KQA}}$. On the other hand, the contribution of the growth of the productivity is measured by υ_t, which is defined by the weighted sum of the growth rate of sectoral productivity, υ_t^j.

In other words, the index of productivity change at the aggregate level as defined by Equation (6.32), υ_t^j is measured as a residual which is defined by the differences between the growth rate of the real value-added, $\frac{\dot{V}}{V}$ and the contribution of the growth rate of factor inputs, labour and capital, $s_L(\frac{\dot{L}}{L}) + s_K(\frac{\dot{K}}{K})$. In this formulation, we are trying to evaluate carefully changes of quality, changes of allocational bias and their interactive effect of both outputs and inputs at the aggregate level. On the other hand, the following definition has often been used as a simple measurement of productivity change at the aggregate level:

$$\upsilon_T^* = \frac{\dot{V^*}}{V^*} - s_L \left(\frac{\dot{L^*}}{L^*} \right) - s_K \left(\frac{\dot{K^*}}{K^*} \right) \qquad (6.34)$$

In Equation (6.34), the index of productivity change at the aggregate level is defined simply by the difference between the growth rate of the simple sum of the real value-added, and the contribution of the growth rate of the simple sum of factor inputs. So far, it is clear that the definition of Equation (6.34), as an index of productivity change at the aggregate level, includes some measurement errors which are identified as allocational biases of outputs and inputs, qualitative changes of inputs, and their interactive effects.

Sources of the measurement errors of TFP

By using the framework given in the previous section, we can identify the measurement errors of the growth rate of TFP. Table 6.2 presents a summary of the sources of Japanese economic growth during the period 1960–92.

Table 6.2 shows the average annual rate of growth of outputs, inputs and productivity at the aggregated level as sources of the economic growth for the economy, which are defined in Equation in (6.32). Values in parentheses in the table represent the ratio of the contribution to economic growth as sources. The first column represents the average annual rate of net aggregate output. It should be noted that while the average rate per year over the whole period 1960–92 reached more than 6.3 per cent, it was remarkably higher (10.4) per cent) during the period of high economic growth, 1960–72, compared with 3.9 per cent per year after the period of the first oil crisis: 1972–92. According to the breakdown of the sources, contributions of labour, capital and productivity are on average 21, 63 and 16 per cent, respectively, over the

Table 6.2 Sources of economic growth (percentage annual growth rate)

	Value added $\dot{V}/V$	Labour		Capital		
		Input $\dot{L}/L$	Contribution $S_L\dot{L}/L$	Input $\dot{K}/K$	Contribution $S_k\dot{K}/K$	TFP v_t
1960–5	10.126	3.343	1.819	12.523	5.688	2.619
	(100)		(18)		–(56)	(26)
1965–70	11.790	3.660	1.956	11.102	5.260	4.575
	(100)		(17)		–(44)	(39)
1970–5	5.009	1.305	0.687	14.456	6.402	–2.080
	(100)		(14)		(128)	(–42)
1975–80	4.277	2.878	1.780	6.582	2.516	–0.019
	(100)		(42)		–(59)	(–1)
1980–5	3.795	1.850	1.130	5.060	1.975	0.690
	(100)		(30)		–(52)	(18)
1985–90	4.629	2.225	1.311	5.859	2.409	0.909
	(100)		(28)		–(52)	(20)
1990–2	2.349	–0.554	–0.326	6.896	2.842	–0.167
	(100)		(–14)		(121)	(–7)
1960–72	10.425	3.372	1.814	12.553	5.829	2.781
	(100)		(18)		–(56)	(26)
1972–92	3.887	1.737	1.050	7.053	2.849	–0.012
	(100)		(27)		–(73)	(–0)
1960–92	6.339	2.350	1.336	9.116	3.967	1.036
	(100)		(21)		–(63)	(16)

whole period. One can see, however, that this average trend of the contribution of growth is completely different between the periods before and after the oil crisis. Before the oil crisis, it was one of the interesting features of the economy that the contribution of productivity growth was higher than 25 per cent, while the contribution of productivity growth was negligible after 1972. Even during the period 1960–72, the contribution of productivity growth reached 26 per cent on average. During the same period, the contributions of capital and labour inputs were 56 and 18 per cent, respectively. On the other hand, after the oil crisis, the contribution of capital inputs increased rapidly, by 73 per cent, and that of productivity decreased by about 20 per cent. During the period before the oil crisis, the growth rates of labour and capital inputs were 3.372 and 12.553 per cent annually, while that of outputs was 10.425 per cent. This means that the partial productivity of labour increased rapidly during the high-growth period, at the cost of the partial productivity of capital. After the oil crisis, the growth rate of capital inputs was also higher than the growth rate of outputs, while the growth rate of labour input was even lower than that. In other words, we can say that the characteristics of the factor substitution between labour and capital have been dominant in Japan since 1960s. It is not necessarily a specific characteristic of recent technology. The contribution of productivity as a source of growth, however, declined to around 16 per cent from 26 per cent before the oil crisis. In particular, after 1990, the growth rate of labour inputs turned out to be negative, and that of capital inputs still continued to be higher than that of outputs. It is impressive that the substitution between labour and capital was rapidly encouraged during this recent period of the Japanese economy. The growth rate of total factor productivity was 1.036 per cent per annum, on average, during the period 1960–92. Before the oil crisis, it was more than 2.781 per cent annually, while after that it declined rapidly to an average negative rate each year.

Table 6.3 represents the results of the breakdown of the sources of economic growth at the aggregate level, which are formulated in Equations (6.29), (6.30) and (6.31). Concerning the growth rate of value added, there were sizeable contributions made by the allocational changes among the industrial sectors. As mentioned above, the positive biases of the output allocation indicates that the efficiency of the economy would be improved by resource allocation. During the period before the oil crisis, almost a third of the total growth of output was attributed to increases of the efficiency of the allocation. In particular during the period 1960–5, the contribution was fairly high. After 1972 the weight of the contribution declined to a level of less than 15 per cent. In particular, during the period 1985–90, it was seen to be negative. It is expected that there would be distortions that disturbed the efficient allocation of the resources.

From the fourth column to the seventh in Table 6.3, we can see the results of the breakdowns of labour input: $\frac{\dot{L}^*}{L^*}$ represents the growth rate of the total man-

Table 6.3 Breakdown of the sources of economic growth (annual growth rate)

	Value added		Labour input				Capital input			
	$\dot{V}^*/V^*$	$\dot{A}_v/A_v$	$\dot{L}^*/L^*$	$\dot{Q}_L/Q_L$	$\dot{A}_L/A_L$	I_{LQA}/I_{LQA}	$\dot{K}^*/K^*$	$\dot{Q}_k/Q_k$	$\dot{A}_k/A_k$	I_{KQA}/I_{KQA}
1960–5	4.435	5.691	1.763	0.277	-0.192	1.495	6.502	0.726	-1.682	6.976
1965–70	9.957	1.833	2.613	0.885	-0.161	0.324	9.258	0.765	-1.432	2.511
1970–5	4.820	0.188	-0.431	1.176	-0.125	0.685	12.792	1.039	-2.153	2.778
1975–80	3.434	0.844	1.715	0.812	-0.013	0.364	6.318	0.063	-0.478	0.679
1980–5	3.572	0.224	0.529	1.056	0.019	0.247	4.964	-0.031	-1.237	1.364
1985–90	4.981	-0.352	1.591	0.463	-0.002	0.173	6.017	0.125	-1.199	0.917
1990–2	2.215	0.134	-1.250	0.661	0.007	0.028	7.179	0.103	-1.562	1.176
1960–72	7.387	3.038	1.954	0.722	-0.194	0.890	8.862	0.817	-1.643	4.517
1972–92	3.589	0.297	0.648	0.800	-0.002	0.291	6.863	0.192	-1.215	1.213
1960–92	5.013	1.325	1.137	0.771	-0.074	0.515	7.613	0.426	-1.376	2.452

hour labour force. $\frac{\dot{Q}_L}{Q_L}$, $\frac{\dot{A}_L}{A_L}$ and $\frac{\dot{I}_{LQA}}{I_{LQA}}$ represents the rate of of qualitative change, the rate of allocational changes, and the rate of their interactive effect, respectively. The rate of qualitative changes of labour input was fairly stable and it had a positive effect of 0.7–0.8 per cent annually. It meant that the qualitative change of labour input contributed an improvement in marginal productivity at a constant annual rate of 0.7–0.8 per cent. On the other hand, the rate of change of the allocation of labour input among industries was mainly negative. As mentioned above, the negative changes of the allocational biases in labour input suggests that labour was shifted from industries with expensive labour costs to industries with less expensive ones. Consequently, this improved the total efficiency of resources allocation in the economy as a whole. We can observe the breakdown of the sources of capital input from the eighth column to the last in the table. The qualitative change of capital input was positive, but it was not constant like that of labour input. The rate of allocational changes of capital input among industries was seen to be negative. This means that the allocational changes of capital inputs contributed to an improvement in the efficiency of capital input in the economy as a whole. Specifically, qualitative change and allocational bias of capital input have recently increased gradually. Also, the interactive effect of qualitative change and allocational bias of capital input are sizeable during the whole period.

Finally, we can summarize the sources of measurement errors of the growth rate of TFP in Table 6.4. The second column represents the growth rate of TFP measured by Equation (6.34). The last column represents the growth rate of he ture TFP as defined by Equation (6.32). Measurement errors of TFP growth rate came from three sources of bias in terms of output, labour and capital. As shown in the table, bias coming from the measurement of output was fairly dominant, while that coming from the measurement of inputs was mainly negative, both in terms of labour and capital, with few exceptions. It is

Table 6.4 Aggregation error of the growth rate of TFP (annual growth rate)

	v_I^*	Decomposition of errors			True TFP v_T
		$Bias_V$	$Bias_L$	$Bias_K$	
1960–5	0.523	5.691	−0.860	−2.735	2.619
1965–70	4.175	1.833	−0.560	−0.874	4.575
1970–5	−0.618	0.188	−0.914	−0.737	−2.080
1975–80	−0.042	0.844	−0.719	−0.101	−0.019
1980–5	1.311	0.224	−0.807	−0.037	0.690
1985–90	1.570	−0.352	−0.374	0.065	0.909
1990–2	−0.008	0.134	−0.410	0.116	−0.167
1960–72	2.220	3.038	−0.763	−1.714	2.781
1972–92	0.426	0.297	−0.658	−0.077	−0.012
1960–92	1.054	1.325	−0.690	−0.654	1.036

interesting that the recent measurement of bias by capital input turned out to be positive. Although there are measurement errors in TFP, which come from allocational bias in the output quantity index, both qualitative changes and allocational biases in labour and capital input index should be taken seriously into account, since the recent declining trends of productivity growth are not necessarily attributable to measurement errors. If we correct the recent measurement error carefully, productivity growth shows a more seriously declining trend. It is one of the interesting suggestions, from discussions of measurement errors, that those attributed to capital input turned out to be positive recently, while the growth rate of labour input turned to be negative. We can understand that these phenomena are characteristics of recent technologies, where partial labour productivity increased rapidly at the cost of increases in partial capital productivity as a result of the substitution between labour and capital. Consequently, since the increases in labour productivity are cancelled out by the decreases in capital productivity, efficiency increases by the measure of total factor productivity would be moderate.

Characteristics of capital formation in Japan

Capital input and capital stock: measurement

According to our approach in the previous section concerning measurement error hypothesis in order to explain the paradoxical trends of recent productivity growth, measurement errors are not necessarily dominant sources of the paradox; although the correction of errors is important in order to measure the true growth of total factor productivity. Nevertheless, we can point out several important findings from such approaches: (i) recently the contribution of capital input to economic growth increased rapidly, while the contribution of labour input turned out to be negative; (ii) while this suggests that the substitution between labour and capital turned out to be dominant, substitution of itself is not necessarily a specific feature in recent technology. This is because we can observe substitution accusing between labour and capital since the 1960s. However, recent changes in the growth rates of labour and capital suggests to us somewhat different patterns of substitution among factors; and (ii) concerning sources of the errors in TFP measurement, sources coming from capital input turned out to be over-whelmingly positive. All these findings suggest to us that we shall have to analyze carefully features of recent capital formation related to new technology.

We assume that all the new technologies are embodied originally in the new investment, and changes of composition of capital stock might have an impact on the substitution of factor inputs and TFP growth. In order to analyze quantitatively the impact of new technologies embodied in capital formation on TFP growth, we need to begin with the estimation of capital flow and stock matrices. Our estimated capital flow and stock matrices are divided into private and government-owned enterprises; capital classified by industry; and social overhead capital unclassified by industry. Both private and government enterprises are classified by forty-three industrial sectors, as shown in Table 6.5. On the other hand, capital formation in each industrial, sector as classified by seventy-eight types of capital goods as types of asset corresponding to the commodity classification in the input–output table.[3] We estimated the capital stock matrix to be consistent with the flow matrices of capital formation.

Let us summarize the findings in the trends of capital formation in Japan during the period 1955–92. Table 6.6 represents average annual rates of growth in capital stock of private enterprises by industry during the period 1955–90, where the period is divided into the following seven sub-periods; 1955–60, 1960–5, 1965–70, 1970–5, 1975–80, 1980–5 and 1985–90 in order to clarify features of accumulation. According to the results in these tables, growth rates of private capital accumulation in all sectors (except water supply) after 1975 clearly slowed down in comparison with the rapid growth before 1975, while those in the 1980s gradually recovered in some sectors such as electrical machinery, motor vehicles, precision instruments, communications, and education. Annual growth rates of capital stock during the three sub-periods after 1960 were significantly higher than those of labour input by sector in the same periods.[4] In particular, during the second sub-period 1960–5, twenty-eight sectors out of forty-three accomplished a high growth of capital stock, at more than 10 per cent annually. These trends continued until 1975. After the oil crisis almost all industries (except electricity, gas, medical and other services) experienced a dramatic slowing down of growth in terms of capital stock.[5] During the fifth sub-period, 1975–80, growth rates of capital stock deteriorated by less than half of the growth rate in the previous sub-periods by sectors. During the period of 1955–75 capital input by sector grews rapidly, showing a higher growth rate of more than the historical standard of the Japanese economy. After 1980, capital formation by sector gradually recovered. Annual growth rate of capital stock increased in sixteen industries during the period 1980–5; and in twenty-six industries after 1985. It is one of the interesting characteristics of the economy that the capital formations in specific industries such as electrical machinery, precision machinery and communications increased rapidly after 1985.[6]

Table 6.7 represents a series of estimated capital stocks by government enterprises. Annual growth rates of capital accumulation in government enterprises show constantly rapid growth such as 6.00, 10.90, 9.77, 13.37, 8.18, 4.55, 2.28 per cent every five years since 1955, respectively. Note that the values after 1989 in the table are not adjusted to take into account the privatization trends in government enterprises.

Structural changes in capital coefficients

Capital stock matrices for private and government enterprises at 1985 constant prices are estimated for every year during the period 1955–92. The

Table 6.5 Industry classification

Sector	Industry name	Abbreviation
1	Agriculture, forestry and fishery	Agriculture
2	Coal mining	Coal mining
3	Other mining	Other mining
4	Construction	Construction
5	Food manufacturing	Foods
6	Textiles	Textiles
7	Apparel	Apparel
8	Woods and related Products	Woods
9	Furniture and fixtures	Furniture
10	Paper and pulp	Paper and pulp
11	Publishing and printing	Publishing
12	Chemical products	Chemicals
13	Petroleum and refinery	Petroleum
14	Coal products	Coal products
15	Rubber products	Rubber products
16	Leather products	Leather products
17	Stone and clay	Stone and clay
18	Iron and steel	Iron and steel
19	Non-ferrous metals	Non-ferrous metals
20	Metal products	Metal products
21	Machinery	Machinery
22	Electric machinery	Electric machinery
23	Motor vehicles	Motor vehicles
24	Other transportation machinery	Other transport machinery
25	Precision instruments	Precision machinery
26	Other manufacturing	Other manufacturing
27	Railroad transport	Railroad transport
28	Road transport	Road transport
29	Water transport	Water transport
30	Air transport	Air transport
31	Storage facility services	Storage
32	Communication	Communication
33	Electricity	Electricity
34	Gas supply	Gas
35	Water supply	Water
36	Wholesale and retail	Trade
37	Finance and insurance	Finance
38	Real estate	Real estate
39	Education	Education
40	Research	Research
41	Medical care	Medical
42	Other services	Other services
43	Public services	Public services

Table 6.6   Annual growth rate of private capital stock (percentages)

	1955–60	1960–5	1965–70	1970–5	1975–80	1980–5	1985–90
1. Agriculture	0.31	7.11	13.90	12.72	4.79	1.76	1.72
2. Coal mining	–6.21	0.62	–1.31	9.89	6.24	1.27	–1.55
3. Other mining	1.24	13.01	9.75	10.57	–0.04	0.48	1.23
4. Construction	9.40	23.56	18.18	19.54	7.78	4.23	6.09
5. Foods	2.15	17.11	12.62	14.48	5.69	5.19	5.46
6. Textiles	–0.29	5.93	9.06	8.34	0.01	1.99	3.30
7. Apparel	8.55	16.92	16.67	9.81	4.58	3.38	5.29
8. Woods	–4.99	10.94	11.38	14.18	0.15	–1.26	2.46
9. Furniture	–3.58	17.17	14.67	14.39	3.11	1.06	4.91
10. Paper and pulp	14.60	10.41	12.88	18.60	5.39	3.39	5.33
11. Publishing	7.57	20.80	14.90	12.73	5.77	7.01	8.34
12. Chemicals	13.64	14.64	12.11	14.03	4.68	4.18	5.02
13. Petroleum	3.47	14.06	18.29	16.63	4.45	3.78	2.82
14. Coal products	11.31	20.66	20.20	14.18	4.26	–0.24	2.01
15. Rubber products	7.58	13.97	17.03	17.82	5.61	6.35	6.38
16. Leather products	5.15	9.59	10.17	6.96	3.92	3.32	5.42
17. Stone and clay	13.34	15.79	13.63	14.47	3.46	4.92	4.81
18. Iron and steel	15.84	11.00	15.52	13.97	5.47	2.36	2.02
19. Non-ferrous metals	3.13	13.41	17.06	13.50	3.65	5.50	5.88
20. Metal products	18.09	17.95	22.18	18.50	7.05	6.76	6.64
21. Machinery	16.63	18.26	20.25	16.13	4.34	6.23	6.45
22. Electric machinery	25.20	8.12	14.29	12.93	6.35	10.85	10.68
23. Motor vehicles	21.58	19.15	16.44	14.81	5.20	8.20	7.87
24. Other transport machinery	2.78	10.48	15.56	23.35	–2.12	–0.23	0.61
25. Precision machinery	7.90	14.59	20.27	20.67	2.63	10.86	8.96
26. Other manufacturing	18.89	23.39	16.83	19.68	4.90	7.31	8.05
27. Railroad transport	11.79	6.11	3.58	12.04	2.66	2.80	15.85
28. Road transport	42.11	1.30	7.96	17.52	8.78	7.20	3.60
29. Water transport	8.90	6.10	10.51	7.52	0.88	3.75	1.05
30. Air transport	40.93	21.51	14.57	11.91	3.22	3.90	4.97
31. Storage	5.91	6.40	8.99	11.11	2.92	2.36	9.65
32. Communication	3.72	17.24	4.27	22.89	6.50	22.74	32.76
33. Electricity	7.81	4.41	6.72	14.14	9.59	5.29	3.86
34. Gas	10.66	6.77	12.50	15.18	10.60	4.40	1.87
35. Water	–14.18	14.05	13.11	12.15	16.54	11.84	15.44
36. Trade	3.18	11.42	9.83	14.02	7.86	3.95	5.93
37. Finance	12.49	15.09	9.61	7.06	3.52	4.10	8.98
38. Real estate	3.47	25.13	15.46	20.02	6.20	5.88	10.98
39. Education	–5.90	6.95	5.77	7.49	5.68	4.68	4.51
40. Research	–0.17	–0.54	2.94	14.50	4.18	17.22	9.38
41. Medical	–26.07	12.58	14.07	28.13	17.43	11.02	9.15
42. Other services	–1.17	4.56	5.41	12.98	10.98	13.18	12.62
Total	6.09	10.02	11.80	14.16	6.22	5.52	6.78

Table 6.7 Estimated capital stock: government enterprises

(units: 1 billion yen at 1985 prices)

	1955	1960	1965	1970	1975	1980	1985	1990
1. Agriculture	730	1 246	2 231	3 979	8 392	13 921	19 406	24 860
3. Other mining	0	0	0	6	9	8	6	10
4. Construction	90	127	226	358	486	490	499	506
5. Foods	176	96	129	145	215	276	218	154
11. Publishing	2	3	27	27	25	26	31	38
12. Chemicals	1	1	1	3	4	5	10	13
20. Metal products	0	1	5	7	8	8	8	9
27. Railroad transport	153	189	421	703	1 192	1 704	1 699	1 505
28. Road transport	1	14	92	196	398	490	645	742
29. Water transport	4	13	35	67	130	158	200	322
30. Air transport	0	0	1	6	19	30	34	59
32. Communication	891	1 572	3 541	6 531	12 751	17 094	18 285	13 881
33. Electricity	1 087	1 467	1 491	1 159	1 172	1 350	1 507	1 273
34. Gas	6	9	15	18	46	77	111	147
35. Water	0	451	1 286	2 757	6 359	9 599	12 070	14 548
36. Trade	5	18	50	123	403	570	629	717
37. Finance	18	19	46	54	75	204	204	522
38. Real estate	1	0	1	2	25	60	148	207
39. Education	1 178	1 630	2 850	4 411	8 448	13 597	16 926	19 758
40. Research	27	110	191	324	747	1 169	1 466	1 956
41. Medical	94	225	585	1 463	3 105	4 848	6 670	8 484
42. Other services	16	59	269	601	1 690	2 742	3 566	4 627
43. Public services	2 906	2 726	3 710	5 095	9 017	13 941	19 071	21 560
Total	7 388	9 975	17 204	28 036	54 716	82 366	103 410	115 898

matrix consists of forty-three commodities in columns, and forty-three industries in rows. The forty-three commodities are aggregated into twelve types of asset: 1. Animals and plants; 2. Construction; 3. Apparel; 4. Wood products; 5. Furniture; 6. Metal products; 7. Machinery; 8. Electrical machinery; 9. Motor vehicles; 10. Other transportation equipment; 11. Precision instruments; and 12. Miscellaneous products. Capital coefficients are defined as follows:

$$b_{ij} = K_{ij} / Z_j \quad (i = 1, \ldots, 12, j = 1, \ldots, 43) \tag{6.35}$$

We can recognize structural changes from trends of capital coefficients by industry. The volume of coefficients designates the degree of capital intensity in industry, and the trend or change of coefficient during the periods represents the patterns of the structural changes, in terms of capital intensity, or capital productivity. We assume that properties of recent new technologies are embodied in the new capital formation and accumulated in the capital stock. Properties embodied in capital should be reflected in changes of capital coefficients as structural parameters. We can investigate the preliminary changes of capital coefficients. Figure 6.1 represents change of capital coefficients at the macro level during the period 1955–92, where the poll in figures stands for the level of capital coefficient and number in each poll corresponds to the asset types classified into twelve categories. We can observe that capital coefficients at the macro level increased from 1.5 in 1955 to 2.5 in 1992 and, moreover, the composition of machinery and electrical machinery among assets have gradually increased over building and construction. The figures also show the relationship between real value added and volume of capital stock by a solid line (*) during the period 1960–92. This also represents a rapid increase in the capital–output ratio in terms of value-added base.

When it comes to the development of technologies, we need to focus on observations at industry level instead of macro level. We can detect certain typical changes of coefficient by industries: 1. Agriculture; 4. Construction; 6. Textiles; 18. Iron; 21. Machinery; 22. Electrical machinery; and 23. Motor vehicles. Capital coefficients in agriculture increased rapidly from 0.3 in 1960 to 3.0 in 1992 in terms of the sum of coefficients, which suggests that capital productivity has been declining historically. Growth rates decreased slightly during the first half of the 1980s, but recovered during the latter half of the 1980s. Although the capital coefficient of machinery has been increasing rapidly, more than 70 per cent of assets are shared by construction. We have to note in the agricultural sector that capital accumulation, especially for construction, was owed mainly to that in government enterprises. Capital productivity in the construction sector has also been declining gradually, and the assets namely consist of own products. In the textile industry changes of coefficients were more characteristic; they were fairly stable in the 1960s, shifted higher in the 1970s and then continued to increase gradually in the

1980s. Volume of coefficients changed from 0.2 in 1960 to 0.7 in 1992. Latterly we can observe rapid increases of capital coefficients in machinery and electrical machinery in the textile industry. In the iron and steel industry, capital coefficients increased from 0.2 in 1960 to 1.0 in 1992, where the rate of increase slowed down, especially after 1985. Here again, the shares of machinery and electrical machinery have increased in assets, while the share of construction has been declining recently. In machinery, the level of capital coefficients in total capital stock shifted after the oil shock from 0.3 to 0.5, where decreases of capital coefficients for construction instead of increases of those in electrical machinery after 1975 are one of the specific characteristics. Electrical machinery is an exceptional example, where the capital coefficients showed a decreasing trend from the beginning of the 1960s. This means that in the electrical machinery sector capital productivity increased rapidly. After 1975, capital coefficients of input for construction in the electrical machinery sector decreased gradually; while those from electrical machinery itself increased rapidly. Capital coefficients of motor vehicles were relatively stable, although after 1975 they indicate a gradually declining trend. While the total volume of capital coefficient in motor vehicles has been stable, the composition of capital coefficient has changed remarkably, where the coefficient of construction has been decreasing and coefficients of machinery and electric machinery have increased rapidly in recent years.

Capital coefficients for private and government capital, including social overhead capital, have been changing since 1960. In particular, capital asset shares of machinery and electrical machinery, in preference to of those of construction, have been increasing rapidly in almost all sectors recently. Simultaneously, we must note that capital productivity in the machinery and electrical machinery sectors have improved historically, and that such trends of capital productivity in these sectors were rare exceptions among the forty-three industries. This seems to be one of the important characteristics of recent movements in capital formation. In the economy, changes of capital coefficients have had an impact on the changes of input coefficients in intermediate and labour inputs as a system of the economy, and, finally, the production efficiency in terms of TFP growth measurement.

Unit structure and dynamic spill-over

According to our findings in the previous section, the composition of general and electrical machinery, as assets in capital formation and stock, increased rapidly in almost all sectors. Furthermore, the partial productivity of labour and capital, and probably total factor productivity in the general and electrical machinery sectors, improved significantly. It is to be expected that the basic knowledge of the new technologies might be embodied in the capital goods, such as general and electrical machinery. Other sectors used to install capital goods as part of their investment. New knowledge of recent technologies is

152

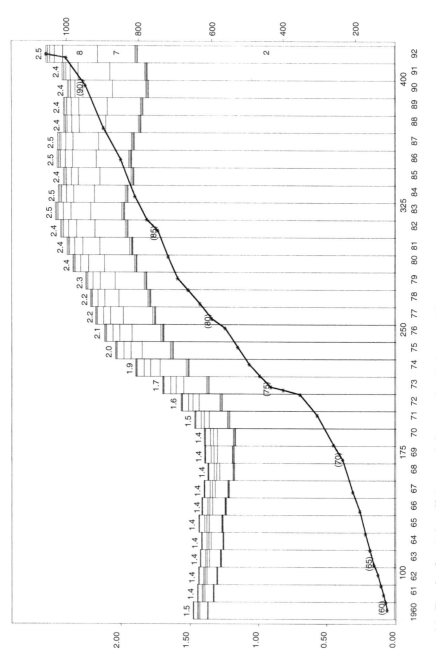

Figure 6.1 Trends of capital coefficients and changes of capital composition

Notes:

1) Dotted line: Plots in time-series of real value-added (x-axis) and capital stocks (y-axis), where x-axis is measured by the upper scale in the bottom with the unit of trillion yen at 1985 constant price and y-axis is measured by the scale in the right-hand side with the unit of trillion yen at 1985 constant price.

2) Poll figure: Trend of capital coefficients in the time-series during the period 1960–92, where x-axis represents the year in the lower scale of the bottom and y-axis is measured by the scale of the capital coefficients by the left-hand side. Numbers in the poll figure represent the number of capital assets, where the capital assets are classified into twelve capital goods; 1. Animals/Plants; 2. Construction; 3. Apparel; 4. Wood products; 5. Furniture; 6. Metal products; 7. Machinery; 8. Electric machinery; 9. Vehicles; 10. Other transport machinery; 11. Precision machinery; 12. Miscellaneous products.

diffused among sectors through their investment. Therefore, when it comes to evaluating the impact of new technologies on productivity in each industrial sector, we have to evaluate direct and indirect impacts of productivity growth in the sectors, in which are embodied the new technologies, such as the general and electrical machinery sectors, on productivity growth in other sectors. New technologies are expected to be embodied in commodities produced in general and electrical machinery sectors, and the new technologies are installed in other sectors through the investment in machinery, such as computers and information facilities. In other words, it suggests to us that we should consider the spill-over effect on productivity measurement among sectors in particular, and beyond the time periods dynamically.

We shall return to our definition of the growth rate of total factor productivity at the macro level formulated in Equation (6.32) and begin to clarify the meanings of the definition of this measure from the viewpoint of the spill-over effect of changes in productivity. Rearranging Equation (6.32) by using the input–output framework of the economy, we can obtain the following relationship:

$$
\begin{aligned}
\upsilon_T^t &= \sum_j \frac{p_T^{jt} Z_T^{jt}}{p_v^t V^t} \upsilon_T^{jt} \\
&= \sum_i \frac{p_i^t f_i^t}{p_i^t V^t} \left(\frac{\dot{f_i}}{f_i}\right)^t - \sum_j \sum_l \frac{p_{Ll}^{jt} L_l^{jt}}{p_v^t V^t} \left(\frac{\dot{L_l^j}}{L_l^j}\right)^t - \sum_j \sum_k \frac{p_{Kk}^{jt} K_k^{jt}}{p_v^t V^t} \left(\frac{\dot{K_k^j}}{K_k^j}\right)^t \\
&= \sum_i \frac{p^t f_i^t}{p_v^t V^t} \left(\frac{\dot{f_i}}{f_i}\right)^t - s_L \left(\frac{\dot{L}}{L}\right)^t - s_K \left(\frac{\dot{K}}{K}\right)^t
\end{aligned}
\tag{6.36}
$$

This is a measure of the growth rate of TFP at the macro level as defined in the second section, above.

The right-hand side of the second equation indicates that the measure of growth rate of TFP at the macro level is explained simultaneously as a difference between the aggregate measure of the growth rate of final demand and that of factor inputs including labour and capital. The aggregate measure of the growth rate of final demand is defined by a divisia growth rate index of final demand components weighted by nominal shares of each component in the nominal GDP. In order to clarify the meanings of the aggregate measure from viewpoints of the spill-over effect of productivity changes, we should propose a concept of 'unit structure'. By using this concept, we can clarify the interdependent relationships among commodities as characteristics of the specific commodity production technology.[7] A unit structure of the specific commodity represents the internal linkages among production, directly and indirectly, which are described by intermediate input coefficients, A_t and factor input coefficients such as labour and capital, l_t and k_t. In this concept, we can define the static measure of the production efficiency for a specific commodity, where the measure defined here is closely related to the traditional measure of 'total factor productivity'.

We begin with the explanation of the concept of 'unit structure'. In the input–output framework, the system of production can be described in terms of the input coefficient matrix, A_t; vector of final demand; F_t vector of output, Z_t vector of value added, V_t; and unit vector, i as follows:

$$A_t Z_t + F_t = Z_t \tag{6.37}$$

$$i' V_t = F_t i \tag{6.38}$$

If A_t is a non-singular matrix, we obtain the following equation system:

$$Z_t = (I - A_t)^{-1} F_t = B_t F_t \tag{6.39}$$

We shall call the following equation the 'unit system' of the j-th commodity production:

$$A_t \hat{B}_j i + f_j^* = B_j \tag{6.40}$$

and

$$i' v^* = f_j^* i \tag{6.41}$$

where $\hat{B}_j$ represents a diagonal matrix with j-th column vector of inverse matrix $(I - A_t)^{-1}$ as elements; f^*_j stands for the final demand vector with unity as the j-th element and zero as other elements; and v^* is a row vector of the unit value added. In the system of Equation (6.40), the following matrix is referred to as the 'static unit structure' peculiar to the j-th commodity:

$$U^{(j)} = u_{ik}^{(j)} = A_t \hat{B}_t \tag{6.42}$$

The technology of the economy is described by the compound system of the 'unit structure' of the various commodities. Each unit structure of the j-th commodity represents the characteristics of the technology involved in production. If we can give factor input coefficients such as labour and capital, l_t and k_t, we can define the vectors of labour and capital inputs corresponding to the unit structure L_t and k_t. These represent the direct and indirect input requirements of labour and capital by sectors in the production of the final demand f_j^*. We understand that a 'unit structure' for the j-th commodity represents the direct and indirect input requirements in terms of intermediate inputs, labour and capital inputs needed to supply one unit of final demand of the j-th commodity. We can define a measure of the production efficiency of any k_{th} ($k = 1, \ldots, \eta$) sector i the production system based on 'unit structure' for the j-th commodity production as follows:

$$v_{Tk}^{jt} = \left(\frac{\dot{Z}_{lk}^j}{Z_{lk}^j} \right)^t - \sum_i s_{xik}^{jt} \left(\frac{\dot{X}_{ik}^j}{X_{ik}^j} \right)^t - s_{Lk}^{jt} \left(\frac{\dot{L}_k^j}{L_k^j} \right)^t - s_{Kk}^{it} \left(\frac{\dot{K}_k^j}{K_k^j} \right)^t \tag{6.43}$$

where Z_{lk}^i, X_{ik}^i, L_k^i, K_k^i, represent output, intermediate inputs, labour and capital inputs of k-th commodity which are needed to supply one unit of the j-th final demand, directly and indirectly, and $S^j{}_{xik}$, $S^j{}_{lk}$, $S^j{}_{kk}$, stand for the cost share of each input, respectively. Note that the TFP measure defined by Equation (6.43) corresponds exactly to an ordinary measure of sectoral TFP. Furthermore, we can define an aggregate measure of the production efficiency in the framework of unit structure as follows:

$$
\begin{aligned}
v_{Tj}^t &= \sum_k \frac{p_T^{kt} Z_T^{kt}}{p_v^t V^t} v_{Tk}^{jt} \\
&= \left(\frac{f_j^*}{f_j^*}\right)^t - \sum_k \frac{L_k^{it} p_{Lk}^t}{p_v^t V^t} \left(\frac{\dot{L}_k}{L_k}\right)^t - \sum_k \frac{K_k^{jt} p_{kk}^t}{p_v^t V^t} \left(\frac{\dot{K}_k}{K_k}\right)^t
\end{aligned}
\tag{6.44}
$$

where p_l^{kt} represents the output price of the k-th commodity, and $p_v^t V^t$ stands for aggregate nominal value-added, which is defined by the sum of sectoral labour and capital compensations, $\sum_k L_k^{jt} p_{Lk}^t$ and $\sum_k K_k^t p_{kk}^t$; v_{Tj}^t is an aggregate measure of production efficiency in term of the unit structure of the j-th commodity. This measure designates the production efficiency of j-th commodity production, where production efficiency is evaluated as a measure of the total factor productivity and as a system needed to supply one unit of the j-th, commodity as final demand. Aggregate measure of TFP growth defined by Equation (6.44) has to be distinguished from growth rate of TFP in the ordinary measure at the macro level. The measure defined here corresponds to an aggregate measure of production efficiency in terms of the unit structure of the j-th commodity. We shall refer to this measure, v_{Tj}^t, as a 'static unit TFP on the j-th commodity as its unit structure.'

In the framework of static unit TFP, we can give a final demand vector, f instead of f_j^g. Here, f stands for a final demand vector which corresponds to the composition of final demand such as consumption, fixed capital formation, exports and so on. We can define the aggregate measure corresponding to Equation (6.44), which suggests a 'static unit TFP on a specific final demand component as a vector'. In particular, if we give the total final demand vector as corresponding to GDP as f, the definition of the aggregate measure in Equation (6.44) is back to the definition of the growth rate of TFP defined Equations in (6.32) or (6.36).

The above concept of 'unit structure' and 'static unit TFP' aims to measure the production efficiency of the j-th commodity in the specific time period t. The production of the j-th commodity at the year t is restricted by the technology embodied in the capital stock at the beginning of the period. Capital stock in the production has already been accumulated over the past period as a result of the investment. Each investment at a certain time in the past is used to embody the knowledge of the technology at that time. Therefore the productivity at a certain time for the production of the j-th the commodity is presumably a result in which all the knowledge in the past is accumulated through a series of investments. Focusing on the historical perspective of capital accumulation, we can define a dynamic concept of the spill-over effect of productivity change. We try to formulate a dynamic measure of the growth rate of TFP embodied in the dynamic production process to realise one unit of the final demand, f_j^{t*}.

We shall turn again to the basic definition of an aggregate measure of the growth rate of TFP, Equation (6.36). In this definition, a term, $\left(\frac{\dot{K}}{K}\right)^t$ represents a divisia growth rate of capital service input at the macro level. We assume that the volume of capital service is proportional to the amount of aggregate capital stock at the beginning of the year t. Aggregate capital stock has been accumulated by the capital formation in past years. The capital formation in each time period of the past was characterized by the technological structure at that time. If there is some installation of facilities embodied within new technologies, it could be influenced by the capital service flow induced from the accumulated capital stock, and the efficiency through input of the capital service in the production process.

We assume a proportional relationship between quantity of capital service at year t and capital stock at the beginning of year t at the macro level. We also assume the following relationship between capital stock at the beginning of year t and $t-1$ and capital formation, I^{t-1} at year $t-1$:

$$S^t = (1-\delta)S^{t-1} + I^{t-1} \tag{6.45}$$

Differentiating (6.45) logarithmically with respect of time t,

$$\left(\frac{\dot{K}}{K}\right)^t = \left(\frac{\dot{S}}{S}\right)^t = (1-\delta)\frac{S^{t-1}}{S^t}\left(\frac{\dot{S}}{S}\right)^{t-1} + \frac{I^{t-1}}{S^t}\left(\frac{\dot{I}}{I}\right)^{t-1} \tag{6.46}$$

where δ stands for the rate of depreciation.

On the other hand, we can define the similar relationship of the growth rate of TFP in the previous year, $t-1$, in Equation (6.36) as follows:

$$
\begin{aligned}
v_T^{t-1} &= \sum_j \frac{p_I^{jt-1} Z_I^{jt-1}}{p_u^{t-1} V^{t-1}} v_T^{jt-1} \\
&= \sum_i \frac{p_i^{t-1} f_i^{t-1}}{p_v^{t-1} V^{t-1}}\left(\frac{\dot{f}_i}{f_i}\right)^{t-1} - \sum_j \sum_l \frac{p_{Ll}^{it-1} z L_{Ll}^{it-1}}{p_v^{t-1} V^{t-1}}\left(\frac{\dot{L}_{Ll}^j}{L_{Ll}^j}\right)^{t-1} - \sum_j \sum_k \frac{p_{Kk}^{jt-1} K_{Kk}^{jt-1}}{p_v^{t-1} V^{t-1}} \\
&\quad \left(\frac{\dot{K}_{Kk}^j}{k_{Kk}^j}\right)^{t-1}
\end{aligned}
\tag{6.47}
$$

When we consider the dynamic production process needed to satisfy a unit of final demand at the year t, f_j^{t*}, real volume of the final demand at year $t-1$

should be equal to real capital formation at year $t - 1$ enough to satisfy the capital service demand at year t. Then we assume the following equation:

$$\left(\frac{\dot{I}}{I}\right)^{t-1} = \sum_i \frac{p_i^{t-1} f_i^{t-1}}{p_v^{t-1} V^{t-1}} \left(\frac{\dot{f}_i}{f_i}\right)^{t-1} \tag{6.48}$$

Rearranging the definition of the growth rate of capital service at the macro level by using Equation (6.48) and (6.46),

$$\sum_j \sum_k \frac{p_{Kk}^{jt} K_{Kk}^{jt}}{p_v^t V^t} \left(\frac{\dot{K}_{Kk}^j}{K_{Kk}^j}\right)^t$$

$$= \frac{p_K^t K^t}{p_v^t V^t} \left[(1-\delta) \frac{S^{t-1}}{S^t} \left(\frac{\dot{S}}{S}\right)^{t-1} + \frac{I^{t-1}}{S^t} \left\{ v_T^{t-1} + \frac{p_L^{t-1} L^{t-1}}{p_v^{t-1} V^{t-1}} \left(\frac{\dot{L}}{L}\right)^{t-1} + \frac{p_K^{t-1} K^{t-1}}{p_v^{t-1} V^{t-1}} \left(\frac{\dot{K}}{K}\right)^{t-1} \right\} \right]$$

$$= \frac{p_K^t K^t}{p_v^t V^t} \frac{I^{t-1}}{S^t} - v_T^{t-1} + \frac{p_K^t K^t}{p_v^t V^t} \frac{I^{t-1}}{S^t} \frac{p_L^{t-1} L^{t-1}}{p_v^{t-1} V^{t-1}} \left(\frac{\dot{L}}{L}\right)^{t-1}$$

$$+ \frac{p_K^t K^t}{p_v^t V^t} \left\{ (1-\delta) \frac{S^{t-1}}{S^t} + \frac{I^{t-1}}{S^t} \frac{p_K^{t-1} K^{t-1}}{p_v^{t-1} V^{t-1}} \right\} \left(\frac{\dot{S}}{S}\right)^{t-1} \tag{6.49}$$

Capital stock at the beginning of year $t - 1$ can be formulated similarly as Equation (6.46),

$$\left(\frac{\dot{K}}{K}\right)^{t-1} = \left(\frac{\dot{S}}{S}\right)^{t-1} = (1-\delta) \frac{S^{t-2}}{S^{t-1}} \left(\frac{\dot{S}}{S}\right)^{t-2} + \frac{I^{t-2}}{S^{t-1}} \left(\frac{\dot{I}}{I}\right)^{t-2} \tag{6.50}$$

On the other hand, we can define a static measure of growth rate of TFP at year $t - 2$ by the definition of Equation (6.47) as follows:

$$v_T^{t-2} = \sum_j \frac{p^{jt-2} Z^{jt-2}}{p_v^{t-2} V^{t-2}} v_T^{jt-2}$$

$$= \sum_i \frac{p_i^{t-2} f_i^{t-2}}{p_v^{t-2} V^{t-2}} \left(\frac{\dot{f}_i}{f_i}\right)^{t-2} - \sum_j \sum_l \frac{p_{Ll}^{jt-2} L_l^{jt-2}}{p_v^{t-2} V^{t-2}} \left(\frac{\dot{L}_l^j}{L_l^j}\right)^{t-2} - \sum_j \sum_k \frac{p_{Kk}^{jt-2} K_k^{jt-2}}{p_v^{t-2} V^{t-2}}$$

$$\left(\frac{\dot{K}_k^j}{K_k^j}\right)^{t-2} \tag{6.51}$$

Therefore, if we can assume equality between real volume of final demand and capital formation at year $t - 2$, we can deduce the following equation as for the third item of the second equation in Equation (6.49):

$$\frac{P_K^t K^t}{p_v^t V^t}\left\{(1-\delta)\frac{S^{t-1}}{S^t}\frac{I^{t-1}}{S^t}\frac{p_K^{t-1}}{p_v^{t-1}}\frac{K^{t-1}}{V^{t-1}}\right\}\left(\frac{\dot{S}}{S}\right)^{t-1}$$

$$=\frac{p_K^t K^t}{p_v^t V^t}\Phi^{t-2}$$

$$\left[(1-\delta)\frac{S^{t-2}}{S^{t-1}}\left(\frac{\dot{S}}{S}\right)^{t-2}+\frac{I^{t-2}}{S^{t-1}}\left\{v_T^{t-2}+\frac{p_L^{t-2}}{p_v^{t-2}}\frac{L^{t-2}}{V^{t-2}}\left(\frac{\dot{L}}{L}\right)^{t-2}+\frac{p_K^{t-2}}{p_v^{t-2}}\frac{K^{t-2}}{V^{t-2}}\left(\frac{\dot{K}}{K}\right)^{t-2}\right\}\right]$$

$$=\frac{p_K^t K^t}{p_v^t V^t}\Phi^{t-2}\frac{I^{t-2}}{S^{t-1}}v_T^{t-2}+\frac{p_K^t K^t}{p_v^t V^t}\Phi^{t-2}\frac{I^{t-2}}{S^{t-1}}\frac{p_L^{t-2}}{p_v^{t-2}}\frac{L^{t-2}}{V^{t-2}}\left(\frac{\dot{L}}{L}\right)^{t-2}$$

$$+\frac{p_K^t K^t}{p_v^t V^t}\Phi^{t-2}\left\{(1-\delta)\frac{S^{t-2}}{S^{t-1}}+\frac{I^{t-2}}{S^{t-1}}\frac{p_K^{t-2}}{p_v^{t-2}}\frac{K^{t-2}}{V^{t-2}}\right\}\left(\frac{\dot{S}}{S}\right)^{t-2} \tag{6.52}$$

where

$$\Phi^{t-2}=(1-\delta)\frac{S^{t-1}}{S^t}+\frac{I^{t-1}}{S^t}\frac{p_K^{t-1}}{p_v^{t-1}}\frac{K^{t-1}}{V^{t-1}} \tag{6.53}$$

Finally, we can trace backwards the process of capital accumulation that is required to satisfy the unit of final demand in year *t*. Since the capital formation invested in the year τ ($\tau = t-1, \ldots, t-\infty$) is assumed to embody the technology at that time, we can evaluate, dynamically, the impact of the growth of efficiency improvement brought about by the installation of new technology by the aggregate measure of static TFP in the following formulation:

$$\left(\frac{\dot{T}}{T}\right)^t=v_T^t+\frac{p_K^t K^t}{p_v^t V^t}\sum_{\tau=t-1}^{-\infty}\Phi^\tau\frac{I^\tau}{S^{\tau+1}}v_T^\tau$$

$$=\sum_i\frac{p_i^t f_i^t}{p_v^t V^t}\left(\frac{\dot{f}_i}{f_i}\right)^t-\frac{p_K^t K^t}{p_v^t V^t}\sum_{\tau=t-1}^{-\infty}\Phi^\tau\frac{I^\tau}{S^{\tau+1}}\frac{p_L^\tau}{p_v^\tau}\frac{L^\tau}{V^\tau}\left(\frac{\dot{L}}{L}\right)^\tau \tag{6.54}$$

where

$$\Phi^\tau=\begin{cases}1 & (\tau=t-1)\\\Phi^{\tau+1}\left\{(1-\delta)\frac{S^{\tau+1}}{S^{\tau+2}}+\frac{I^{\tau+1}}{S^{\tau+2}}\frac{K^{\tau+1}}{p_v^{\tau+1}}\frac{\tau}{V^{\tau+1}}\right\} & (\tau=t-2,\cdots,-\infty)\end{cases} \tag{6.55}$$

We refer to this measure $(\frac{\dot{T}}{T})^t$ as the growth rate of 'dynamic unit TFP'. By using the concept of 'dynamic unit TFP', we can recognize the dynamic and static spill over impacts of the structural changes in inputs including the intermediate inputs, labour and capital of the specific commodity production on the whole economic system.

As mentioned above, the recent trend of capital coefficients indicates that the share of machinery and electrical machinery has increased rapidly.

Productivity changes in industries which could implement the newly-developed technology are expected to have an impact on productivity changes in all the other sectors, directly and indirectly through the dynamic process of capital formation in each sector.

Structural change and efficiency trends in Japan

We begin with a comparison between ordinary measures of growth rate of sectoral TFP and the growth rate of static unit TFP as unit structure of the *j*-th commodity as shown in Tables 6.8 and 6.9, respectively. Ordinary measures of sectoral TFP represent the efficiency of *j*-th commodity production on its own. On the other hand, static unit TFP, based on unit structure, indicates the total efficiency in *j*-th commodity production, where we can evaluate the efficiency of direct and indirect linkages of the technology as a system of *j*-th commodity production. According to the results shown in Table 6.8, high growth of TFP in the 1960s deteriorated rapidly during the first half of the 1970s, in almost all industries. After a slight recovery during the second half of the 1970s was observed in some sectors, growth of TFP turned out to be lower again during the second half of the 1980s. It should be noted, however, that there were some exceptional sectors such as chemicals, rubber products metal products, machinery, electrical machinery, precision instruments, communications and trade, where TFP grew at a stable rate during these periods. On the other hand, according to the results shown in Table 6.9, efficiency based upon unit structure seems to be exaggerated by the interdependency of the production linkages. During the first half of the 1970s, when TFP growth in almost all of sectors deteriorated, growth rates of 'static unit TFP' worsened in comparison with those of ordinary TFP in almost all industries except rubber products. Conversely, in the 1980s, growth rates of static unit TFP indicated a smooth recovery of production efficiency in many sectors. This suggests that efficiency gains in the sectors in which the efficiency of their own technology has improved could compensate for efficiency loss in the sectors in which their own efficiency has deteriorated. In particular, it might be expected that there were some leading sectors where production efficiency has increased rapidly in recent years. For example, in the agricultural sector, growth rates of static unit TFP have been compensated by the technology linkages to other sectors during this period, apart from the first half of the 1970s, while its own efficiency has deteriorated during the whole period apart from the period 1980–5. In machinery and electrical machinery, the efficiency gain increased in the unit measures rather than in its own measure during the whole period.

Let us now turn to the dynamic approach. By using the framework of the dynamic inverse, we can estimate sectoral output requirements in the past which are needed to supply a certain amount of final demand in the reference year. Dynamic output requirements of all commodities for the final demand

Table 6.8   Annual growth rate of ordinary TFP (percentages)

	1960–65	1965–70	1970–75	1975–80	1980–85	1985–90	1970–90
1. Agriculture	−1.549	−4.079	−4.488	−3.077	1.263	−0.315	−1.654
2. Coal mining	6.490	2.607	2.541	−2.115	0.717	−1.369	−0.056
3. Other mining	4.013	8.934	−4.068	4.967	−2.450	2.512	0.240
4. Construction	−1.222	1.044	−0.639	−1.930	0.205	0.813	−0.388
5. Foods	−0.350	0.364	−1.394	1.851	0.247	−1.268	−0.141
6. Textiles	0.885	1.305	0.756	1.429	0.937	1.515	1.159
7. Apparel	0.641	1.417	0.731	1.380	−0.137	−0.654	0.330
8. Woods	1.632	1.222	1.890	−3.298	4.409	−1.225	0.444
9. Furniture	−0.862	1.250	0.217	1.126	0.834	0.439	0.654
10. Paper and pulp	2.144	2.463	−1.457	0.441	1.259	2.216	0.615
11. Publishing	−4.456	−3.501	−2.241	−0.216	0.066	0.832	−0.390
12. Chemicals	2.672	4.712	−1.630	1.062	2.319	1.341	0.773
13. Petroleum	4.867	0.764	−5.757	−1.423	0.044	7.570	0.108
14. Coal products	0.004	2.139	−5.109	−7.431	−0.010	2.018	−2.633
15. Rubber products	3.282	3.534	−3.538	−0.600	2.860	3.045	0.442
16. Leather products	3.212	−0.674	2.921	−2.232	1.550	−0.926	0.328
17. Stone and clay	2.455	1.150	−2.122	0.682	0.971	1.038	0.142
18. Iron and steel	0.218	1.991	0.035	0.828	−0.428	0.166	0.150
19. Non-ferrous metals	−0.402	1.035	2.951	2.224	2.007	0.260	1.861
20. Metal products	2.171	3.634	−1.893	1.582	0.794	1.425	0.477
21. Machinery	−0.993	3.415	−1.624	3.105	1.413	0.456	0.838
22. Electric machinery	2.861	6.300	1.396	5.430	1.895	3.034	2.939
23. Motor vehicles	1.409	4.816	2.098	3.326	0.558	0.629	1.653
24. Other transport machinery	4.577	1.189	−5.089	0.678	1.479	1.987	−0.236
25. Precision machinery	3.027	4.960	0.186	6.220	1.527	−0.356	1.894
26. Other manufacturing	2.511	3.960	−2.237	1.440	0.797	0.755	0.189
27. Railroad transport	1.913	−2.511	3.900	−11.994	2.232	−2.088	−1.988
28. Road transport	2.731	4.781	−6.400	1.939	−2.365	0.091	−1.684
29. Water transport	−0.566	7.234	2.090	−2.196	4.152	−3.668	0.095
30. Air transport	4.061	9.564	8.874	−0.869	2.060	0.828	2.723
31. Storage	1.433	3.474	−5.768	8.065	0.601	0.009	0.727
32. Communication	1.814	2.139	0.937	2.138	5.679	2.808	2.891
33. Electricity	4.389	5.526	−3.162	−1.639	2.018	1.449	−0.334
34. Gas	3.549	1.178	0.673	−0.326	1.118	3.036	1.125
35. Water	−2.742	−3.143	−2.968	−5.937	0.061	−1.621	−2.616
36. Trade	5.571	5.524	−0.181	2.314	−0.296	3.454	1.323
37. Finance	5.465	1.270	−0.620	−0.677	3.671	0.839	0.803
38. Real estate	5.596	−0.204	−2.993	−0.461	0.719	−0.433	−0.792
39. Education	0.867	3.563	0.994	−5.014	−3.558	−1.481	−2.265
40. Research	5.950	2.695	−2.707	4.041	−2.108	−0.236	−0.253
41. Medical	1.628	−0.592	5.186	−1.912	−1.262	−3.715	−0.426
42. Other services	−5.507	1.719	−3.803	0.252	−0.776	−2.372	−1.675
43. Public services	4.087	2.480	6.916	−4.955	−0.843	0.451	0.392

Table 6.9 Annual growth rate of static unit TFP (percentages)

	1960–65	1965–70	1970–75	1975–80	1980–85	1985–90	1970–90
1. Agriculture	−1.243	−3.888	−6.360	−3.241	2.082	0.072	−1.862
2. Coal mining	7.135	4.615	0.514	−2.368	1.406	−1.024	−0.368
3. Other mining	5.327	10.454	−5.503	5.447	−1.826	3.680	0.449
4. Construction	1.023	5.157	−2.623	−1.230	1.077	1.651	−0.281
5. Foods	−0.500	−0.364	−5.146	1.046	1.321	−1.014	−0.948
6. Textiles	2.731	4.459	−1.120	2.404	2.769	3.284	1.834
7. Apparel	3.138	5.126	−0.589	2.656	1.179	1.095	1.085
8. Woods	1.689	0.269	−1.606	−5.074	6.337	−0.878	−0.305
9. Furniture	1.176	4.161	−1.525	0.731	2.725	1.093	0.756
10. Paper and pulp	4.507	5.833	−4.524	0.205	3.282	4.150	0.778
11. Publishing	−3.017	−1.174	−4.458	−0.007	1.259	1.990	−0.304
12. Chemicals	5.724	9.352	−4.811	1.777	4.266	2.806	1.010
13. Petroleum	5.056	1.094	−6.473	−1.417	0.272	8.168	0.138
14. Coal products	3.187	5.328	−6.531	−8.716	0.650	2.474	−3.031
15. Rubber products	5.544	7.420	−5.582	0.037	4.486	4.387	0.832
16. Leather products	7.497	1.639	2.839	−2.525	3.134	−0.520	0.732
17. Stone and clay	4.768	5.448	−4.899	1.663	1.438	2.277	0.120
18. Iron and steel	2.314	7.936	−1.974	0.507	−0.051	1.071	−0.112
19. Non-ferrous metals	3.141	9.548	1.717	5.120	3.974	1.495	3.076
20. Metal products	3.722	7.670	−3.200	2.226	1.353	2.141	0.630
21. Machinery	0.283	8.520	−3.196	5.639	2.768	1.404	1.654
22. Electric machinery	5.221	12.347	0.574	8.207	3.475	5.041	4.324
23. Motor vehicle	3.800	10.786	1.506	6.176	1.906	2.205	2.948
24. Other transport machinery	6.874	5.901	−7.290	2.158	2.841	3.332	0.260
25. Precision machinery	4.986	9.355	−0.556	8.395	2.873	0.391	2.776
26. Other manufacturing	4.981	8.107	−4.854	2.135	2.663	2.020	0.491
27. Railroad transport	3.608	−0.773	1.675	−11.552	2.910	−1.924	−2.223
28. Road transport	3.822	6.436	−7.188	2.281	−2.016	0.665	−1.564
29. Water transport	0.411	10.121	2.473	−3.215	6.572	−3.793	0.509
30. Air transport	5.997	12.093	7.662	−0.949	3.172	1.894	2.945
31. Storage	1.796	4.571	−7.609	8.018	1.154	−0.122	0.360
32. Communication	1.984	2.655	0.250	2.305	5.695	2.822	2.768
33. Electricity	5.199	6.380	−4.926	−2.146	2.276	1.905	−0.723
34. Gas	4.518	2.484	−0.051	2.660	1.177	3.173	1.740
35. Water	−2.330	−2.060	−5.024	−6.487	1.017	−1.117	−2.903
36. Trade	6.539	6.946	−1.234	2.400	0.279	3.677	1.280
37. Finance	5.252	2.111	−1.709	−0.600	4.143	0.623	0.614
38. Real estate	5.758	0.413	−3.360	−0.585	0.961	−0.422	−0.852
39. Education	0.607	4.487	0.511	−5.066	−3.403	−1.387	−2.336
40. Research	5.426	3.734	−3.938	4.046	−1.877	−0.181	−0.488
41. Medical	3.127	1.899	3.515	−1.480	−0.251	−2.903	−0.280
42. Other services	−4.381	3.691	−5.600	0.451	−0.029	−1.876	−1.763
43. Public services	4.971	3.769	5.889	−4.919	−0.514	0.641	0.274

change of one dollar's worth at the certain period could be observed during the past eight to ten years with certain diminishing impacts. The value of the dynamic multiplier in investment goods such as construction, chemical, stone, iron, metal, machinery, electrical machinery and vehicles, and services, continues to remain fairly high. We can estimate a measure of dynamic unit TFP defined in Equation (6.54), in which we can evaluate dynamically the total efficiency of production which is directly, and indirectly required to supply one unit of *j*-th commodity final demand at year t. Table 6.10 shows the results. As mentioned above, the dynamic impact of production chains for one unit change of the *j*-th commodity of final demand at certain year seems to continue during the past eight to ten years. Therefore, in the case we could observe after 1960, the estimates of dynamic TFP can be evaluated only during the period after 1970. In Table 6.10 we show the annual growth rate of this measure for every five years since 1970 in each sector.

Each value in the table represents the average annual growth rate of dynamic unit TFP as a measure of the impact of structural change during each sub-period. The growth rate is evaluated by the difference per year between the dynamic unit TFP corresponding to the structure of the beginning, year, and that of the ending year, in each sub-period. Then each value in the table indicates the degree of annual impact caused by the structural changes during each sub-period. According to our results, the impact of structural changes was fairly high in every sector. We try to focus on the impact of new technologies on TFP growth during the period 1985–90. As mentioned above, the values of capital coefficients of machinery and electrical machinery have increased rapidly in almost all of the sectors where these changes of composition in capital coefficients are expected to embody recent new development of technologies in production. In spite of this hypothesis, it is quite difficult to detect the impact on productivity growth in the results of ordinary measures of TFP growth, as shown in the last column of Table 6.8. In twenty-three out of forty-three sectors, annual growth rates of TFP in the ordinary measures deteriorated during the period 1985–90 rather than in the previous sub-period. It might suggest that there are initial intuitive questions regarding the so-called 'productivity paradox' in recent years. When it comes to focusing on the measures defined by the static unit TFP (as shown in Table 6.9), the number of industries showing a deterioration of TFP growth during the period 1985–90 decreased from twenty-three in the ordinary measures to twenty in the static unit TFP measures. On the other hand, if we try to measure TFP growth in the dynamic unit TFP concept (as shown in Table 6.10), the deterioration of TFP growth can be observed only in eleven out of forty-three sectors. In comparison with the static unit TFP, the dynamic unit TFP represents an improvement of production efficiency in almost all sectors, except coal mining, coal products and real estate. We can conclude that there was a fairly dominant impact of new technologies on TFP growth even in these sectors. This can be verified by changes in capital coefficients, especially in the capital

Table 6.10   Annual growth rate of dynamic unit TFP (percentages)

	1970–75	1975–80	1980–85	1985–90	1970–90
1. Agriculture	–5.730	–3.401	2.560	1.507	–1.266
2. Coal mining	1.847	–1.952	2.406	0.108	0.602
3. Other mining	–3.748	6.313	–0.475	5.215	1.826
4. Construction	–1.321	–0.762	1.861	2.943	0.680
5. Foods	–4.742	1.031	2.087	0.351	–0.318
6. Textiles	–0.297	2.777	3.397	4.148	2.506
7. Apparel	0.310	2.955	1.750	2.050	1.766
8. Woods	–0.957	–5.043	6.890	0.305	0.299
9. Furniture	–0.525	0.938	3.358	2.352	1.531
10. Paper and pulp	–3.255	0.947	4.337	5.649	1.919
11. Publishing	–3.410	0.511	2.119	3.142	0.590
12. Chemicals	–3.485	2.438	5.212	4.476	2.160
13. Petroleum	–5.350	–1.120	0.621	9.331	0.871
14. Coal products	–5.206	–9.425	2.017	4.406	–2.052
15. Rubber products	–4.518	0.662	5.378	5.686	1.802
16. Leather products	3.915	–2.242	3.839	0.662	1.543
17. Stone and clay	–3.298	1.962	2.195	3.559	1.105
18. Iron and steel	–0.450	1.244	1.062	2.806	1.165
19. Non-ferrous metals	3.626	5.448	4.933	2.998	4.251
20. Metal products	–1.853	2.540	2.025	3.428	1.535
21. Machinery	–1.821	6.321	3.923	2.949	2.843
22. Electric machinery	2.427	8.843	4.398	6.658	5.582
23. Motor vehicles	2.716	6.941	2.970	3.453	4.020
24. Other transport machinery	–5.673	2.624	3.669	4.484	1.276
25. Precision machinery	0.738	9.082	3.867	1.664	3.838
26. Other manufacturing	–3.717	2.639	3.548	3.443	1.478
27. Railroad transport	2.441	–11.593	3.182	–0.747	–1.679
28. Road transport	–6.603	2.253	–1.802	1.572	–1.145
29. Water transport	5.115	–3.854	7.205	–2.409	1.514
30. Air transport	10.510	–1.258	4.060	3.474	4.197
31. Storage	–6.623	8.574	2.090	1.305	1.337
32. Communication	1.906	2.868	6.545	4.665	3.996
33. Electricity	–2.510	–1.588	3.291	4.364	0.889
34. Gas	1.402	3.484	1.796	4.534	2.804
35. Water	–3.906	–6.149	1.540	0.490	–2.006
36. Trade	0.281	2.810	0.953	4.931	2.244
37. Finance	–0.188	–0.049	4.965	2.183	1.728
38. Real estate	–2.021	–0.435	1.837	2.355	0.434
39. Education	0.837	–4.953	–3.175	–0.893	–2.046
40. Research	–3.365	4.322	–1.437	0.624	0.036
41. Medical	5.103	–0.951	0.513	–1.592	0.769
42. Other services	–4.029	1.117	0.970	–0.430	–0.593
43. Public services	6.750	–4.692	–0.126	1.189	0.780

coefficients of machinery and electrical machinery in which new technologies are expected to be embodied new technologies in recent years.

Finally, we can evaluate the impact of new technology development on productivity growth at the macro level by using the framework of static and dynamic TFP measures. In order to evaluate these impacts at the aggregate level, we can estimate measures of static and dynamic TFP growth rates by giving one unit of final demand along with observed weights of commodities in a specific final demand instead of one unit of a special commodity as a final demand. As weights of commodities in final demand, we can select alternative weights on consumption, investment, export and total domestic final demand as final demand, respectively. By using the formulations in equations (6.44) and (6.54) separately, we can estimate TFP growth rates at the macro level, in terms of the static and dynamic TFP measures, in order to realize one unit of the specific final demands such as consumption, investment, export and total domestic final demand. Table 6.11 represents the results. The first row in Table 6.11 represents the growth rates of ordinary TFP measure at the macro level. We can confirm, from the results of the trend of the ordinary TFP measures, that the growth rate of TFP declined at the beginning of the 1970s, and continued at a lower, stable level after 1975; even though a slight recovery could be observed after 1985. In the ordinary measure of TFP, we cannot identify the impact of new technology on the productivity growth at the macro level. This is because the deterioration of TFP growth needed to realize one unit of consumption contributed sharply to the decline of TFP growth in terms of total final demand. On the other hand, if we try to evaluate TFP growth by dynamic measures at the macro level, we can see a strong recovery of TFP growth after 1975, especially after 1985. On the other hand, we can evaluate TFP growth by dynamic measures at the macro level. We can define the dynamic TFP growth rate alternatively along with the different weights of the final demand such as total domestic final demand, consumption, investment and export respectively. All measures of dynamic TFP growth rate with alternative weights show rapid recovery of the growth after 1975, especially after 1985. The growth rate of the dynamic TFP measured with total domestic final demand as weights increased continuously at 0.5233, 1.6005 and 2.2004 per cent per annum during the periods 1975–80, 1980–5 and 1985–90 respectively. In the case of the dynamic TFP measured with consumption as weights, we could observe the gradual recovery of the growth rate after 1975. Also, in the case of the dynamic TFP measured with investment and export as weights, the growth rates of dynamic TFP showed the complete recovery after 1975.

Conclusion

In this chapter we have tried to evaluate the impact of new technology on TFP growth. We started from the intuitive observation of TFP growth in countries that have joined the OECD. Statistics of macro TFP measures in OECD

Table 6.11 Comparison of alternative measures of TFP at aggregated levels (annual growth rate)

	Demand Item	1960–65	1965–70	1970–75	1975–80	1980–85	1985–90
Ordinary TFP		2.360	4.831	–1.999	0.499	1.074	0.921
Static-Unit TFP	Consumption	2.146	2.850	–3.022	0.540	0.972	0.352
	Investment	1.841	6.436	–2.166	0.911	1.587	2.159
	Export	2.947	7.601	–1.990	3.034	2.644	2.322
	Domestic F.D.	2.104	4.227	–2.141	0.172	0.902	0.824
Dynamic-Unit TFP	Consumption	–	–	–1.711	0.795	1.657	1.883
	Investment	–	–	–0.802	1.453	2.399	3.478
	Export	–	–	–0.379	3.330	3.478	3.715
	Domestic F.D.	–	–	–0.814	0.523	1.601	2.200

countries designate the so-called 'productivity paradox', where TFP growth has been deteriorating recently, in spite of increases in real investment. The 'productivity paradox' should stop in order to evaluate the real impact of new technology on productivity growth. Several alternative hypotheses have been proposed to explain and solve these paradoxical trends in recent productivity growth. We began with a consideration of the measurement error hypothesis. Broadly speaking, there are two main sources of measurement error. One involves the measurement errors arising from the evaluation of qualitative changes in input and output measures; the other is the aggregation bias in the measurement of inputs and outputs. According to our results, although the measurement errors are one of the important issues in estimating growth rates of productivity correctly, they do not explain sufficiently recent puzzling trends in productivity. When we tried to measure carefully the qualitative changes of inputs and allocational biases of outputs and inputs, we observed that the partial productivity of labour has increased rapidly, while that of capital has deteriorated gradually since the 1960s in Japan. Furthermore, these trends have been exaggerated recently. In particular, the growth rate of labour input in the 1990s turned out to be negative, while that of capital input continued to increase positively.

We can assume that such new technology might be embodied in new investments, and that changes in composition by assets in capital stock, along with new investments, should have an impact on TFP growth. We try to measure the changes in the composition of assets in capital stock caused by the new technology as distinct from changes in trends of capital coefficients in each industrial sector. We can observe remarkable changes in the capital coefficients, where those of machinery and electrical machinery as capital goods have increased rapidly in each sector, compared to the decreases in construction as capital, goods in almost all sectors recently. In order to clarify the implications of observed substitutions between labour and capital, and evaluate the impact of the changes of composition in capital coefficients, we proposed new measures of TFP growth. In this case, TFP growth in specific commodity production is evaluated by a unit system, in which the spill-over effect of productivity is taken into account both directly and indirectly, as an extension of ordinary TFP growth measures. New measurements of TFP growth are divided into two concepts: 'static unit TFP' and 'dynamic unit TFP'. In the measure of static unit TFP, direct and indirect spill-over effects of TFP growth dynamically. Dynamic unit TFP growth represents the reasonable impact of the new developments in technology. It implies that there have been no paradoxical movements in recent years from the viewpoint of the relationships between TFP growth and new investment.

Although we have tried to present one of the implications concerning the 'productivity paradox' in recent years, the analysis of the conceptualization in productivity growth still has several remaining issues. One is the evaluation of the impact of new technologies on the labour market. In our context, we can extend our analysis to the evaluation of changes in labour coefficients related to those of capital coefficients. These might have an impact on the substitutability among labour and capital from new technology. This might be expected to involves some time lag in the changes of labour coefficients in the adjustment process to new technologies. The other issue remaining here is the effect of the externality of the new technologies. In particular, new information technology might be expected to have some impact on the externality, along with networks in society.

Notes

1. Greenspan (1995, 1996).
2. In our analysis, labour inputs are cross-classified by sex, age, education and employment status by industry.
3. Commodity classification of capital goods corresponds to the commodities in the Basic Japanese Input–Output Table classified by 541 commodities, and capital goods are divided into 78 commodities in the table.
4. See Table 6.3
5. In Japan, where more than 90 per cent of energy sources are imported, the impact of the oil crisis was unexpectedly serious. Trends of capital formation in almost all the industries were shifted downwards. The few exceptions such as electricity, gas, medical and other services were because of the investment promotion policy in utility sectors, supported by the government, in order to avoid a serious deterioration in the economy.
6. Japan National Railway and National Telecommunication Company were privatized in 1987 and 1985 respectively. Growth rates of both industries in Table 6.6 include their impacts.
7. Ozaki* (1984).

References

Arrow, K., Chenery, H., Minhas, B. and Solow, R. (1961) 'Capital–Labour Substitution and Economic Efficiency', *The Review of Economics and Statistics*.

Biørn, E. (1989) *Taxation, Technology and the User Cost of Capital*, (Amsterdam: North-Holland)

Coen, R. (1975) 'Investment Behaviour, The Measurement of Depreciation, and Tax Policy', *American Economic Review*, vol. 65, pp. 59–74.

Diewert, W. E. (1986) *The Measurement of the Economic Benefits of Infrastructure Services*, vol. 278, Berlin, Springer–Verlag)

Feldstein, M. S. and Rothschild, M. (1974) 'Towards an Economic Theory of Replacement Investment', *Econometrica*, vol. 42, pp. 393–423.

Greenspan, A. (1995) Speech at the Economic Club of Chicago.

Greenspan, A. (1996) Keynote Speech at the Conference held by the Federal Reserve Bank of Kansas.

Hall, R. E. (1968) 'Technical Change and Capital from the Point of View of the Dual', *Review of Economic Studies*, vol. 35, pp. 35–46.

Hall, R. E. (1971) 'The Measurement of Quality Change from Vintage Price Data', in Z. Griliches, (ed.), *Price Indexes and Quality Change: Studies in New Methods of Measurement* (Harvard University Press) ch. 8, pp. 240–71.

Hall, R. E. and Jorgenson, D. W. (1967) 'Tax Policy and Investment Behaviour', *American Economic Review*, vol. 57, pp. 391–414.

Hulten, C. R. (1990) 'The Measurement of Capital', in E. R. Berndt and J. E. Triplett (eds), *Fifty Years of Economic Measurement: The Jubilee of the Conference on Research in Income and Wealth*, (University of Chicago Press), ch. 4; pp. 119–58.

Hulten, C. R. and Wykoff, F. C. (1981a) 'Economic Depreciation and Accelerated Depreciation: An Evaluation of the Conable–Jones 10–5–3 Proposal', *National Tax Journal*, vol. 34, pp. 45–60.

Hulten, C. R. and Wykoff, F. C. (1981b) 'The Estimation of Economic Depreciation Using Vintage Asset Prices: An Application of the Box–Cox Power Transformation', *Journal of Econometrics*, vol. 15, pp. 367–96.

Hulten, C. R. and Wykoff, F. C. (1981c) 'The Measurement of Economic Depreciation', in C. R. Hulten (ed.), *Depreciation, Inflation, and the Taxation of Income from Capital*, (Washington DC: Urban Institute Press), pp. 81–125.

Jorgenson, D. W. (1963) 'Capital Theory and Investment Behaviour', *American Economic Review*, vol. 53, pp. 247–74.

Jorgenson, D. W. (1974) 'The Economic Theory of Replacement and Depreciation', in W. Sellekaerts (ed.), *Econometrics and Economic Theory: Essays in Honour of Jan Tinbergen* (New York: Macmillan), ch. 10, pp. 189–221.

Jorgenson, D. W. (1989) 'Capital as a Factor of Production', in D. W. Jorgenson and R. Landau (eds), *Technology and Capital Formation*, (Cambridge, Mass: MIT Press), ch. 1, pp. 1–35.

Jorgenson, D. W. and Griliches, Z. (1967) 'The Explanation of Productivity Change', *Review of Economic Studies*, vol. 34, pp. 249–283.

Kuroda, M. (1988) 'A method of Estimation for Updating Transaction Matrix in the input–Output Relationships', in K. Uno, and S. Shishido (eds), *Statistical Data Bank Systems, Socio-economic Database and Model Building in Japan* (Amsterdam: North-Holland), ch. 2, pp. 128–48.

Leontief, W. W. (1970) 'The Dynamic Inverse', in A. P. Carter and A. Brody (eds), *Contributions to Input–Output Analysis* (Amsterdam: North-Holland), pp. 17–46.

Ohta, M. and Griliches, Z. (1975) 'Automobile Prices Revisited: Extensions of the Hedonic Price Hypothesis', in N. E. Terleckyj (ed.), *Household Production and Consumption* (New York: Columbia University Press), pp. 325–90.

Ozaki, I. and Shimuzu, M. (1984) 'Technological Change and the Pattern of Economic Development', *Proceedings of the Seventh International Input–Output Techniques* (New York: United Nations).

Solow, R. M. (1955) 'The Production Function and the Theory of Capital', *The Review of Economic Studies*, vol. 23, pp. 101–8.

Solow, R. M. (1962) 'Substitution and Fixed Proportions in the Theory of Capital', *The Review of Economic Studies*, vol. 29, pp. 207–18.

Solow, R. M. (1963) 'Heterogeneous Capital and Smooth Production Function: An Experimental Study', *Econometrica*, vol. 31, pp. 623–45.

Comments

Jørgen Elmeskov[*]

The chapter by Professors Kuroda and Nomura takes as its point of departure the international productivity slowdown following the high-growth period of the 1960s. Basically, it aims to solve the so-called Solow Paradox, that is the fact that both labour and total factor productivity as conventionally measured slowed down despite what seems to be strong investment in new technology. In its attempt to solve the paradox, the chapter employs some interesting techniques and an impressive Japanese dataset. The chapter concludes that there is no paradox because, at least in the case of Japan, productivity did not slow down. On the contrary, when measured appropriately productivity growth has risen since the early 1970s.

The chapter takes two novel approaches to show that there is no paradox. First, it looks at TFP from the demand side and aims to measure TFP in producing the output corresponding to various components of final delivery. Second, it aims to take into account the fact that capital is produced. When it calculates TFP, it therefore not only includes current inputs but also the inputs that, in previous years, went into producing the current capital stock. I shall deal with these two approaches in turn.

Broadly speaking, it may be useful – as an alternative way of looking at sectoral TFP trends – to calculate TFP growth in providing a unit of final demand from a sector rather than in just producing a unit of output. The sectoral TFP growth rates obtained from this approach are significantly different from the traditional measures based on total output, although not radically so. It may seem noteworthy that these demand-based TFP growth rates are higher than the output-based growth rates for virtually all sectors (this can be seen by comparing Tables 6.5 and 6.6 in the chapter). Nevertheless, when the authors aggregate these demand-based TFP growth rates using final domestic demand weights and compare them with those based on total output, the differences are relatively moderate. In fact, the growth rates based

* The views presented in these comments are those of the author and do not necessarily reflect those of the OECD.

170

on final domestic demand are slightly lower than the output-based ones (see Table 6.8).

The calculations leave some questions which might usefully have been discussed in the chapter. First, the reader may need a bit of help in interpreting a demand-based measure of TFP. For example, the calculations show a demand-based (or static unit) TFP growth rate of 2.7 per cent between 1985 and 1990 in the motor industry, as opposed to only 0.7 per cent when based on total output in the same industry. The sources of this difference are not quite clear and might have been spelled out. One hypothesis is that it reflects very high TFP growth in some other sectors who contribute to delivering a final unit of demand from the motor industry. A second question refers to the above-mentioned observation that virtually all period- and sector-specific growth rates becomes higher when looked at from the demand side rather than the output side. The reasons for this tendency might have been spelled out, together with the reason why a similar tendency is not found when comparing aggregate TFP growth rates from, respectively, the demand and output sides.

The second approach followed by the authors consists of taking into account the fact that capital goods are produced. Instead of treating capital as a contemporaneous input when calculating TFP, the chapter calculates TFP using the inputs which historically went into producing the different vintages of the current capital stock. This then implies that TFP growth in the sectors that use the capital goods will tend to look higher to the extent that the capital intensity of production is rising at the same time as capital goods producing sectors have relatively high TFP, to the extent that TFP is rising rapidly in sectors that produce capital goods, and to the extent that there are compositional changes of the capital stock towards assets produced with higher and more rapidly rising TFP. Indeed, many of the sectoral (demand-based) TFP growth rates calculated in this way show a tendency to increase over time (Table 6.7). The tendency for rising TFP growth over time shows up also in aggregate measures based on different demand components (Table 6.8).

The tendency for rising aggregate TFP growth is particularly strong for production aimed at investment demand. This raises the question whether the rise in TFP growth in production for investment should be considered in this type of analysis. When treating capital as a produced input it is not obvious that one should at the same time include investment as a final demand component; in some sense, rapid TFP growth in capital-goods-producing sectors will then be counted in both deliveries to investment and through the treatment of capital as a produced input. To give a concrete example, the question is whether it is appropriate, on the one hand, to count in the high TFP growth of computer producers as contributing to TFP growth in other sectors via their delivery of capital stocks and, at the same time, counting the high TFP growth of computer producers as delivering final outputs. It should be noted, however, that even when looking at TFP in production for consumption alone there is some, albeit much weaker, tendency for its growth rate to increase over time.

Summing up, the international slowdown in productivity growth after the 1960s is frequently seen as paradoxical in the sense that it took place at the same time as a range of new technologies were introduced. Against that, this chapter tells a different story, according to which productivity growth has been increasing since the early 1970s. The chapter backs up its story with impressive data material. Has the paper then rejected the Solow Paradox? A few questions on the calculations presented in the chapter were asked above. One additional point is that the paradox as originally stated seemed primarily to be about the use of computers and other new technology as a means of raising productivity in the user industries. What the chapter does is to correct for higher productivity in the *production* rather than the *use* of capital goods. Another, and somewhat related, point is that even if one accepts that the paradox disappears when TFP is looked at in terms of both current and past inputs via the capital stock, this may not qualify as a rejection of the paradox. In terms of contemporaneous inputs, the authors still find that TFP growth has remained low. And this still seems to be a paradox given that current inputs comprise a lot of new technologies. In any case, recent evidence pointing to accelerating productivity in the United States and some other countries may be about to solve that puzzle and thereby the Solow Paradox.

Comments

Kazumi Asako

Professor Kuroda and Mr Nomura propose a new hypothesis that attempts to explain the so-called conceptualization problem or the productivity paradox, that is, an apparently puzzling phenomenon that recent and technologically high investment has not driven high productivity growth in many OECD countries. The authors analyze the Japanese data very carefully and conclude that, once properly constructed measures are introduced in place of an ordinary TFP (total factor productivity) measure, there is no difficulty in understanding the recent relationship between investment and productivity growth, and thereby the productivity paradox is easily resolved. Basically I am persuaded by the reasons given by the authors, and only the following four comments or questions remain.

First, although the authors understandably attempt to identify the effect of conceptualization with changes in capital coefficient, Figure 6.2 shows that the capital coefficient itself has remained rather stable since the early 1980s up to the present time, after experiencing stable movement during the 1960s and a rapid rise from a level of around 1.4 to around 2.5 through the 1970s. Of course, this is a macroeconomic observation and the microeconomic situations of such industries as electronic machinery and communications, which have something to do with conceptualization, may be somewhat different. But yet the capital coefficient seems to have been kept fairly intact throughout the 1980s and the early 1990s. Is this because of the dynamics of decision-making of economic agents, or the time lags between the date of investment and the day when the effect of conceptualization materializes? To put it differently, why did the capital coefficient increase during, and virtually only during, the 1970s? Professor Kuroda and Mr Nomura are asked to answer this question. My naïve observation picks up such possible candidates as a slowdown of output growth (which causes the denominator of capital coefficient to be relatively small) because of the end of area of rapid economic growth, or increases in replacement investment and pollution abatement, or energy saving investment (which render the numerator of capital coefficient relatively large). But these factors do not seem to be particularly relevant to the conceptualization problem.

Second, the authors' original and successful attempt to construct new measures of the TFP that is, static unit TFP and dynamic unit TFP, by taking into account the inter-industry spill-over effect of production activities is admirable. However, if we interpreted the ordinary measure of TFP as the one that captures the eventual and overall effect of conceptualization, the portion of the additional conceptualization effect, computed as the difference between the authors' measure of the TFP and the overall effect, must just be cancelled eventually by another, opposite, effect. What is this offsetting effect?

My third comment is related to my second one above. In general, when we decompose the overall effect into two in such a way that one is that portion of effect that captures conceptualization and the other is that portion of effect that has nothing to do with conceptualization, should this be done uniquely? Is the authors' proposed way of decomposition that utilizes input – output tables justifiable, on the theoretical basis, for example, that the decomposed portions are orthogonal to each other? Another way of positing this question may be whether the authors' measures of TFP are subject to any systematic bias towards over- or under-valuation because of, for example, double-counting of the same effect, or the possibility of missing channels of input–output interaction.

Fourth, as Professor Kuroda and Mr Nomura point out, structural changes occur not only in intermediate input coefficient and capital coefficients but also in labour input coefficients. As a trend in Japan, the amount of labour input has decreased significantly since the 1970s – for example, yearly working hours have decreased from 2251 in 1970 to 2104 in 1980, and to 1912 in 1996. This indicates that the labour input coefficient has changed accordingly since entering the 1980s, and this fact in turn is to be contrasted with fairly stable movements of capital coefficients during the same period, which I touched on above in my first comment. So the role of the labour input coefficient may be very important in explaining the productivity paradox. It is probably one of the most important factors of the opposite effect of conceptualization, which I pointed out in my second comment above.

7
The Productivity Paradox and Mismeasurement of Economic Activity

W. E. Diewert and Kevin J. Fox*

Introduction

Good policy may be possible without good measurement, but without good measurement it is unlikely that the costs and benefits of policies can be assessed accurately. While there has been some progress in both the theory and practice of measurement (particularly for inputs), the modern economy presents some new measurement complications, and amplifies some old ones. The assessment of economic performance for countries may be seriously affected by these difficulties.

In particular, there has been much attention paid recently to what has become known as the 'productivity paradox'. Basically, the paradox is that we have not seen the expected productivity improvement from new technology in the official statistics. In fact, there has been a measured productivity slowdown in industrialized countries since the mid-1970s, the very time when we would have expected to see large increases in productivity growth because of rapid technological change.

Diewert and Fox (1998) reported productivity growth estimates for eighteen OECD countries, which showed that average total factor productivity growth fell from 3.25 per cent for 1961–73 to 1.09 per cent for 1974–92. Labour productivity growth fell from 4.41 per cent in the earlier period to 1.81 per cent in the later period. These falls in productivity growth are not trivial, hence the many recent attempts to try to explain this 'paradox'. In particular, there has been a great deal of focus on the role of computers – perhaps the most visible of technological improvements in since the 1970s – and whether or not they can produce the productivity payoff expected of them. In broader terms, the productivity slowdown still seems puzzling, even if computers have not contributed to productivity growth.

* The authors gratefully acknowledge financial support from the Canadian Donner Foundation and the Australian Research Council. The second author is also grateful for the hospitality provided by the Department of Economics at the University of Georgia.

In this chapter we review the evidence that there may be some serious measurement problems faced by under-resourced statistical agencies. Given the nature of current technological change, these measurement difficulties are becoming more serious, leading to productivity measures being biased downwards. Possible measurement errors come from a variety of sources. Some are caused by the difficulty in defining an appropriate measure of output, which is a problem particularly in the service industries. Others are caused by national income accounting conventions which have traditionally been used, but which are not appropriate to deal with the nature of a modern economy. The treatment of interest is one such example. However, many of the measurement problems to be, examined do not have simple solutions.

The chapter is organised as follows. The second section looks at the debate over the apparent absence of a productivity payoff from computers, and the third to sixth section examine various sources of economic mismeasurement which may be obscuring the true level of productivity growth. Hence this provides a direct explanation for the paradox – we are more productive than we think, it is just that we cannot show it. The seventh section looks at reasons why we may not be as productive as we could be, many of which are related to measurement problems.

Where is the productivity payoff from computers?

Much of the attention that has focused on the productivity paradox has resulted from anecdotal evidence on the proliferation of computers, the variety of uses to which they are put, potential applications, and the enormous increase in raw computing power in a startlingly short period of time. This has occurred at a time that measured productivity growth has been slow. Hence we are puzzled why we do not see a 'productivity dividend' from the rapid spread of computer technology.

One explanation is that there *has* been a productivity payoff from computers, but because of the measurement problems to be discussed below, we have not been able to see it. This seems to be the favoured explanation of Griliches (1994):

> Why has this [computer investment] not translated itself into visible productivity gains? The major answer to this puzzle is very simple ... This investment has gone into our 'unmeasurable sectors' and thus its productivity effects, which are likely to be quite real, are largely invisible in the data. (Griliches, 1994, p. 11)

Triplett (1999) provides a quite comprehensive review of the arguments put forward concerning the computer productivity paradox. Among these arguments is one that measurement error is not responsible for the paradox; that, in fact, there is no paradox – computers are simply not (yet) as productive as we think. One example of thinking along these lines is that given by David (1990), using the comparison in the delay in the payoff seen from the use of electricity:

> Factory electrification did not ... have an impact on productivity growth in manufacturing before the early 1920's. At that time only slightly more than half of factory mechanical drive capacity had been electrified ... This was four decades after the first central power station opened for business. (David, 1990, p. 357)

Triplett (1999) argues convincingly that the pattern of price decline of computing power is such that it makes the analogy with electrification suspect. The more rapid decline in the price of computers has meant that the diffusion process has also been fundamentally different.

> In the computer diffusion process, the *initial* applications supplanted older technologies for computing. Water and steam power long survived the introduction of electricity; but old pre-computer age devices for doing calculations disappeared long ago ... The vast continuous decline in computing prices has long since been factored into the decision to replace the computational analogy to the old mill by the stream – electric calculators, punched-card sorters, and the like – with modern computers. (Triplett, 1999)

Another common argument as to why computers may not have been able to provide a productivity payoff comes from considering growth accounting equations:

> It is a basic rule of growth accounting that large changes in investment cause only small changes in output. The reasons for this are that investment is a small fraction of GNP and that the marginal product of capital is small. Since computers are a quite small part of total investment, a vast increase in investment in computers would yield only a small increase in measured output even if all the computers were being used productively and were generating measured output ... These calculations imply that if computers are being used productively [in the USA], they have raised the average annual growth rate of output over the past two decades by roughly a twenty-fifth of a percentage point. (Romer, 1988, p. 427)

However, one wonders if this is the correct framework in which to think about the role of computer capital. A computer does not seem to be like any other piece of capital. It can be used to control other capital (and labour), so that the other capital (and labour) is used more efficiently – for example, the management of a warehouse, or co-ordinating the movement of transport.

Placing a new computer in a warehouse may be expected to have a similar effect to placing a better microchip in a computer – that extra piece of capital makes all the surrounding capital more productive. Considering only the small share of computer capital in investment seems to undervalue the capacity of computers to improve the efficient use of other resources.

However, this capacity may point to a reason for the lack of an observed productivity payoff from computers. Investment in computers not only involves substitution away from investment in other kinds of physical capital, but it may also involve substitution away from human capital. Many of the roles formerly played by humans in co-ordinating production are now performed by computers. The myriad tasks that bank tellers used to have to perform have been reduced through the spread of Automatic Teller Machines (ATMs). School test scores (in the USA at least) have fallen at the same time that schools are investing heavily in computer learning. Perhaps when we look for the productivity payoff, we are ignoring the substitution of computer capital for human capital.

Even if computers have not lead to a productivity payoff, but have just substituted for other inputs, it is still puzzling why the rate of productivity growth since the mid-1970s is relatively low compared to the previous fifty years. We turn now to measurement problems that may explain this lack of observed productivity growth.

Measuring the benefits of new products

> Gains and losses that results from price changes would be measurable easily enough by our regular index-number technique, if we had the facts; but the gains which result from the availability of new commodities, which were previously not available at all, would be inclined to slip through ... The variety of goods available is increased, with all the widening of life that that entails. This is a gain which quantitative economic history which works with index-numbers of real income, is ill-fitted to measure or even describe. (Hicks, 1969, pp. 55–6)

The argument for a role of mismeasurment of the benefits of new products in explaining the productivity paradox hinges on there having been an increase in the number of new products. In other words, assuming that statistical agencies have not become worse at measuring economic activity, the measurement problem must have become more difficult. Triplett (1999) is sceptical that new products have appeared more rapidly since the mid-1970s than in previous years. He feels that much of the perception that there has been a massive increase in new goods comes about through thinking in terms of an arithmetical scale rather than the appropriate logarithmic scale: that is it is the growth in new products that matters, rather than their absolute numbers. He argues that there is simply not enough evidence to put the current growth in new products in an historical context. However, while definitive research on this topic would be very desirable, the anecdotal evidence presented in Baily and Gordon (1988), Nakamura (1997), Diewert and Smith (1994), and Diewert and Fox (1998) has been enough to convince us that there is a strong possibility that the rate of introduction of new products has increased. One only has to consider the enormous expansion in services over the Internet (and the difficulty in measuring the introduction of these new products), to see that this is a real possibility. Hence, we now examine how the introduction of new products may have helped to obscure actual productivity growth.

While the measurement of the costs of the development and introduction of new products does not seem to be a problem, certainly the benefits of new products pose a difficult measurement problem. It is important to be able to measure these benefits, not only for the firms that introduce them, but also for the economy as a whole. Consider the following:

> Every real economy is presented with an almost incomprehensible number of new goods that can be introduced ... They would increase utility. Many others, perhaps the great majority of all possible new goods, would not be worth introducing. The fixed costs are too high and the benefits too low. (Romer, 1994, p. 14)

Similar concerns about the trade-offs between costs and benefits of new products have been expressed by others, such as Nordhaus (1988, p. 423):

> Are we better off because of all the proliferation of Corn Pops and Freakies? The issue of the optimal amount of product differentiation is a profound one, and industrial organization economists reason that even if tastes are not manipulated, a market economy can easily produce excessive quality change because of setup costs of product differentiation.

If we are measuring the costs of the introduction of new goods well, but the benefits poorly, we may well end up with the conclusion that we have been made worse off by the introduction of new goods, when the opposite is true. Statistical agencies try to deal with the expansion in the set of available goods, but run into some problems, as explained by Diewert (1996, p. 31):

> *Quality adjustment bias or linking bias* is the bias that can occur when a variety or model of a good is replaced by a new variety. Suppose that a new model appears that is more efficient in some dimension than an existing model. After two or more periods, the statistical agency places a price ratio for the new goods into the relevant elementary price index, but the absolute decline in price going from the old to new variety is never reflected in the relevant elementary price index. This source of bias was recognized

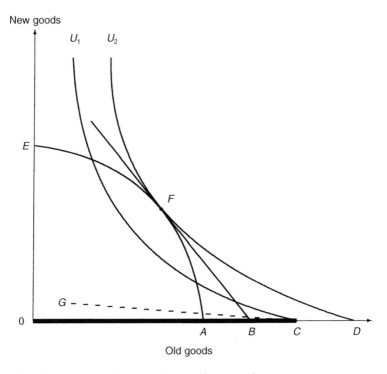

Figure 7.1 Fixed costs and the introduction of new goods

by Griliches (1979, p. 97), Gordon (1981, pp. 130–3) (1990) (1993) and many others.

We can illustrate the above problems by using a diagram based essentially on Romer (1994; pp. 12–14), and discussed in Diewert and Fox (1998) (see Figure 7.1).

Prior to the introduction of the new good, the economy could produce the amount *OC* of old goods. The fixed costs of introducing the new good can be represented by the line segment *AC*. Once these fixed costs have been incurred, the production possibilities set for the economy over old and new goods is represented by the traditionally-shaped production frontier *EA*. Turning now to the consumer side of the model, we follow the example of Hicks (1940, p. 114) and assume that the consumer has well-defined preferences over combinations of old and new goods; two representative indifference curves are indexed by U_1 and U_2 in Figure 7.1. In the period prior to the introduction of the new good, the amount *OC* of old goods is consumed and the utility level U_1 is achieved. In the subsequent period, when the new good is introduced, the consumer ends up at point F and attains the higher utility level U_2. The equivalent amount of old goods that attains the utility level U_2 is OD, so the consumer ends up with the net gain (in terms of old goods) of CD because of the introduction of the new commodity. However, note that if the fixed costs were large enough, it can easily happen that the point D lies to the left of C, indicating that from the welfare point of view, it was a mistake to introduce the new commodity.

In terms of Figure 7.1, linking bias will lead the statistical agency to estimate the amount of old goods that is equivalent to the utility level associated with the point F to be OB instead of the true amount OD. The only way the bias BD will be reduced to zero is if the consumer's indifference curve through F is the straight line FB instead of the curved line FD.

As has already been noted, standard accounting practices will recognize the costs of introducing new products. Now we see that *existing statistical agency practices ensure that the benefits of new products are biased downwards* by the amount of curvature in consumers' indifference curves. This leads to the underestimation of productivity gains.

Hicks (1940, p. 114) proposed a theoretical solution to the problem of measuring the benefits of new products: if we could estimate the slope of the (dashed) line that is just tangent to the indifference curve that passes through the consumer's initial consumption point C, then a shadow or reservation price for the new good could be constructed for the new commodity in the period prior to its introduction, and normal index number theory could be applied. Of course, the problem facing a statistical agency is how it can produce estimated reservation prices on a large scale and on a timely basis.

While this is a complex problem, perhaps some progress has been made. Diewert (1980, pp. 501–3) proposed an econometric approach to the estimation of the relevant shadow prices. Recently, Hausman (1996) utilized such an approach for breakfast cereals using supermarket scanner data. The fact that statistical agencies seem reluctant to follow Hausman's lead, and broadly implement the estimation of shadow prices, suggests that there are still significant practical difficulties involved.

Service sector outputs

Baily and Gordon (1988) and the contributors in Griliches (1992) discussed many of the problems involved in measuring the outputs of certain service industries. For the most part, these problems are still with us as we enter the twenty-first century. In this section, we shall review some of these measurement problems for nine service sectors.

Real estate

In the USA, the real and nominal output of the real estate industry was defined as follows:

The real estate industry's output is the rental income it receives and the commissions of realtors. This nominal output is deflated using rental cost indexes for residential and commercial rents. The problem in using the available rent indexes as deflators is that they do not adjust for changes in the quality of the property being rented. (Baily and Gordon, 1988, pp. 396–7)

In addition to the likely downward bias in measuring the real output of the rental segment of real-estate output identified by Baily and Gordon, it is likely that the commissions part of real-estate deflated output is also biased downwards. Real-estate agents assist in the buying and selling of real property. This portion of real-estate output should be measured in real terms as either the number of completed transactions or as the real value of the property transacted. The nominal value of this part of real-estate output is equal to the commissions received by real-estate agents, which is correctly measured by statistical agencies. Note that this part of the output of the real-estate industry can be viewed as a margin industry, like retailing and wholesaling: the price of the output of a margin industry is the difference between the sale price of the vendor and the purchase price of the buyer. A little algebra may help to clarify the measurement of the real output of a margin industry. Thus, let p_t denote the average purchase price of the real property sold during period t and let q_t denote the corresponding quantity sold. Let m_t denote the period t commission rate that real-estate agents received. Then period t nominal output is $m_t p_t q_t$, and the period t price and quantity indexes relative to period 0 should be $(m_t/m_0)(p_t/p_0)$ and q_t/q_0 respectively. However, if the statistical agency uses an inappropriate price index P_t/P_0 in order to deflate the ratio of nominal commissions in period t relative to period 0, then the following incorrect quantity index will be obtained:

$$Q_t/Q_0 = [(p_t/p_0)/(P_t/P_0)][m_t/m_0][q_t/q_0] \tag{7.1}$$

which should be compared to the correct quantity index, q_t/q_0. Baily and Gordon (1988, 397) hypothesized that the term $[(p_t/p_0)/(P_t/P_0)]$ was less than one for the US real estate industry – that is, that the official statistical agency deflator P_t/P_0 was greater than the quality adjusted selling price index, p_t/p_0. Our additional hypothesis is that the margin ratio, m_t/m_0, is likely to have been less than one in recent years because of increased competition placing pressure on margins. For example, many properties in North America and Australia are now listed on the Internet. This means that Internet-connected potential buyers of real estate can now do a preliminary screening of properties through their computer. This screening saves some time and effort for real-estate agents, who in turn can offer lower commission rates to customers. Thus the Baily and Gordon hypothesis and our hypothesis both lead to a downward bias in the official output growth measure Q_t/Q_0 defined by Equation (7.1) relative to the 'true' real output index, q_t/q_0.

Retailing and wholesaling

These industries are straightforward margin-type industries, they buy goods q in period t at the price $(1 - m_t)\, p_t$ and sell them at the price p_t, where m_t is the period t margin rate. As was the case with property sales, the correct period t price and quantity indexes are $(m_t/m_0)\,(p_t/p_0)$ and q_t/q_0, respectively. If the statistical agency constructs its quantity index Q_t/Q_0 by deflating industry value added by the price index P_t/P_0 in place of the 'true' price index (m_t/m_0) (p_t/p_0) then the official index Q_t/Q_0 will again be defined by Equation (7.1) above. Typically, P_t/P_0 will be greater than p_t/p_0 because of outlet substitution bias – that is, the statistical agency will tend to follow prices in established high-cost outlets and fail to weight adequately the lower prices that appear in newer discount outlets.[1] Second, the use of deflated value added by the statistical agency as an output measure will again lead to a downward bias in output growth, because any declines in margins because of increased efficiencies in marketing and inventory management will be missed – that is, as in the case of real estate, m_t/m_0 will tend to be less than one.[2] However, statistical agencies are often unable to calculate the value added for the distribution trades, except for sporadic Census years. Thus, they are unable to calculate the margins m_t for each period t, and they are forced to assume that the base period margin rate m_0 is still applicable in period t. In this case, the statistical agency will estimate period t real output as (incorrectly) deflated period t sales, $p_t q_t / P_t$, and the resulting official statistical agency output quantity index becomes Equation (7.2) below instead of Equation (7.1) above:

$$Q_t/Q_0 = [(p_t/p_0)/(P_t/P_0)][q_t/q_0] \qquad (7.2)$$

Assuming that m_t/m_0 is less than one, it can be seen that the downward bias in the measurement of real output growth in the distributive trades will generally be lower if the statistical agency uses the formula in Equation (7.2) in place of Equation (7.1). However, in both cases, the term $[(p_t/p_0)/(P_t/P_0)]$ will tend to be less than one because of outlet substitution bias, and so official output growth will be understated.

Financial services

Stock market trading can be viewed as another margin-type-industry. The period t nominal output for this industry can be represented approximately by the formula $m_t p_t n_t$ where m_t is the average transactions cost for trading one share of a stock during period t, p_t is the average purchase price of a stock, and n_t is the number of shares traded during period t. To convert the industry period t nominal value into a real value, divide by the period t price for a representative basket of goods, say, P_t. Then we can decompose the period t nominal output value as follows:

$$m_t\, p_t\, n_t = [m_t\, P_t][(p_t/P_t)n_t] \qquad (7.3)$$

and we identify $m_t P_t$ as the period t output price and $(p_t/P_t)\, n_t$ as the period t real output of the stock trading industry. Thus the period t real output index for this industry can be defined as:

$$q_t/q_0 = [p_t/p_0][n_t/n_0]/[P_t/P_0] \tag{7.4}$$

For most industrialized countries, the value of stock market trading $p_t n_t$ has increased tremendously, driven by the large declines in commission rates m_t that have been stimulated by the growth of discount brokers and cheap internet trading in stocks. Thus the 'true' q_t/q_0 defined by Equation (7.4) above has grown tremendously relative to official statistical agency estimates of financial services output growth, which tend to be based on the growth of labour input.[3] Baily and Gordon (1988, p. 398) indicate that the number of shares traded in US stock exchanges increased from 2 billion in 1961 to 10.8 billion in 1979, and then to 63.8 billion in 1987. Baily and Gordon (1988, p. 399) go on to show that official statistics do not reflect the tremendous productivity gains that have taken place in this industry.

It is possible to treat investing in risky securities as a form of gambling.[4] We discuss the gambling industry below.

Transportation

Baily and Gordon (1988, p. 416) noted that US measures of airline output were biased downwards, because statistical agencies forgot to take account of discount airline fares.[5] In recent years, the problems faced by statistical agencies in measuring airline fares have probably become even more difficult because of airline deregulation. For example, a typical midday, midweek return flight from Vancouver to Toronto in early June 1998 would have had passengers travelling on at least six different fares, ranging from $379 to $1813. Business class passengers would have paid $2682, but 10 per cent to 15 per cent of the passengers in both business and economy would have been flying 'free' on frequent-flyer plans. Some airlines now auction off seats, with prices rising as the flight fills. There are also further measurement complications because of the new availability of non-stop direct flights between cities that were not directly connected before the advent of deregulation. For example, in 1998, it was possible to take a non-stop flight between Vancouver and Washington DC for the first time, with a resulting increase in utility at no extra cost. To work out an accurate price index for air travel under the above conditions is a very difficult problem, but simply pricing out a few fares without taking into account discount fares, the increased availability of direct flights and increased popularity of frequent-flyer plans will tend to under-estimate real output growth in this industry.

Telecommunications

This industry is similar to airline transportation in that the world-wide introduction of competition and deregulation has led to an incredible array of different discount plans and rate systems. Thus the usual statistical agency procedure of pricing out a few local calls and a few long distance calls at standard rates will again miss out on the effects of discount plans. Another complication is the increased use of the Internet. Internet rates are very low, and so an increasing volume of communication that used to take place by ordinary mail and traditional telephone services is now taking place via this medium. The resulting drop in the average price of communication services is missed by statistical agencies because of the difficulties in determining precisely how much substitution from traditional services has taken place.[6]

Banking

The treatment of interest in the system of national accounts leads to a rather flawed measure of banking output. Basically, banks produce two main classes of outputs: (i) checking and deposit services and (ii) financial intermediation services – that is, banks have access to funds at relatively low rates of interest and they loan these funds out at higher rates of interest. Thus, with respect to this second class of outputs, banks act like a margin-type industry: their nominal period t output is the value of loans v_t times the period t markup rate m_t (which is the difference between the average period t lending and borrowing rates). The corresponding period t output price index can be defined as $[P_t/P_0]$ $[m_t/m_0]$, where p_t/p_0 is the consumer price index and the corresponding real output index can be defined as

$$q_t/q_0 = [v_t/v_0]/[P_t/P_0] \qquad (7.5)$$

For a more rigorous approach to measuring the output of banks, see Fixler and Zieschang (1991,1992), who draw on the various user costs of money proposed by Diewert (1974), Barnett (1978), Donovan (1978) and Hancock (1985).[7]

More recently, Fixler and Zieschang (1998) have compared the traditional (flawed) national accounts measure of real output growth for the US banking industry with their user cost approach for the years 1977–94. They found that the real output growth using their user-cost approach averaged about 7.4 per cent per year, while the traditional measure grew by about 0.7 per cent per year over this period. This is a rather substantial difference in rates of growth!

Insurance

In some ways, insurance can be viewed as another margin-type industry: individuals pay premiums to an insurance company and the company returns to claimants much of the money collected. The margin rate in this industry is premiums minus claims divided by premiums. The lower the margin rate, the more efficient the industry. Premiums less claims is known as the net premiums measure of nominal insurance output. How do statistical agencies measure the corresponding real output? Baily and Gordon describe the US method as follows:

The deflators used for the insurance industry are those developed for the industries being covered by the insurance. The auto repair cost index is used for auto insurance, medical costs for medical insurance, and so on ... Thus, the productivity weakness in the insurance sector is being driven by the escalation of cost indexes in the medical care area and in repair services, even though the insurance industry is engaged in an entirely different productive activity. (Baily and Gordon, 1988, p. 395)

The nature of the insurance industry's productive activity requires some discussion. Note that defining the nominal output of the insurance industry as premiums less claims has the rather unpalatable implication that a perfectly efficient industry that had no transaction costs would end up contributing nothing to national output. To avoid this unpleasant implication, Denny (1980), Ruggles (1983, p. 67) and Hornstein and Prescott (1991) suggested that gross premiums paid (rather than net premiums or premiums less claims) is a more appropriate measure of the nominal output of the insurance industry. In this view, consumers are buying protection services rather than forming a club to pool risk. In the gross-premiums view, the payment of claims by insurance companies appears on the balance sheets of households as offsets to their insured losses. This protection services view of insurance services will give rise to a much larger nominal gross output for the insurance industry than the traditional net claims approach, which leads to zero or negative nominal output in years when claims are large.[8]

There are some additional difficult conceptual issues that need to be resolved when measuring the output of the insurance industry. One such difficulty is the fact that consumers must pay for insurance protection services at the beginning of the protected period. If we view the protection services as being delivered in equal increments over the entire period, then the consumer's premium payments for each increment of protection services (except, perhaps, the first increment) can be viewed as an intertemporal prepayment for services to be delivered in the future, and the consumer should add an (implicit) opportunity cost of interest forgone to each incremental premium payment. On the other hand, the insurance company receives premium revenues well in advance of any claim costs and thus can earn (explicit) interest on these premium prepayments. Thus a major output of the insurance industry is interest and investment income earned.[9] The need for the insurance industry to have reserves to cover abnormal claim years will increase this financial component of insurance industry output.

Another difficult conceptual problem is the deflation of the nominal insurance output measure into a real measure. If we take the insurance as protection services point of view, then premiums should be deflated by the real value of the insurance coverage. However, this approach neglects any changes in risk. In order to deal with changes in risk, we could use the expected utility model to work out the incremental utility gain provided by insurance.[10]

However, Diewert (1993, pp. 418–19; 1995) proposed a more flexible non-expected utility approach to modelling the demand for insurance, and this approach could also be used to develop a measure for the real output of the protection services part of insurance industry output that would be valid under conditions of changing risk. All of these alternative approaches to measuring insurance outputs will lead to larger estimates of output growth than the traditional deflated net premiums approach.

Gambling

Gambling is another industry that could be viewed as a margin-type industry. Consumers wager a certain amount of funds and get a fraction back as prizes or winnings; the difference between the wagers and the prizes divided by wagers is the average margin rate. The smaller the margin rate, the more efficient the industry.[11] On the other hand, the national accounts treatment of nominal gambling output is similar to insurance: namely, output is approximately equal to transactions cost. Hence, again, we have the anomalous result that a fully efficient industry would have zero nominal output. The counterpart to the gross premiums approach to measuring insurance output is the gross wagers approach: the nominal output of the gambling industry is the total amount wagered during the accounting period, and the service being provided by the industry is entertainment. Prize money paid out is treated as an intermediate input expense just as claims paid out were treated as an intermediate expense in the gross premiums approach to measuring insurance output. If we followed the insurance industry analogy completely, then on the household accounts, prize money won would appear in the household balance sheets as an increase in assets. However, the case for putting winnings in the balance sheets is not as persuasive as in the insurance case, where claims paid were simply a balance sheet offset for insured losses. However, the alternative net wagers approach (where nominal gambling output is set equal to wagers less winnings) is not particularly attractive either, because of the problem of a zero nominal output for a fully efficient industry.

How should the real output of the gambling industry be measured? If we take the gross wagers approach, then nominal wagers should be deflated by a general measure of purchasing power such as the consumer price index. This approach will be satisfactory if the probability of winning remains constant (or, alternatively, if the average margin rate remains constant). However, as the gambling industry has grown rapidly in recent years, so too has competition. Thus the gambling industry at the beginning of the twenty-first century faces (like most industries) competitive pressures to increase payouts and reduce margins. As in the case of insurance, we could appeal to the expected utility approach to gambling to determine the incremental gain in utility that gambling provides to (non-addicted) consumers under changing risk conditions. However, the expected utility approach to modelling the demand to gamble does not provide an adequate approximation to empirical behaviour; hence, non-expected utility models will have to be used to measure the real output of the gambling industry.[12] It is likely that these new approaches to measuring the output of the gambling industry will give higher rates of growth in real output than the traditional approach.

Business services

A final problem industry where actual real output growth is likely to be greater than measured real growth is business services. For example, the effective price of accounting services will probably drop dramatically in the future as small businesses adopt computer-driven accounting packages such as Quicken, Quickbooks and Simply Accounting. However, it is likely that this effective drop in price will be missed by traditional statistical agency procedures.[13] Another example of a class of new business services that has the potential to lower prices dramatically is the development of Internet sites that compare prices for the same product from different suppliers. Such services exist for computers, standard insurance policies, airline fares, motor vehicles and many other commodities.[14] The effect of these sites will be to expand the sales of the most efficient suppliers and eventually to bankrupt the suppliers who are unable to compete effectively. However, existing statistical agency pricing procedures will tend to miss this shift to low-cost suppliers: that is, the sampled prices of the efficient suppliers will not be weighted according to sales and it is not until the inefficient suppliers disappear that their price quotes will be dropped. Thus the growth of Internet sites that compare prices, and the growth of Internet sales for the low-cost suppliers will lead to large outlet substitution biases unless statistical agencies are given additional funds to take remedial action.

We believe that it is possible for statistical agencies to measure the outputs of service sector industries more accurately, but the resources that will be required to accomplish this are considerable. Because statistical agencies have not stressed these measurement difficulties, the public at large remains unaware of the problems and has not insisted on having governments make the required resource investments. As a result, output growth is almost certainly greatly underestimated because of: (a) the difficulties in measuring outputs that involve uncertainty or interest; (b) the pervasive presence of new goods and services; and (c) the outlet substitution biases that have been stimulated by computers and the Internet.

Have consumption expenditures become business expenses?

Consumption expenditures are final 'goods' and hence appear as part of GDP. Business expenses are intermediate 'goods' and do not appear as a positive part of GDP. The expansion of business expense accounts, and various fringe benefits, may have caused many consumption items to be classified now as intermediate goods. Entertainment expenses, as well as company gyms, daycare centres, cars, home loans and parts of business travel, are all former consumption expenditures that will not appear in final aggregate demand (Triplett, 1997; Diewert and Fox, 1998).[15]

A recent Japanese study (reported in the *Asahi Shimbun*, 1995) hinted at the extent that such a reclassification of consumption expenditures had taken place. An index of economic activity was found to be very highly correlated with blood sugar levels of Japanese businessmen. When there was a decline in the economic-activity index around 1990, blood sugar levels fell correspondingly. A possible reason for this remarkable correlation is that entertainment expense accounts expand with economic growth, and dietary habits change as a result. If Japanese businessmen consume more and richer food (perhaps Western food) when they dine out than when they eat at home, this could explain this correlation. Larger expense accounts means more entertaining of guests and more dining out, hence higher blood sugar levels. If this is indeed the reason behind the correlation, then this suggests that actual GDP is growing faster than measured GDP during economic booms, and slower than measured GDP during downturns – cuts in expense accounts result in a reclassification of consumption back to final demand expenditures, which would contribute to measured GDP growth.

There are other examples of such misclassification of final demand expenditures as business intermediate expenditures. The impact of pollution control and environmental preservation regulations on productivity have been examined by, for example, McConnell (1979, p. 44), Malkiel (1979, pp. 83–4), Nordhaus (1982, p. 138), Mairesse (1982, p. 161), and Baily and Gordon (1988, p. 362). Estimates of the contribution to the productivity slowdown from these sources range from 0.2 per cent to 0.5 per cent per year. We can note that these results are related to the much publicized arguments put forward primarily by Porter (1990), and Porter and van der Linde (1995) on the possibility of productivity-improving environmental regulation. It may be more appropriate for expenses that firms incur in preserving the environment to be treated as final demand expenditures, rather than as intermediate business expenses. At least, if these expenditures are to be classified as costs for firms, there should be appropriate measures of the 'output', that is, the resulting improvement in the environment. Taking this into account would increase the productivity growth measures for the sectors subject to such regulation, and the economy as a whole.

Similarly, improvements in workplace safety and amenities have been suggested as practical explanations of the productivity slowdown by Summers (1982, p. 167), and Baily and Gordon (1988, p. 409).

Land and productivity

The current system of national accounts has no role for land as a factor of production, perhaps because it is thought that the quantity of land in use remains roughly constant over time, and hence it can be treated as a fixed, unchanging factor in the analysis of production. However, the quantity of land in use by any particular firm or industry does change over time. Moreover, the price of land can change dramatically and thus the user cost of land will also change over time. This changing user cost will, in general, affect correctly measured productivity. For example, during the period 1955–87, the price of land (non-reproducible tangible assets) in Japan grew by approximately 16 per cent per year. Inserting an appropriate user cost of land into the aggregate productivity (index number) formula for Japan (versus merely omitting land from the computation) leads to a 0.5 per cent per year increase in Japanese total factor productivity. Thus it is important not to neglect the role of land when computing the total factor productivity of a producer unit.

There are other important issues related to the treatment of land as a factor of production. Land ties up capital just as inventories do (both are zero depreciation assets). Hence, when computing *ex-post* rates of return earned by a production unit, it is important to account for the opportunity cost of capital tied up in land. Neglect of this factor can lead to very biased rates of return on financial capital employed.

Also, property taxes that fall on land must be included as part of the user cost of land. It may not be easy to separate the land part of property taxes from the structures part. Note that, in the national accounts, property taxes (which are input taxes) are lumped together with other indirect taxes that fall on outputs. This is another shortcoming of the current system of accounts.

Price and regulatory distortions and productivity

Individual firms or establishments could be operating efficiently (that is, be on the frontiers of their production possibilities sets) but yet the economy as a whole may not be operating efficiently. The explanation for this phenomenon was given by Gerard Debreu (1951): there is a loss of system-wide output (or waste, to use Debreu's term) because of the imperfection of economic organization – that is, different production units, while technically efficient, face different prices for the same input or output, and this causes net outputs aggregated across production units to fall below what is attainable if the economic system as a whole were efficient. In other words, a condition for system-wide efficiency is that all production units face the same price for each separate input or output produced by the economy as a whole. Thus, if producers face different prices for similar commodities and if production functions exhibit some substitutability, then producers will be induced jointly to supply an inefficient economy-wide net output vector. Some sources of system-wide waste are as follows:

1. Industry-specific taxes or subsidies that create differences in prices faced by production-units for the same commodity; for example, an industry-

specific subsidy for an output or a tax on the output of one industry where that output is used as an input by other industries (an example of the latter is a petroleum tax).
2. Tariffs on imports, or subsidies or taxes on exports.
3. Monopolistic or monopsonistic mark-ups on commodities by firms, or any kind of price discrimination on the part of firms.
4. A source of commodity price wedges that is related to the last source above is the difficulty that multi-product firms have in pricing their outputs, particularly when there are large fixed costs involved in producing new (or old) products (Romer, 1994), and particularly when there is high inflation and historical cost accounting techniques for pricing products break down (Diewert and Fox, 1998).
5. Imperfect regulation; it is very difficult for government regulators to set 'optimal' prices for the commodities that are regulated. If the regulators are unable to determine the 'optimal' prices for regulated commodities, then the other producers that use the regulated outputs as inputs will generate system-wide waste. Examples of imperfect regulation might include marketing boards; telecommunications; environmental protection; and health and safety regulations; the regulation of labour markets including the collective bargaining framework; regulation of the radio/TV spectrum; municipal zoning and building code regulations; and the patent system.
6. Another source of market imperfections between economic agents might be the legal system: are property rights well defined and enforceable? If not, the resulting uncertainty prevents the market from assigning a definite value to the asset or resource under dispute, and this uncertainty will generally prevent the asset from being put to its most profitable use.
7. A related source of price wedges between economic agents is the existence of widespread bribery and corruption. A bribe has roughly the same effect as an uncertain tax on a transaction and will create distortion wedges between business units.
8. A final source of Allais–Debreu intersectoral waste is the system of business income taxation that is in place in most countries. The lack of indexation of depreciation allowances for inflation causes a divergence between the value of a depreciable asset to the producer of the asset and the value to the purchaser of the asset: in periods of high inflation, the discounted value of the depreciation allowances allowed for tax purposes will be much less than the purchase price of the asset and thus the using firm will have to charge itself a much higher price than the purchase price for the asset to overcome this tax-induced penalty for using the asset (Diewert and Fox, 1998). The higher internal (to the firm) price of capital will cause firms to economize on its use. This may help to explain the investment slowdown and the subsequent rise in the average age of capital in many countries that experienced high inflation in the 1970s. See, for example, Wolff (1996) for a possible explanation for the productivity paradox through the increased

average age of capital. There are many other distortions between sectors and assets that the typical system of business income taxation induces. Some references to the literature include Harberger (1974), Jorgenson and Yun (1986), Feldstein (1978), Ballard *et al.* (1985), and Shoven and J. Whalley (1984).

Note that the above sources of intersectoral waste are mainly induced by governments (non-optimal taxes and non-optimal regulations and institutions), but some waste is induced by the fixed costs of establishing new plants and developing new products and processes, which in turn leads to monopolistic (or somewhat random) pricing of outputs on the part of business units. However, it is difficult for governments to determine 'optimal' taxes or 'optimal' prices for the outputs of regulated businesses and it is just as difficult for multi-product firms that are constantly developing new products or experimenting with new processes to price their products at socially efficient levels.

What are the implications of intersectoral waste for statistical agencies? The current input–output system of industry accounts is two-dimensional: current and constant dollar value flows are classified by industry and by commodity. There is an urgent need to make the classification three-dimensional and add a table that lists taxes paid (or subsidies received) by industry and by commodity. This would enable applied general equilibrium modellers to calculate estimates of the waste or excess burdens that are induced by the tax-subsidy wedges that are pervasive in most economies. The present system of national income accounts just adds a row to the usual input–output table that simply sums up all indirect commodity taxes paid by the industry without telling users what the incidence of the taxes are by commodity. For regulated industries, there is a need for statistical agencies to provide estimated marginal costs (or producer prices) for the regulated commodities, and estimated user values (or consumer prices) as well as quantities supplied. This is a somewhat utopian request given the limited resources that statistical agencies have at their disposal at present, and given the practical and conceptual difficulties in constructing producer and consumer prices for regulated commodities. Perhaps this is a fruitful area for the academic community to till.

Conclusion

This chapter has reviewed the productivity paradox from the point of view of economic measurement. Our tentative conclusion is that various measurement problems could explain the productivity slowdown that has occurred in most advanced industrial economies since the mid-1970s

In the third section we argued that economic growth since around 1980s has been driven by the development of new products, and since current statistical agency procedures do not capture the full benefits of new products (or outlets, for that matter), actual growth has been much higher than measured growth. In the fourth section we followed the example of Griliches (1994) in noting that in recent decades, growth has been concentrated in the service sectors of advanced economies, and that outputs are difficult to measure in many of these sectors. In particular, service sectors involving margins, complex products, interest payments and uncertainty tend to be poorly measured. We gave several examples where poor measurement resulted in output measures that were biased downwards. In the fifth section we noted that the growth of white-collar employment may have led to an increase in business intermediate expenditures (which reduces measured productivity), which were, in fact, consumption expenditures. In part, this growth of consumption-type intermediate expenditures may have been driven by increasing rates of personal income taxation. In the sixth section we noted that current statistical agency methods for measuring productivity (with a few exceptions) ignore the role of land as a productive input, and hence if land prices are rising rapidly (as they did in many countries during the 1970s and 1980s), then measured productivity will be biased downwards. In the seventh section, we argued that increased government spending during the 1970s and 1980s eventually lead to increased taxes, which in turn led to an economy-wide loss of productive efficiency.

Putting together all of the above measurement problems could explain the productivity slowdown. However, in order to obtain definitive proof of this, governments will have to allocate more funds so that statistical agencies can better measure the benefits of new products, and can better measure service-sector outputs. Thus it seems essentially that the 'data constraint' must be relaxed by providing statistical agencies with the support and resources necessary to produce more accurate statistics which are useful for policy analysis.

Notes

1. For some evidence at higher levels of aggregation that this effect occurs, see Reinsdorf (1993), McDonald (1995) and Triplett (1997, p. 17). For evidence at lower levels of aggregation, many scanner data studies have been done that track market transactions data for specific commodities. These studies (which are reviewed in Diewert, 1998, pp. 54–5) tend to show that unit values or superlative price indexes (which are constructed using detailed price and quantity data rather than a few sampled prices) show lower rates of price increase than the corresponding consumer price index inflation rates.
2. For some limited evidence of productivity gains resulting from more efficient management of inventories, see Diewert and Smith (1994).
3. 'The output of the financial service industry is measured on the basis of labor input and thus ignores any output per hour gain by definition'. (Baily and Gordon, 1988).
4. See Diewert (1993, pp. 427–32).
5. See also Gordon (1992, p. 377) for additional material on biases in US transportation indexes.

6. This problem is similar to that faced by statistical agencies when the methods of delivering light (in lumens) changed over the years through technological progress. As new delivery systems were introduced, agencies tended to ignore the new method until it became very important. Finally, prices for the new commodity were collected for two periods, and then the resulting price relative for the new delivery system was averaged together, with the price relatives for the old existing commodities, so that the absolute drop in the price per lumen did not show up in the official indexes; see Nordhaus (1997, pp. 46–7).
7. The user cost idea dates back to the economist Walras (1954, p. 269) and the industrial engineer Church (1901, pp. 907–8).
8. However, the nominal value added of the insurance industry will still be approximately equal to net claims, since claims must be viewed as an intermediate input cost.
9. Sherwood (1998) notes the importance of including this financial output of the insurance industry in the nominal output of the industry, since if it is not included, net claims in the US insurance industry are negative for some years.
10. See von Neumann and Morgenstern (1947), Arrow (1951, 1984) and Mossin (1968). The modern actuarial literature uses the expected utility approach to model the demand for insurance; see Bowers *et al.* (1986).
11. However, we note that this does not take into account the entertainment value of the gambling experience, such as free drinks and lavish settings.
12. See Diewert (1993, pp. 424–7; 1995, pp. 143–4) for non-expected utility theory approaches to gambling.
13. Recall the Nordhaus (1997) price of light problem.
14. There are also Internet auction sites that deal with a wide variety of goods.
15. 'Salary sacrifice' schemes are becoming an increasingly common way of avoiding taxes in many countries. Under these schemes, employees may give up same salary and be compensated in kind through, for example, the use of a company car. The expansion of these schemes has attracted the attention of the Australian government: 'Salary packaging, elaborate tax schemes used by the wealthy and increasing numbers of multinational companies, have been cited as some of the prime risks to the tax system ... The Treasury did not give any indication of the numbers of people involved in these schemes, but the mention of salary sacrifice schemes indicates that they pose a significant threat to revenue' (*Sydney Morning Herald*, 14 May 1998).

References

Arrow, K. J. (1951) 'Alternative Approaches to the Theory of Choice in Risk Taking Situations', *Econometrica*, vol. 19, pp. 404–37.

Arrow, K. J. (1984) *Individual Choice under Certainty and Uncertainty* (Cambridge; Mass.: Harvard University Press).

Baily, M. N. and Gordon, R. J. (1988) 'The Productivity Slowdown, Measurement Issues, and the Explosion of Computer Power', *Brookings Papers on Economic Activity*, 1988;2, pp. 347–420.

Ballard, C. L., Shoven, J. B. and Whalley, J. (1985) 'General Equilibrium Computations of the Marginal Welfare Costs of Taxes in the United States', *American Economic Review*, vol. 75, pp. 128–38.

Barnett, W. (1978) 'The User Cost of Money', *Economic Letters*, vol. 2, pp. 145–9.

Bowers, N. L., Gerber, H. U., Hickman, J. C., Jones, D. A. and Nesbitt C. J. (1986) *Actuarial Mathematics* (Itasca, Ill.: Society of Actuaries).

Church, A. H. (1901) 'The Proper Distribution of Establishment Changes', Parts I, II and III, *The Engineering Magazine*, vol. 21, pp. 508–17; 725–34; 904–12.

David, P. A. (1990) 'The Dynamo and the Computer: An Historical Perspective on the Modern Productivity Paradox', *American Economic Review*, vol. 80, pp. 355–61.

Denny, M. (1980) 'Measuring the Real Output of the Life Insurance Industry: A Comment', *The Review of Economics and Statistics*, vol. 62, pp. 150–2.

Debreu, G. (1951) 'The Coefficient of Resource Utilization', *Econometrica*, vol. 19, pp. 273–92.

Diewert, W. E. (1974) 'Intertemporal Consumer Theory and the Demand for Durables', *Econometrica*, vol. 42, pp. 497–516.

Diewert, W. E. (1980) 'Aggregation Problems in the Measurement of Capital', in Dan Usher (ed.), *The Measurement of Capital* (University of Chicago Press), pp. 433–528.

Diewert, W. E. (1993) 'Symmetric Means and Choice Under Uncertainty', in W. E. Diewert and A. O. Nakamura (eds), *Essays in Index Number Theory*, vol. 1 (Amsterdam: North-Holland), pp. 355–433.

Diewert, W. E. (1995) 'Functional Form Problems in Modeling Insurance and Gambling', *The Geneva Papers on Risk and Insurance Theory*, vol. 20, pp. 135–50.

Diewert, W. E. (1996) 'Comment on CPI Biases', in *Business Economics*, vol. xxxi, no. 2, pp. 30–5.

Diewert, W. E. (1998) 'Index Number Issues in the Consumer Price Index', *Journal of Economic Perspectives*, vol. 12 no. 1 (Winter), pp. 47–58.

Diewert, W. E. and Smith, A. M. (1994) 'Productivity Measurment for a Distribution Firm', *The Journal of Productivity Analysis*, vol. 5, pp. 335–47.

Diewert, W. E. and Fox, K. J. (1999) 'Can Measurement Error Explain the Productivity Paradox?', *Canadian Journal of Economics* 32, 251–80.

Donovan, D. (1978) 'Modeling the Demand for Liquid Assets: An Application to Canada', *International Monetary Fund Staff Papers*, vol. 25, pp. 676–704.

Feldstein, M. S. (1978) 'The Welfare Cost of Capital Income Taxation', *Journal of Political Economy* vol. 86, pp. S29–51.

Fixler, D. and Zieschang, K. (1991) 'Measuring the Nominal Value of Financial Services in the National Income Accounts', *Economic Inquiry*, vol. 29, pp. 53–68.

Fixler, D. and Zieschang, K. (1992) 'User Costs, Shadow Prices, and the Real Output of Banks', in Z. Griliches (ed.), *Output Measurement in the Service Sectors* (University of Chicago Press), pp. 219–43.

Fixler, D. and Zieschang K. (1999) 'The Productivity of the Banking Sector: Intergrating Financial and Production Approaches to Measuring Financial Service Output', *Canadian Journal of Economics*, vol. 32, 547–69.

Gordon, R. J. (1981) 'The Consumer Price Index: Measuring Inflation and Causing it', *The Public Interest*, vol. 63 (Spring), pp. 112–34.

Gordon, R. J. (1990) *The Measurement of Durable Goods Prices* (Chicago: University of Chicago Press and National Bureau of Economic Research).

Gordon, R. J. (1992) 'Productivity in the Transportation Sector', in Z. Griliches (ed.), *Output Measurement in the Service Sectors* (University of Chicago Press), pp. 371–422.

Gordon, R. J. (1993) 'Measuring the Aggregate Price Level: Implications for Economic Performance and Policy', in K. Shingehara (ed.), *Price Stabilization in the 1990s* (London: Macmillan), pp. 233–76.

Griliches, Z. (1979) 'Issues in Assessing the Contribution of Research and Development to Productivity Growth', *Bell Journal of Economics*, vol. 10 (Spring), pp. 92–116.

Griliches, Z. (ed.) (1992) *Output Measurement in the Service Sectors* (University of Chicago Press).

Griliches, Z. (1994) 'Productivity, R&D, and the Data Constraint', *American Economic Review*, vol. 84, pp. 1–23.

Hancock, D. (1985) 'The Financial Firm: Production with Monetary and Non-Monetary Goods', *Journal of Political Economy*, vol. 93, pp. 859–80.

Harberger, A. C. (1974) *Taxation and Welfare* (Boston, Mass.: Little, Brown).

Hausman, J. A. (1996) 'Valuation of New Goods Under Perfect and Imperfect Competition', in T. Bresnahan and R. J. Gordon (eds), *The Economics of New Goods* (University of Chicago Press).

Hicks, J. R. (1940) 'The Valuation of the Social Income', *Economical*, vol. 7, pp. 105–40.

Hicks, J. R. (1969) *A Theory of Economic History*, (Oxford University Press).

Hornstein, A. and Prescott, E. D. (1991) 'Measuring the Real Output of the Life Insurance Industry', *Review of Economics and Statistics*, vol. 59, pp. 211–19.

Jorgenson, D. W. and Yun, K.-Y. (1986) 'The Efficiency of Capital Allocation', *Scandinavian Journal of Economics*, vol. 88, pp. 85–107.

Mairesse, J. (1982) 'Comments', *European Economic Review*, vol. 18, pp. 159–62.

Malkiel, B. G. (1979) 'Productivity – the Problem Behind the Headlines', *Harvard Business Reviews*, vol. 57, no. 3, pp. 81–91.

McConnell, C. R. (1979) 'Why is U.S. Productivity Slowing Down?', *Harvard Business Review*, vol. 57, no. 2, pp. 36–60.

McDonald, J. M. (1995) 'Consumer Price Index Overstates Food-Price Inflation', *Food Review*, vol. 18, no. 3, pp. 28–32.

Mossin, J. (1968) 'Aspects of Rational Insurance Purchasing', *Journal of Political Economy*, vol. 76, pp. 553–68.

Nakamura, L. I. (1997) 'The Measurement of Retail Output and the Retail Revolution', Paper presented at the CSLS Workshop on Service Sector Productivity and the Productivity Paradox, Ottawa, April 1997.

Nordhaus, W. D. (1982) 'Economic Policy in the Face of Declining Productivity Growth', *European Economic Review*, vol. 18, pp. 131–57.

Nordhaus, W. D. (1988) 'Comment', *Brookings Papers on Economic Activity*, vol. 2, pp. 421–5.

Nordhaus, W. D. (1997) 'Do Real Output and Real Wage Measures Capture Reality? The History of Light Suggests Not', in T. Bresnahan and R.J. Gordon (eds), *The Economics of New Goods*, NBER Studies in Income and Wealth (University of Chicago Press).

Porter, M. E. (1990) *The Competitive Advantage of Nations* (New York: Free Press).

Porter, M. E. and van der Linde, C. (1995) *Journal of Economic Perspectives*, vol. 9, pp. 97–118.

Reinsdorf, M. (1993) 'The Effects of Outlet Price Differentials in the U.S. Consumer Price Index', M. F. Foss, M. E. Manser and A. H. Young (eds)., in *Price Measurements and their Uses*, NBER Studies in Income and Wealth, vol. 57 (University of Chicago Press), pp. 227–54.

Romer, D. (1988) 'Comment', *Brookings Papers on Economics Activity*, vol. 2, pp. 425–8.

Romer, P. (1994) 'New Goods, Old Theory and the Welfare Costs of Trade Restrictions', *Journal of Development Economics* vol. 43, pp. 5–38.

Ruggles, R. (1983) 'The United States National Income Accounts, 1947–1977: Their Conceptual Basis and Evolution', in M. Foss (ed.), *The U.S. National Income and Product Accounts: Selected Topics* (University of Chicago Press), pp. F15–96.

Sherwood, M. K. (1999) 'Output of the Property and Causalty Insurance Industry', *Canadian Journal of Economics*, 32 518–46.

Shoven, J. B. and Whalley, J. (1984) 'Applied General-Equilibrium Models of Taxation and International Trade: An Introduction and Survey', *Journal of Economic Literature*, vol. 22, pp. 1007–51.

Steindel, C. (1999) 'The Impact of Reduced Inflation Estimates on Real Output and Productivity Growth', Federal Reserve Bank of New York, *Current Issues in Economics and Finance*, vol. 5, no. 9, June.

Summers, L. H. (1982) 'Comments', *European Economic Review*, vol. 18, pp. 163–9.

Triplett, J. E. (1997) 'Measuring Consumption: The Post-1973 Slowdown and the Research Issues', *Federal Reserve Bank of St. Louis Review*, (May–June), vol. 79, no. 3, pp. 9–43.

Triplett, J. E. (1999) 'The Slow Productivity Paradox: What Do Computers Do to Productivity?' *Canadian Journal of Economics* 32, 309–34.

von Neumann, J. and Morgenstern, O. (1947) *Theory of Games and Economic Behavior*, 2nd edn (Princeton, NJ: Princeton University Press).

Walras, L. (1954) *Elements of Pure Economics*, trans. W. Jaffe, (first pub. 1874) (London: George Allen & Unwin).

Wolff, E. N. (1996) 'The Productivity Slowdown: The Culprit at Last? Follow-Up on Hulten and Wolff', *American Economic Review*, vol. 86, pp. 1239–52.

Comments

Charles Steindel[1]

The chapter by Diewert and Fox addresses a number of ways that existing data structures and procedures may produce understatements of real output growth. In my comments I shall focus on three topics: (i) the possible overstatement of aggregate inflation when new products are introduced; (ii) some of the possible understatements of real output growth in a number of major US service industries; and (iii) the potential these data problems have for explaining the reported sluggishness in US productivity growth since the 1970s.

New products

The introduction of new products has always posed a major challenge to the construction of aggregate price and output indexes. Diewert and Fox note the correct theoretical way of handling new products in a cost-of-living index: essentially, compute the consumer surplus earned by the introduction of the new product. We might in practice do this by using econometric results to compute the price at which none of the new product would be purchased. The area under the demand curve for the new product from zero to the actual quantity purchased is an estimate of the consumer surplus arising from its introduction. Diewert and Fox assert that this technique will always result in a slower growth in the cost of living than the linking technique, where price relatives for the new product replace those for an old one in the formula for computation of inflation.

There is no theoretical problem with this argument under the conditions posed by Diewert and Fox. Obviously, as they note, there would be enormous practical and statistical problems involved in implementing this programme in real-world statistics in anything like real time. I would also point out that the exercise involves more than extrapolation from a conventional demand curve estimated after a product is introduced. In particular, I do not think that the introduction of a new product can be viewed as merely the reduction in its price so that there is non-zero usage. As the quote from Nordhaus on page 179

198

suggests, marketing efforts involve not only the introduction of new products but also often the withdrawal of old ones – the supply conditions in the marketplace often change radically when a new product is launched. In addition, as Bob Gordon noted in his chapter (Chapter 11), the consumer's time constraint is not lessened by a new product, and indeed, time must be expended learning about it. Correct computation of the consumer surplus gained by a new product is a formidable undertaking.

I am also not sure that more rapid linking of new products into a price index is a practical fix for the new-product problem. It may be true that price relatives for new products are often folded into indexes after the most rapid declines in their prices – but rapid declines in the price of a new product could well reflect the liquidation of a failure. Linking-in such a product could work to understate true inflation, since it is not part of anybody's market basket! As a practical matter, dealing with more rapid change in the marketplace would probably involve more frequent updating of the product mix in the price indexes.

Understatements of service industry output

In the section on industries, Diewert and Fox produce examples of how existing procedures may well understate output growth and overstate price inflation, particularly in the service sector. In the financial sector, at least, I am not sure that I grasp the merits of their proposals: they seem to be saying that the typical products are consumer deposits and loans for banking, while for the other financial industries the representative product is a trade of one share. I do not believe that these products typify the US financial sector any more, so it might be inadvisable to go very far along the road of using these as guides to activity in these industries. I feel that the difficult problems with pricing and computing the real output of the modern financial system stem from the enormous conceptual difficulty of defining its products in any sort of standardized way that is susceptible to price measurement.

More fundamentally, a basic issue is whether biases in industry price and output series have increased, not just whether or not they exist. The policy-maker often needs to know whether inflation or real growth is higher today than in some reference period; the absolute level of the numbers could be secondary. Diewert and Fox contend that advances in computer technology have caused an acceleration in the number of new products and refinements in old products, effectively increasing real output and reducing the cost of living through the consumer surplus arguments sketched above. While this may be true, a major question is whether or not the statistical agencies are falling further and further behind the marketplace, resulting in increasing biases.

We know very little about these issues. In the USA, at least, the statistical agencies do make earnest efforts to keep up with marketplace changes – the adoption of hedonic pricing techniques for computers themselves is the most notable change – and I do not see why there should be a presumption that they are falling further and further behind in these efforts. Besides, there is some impression that innovations lost to the statistics may have been larger in the past, though perhaps smaller in number: the introduction of jet aircraft and containerization in the transportation industry; the introduction of direct-dialing long distance in communications and so on. For example, one industry where it has been seriously argued that current statistical procedures – at least those in place from 1978 to very recently in the USA – result in overstatements of price increases is retailing, especially that of food. This is the so-called 'formula bias problem'. However, there clearly been profound innovations in retailing in the past, such as the development of the supermarket and the shopping mall, which were probably lost to the price and output indexes.

Can increased biases explain the productivity shortfall?

Even if we believe that there have been growing biases in the price numbers in large parts of the service economy, would it be enough to explain the reported post-1973 slowdown in aggregate US productivity growth? Many of the specific industries Diewert and Fox discuss make, in the main, intermediate products, not items used in final demand for goods and services. Thus, mismeasurement in their output would not affect the aggregate series very much. For example, mismeasurement of financial sector output would generally be reflected in an equal and opposite mismeasurement of the output of some business customer, since business provides the bulk of financial revenues. The shift of the economy to harder-to-measure sectors has been less marked in final demand categories. Daniel Sichel and I have both noted that the shift of final demand to sectors such as finance and medicine – where we think that not only are the biases in the price numbers larger than elsewhere, but have also arguably increased – has not been large enough to introduce new first-order distortions to the aggregate output and inflation numbers. No matter how it is sliced, we cannot plausibly say that increased price measurement error has been hiding a resurgence of aggregate US productivity growth back to the pace of the 1960s.[2] We do want to know what is really going on, industry by industry, and I think measurement error is an issue that has to be confronted here, and where the arguments of Diewert and Fox have their punch. I think, though, that it is very risky to expect measurement error to explain the aggregate 'productivity paradox'.

Notes

1. The views expressed are those of the author and do not necessarily reflect the position of the Federal Reserve Bank of New York or the Federal Reserve System.
2. Diewert and Fox contend that measured productivity growth may have been held down by the increased subsidization of consumption by employers, which displaces

a final product by an intermediate product in national income accounting. The empirical question is whether there has been an acceleration of fringe benefit growth. Also, getting to the heart of the question about the purpose of economic activity, at some point it would be useful to know the fraction of these fringe benefits and some other items that are welfare-enhancing, rather than income-improving. As an offset to fringes, spending on 'personal business expenses' – items such as financial charges and legal expenses – have grown quite rapidly in the USA. While these items are classified as part of personal consumption expenses, perhaps they should be subtracted from spending if we want to look at some measure of household utility.

References

Sichel, D. (1997) 'The Productivity Slowdown: Is a Growing Unmeasurable Sector the Culprit?', *Review of Economics and Statistics*, vol. 79, no. 3, (August), pp. 367–70.
Steindel, C. (1997) 'Measuring Economic Activity and Economic Welfare: What Are We Missing?' Federal Reserve Bank of New York Research Paper No. 9732 (October).

Part IV

Implications of a Knowledge-based Economy on Economic Growth and the Labour Market

8
Whatever Happened to Productivity? Investment and Growth in the G7

*Dale W. Jorgenson and Eric Yip**

Introduction

In this chapter we present international comparisons of patterns of economic growth among the G7 countries over the period 1960–95. Between 1960 and 1973 productivity growth accounted for more than half of growth in output per capita for France, Germany, Italy, Japan and the UK, and somewhat less than half of output growth in Canada and the USA. The relative importance of productivity declined substantially after 1973, accounting for a predominant share of growth between 1973 and 1989 for France alone.

Since 1989, productivity growth has almost disappeared as a source of economic growth in the G7 countries. Between 1989 and 1995 productivity growth was negative for five of the G7 countries, with positive growth only for Japan and the USA. The level of productivity for Canada in 1995 fell almost to the level first achieved in 1973, while declines in Italy and the UK brought productivity down to the levels of 1974 and 1978, respectively. Since 1989, input per capita has grown more slowly than the average for the period 1960 to 1989, except for Germany.

The USA has retained its lead in output per capita throughout the period 1960–95. The USA has also led the G7 countries in input per capita, while relinquishing its lead in productivity to France. However, the US has lagged behind Canada, France, Germany, Italy and Japan in the growth of output per capita, surpassing only the UK. Apart from Germany and the UK, the USA has lagged behind all the G7 countries in growth of input per capita, while US productivity growth has exceeded only that of Canada and the UK.

Japan exhibited considerably higher growth rates in output per capita and productivity than the other G7 countries from 1960 to 1995, but most of these gains took place before 1973. Japan's productivity level, along with the levels

* We gratefully acknowledge financial support by the Program on Technology and Economic Policy of Harvard University. Responsibility for any remaining deficiencies rests solely with the authors.

of Germany and Italy, remains among the lowest in the G7. Japan's performance in output per capita owes more to high input per capita than to high productivity. The growth of Japanese input per capita greatly exceeded that for other G7 countries, especially prior to 1973.

During the period 1960–95, economic performance among the G7 countries became more uniform. The dispersion of levels of output per capita fell sharply before 1970 and declined modestly after that. The dispersion in productivity levels also fell before 1970 and has remained within a narrow range. The dispersion of levels of input per capita has been stable throughout the period 1960–95. However, the relative positions of the G7 countries have been altered considerably with the dramatic rise of Japan and the gradual decline of the UK.

We can rationalize the important changes in economic performance that have taken place among the G7 countries on the basis of Robert Solow's (1956) neoclassical theory of economic growth, extended to incorporate persistent differences among countries. Productivity growth is exogenous, while investment is endogenous to the theory. Obviously, the relative importance of exogenous productivity growth has been greatly reduced, while a more prominent role must be assigned to endogenous investment in tangible assets and human capital.

In the second section we describe the methodology for allocating the sources of economic growth between investment and productivity. We introduce constant quality indices of capital and labour inputs that incorporate the impacts of investments in tangible assets and human capital. The constant quality index of labour input combines different types of hours worked by means of relative wage rates. The constant quality index of capital input weights different types of capital stocks by rental rates, rather than the asset prices used for weighting capital stocks.

Differences in wage rates for different types of labour inputs reflect investments in human capital through education and training, so that a constant quality index of labour input is the channel for the impact of these investments on economic performance. The constant quality index of capital input includes a perpetual inventory of investments in tangible assets. The index also incorporates differences in rental prices that capture the differential impacts of these investments.

In the third section we analyze the role of investment and productivity as sources of growth in the G7 countries over the period 1960–95. We sub-divide this period at 1973 to identify changes in performance after the first oil crisis. We employ 1989 as another dividing point to focus on the most recent experience. We decompose growth of output per capita for each country between growth of productivity and growth of input per capita. Finally, we decompose the growth of input per capita into components associated with investments in tangible assets and human capital.

International comparisons reveal important similarities among the G7 countries. Investments in tangible assets and human capital now account for the overwhelming proportion of economic growth in the G7 countries, and also explain the predominant share of international differences in output per capita. Heterogeneity in capital and labour inputs, and changes in the composition of these inputs over time are essential for identifying persistent international differences and accounting for growth.

In the fourth section we test the important implication of the neoclassical theory of growth that relative levels of output and input per capita must converge over time. For this purpose we employ the coefficient of variation to measure convergence of levels of output per capita, input per capita, and productivity among the G7 countries over the period 1960–95. As before, we divide the period at 1973 and 1989. We also analyze the convergence of capital and labour inputs per capita implied by the theory.

In the fifth section we summarize the conclusions of our study and outline alternative approaches to endogenous growth through broadening the concept of investment. The mechanism for endogenous accumulation of tangible assets captured in Solow's theory provides the most appropriate point of departure. Investments in human capital, especially investment in education, can now be incorporated into the theory. When measures of the output of research and development activities become available, investment in intellectual capital can be made endogenous.

Investment and productivity

Ongoing debates over the relative importance of investment and productivity in economic growth coincide with disputes about an appropriate role for the public sector. Productivity can be identified with 'spill-overs' of benefits that fail to provide incentives for actors within the private sector. Advocates of a larger role for the public sector suggest that these spill-overs can be guided into appropriate channels by an all-wise and beneficent government. By contrast, proponents of a smaller government search for methods of decentralizing investment decisions among participants in the private sector.

Profound differences in policy implications militate against any simple resolution of the debate on the relative importance of investment and productivity. Proponents of income redistribution will not lightly abandon the search for a 'silver bullet' that will generate economic growth without the necessity of providing incentives for investment. Advocates of growth strategies based on capital formation will not readily give credence to claims of spill-overs to beneficiaries who are difficult, or impossible, to identify.

To avoid the semantic confusion that pervades popular discussions of economic growth it is essential to be precise in defining investment. Investment is the commitment of current resources in the expectation of future returns, and can take a multiplicity of forms. The distinctive feature of investment as a source of economic growth is that the returns can be internalized by the investor. The most straightforward application of this definition is to invest in tangible assets that create property rights, including rights to the incomes that accrue to the owners of the assets.

The mechanism by which tangible investments are translated into economic growth is well understood. For example, an investor in a new industrial facility adds to the supply of these facilities and generates a stream of property income. Investment and income are linked through markets for capital assets and their services. The increase in capital input contributes to output growth in proportion to the marginal product of capital. The stream of property income can be divided between capital input and its marginal product. Identifying this marginal product with the rental price of capital provides the basis for a constant quality index of capital input.

The seminal contributions of Gary Becker (1993), Fritz Machlup (1962), Jacob Mincer (1974) and Theodore Schultz (1961) have given concrete meaning to a notion of wealth, including investments that do not create property rights. For example, a student enrolled in school or a worker participating in a training programme can be viewed as an investor. Although these investments do not create assets that can be bought or sold, the returns to higher educational qualifications or better skills in the workplace can be internalized by the investor.

An individual who completes a course of education or training adds to the supply of people with higher qualifications or skills. The resulting stream of labour income can be divided between labour input and its marginal product. The increase in labour contributes to output growth in proportion to the marginal product. Identifying this marginal product with the wage rate provides the basis for a constant quality index of labour input. While there are no asset markets for human capital, investments in human and non-human capital have in common that returns to these investments can be internalized.

The defining characteristic of productivity as a source of economic growth is that the incomes generated by higher productivity are external to the economic activities that generate growth. Publicly supported research and development programmes are a leading illustration of activities that stimulate productivity growth. These programmes can be conducted by government laboratories or financed by public subsidies to private laboratories, but the resulting benefits are external to the economic units conducting the research and development. These benefits must be distinguished carefully from the private benefits of research and development that can be internalized through the creation of intellectual property rights.[1]

The allocation of sources of economic growth between investment and productivity is critical for assessing the explanatory power of growth theory. Only substitution between capital and labour inputs resulting from investment in tangible assets is endogenous in Solow's (1956) neoclassical theory of growth. However, substitution among different types of labour inputs is the consequence of investment in human capital, while investment in tangible assets induces substitution among different types of capital input. Neither form of substitution is incorporated into Solow's (1957) model of production.

The distinction between substitution and technical change emphasized by Solow (1957) parallels the distinction between investment and productivity as sources of economic growth. However, Solow's definition of investment, like that of Simon Kuznets (1971), was limited to tangible assets. Both specifically excluded investments in human capital by relying on increases in undifferentiated hours of work as a measure of the contribution of labour input.

The contribution of investment in tangible assets to economic growth is proportional to the rental price of capital, which reflects the marginal product of capital. By contrast, the asset price of capital reflects the present value of the income from a capital asset over its entire lifetime. Both Kuznets (1971) and Solow (1970) identified the contributions of tangible assets to growth with increases in the stock of capital, weighted by asset prices. By failing to employ the marginal products of tangible assets as weights, Kuznets and Solow misallocated the sources of economic growth between investment in tangible assets and productivity.[2]

Investment can be made endogenous within a neoclassical growth model, while productivity growth is exogenous. If productivity greatly predominates among sources of growth, as indicated by Kuznets (1971) and Solow (1970), most growth is determined exogenously. Reliance on the 'Solow residual' as an explanatory factor is a powerful indictment of the limitations of the neoclassical framework. This viewpoint was expressed by Moses Abramovitz (1956), who famously characterized the Solow residual as 'A Measure of Our Ignorance'.

Jorgenson and Griliches (1967) introduced constant quality indices of capital and labour inputs and a constant quality measure of investment goods output in allocating the sources of growth between investment and productivity. This broadened greatly the concept of substitution employed by Solow (1957) and altered, irrevocably, the allocation of economic growth between investment and productivity. They showed that 85 per cent of US economic growth could be attributed to investment, while productivity accounted for only 15 per cent.[3]

The measure of labour input employed by Jorgenson and Griliches combined different types of hours worked, weighted by wage rates, into a constant quality index of labour input, using methodology Griliches (1960) had developed for US agriculture.[4] Their constant quality index of capital input combined different types of capital inputs by means of rental rates, rather than the asset prices appropriate for measuring capital stock. This model of capital as a factor of production was introduced by Jorgenson (1963) and made it possible to incorporate differences in capital consumption and the tax treatment of different types of capital income.[5]

Jorgenson and Griliches identified technology with a production possibility frontier. This extended the aggregate production function – introduced by Paul Douglas (1948) and developed by Jan Tinbergen (1942) and Solow (1957) – to include two outputs: investment, and consumption goods. Jorgenson (1966) showed that economic growth could be interpreted equivalently as 'embodied' in investment in the sense of Solow (1960), or 'disembodied' in productivity growth. Jorgenson and Griliches removed this indeterminacy by introducing constant quality indices for investment goods.[6] Christensen and Jorgenson (1969, 1970) imbedded the measurement of productivity in a complete system of US national accounts. They provided a much more detailed model of capital input based on the framework for the taxation of corporate capital income developed by Hall and Jorgenson (1967, 1969, 1971). Christensen and Jorgenson extended this framework to include non-corporate and household capital incomes. This captured the impact of differences in returns to different types of capital inputs more fully.

Christensen and Jorgenson identified the production account with a production possibility frontier describing technology, and the income and expenditure account with a social welfare function describing consumer preferences. Following Kuznets (1961), they divided the *uses* of economic growth between consumption and saving. They linked saving to the wealth account through capital accumulation equations for each type of asset. Prices for different vintages of assets were linked to rental prices of capital inputs through a parallel set of capital asset pricing equations.

In 1973, Christensen and Jorgenson constructed internally consistent income, product and wealth accounts. Separate product and income accounts are integral parts of both the US Income and Product Accounts[7] and the United Nations (1968) *System of National Accounts* designed by Richard Stone.[8] However, neither system included wealth accounts consistent with the income and product accounts.

Christensen and Jorgenson constructed income, product and wealth accounts paralleling the US National Income and Product Accounts for the period 1929–69. They also implemented a vintage accounting system for the USA on an annual basis. The complete system of vintage accounts gave stocks of assets of each vintage and their prices. The stocks were cumulated to obtain asset quantities, providing the perpetual inventory of assets employed by Raymond Goldsmith (1955–6, 1962).

The key innovation was the use of asset pricing equations to link the prices used in evaluating capital stocks, and the rental prices employed in the constant quality index of capital input.[9] In a prescient paper on the measurement of welfare, Paul Samuelson (1961) had suggested that a link between asset and rental prices was essential for the integration of income and wealth accounting.[10] The vintage system of accounts employed the specific form of this relationship developed by Jorgenson (1967).

Christensen *et al.* (1981) presented annual estimates of sources of economic growth for the USA and its major trading partners for the period 1960–73. These estimates included constant qualityindexes of capital and labour input for each country. Our first objective in this chapter is to extend these estimates to 1995 for the G7 countries.[11] We have chosen GDP as a measure of output. We include imputations for the services of consumers' durables as well as land, buildings and equipment owned by non-profit institutions in order to preserve comparability in the treatment of income from different types of capital.

Our constant quality index of capital input is based on a disaggregation of the capital stock among the twenty-one categories given in Table 8.1. These are classified by asset type and ownership to reflect differences in capital consumption and tax treatment among assets. We derive estimates of capital stock and property income for each type of capital input from national accounting data. Similarly, our constant quality index of labour input is based on a disaggregation of the workforce among the twenty categories presented in Table 8.2. These are classified by sex, educational attainment and employment status. For each country we derive estimates of hours worked and labour compensation for type of labour input from labour force surveys.

Table 8.1 Disaggregation of capital by asset characteristics

Asset type	Ownership sector
1. Equipment	1. Corporations and government
2. Non-residential structures	2. Unincorporated businesses
3. Residential structures	3. Households and non-profit institutions
4. Non-farm inventories	4. General government
5. Farm inventories	
6. Consumer durables	
7. Residential land	
8. Non-residential land	

Table 8.2 Disaggregation of labour by demographic characteristics

Sex

Educational attainment:
1. 1–8 years grade school
2. 1–3 years secondary school
3. Completed secondary school
4. 1–3 years college
5. 4 or more years of college

Employment Status
1. Business sector employee
2. Self-employed or unpaid family worker
3. General government employee

Sources of growth

In Table 8.3 we present output per capita for the G7 countries over the period 1960–95, expressed relative to the US in 1985. We use 1985 purchasing power parities from the OECD (1987) to convert quantities of output per capita from domestic currencies for each country into US dollars. The USA was the leader in per capita output throughout the period, while Canada ranked second for most of the period. Among the remaining five countries, the UK started at the top and Japan at the bottom; by 1995, these roles were interchanged, with Japan overtaking all four European countries and the UK lagging behind among all these countries except Italy.

In Table 8.4 we present input per capita for the G7 countries over the period 1960–95, relative to US input per capita in 1985. We express quantities of input per capita in US dollars, using purchasing power parities constructed for this study.[12] The US was the leader in per capita input as well as output throughout the period. Germany started in second place, but lost its position to Canada in 1975, and to Japan in 1976. In 1995, Japan ranked next to the USA input per capita, with Canada third. France started at the bottom of the ranking and remained there for most of the period. Canada, France, Italy, and Japan grew relative to the USA while Germany and the UK declined.

Table 8.3 Growth in output and input per capita, and productivity (percentages)

Year	USA	Canada	UK	France	Germany	Italy	Japan
Output per capita							
1960–73	2.89	3.20	2.74	4.26	3.74	4.62	8.77
1973–89	1.90	2.45	1.75	2.04	2.15	2.69	2.71
1973–95	1.65	1.68	1.38	1.74	2.02	2.34	2.46
1989–95	0.97	−0.37	0.42	0.92	1.66	1.40	1.81
1960–89	2.34	2.79	2.19	3.04	2.86	3.56	5.43
1960–95	2.11	2.24	1.89	2.68	2.66	3.19	4.81
Input per capita							
1960–73	1.53	1.70	0.98	2.15	1.24	0.79	2.42
1973–89	1.45	2.21	1.10	0.74	1.25	2.42	2.15
1973–95	1.24	1.67	1.28	0.91	1.39	2.17	2.01
1989–95	0.88	0.21	1.77	1.37	1.78	1.49	1.63
1960–89	1.49	1.98	1.04	1.37	1.25	1.69	2.27
1960–95	1.35	1.68	1.17	1.37	1.34	1.66	2.16
Productivity							
1960–73	1.36	1.51	1.76	2.11	2.50	3.82	6.35
1973–89	0.45	0.23	0.65	1.31	0.90	0.27	0.56
1973–95	0.41	0.01	0.10	0.83	0.62	0.17	0.45
1989–95	0.29	−0.59	−1.35	−0.45	−0.11	−0.10	0.18
1960–89	0.86	0.80	1.15	1.67	1.62	1.86	3.16
1960–95	0.76	0.57	0.72	1.30	1.32	1.53	2.65

Table 8.4 Levels of output and input per capita, and productivity (USA = 100.0 in 1985)

Year	USA	Canada	UK	France	Germany	Italy	Japan
Output per capita							
1960	55.6	43.1	37.5	29.2	32.9	22.7	17.3
1973	80.9	65.4	53.6	50.9	53.6	41.4	54.0
1989	109.7	96.7	70.8	70.6	75.6	63.7	83.3
1995	116.3	94.6	72.6	74.6	83.5	69.2	92.8
Input per capita							
1960	70.2	55.6	53.0	42.5	61.7	44.8	50.1
1973	85.6	69.4	60.1	56.3	72.5	49.7	68.6
1989	108.0	98.8	71.7	63.3	88.5	73.2	96.7
1995	112.5	100.1	79.7	68.7	98.5	80.1	106.7
Productivity							
1960	79.2	77.5	70.9	68.8	53.4	50.7	34.5
1973	94.5	94.3	89.1	90.5	73.9	83.3	78.7
1989	101.6	97.9	98.8	111.5	85.4	87.0	86.1
1995	103.4	94.5	91.1	108.6	84.8	86.5	87.0

Finally, in Table 8.4 we present productivity levels for the G7 countries over the period 1960–95, where productivity is defined as the ratio of output to input. In 1960 the US was the productivity leader, with Canada close behind. In 1970, Canada became the first country to overtake the US, remaining slightly above the US level for most of the period ending 1984. France surpassed the USA in 1979 and became the international productivity leader after 1980. The UK overtook Canada and nearly overtook the USA in 1987, but fell behind both countries in 1990. Japan surpassed Germany in 1970 and Italy in 1990, while Italy overtook Germany in 1963 and maintained its lead during most of the period ending 1995.

We summarize growth in output and input per capita and productivity for the G7 countries in Table 8.3. We present annual average growth rates for the period 1960–89 and 1960–95, and the sub-periods 1960–73, 1973–89 and 1989–95. Japan was the leader in output growth for the period as a whole and before 1973. The UK grew more slowly than the remaining six countries during the period as a whole and after 1960. Output growth slowed in all the G7 countries after 1989, and Canada's growth rate was negative. Differences in growth rates among the G7 countries declined substantially after 1973.

Japan also led the G7 in growth of input per capita for the period 1960–95 and before 1973. Italy was the leader during the sub-period 1973–89, and Germany led during 1989–95. There is little evidence of a slowdown input growth after 1973; differences among input growth rates are much less than among output growth rates. Japan led the G7 in productivity growth for the period as a whole and before 1973, while France was the leader from 1973 to

1989. All the G7 countries – with the exception of Japan and the USA – experienced negative productivity growth after 1989. The USA had a slightly higher productivity growth rate than Japan during this period.

Our constant quality index of capital input weights capital stocks for each of the twenty-one categories given in Table 8.1 by rental prices, defined as property compensation per unit of capital. By contrast, an index of capital stock weights different types of capital by asset prices rather than the rental prices appropriate for capital input. The ratio of capital input to capital stock measures the average quality of a unit of capital, as reflected in its marginal product. This enables us to assess the magnitude of differences between the constant quality index of capital input and the unweighted index of capital stock employed by Kuznets (1971) and Solow (1970).

In Table 8.6 we present capital input per capita for the G7 countries over the period 1960–95, expressed relative to the USA in 1985. The US was the leader in capital input per capita up to 1991, when Canada emerged as the international leader. All countries grew substantially relative to the USA but only Canada surpassed the US level. Germany led the remaining five countries throughout the period, while the UK was the laggard among these countries, except for the period 1962–73, when Japan ranked lower.

The picture for capital stock per capita has some similarities to capital input, but there are important differences. The USA led throughout the period in capital stock, while Canada overtook the USA in capital input. France, Germany and Italy had similar stock levels throughout the period, with Italy leading this group of three countries in 1995. Similarly, Japan and the UK had similar stock levels throughout the period; Japan ranked last until 1976, but surpassed the UK in that year. Capital stock levels do not reflect accurately the substitutions among capital inputs that accompany investments in tangible assets.

Capital quality, presented in Table 8.6, is the ratio of capital input to capital stock. The behaviour of capital quality highlights the differences between the constant quality index of capital input and capital stock. Germany was the international leader in capital quality through most of the period 1960–95, while the US ranked at the bottom. There are important changes in capital quality over time, and persistent differences among countries. Heterogeneity of capital input within each country and between countries must be taken into account in international comparisons of economic performance.

We summarize growth in capital input and capital stock per capita and capita quality for the G7 countries in Table 8.5. Italy was the international leader in capital input growth and the US the laggard for the period 1960–95. There was a modest slowdown in capital input growth after 1973 and again after 1989, and similar slowdowns in capital stock growth. Italy was the leader in capital quality growth and Japan the laggard.

Our constant quality index of labour input weights hours worked for each of the twenty categories given in Table 8.2 by wage rates defined in terms of labour compensation per hour. An index of hours worked adds together

Table 8.5 Growth in capital input and capital stock per capita, and capital quality (percentages)

Year	USA	Canada	UK	France	Germany	Italy	Japan
Capital input per capita							
1960–73	2.32	3.03	3.34	5.15	6.00	6.20	2.93
1973–89	2.03	3.40	3.02	3.06	3.02	4.65	3.63
1973–95	1.68	2.98	2.82	2.82	2.95	4.23	3.51
1989–95	0.74	1.85	2.29	2.19	2.77	3.12	3.18
1960–89	2.16	3.24	3.17	4.00	4.36	5.34	3.32
1960–95	1.92	3.00	3.02	3.69	4.09	4.96	3.29
Capital stock per capita							
1960–73	1.77	2.54	3.06	5.42	5.54	5.01	2.97
1973–89	1.28	2.73	2.68	3.17	2.63	3.52	3.94
1973–95	1.11	2.23	2.48	2.88	2.71	3.42	3.80
1989–95	0.64	0.91	1.94	2.08	2.92	3.15	3.42
1960–89	1.50	2.65	2.85	4.18	3.93	4.18	3.51
1960–95	1.35	2.35	2.69	3.82	3.76	4.01	3.49
Capital quality							
1960–73	0.55	0.49	0.29	–0.27	0.46	1.19	–0.04
1973–89	0.75	0.67	0.35	–0.11	0.40	1.13	–0.32
1973–95	0.57	0.75	0.35	–0.05	0.25	0.81	–0.30
1989–95	0.09	0.95	0.34	0.10	–0.15	–0.03	–0.24
1960–89	0.66	0.59	0.32	–0.18	0.43	1.16	–0.19
1960–95	0.56	0.65	0.32	–0.14	0.33	0.95	–0.20

Table 8.6 Levels of capital input and capital stock per capita, and capital quality (USA = 100.0 in 1985)

Year	USA	Canada	UK	France	Germany	Italy	Japan
Capital input per capita							
1960	58.5	41.7	21.0	24.0	26.0	17.1	21.6
1973	79.0	61.9	32.4	46.8	56.6	38.4	31.6
1989	109.4	106.7	52.6	76.4	91.9	80.7	58.4
1995	114.3	119.2	60.4	87.1	108.5	97.3	68.3
Capital stock per capita							
1960	68.2	43.3	18.8	18.8	20.1	19.6	17.3
1973	85.8	60.3	28.0	38.1	41.3	37.5	25.4
1989	105.3	93.3	42.9	63.4	62.9	65.9	47.8
1995	109.4	98.5	48.2	71.8	74.9	79.6	58.7
Capital quality							
1960	85.8	96.3	111.8	127.2	129.1	87.6	124.7
1973	92.1	102.7	116.1	122.8	137.1	102.2	124.1
1989	103.9	114.3	122.7	120.6	146.1	122.5	118.0
1995	104.5	121.0	125.2	121.3	144.8	122.2	116.3

different types of hours without taking quality differences into account. The ratio of labour input to hours worked measures the average quality of an hour of labour, as reflected in its marginal product. This enables us to assess the magnitude of differences between the constant quality index of labour input and the unweighted index of hours worked employed by Kuznets (1971) and Solow (1970).

In Table 8.8 we present labour input per capita for the G7 countries for the period 1960–95, relative to the USA in 1985. The UK led until 1969, but was overtaken by Japan in that year. The USA surpassed the UK in 1981, but the two countries grew in parallel through 1995, with the USA maintaining a slight lead for most of the period. France ranked at the bottom of the G7 for most of the period, but led Italy from 1963 to 1979. Japan remained the international leader through 1995 with levels of labour input from 10–15 per cent above the USA and the UK and almost double that of France.

The picture for hours worked per capital has some similarities to labour input, but there are important differences. Japan was the international leader in hours worked per capital throughout the period, while Germany led the four European countries for most of the period. The US overtook France in 1975, and Germany and the UK in 1977. At the beginning of the period, Canada ranked last, but lost this position to Italy in 1965. Italy was the laggard in hours worked until 1983, when France fell to the bottom of the G7, remaining there through 1995. Hours worked do not accurately reflect the substitutions among labour inputs that accompany investments in human capital.

Labour quality, presented in Table 8.8, is the ratio of the constant quality index of labour input to the unweighted index of hours worked. The behaviour of labour quality highlights the differences between labour input and hours worked. The UK was the leader in labour quality, but was surpassed by Canada in 1981; labour quality in the two countries grew in parallel through 1995. Japan was the laggard among G7 countries in labour quality throughout most of the period 1960–95, briefly surpassing France in 1977; and the two countries grew in parallel for the rest of the period. There are important changes in labour quality over time and persistent differences among countries. Heterogeneity within each country and between countries must be taken into account in international comparisons of economic growth.

We summarize growth in labour input and hours worked per capita and labour quality in Table 8.7. Japan led the G7 countries in labour input growth for the period 1960–95 and before 1973. Canada was the international leader during the subperiod 1973–89, while the USA was the leader after 1989. The USA led growth in hours worked for the period as a whole and after 1989, while Japan was the leader before 1973, and Italy led between 1973 and 1989. Growth was positive throughout the period for Japan and the USA, mostly negative for the four European countries, and alternately positive and negative

Table 8.7 Growth in labour input and hours worked per capita, and labour quality (percentages)

Year	USA	Canada	UK	France	Germany	Italy	Japan
Labour input per capita							
1960–73	1.16	1.23	–0.48	0.31	–1.20	–1.25	1.96
1973–89	0.92	1.23	–0.03	–0.82	0.13	1.21	1.13
1973–95	0.88	0.66	0.40	–0.41	0.34	0.97	0.98
1989–95	0.78	–0.87	1.54	0.68	0.90	0.34	0.60
1960–89	1.02	1.23	–0.23	–0.32	–0.47	0.11	1.50
1960–95	0.98	0.87	0.07	–0.14	–0.23	0.15	1.35
Hours worked per capita							
1960–73	0.37	0.31	–1.01	–0.57	–1.53	–1.38	0.60
1973–89	0.56	0.69	–0.26	–1.41	–0.34	0.86	0.21
1973–95	0.44	0.03	0.01	–1.24	–0.16	0.55	0.21
1989–95	0.13	–1.70	0.72	–0.79	0.34	–0.27	0.21
1960–89	0.47	0.52	–0.60	–1.03	–0.87	–0.15	0.38
1960–95	0.42	0.14	–0.37	–0.99	–0.67	–0.17	0.35
Labour quality							
1960–73	0.79	0.92	0.53	0.88	0.32	0.13	1.36
1973–89	0.36	0.54	0.23	0.58	0.47	0.35	0.92
1973–95	0.44	0.62	0.39	0.83	0.50	0.42	0.78
1989–95	0.65	0.84	0.82	1.47	0.56	0.62	0.39
1960–89	0.55	0.71	0.37	0.72	0.40	0.25	1.12
1960–95	0.57	0.73	0.44	0.85	0.43	0.31	0.99

Table 8.8 Levels of labour input and hours worked per capita, and labour quality (USA = 100.0 in 1985)

Year	USA	Canada	UK	France	Germany	Italy	Japan
Labour input per capita							
1960	78.3	70.3	106.2	68.0	100.6	71.6	79.5
1973	91.0	82.4	99.8	70.8	86.0	60.8	102.6
1989	105.4	100.4	99.3	62.0	87.8	73.8	122.9
1995	110.5	95.3	108.9	64.6	92.7	75.4	127.4
Hours worked per capita							
1960	91	80	110	105	120	89	134
1973	95.5	83.7	96.6	97.4	98.7	74.6	145.3
1989	104.5	93.4	92.7	77.8	93.5	85.5	150.2
1995	105.3	84.3	96.8	74.2	95.4	84.2	152.1
Labour quality							
1960	86.0	87.4	96.4	64.8	83.6	80.3	59.2
1973	95.3	98.5	103.2	72.6	87.2	81.6	70.6
1989	100.9	107.5	107.1	79.7	94.0	86.3	81.8
1995	104.9	113.0	112.5	87.1;	97.2	89.6	83.7

for Canada. Growth in labour quality was positive for all seven countries, with a modest decline after 1973 and a revival after 1989. In Table 8.8 we present labour input and hours worked per capita and labour quality relative to the USA in 1985.

In Figure 8.1 we assess the relative importance of investment and productivity in per capita growth for the G7 countries. For Canada, the UK, and the USA, investments in tangible assets and human capital greatly predominated as sources of growth over the period 1960–95. We attribute slightly more than half of Japanese growth to productivity, while proportions for the four European countries – France, Germany, Italy and the UK – are slightly less than half. After 1973, growth in output and productivity declined for all seven countries; however, growth in input has not declined, so that the relative importance of productivity has diminished sharply.

In Figure 8.2 we combine estimates of growth in capital input, capital stock and capital quality to assess the importance of changes in quality. Capital input growth is positive for all countries for the period 1960–95, and all three sub-periods. Capital quality growth is positive for the period as a whole for all G7 countries except France and Japan. Although capital stock greatly predominates in capital input growth, capita quality is quantitatively significant, so that the heterogeneity of capital must be taken into account in assessing the role of investment in tangible assets.

Finally, in Figure 8.3 we combine estimates of growth in labour input, hours worked and labour quality to assess the importance of hours and quality. Labour input growth in negative for the period 1960–95 in France and Germany, near zero for the UK, and slightly positive for Italy. Growth in hours worked is mainly negative for all four countries throughout the period. However, growth in labour quality has helped to offset the decline in hours worked in Europe. For Canada, Japan and the USA, labour quality predominates in the growth of labour input, so that the heterogeneity of labour input is essential in assessing the role of investment in human capital.

Convergence

The objective of modelling economic growth is to explain the *sources* and *uses* of growth endogenously. National income is the starting point for assessments of the *uses* of growth through consumption and saving. The concept of a 'measure of economic welfare', introduced by William Nordhaus and James Tobin (1972), is the key to augmenting national income to broaden the concepts of consumption and saving. Similarly, gross domestic product is the starting point for attributing the *sources* of economic growth to growth in productivity and investments in tangible assets and human capital.

Denison (1967) compared differences in growth rates for national income per person employed for the period 1950–62, with differences of levels in

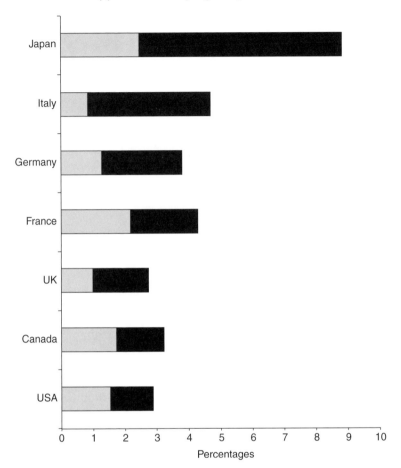

(a) Sources of output growth, 1960–73

Figure 8.1   Sources of output growth, 1960–95

1960 for eight European countries and the USA. However, he overlooked the separate roles for a production account with the national product and inputs of capital and labour services, and an income and expenditure account with national income, consumption, and saving. From an economic point of view this ignored the distinction between the *sources* and *uses* of economic growth.

Denison compared differences in both growth rates and levels of national income per person employed. The eight European countries were characterized overall by more rapid growth and a lower level of national income per

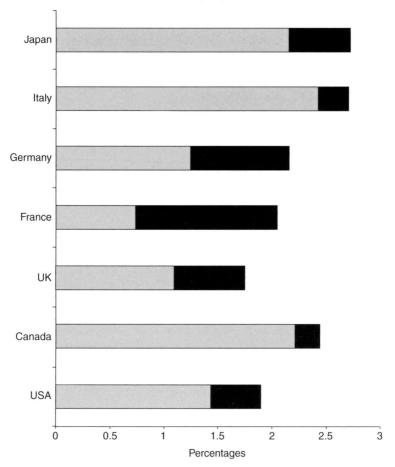

(b) Sources of output growth, 1973–89

Figure 8.1   (continued)

capita. Although this association was not monotonic for comparisons between individual countries and the USA, Denison concluded that:[13]

> Aside from short-term aberrations Europe should be able to report higher growth rates, at least in national income per person employed, for a long time. Americans should expect this and not be disturbed by it.

Kuznets (1971) provided elaborate comparisons of growth rates for the fourteen countries included in his study. Unlike Denison (1967), he did not

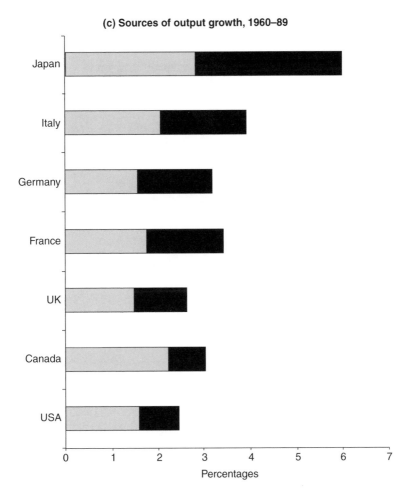

(c) Sources of output growth, 1960–89

Figure 8.1 (*continued*)

provide level comparisons. Maddison (1982) filled this gap by comparing levels of national product for sixteen countries[14] on the basis of estimates of purchasing power parities by Kravis *et al.* (1978).[15] These estimates have been updated by successive versions of the Penn World Table and made it possible to reconsider the issue of convergence of output per capita raised by Denison (1967).[16]

Abramovitz (1986) was the first to take up the challenge of analyzing convergence of output per capita among Maddison's sixteen countries. He found that convergence appeared to characterize output levels in the postwar period, but not the period before 1914 and the interwar period. Baumol (1986)

(d) Sources of output growth, 1989–95

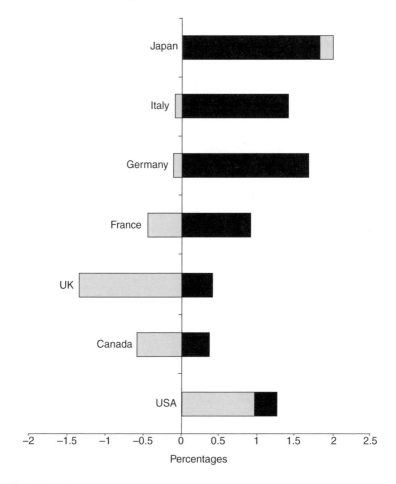

Figure 8.1   (continued)

formalized these results by running a regression of growth rate of GDP per hour worked over the period 1870–1979 on the 1870 level of GDP per hour worked.[17] A negative regression coefficient is evidence for 'beta-convergence' of GDP levels.

In a notable paper on 'Crazy Explanations for the Productivity Slowdown', Romer (1987) derived a version of the growth regression from Solow's (1970) growth model with a Cobb–Douglas production function. Romer also extended the data set for growth regressions from Maddison's (1982) group

(e) Sources of output growth, 1960–95

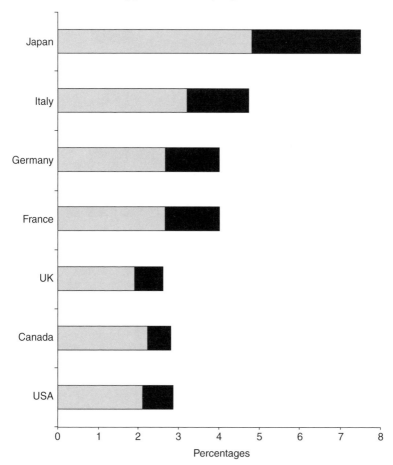

Figure 8.1   (continued)

of sixteen advanced countries to the 115 countries included in Penn World Table (Mark 3), presented by Summers and Heston (1984). Romer's key finding was that an indirect estimate of the Cobb–Douglas elasticity of output with respect to capital was close to three-quarters. The share of capital in output implied by Solow's model was less than half as great on average.[18]

Mankiw *et al.* (1992) undertook a defence of the neoclassical framework of Kuznets (1971) and Solow (1970). The empirical portion of their study is based on data for ninety-eight countries from the Penn World Table (Mark 4), presented by Summers and Heston (1988). Like Romer (1987), Mankiw *et al.*

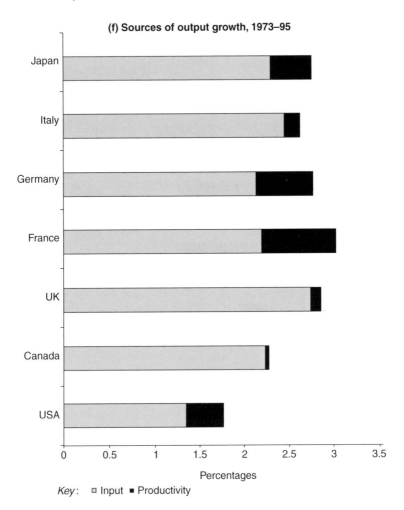

Figure 8.1   (continued)

(1992) derived a growth equation from the Solow (1970) model; however, they also augmented this model by allowing for investment in human capital.

The results of Mankiw *et al.* (1992) provided empirical support for the augmented Solow model. There was clear evidence of the convergence predicted by the model, where convergence was conditional on the ratio of investment to GDP and the rate of population growth; both are determinants of steady-state output. In addition, the estimated Cobb–Douglas elasticity of

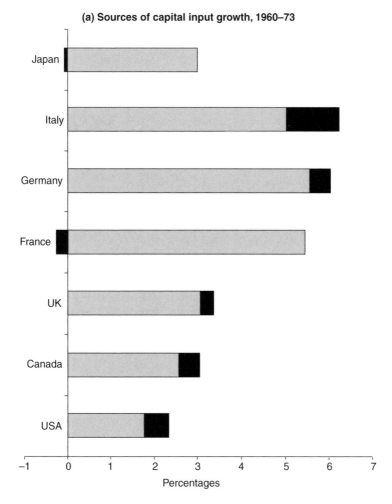

Figure 8.2 Sources of capital input growth, 1960–95

output with respect to capital coincided with the share of capital in the value of output. However, the rate of convergence of output per capita was too slow to be consistent with 1970 version of the Solow model.

Islam (1995) exploited an important feature of the Summers and Heston (1988) data overlooked in previous empirical studies – namely, benchmark comparisons of levels of the national product at five-year intervals beginning in 1960 and ending in 1985. Using econometric methods for panel data, Islam

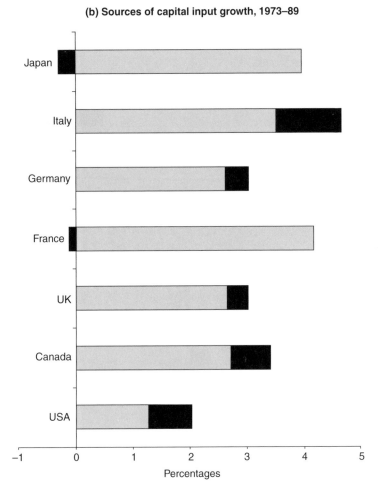

(b) Sources of capital input growth, 1973–89

Figure 8.2   (continued)

tested an assumption maintained in growth regressions, such as those of Mankiw *et al.* (1992). Their study, like that of Romer (1987), assumed identical technologies for all countries included in the Summer–Heston data sets.

Substantial differences in levels of productivity among countries have been documented by Denison (1967), Christensen *et al.* (1981), and in the second section, above. By introducing panel data techniques, Islam (1995) was able to allow for these differences. He corroborated the findings of Mankiw *et al.* (1992) that the elasticity of output with respect to capital input coincided with

(c) Sources of capital input growth, 1960–89

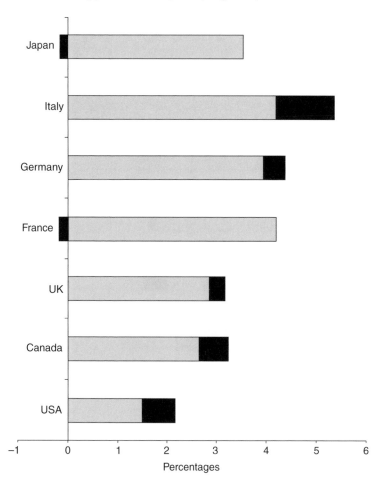

Figure 8.2 (continued)

the share of capital in the value of output. This further undermined the empirical support for the existence of the increasing returns and spill-overs analyzed in the theoretical models of Romer (1986, 1990).

In addition, Islam (1995) found that the rate of convergence of output per capita among countries in the Summers and Heston (1988) data set was precisely that required to substantiate the *un-augmented* version of the Solow (1970). In short, 'crazy explanations' for the productivity slowdown, like those

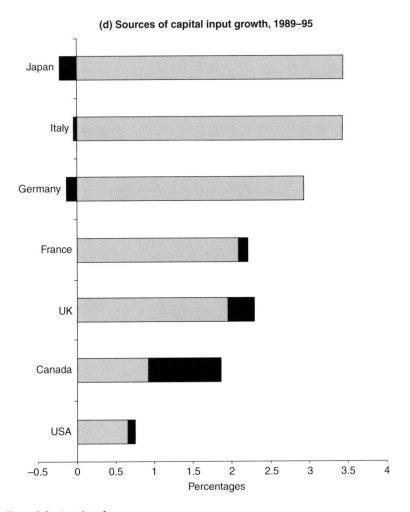

Figure 8.2   (continued)

propounded by Romer (1987, 1994), are not required. Moreover, the model did not require augmentation, as suggested by Mankiw *et al.* (1992). However, differences in productivity among these countries must taken into account in modelling differences in growth rates.

The conclusion from Islam's (1995) research is that the Solow model is the appropriate point of departure for modelling the accumulation of tangible assets. For this purpose it is unnecessary to endogenize investment in human capital as well. The rationale for this key empirical finding is that the transition

(e) Sources of capital input growth, 1960–95

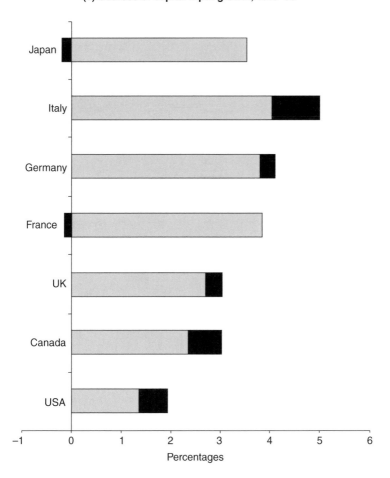

Figure 8.2 (*continued*)

path to balanced growth equilibrium requires decades after a change in policies that affect investment in tangible assets, such as tax policies. By contrast, the transition after a change in policies affecting investment in human capital requires as much as a century.

In Figure 8.4 we present coefficients of variation for levels of output and input per capita and productivity for the G7 countries annually for the period 1960–95. The coefficients for output decline by almost a factor of two between 1960 and 1974, but then remain stable throughout the rest of the period.

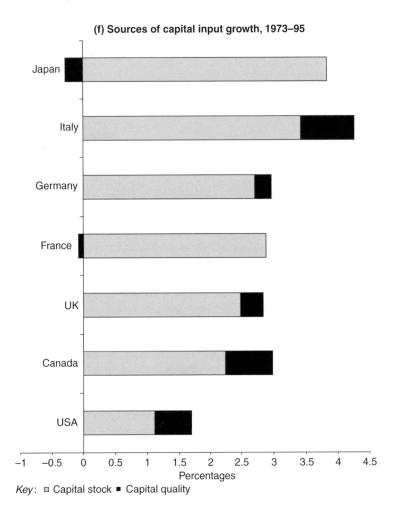

Figure 8.2   (continued)

Coefficients for productivity decline by more than a factor of two between 1960 and 1970, and then stabilize. Coefficients for input per capita are nearly unchanged throughout the period. This is evidence for the 'sigma-convergence' of output and input per capita and productivity implied by Solow's neoclassical theory of growth, allowing for differences in productivity of the type identified by Islam.

Figure 8.5 presents coefficients of variation for levels of capital input and capital stock per capita and capital quality for the G7 countries. The coefficients for capital input decline gradually throughout the period.

(a) Sources of labour input growth, 1960–73

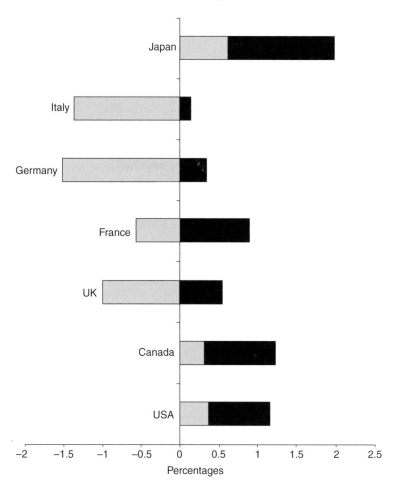

Figure 8.3 Sources of labour input growth, 1960–95

Coefficients for capital stock are slightly larger than those for capital input, but behave in a similar manner. Coefficients for capital quality are stable until 1968 and then decline to a slightly lower level after 1971. This is also evidence of the sigma-convergence implied by Solow's growth model with persistent differences in levels of capital quality among countries.

Finally, coefficients of variation for levels of labour input and hours worked per capita and labour quality for the G7 are given in Figure 8.6. The coefficients for labour input are stable through 1983 and then rise gradually. The

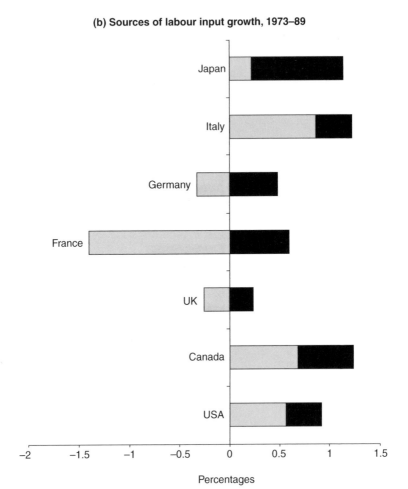

(b) Sources of labour input growth, 1973–89

Figure 8.3   (continued)

coefficients for hours worked rise gradually until 1964 and then stabilize for most of the period. The coefficients for labour quality decline gradually. Again, this is evidence for sigma-convergence with persistent international differences in labour quality.

The evidence of sigma-convergence among the G7 countries presented in Figures 8.4, 8.5 and 8.6 is consistent with a new version of Solow's neoclassical growth model, characterized by persistent but stable international differences in productivity, capital quality, labour quality, and hours worked per capita. A simpler version of Solow's model with constant

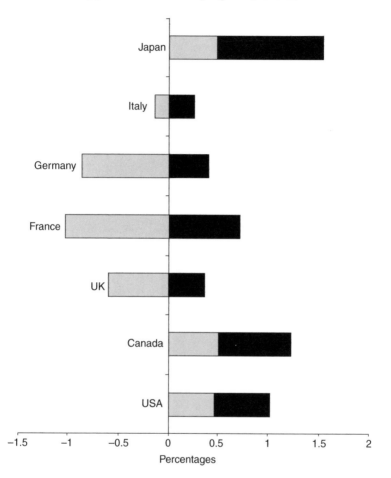

(c) Sources of labour input growth, 1960–89

Figure 8.3 (continued)

differences in productivity among countries was identified in Islam's research on beta-convergence. This version successfully rationalizes differences in growth of per capita output among a much broader group of countries over the period 1960–85.

Endogenizing growth

Constant quality indices of labour input are an essential first step in incorporating investments in human capital into empirical studies of

(d) Sources of labour input growth, 1989–95

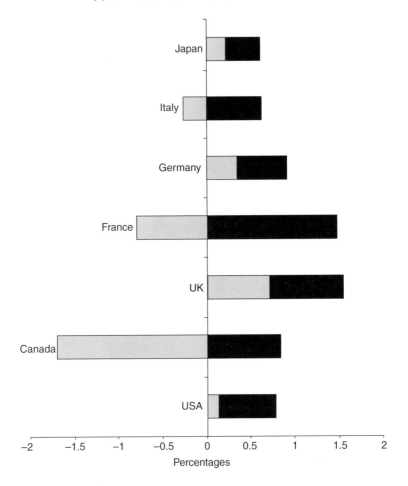

Figure 8.3   (continued)

economic growth. Jorgenson and Fraumeni (1989) extended the vintage accounting system developed by Christensen and Jorgenson (1973) to incorporate these investments. The essential idea is to treat individual members of the US population as human assets with 'asset prices' given by their lifetime labour incomes. Jorgenson and Fraumeni implemented the vintage accounting system for both human and non-human capital for the USA on an annual basis for the period 1948–84.

(e) Sources of labour input growth, 1960–95

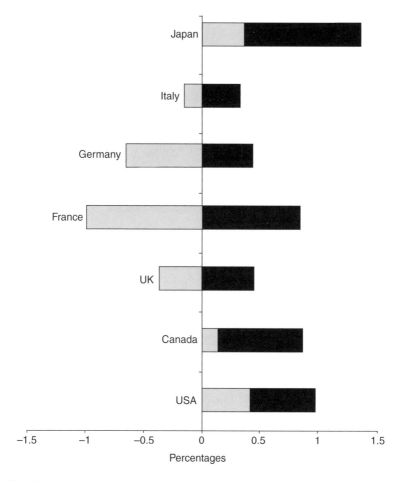

Figure 8.3 (continued)

Asset prices for tangible assets can be observed directly from market transactions in investment goods; intertemporal capital asset pricing equations are used to derive rental prices for capital services, because human capital wage rates correspond to rental prices and can be observed directly from transactions in the labour market. Lifetime labour incomes are derived by applying asset pricing equations to these wage rates. Lifetime incomes are analogous to the asset prices used in accounting for investment in tangible assets.

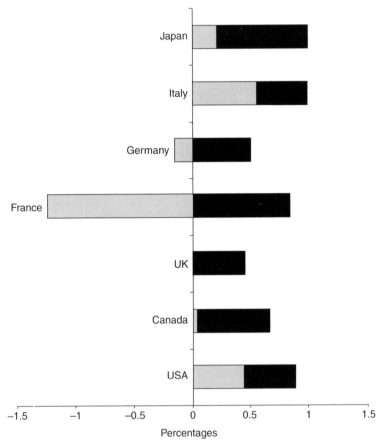

(f) Sources of labour input growth, 1973–95

Key: □ Hours worked ■ Labour quality

Figure 8.3   (continued)

Jorgenson and Fraumeni (1992b) have developed a measure of the output of the US education sector. The point of departure is that, while education is a service industry, its output is investment in human capital. Investment in education can be measured from the impact of increases in educational attainment on lifetime incomes of all individuals enrolled in school. Investment in education, measured in this way, is similar in magnitude to the value of working time for all individuals in the labour force.

Second, Jorgenson and Fraumeni (1992a) measured the inputs of the education sector, beginning with the purchased inputs recorded in the outlays

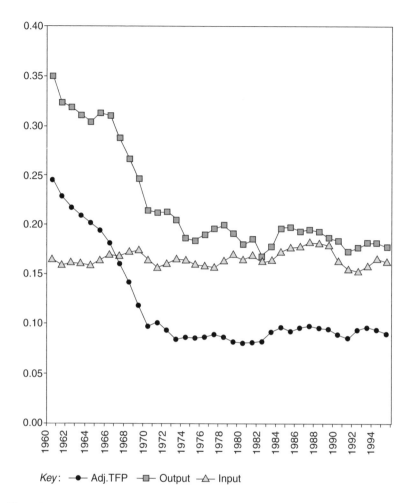

Figure 8.4 Convergence of output and input per capita, and productivity

of educational institutions. A major part of the value of the output of educational institutions accrues to students in the form of increases in their lifetime incomes. Treating these increases as compensation for student time, this time is evaluated as an input into the educational process. Given the outlays of educational institutions and the value of student time, the growth of the education sector can be allocated to its sources.

An alternative approach, employed by Schultz (1961), Machlup (1962), Nordhaus and Tobin (1972), and many others, is to apply Goldsmith's (1955–6) perpetual inventory method to private and public expenditure on educational

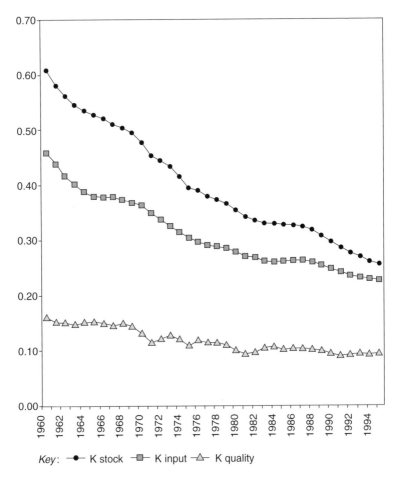

Figure 8.5   Convergence of capital input, capital stock per capita, and capital quality

services. Unfortunately, the approach has foundered on the absence of a satisfactory measure of the output of the educational sector and the lack of an obvious rationale for capital consumption.[19]

Given vintage accounts for human and non-human capital, Jorgenson and Fraumeni (1989) constructed a system of income, product and wealth accounts, paralleling the system Jorgenson had developed with Christensen. In these accounts, the value of human wealth was more than ten times the value of non-human wealth, while investment in human capital was five times the investment in tangible assets. 'Full' investment in the US economy is defined as the sum of these two types of investment. Similarly, the value of non-market labour activities is added to personal consumption expenditures

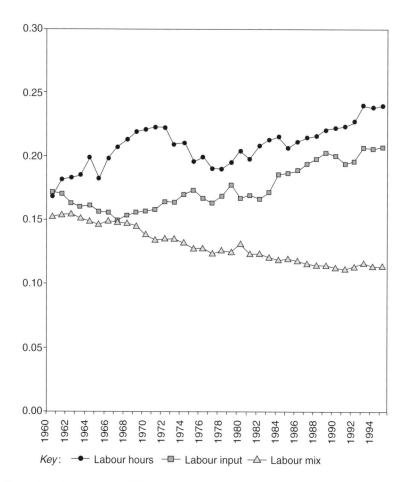

Figure 8.6 Convergence of labour input and hours worked per capita, and labour quality

to obtain 'full' consumption. The product measure included these new measures of investment and consumption.

Since the complete accounting system included a production account with 'full' measures of capital and labour inputs,[20] Jorgenson and Fraumeni were able to generate a new set of accounts for the *sources* of US economic growth. The system also included an income and expenditure account with income from labour services in both market and non-market activities, and an allocation of 'full' income between consumption and saving. This provided the basis for the *uses* of US economic growth, and a new Measure of Economic Welfare. The system was completed by a wealth account containing both human wealth and tangible assets.

Jorgenson and Fraumeni aggregated the growth of education and non-education sectors of the US economy to obtain a new measure of US economic growth. Combining this with measures of input growth, they obtained a new set of accounts for the sources of growth. Productivity contributes almost nothing to the growth of the education sector and only a modest proportion to output growth for the economy as a whole, so that productivity accounts for only 17 per cent of growth.

The introduction of endogenous investment in education increases the explanatory power of the theory of economic growth to 83 per cent. However, it is important to emphasize that growth is measured differently. The traditional framework for economic measurement of Kuznets (1971) and Solow (1970) excludes non-market activities, such as those that characterize the major portion of investment in education. The intuition is familiar to any teacher, including teachers of economics: what the students do is far more important than what the teachers do, even if the subject matter is the theory of economic growth.

A third approximation to the theory of economic growth results from incorporating all forms of investment in human capital, including education, child-rearing, and the addition of new members to the population. Fertility could be made endogenous by using the approach of Barro and Becker (1989), and Becker and Barro (1988). Child-rearing could be made endogenous by modelling the household as a producing sector along the lines of the model of the educational sector outlined above. The results presented by Jorgenson and Fraumeni (1989) show that this would endogenize 86 per cent of US economic growth. This is a significant, but not overwhelming, gain in explanatory power.

In principle, investment in new technology could be made endogenous by extending the accounting framework to incorporate investment in new technology. BEA (1994) has provided a satellite system of accounts for research and development, based on Goldsmith's (1955–6) perpetual inventory method, applied to private and public expenditure. Unfortunately, this is subject to the same limitations as the approach to human capital of Schultz (1961) and Machlup (1962). The BEA satellite system has foundered on the absence of a satisfactory measure of the output of R&D and the lack of an appropriate rationale for capital consumption.

The standard model for investment in new technology, formulated by Griliches (1973) is based on a production function incorporating inputs of services from intellectual capital accumulated through investment in R&D. Intellectual capital is treated as a factor of production in precisely the same way as tangible assets were in the second section, above. Hall (1993) has developed the implications of this model for the pricing of the services of intellectual capital input and the evaluation of intellectual capital assets.

The model of capital as a factor of production first proposed by Jorgenson (1963) has been applied successfully to tangible assets and human capital.

However, implementation for intellectual capital would require a system of vintage accounts, including not only accumulation equations for stocks of accumulated research and development, but also asset pricing equations. These equations are essential for separating the revaluation of intellectual property because of price changes over time from depreciation of this property due to ageing. This is required for measuring the quantity of intellectual capital input and its marginal product.

Notes

1. Zvi Griliches (1992, 1995) has provided detailed surveys of spill-overs from investment in research and development. Griliches (1992) gives a list of survey papers on spill-overs.

2. The measurement conventions of Kuznets and Solow remain in common use. See the references given by Jorgenson (1990) and the following recent examples: Baily and Schultze (1990); Robert Gordon (1990); Steven Englander and Andrew Gurney (1994); Lawrence Lau (1996); and Robert Hall and Charles Jones (1997).

3. Jorgenson and Griliches (1967), table IX, p. 272, attributed 13 per cent of growth to the relative utilization of capital, measured by energy consumption as a proportion of capacity, however, this is inappropriate at the aggregate level, as Edward Denison (1974, p. 56) pointed out. For additional details, see Jorgenson *et al.* (1987), especially pp. 179–81.

4. Constant quality indices of labour input are discussed in detail by Jorgenson *et al.* (1987), 3 and 8, pp. 69–108 and 261–300; Bureau of Labour Statistics (1993); and Ho and Jorgenson (1998).

5. Detailed surveys of empirical research on the measurement of capital input are given by Jorgenson (1996) and Triplett (1996). BLS (1983) compiled a constant quality index of capita input for its official estimates of productivity, renamed as *multifactor productivity*. BLS retained hours worked as a measure of labour input until 11 July 1994, when it released a new multifactor productivity measure incorporating a constant quality index of labour input.

6. A detailed history of constant quality price indices is given by Ernst Berndt (1991). Gordon (1990) constructed constant quality indices for all types of producers' durable equipment in the national accounts, and Paul Pieper (1989, 1990) provided constant quality indices for structures.

7. See Bureau of Economic Analysis (1995).

8. The United Nations System of National Accounts (SNA) is summarized by Stone (1992) in his Nobel Prize address. The SNA has been revised by the Inter-Secretariat Working Group on National Accounts (1993).

9. Constant quality price indices for investment goods of different ages or vintages were developed by Hall (1971). This made it possible for Charles Hulten and Frank Wykoff (1982) to estimate relative efficiencies by age for all types of tangible assets, putting the measurement of capital consumption required for constant quality index of capital input on to a firm empirical foundation. BEA (1995) has adopted this approach in the latest benchmark revision of the US National Income and Product Accounts, following methodology described by Fraumeni (1997).

10. See Samuelson (1961), esp. p. 309.

11. Dougherty and Jorgenson (1996, 1997) have updated the estimates of Christensen *et al.* (1981) through to 1989.

12. Our methodology is described in detail by Dougherty (1992).

13. See Denison (1967) esp. ch. 21, 'The Sources of Growth and the Contrast between Europe and the United States', pp. 296–348.
14. Maddison added Austria and Finland to Kuznets' list and presented growth rates covering periods beginning as early as 1820 and extending 1979. Maddison (1991, 1995) has extended these estimates to 1992.
15. For details, see Maddison (1982), pp. 159–68. Purchasing power parities were first measured for industrialized countries by Gilbert and Kravis (1954) and Gilbert *et al.* (1958).
16. A complete list upto Mark 5 is given by Summers and Heston (1991), while the results of Mark 6 are summarized by the World Bank in the *World Development Report 1993*.
17. This 'growth regression' has spawned a vast literature, summarized by Levine and Renelt (1992), Baumol (1994), and Barro and Sala-i-Martin (1994). Much of this literature has been based on successive versions of the Penn World Table.
18. Unfortunately, this Mark 3 data set did not include capital input. Romer's empirical finding has spawned a substantial theoretical literature, summarized at an early stage by Robert Lucas (1988) and, more recently, by Grossman and Helpman (1991, 1994), Romer (1994), and Barro and Sala-i-Martin (1994). Romer's own important contributions to this literature have focused on increasing returns to scale, as in Romer (1986), and spill-overs from technological change, as in Romer (1990).
19. For more detailed discussion, see Jorgenson and Fraumeni (1989).
20. Our terminology follows that of Becker's (1965, 1993) theory of time allocation.

References

Abramovitz, M. (1956) 'Resources and Output Trends in the United States since 1870', *American Economic Review*, vol. 46, no. 2 (May), pp. 5–23.

Abramovitz, M. (1986) 'Catching Up, Forging Ahead, and Falling Behind', *Journal of Economic History*, vol. 46, no. 2 (June), pp. 385–406.

Baily, M. N. and Schultze, C. L. (1990) 'The Productivity of Capital in a Period of Slower Growth', *Brookings Papers on Economic Activity: Macroeconomics*, vol. 1, pp. 369–406.

Barro, R. J. and Becker, G. S. (1989) 'Fertility Choice in a Model of Economic Growth', *Econometrica*, vol. 7, no. 2 (March), pp. 481–502.

Barro, R. J. and Sala-i-Martin, X. (1994) *Economic Growth* (New York: McGraw-Hill).

Baumol, W. J. (1986) 'Productivity Growth, Convergence, and Welfare', *American Economic Review*, vol. 76, no. 5 (December), pp. 1072–85.

Baumol, W. J. (1994) 'Multivariate Growth Patterns: Contagion and Common Forces as Possible Sources of Convergence', in W. J. Baumol, R. R. Nelson, and E. N. Wolff (eds), *Convergence of Productivity* (New York, Oxford University Press), pp. 62–85.

Becker, G. S. (1965) 'A Theory of the Allocation of Time', *Economic Journal*, vol. 75, no. 296, (September), pp. 493–517.

Becker, G. S. (1967) 'Human Capital and the Personal Distribution of Income: An Analytical Approach', Woytinsky Lecture No. 1 (Ann Arbor, Mich.: Institute of Public Administration, University of Michigan).

Becker, G. S. (1993) *Human Capital*, 3rd edn (1st edn, 1964; 2nd edn, 1975) (University of Chicago Press).

Becker, G. S. and Barro, R. J. (1988) 'A Reformulation of the Economic Theory of Fertility', *Quarterly Journal of Economics*, vol. 103, no. 1 (February), pp. 1–25.

Berndt, E. R. (1991) *The Practice of Econometrics: Classic and Contemporary* (Reading, Mass.: Addison-Wesley).

Bureau of Economic Analysis (1994) 'A Satellite Account for Research and Development', *Survey of Current Bussiness*, vol. 74, no. 11 (November), pp. 37–71.

Bureau of Economic Analysis (1995) 'Preview of the Comprehensive Revision of the National Income and Product Accounts: Recognition of Government Investment and Incorporation of a New Methodology for Calculating Depreciation', *Survey of Current Business*, vol. 75, no. 9 (September), pp. 33–41.

Bureau of Labor Statistics (1983) *Trends in Multifactor Productivity*, Bulletin No. 2178 (Washington, DC: US Department of Labour).

Bureau of Labor Statistics (1993) *Labour Composition and U.S. Productivity Growth, 1948–90*, Bulletin No. 2426, (Washington, DC: US Department of Labor).

Bureau of Labor Statistics (1994) 'Multifactor Productivity Measures, 1991 and 1992', *News Release USDL 94–327*, July 11.

Christensen, L. R. and Jorgenson, D. W. (1969) 'The Measurement of U.S. Real Capital Input, 1929–1967', *Review of Income and Wealth*, Series 15, no. 4 (December), pp. 293–20.

Christensen, L. and Jorgenson, D. W. (1970) 'U.S. Real Product and Real Factor Input, 1929–1967', *Review of Income and Wealth*, Series 16, no. 1 (March), pp. 19–50.

Christensen, L. and Jorgenson, D. W. (1973) 'Measuring Economic Performance in the Private Sector', in M. Moss (ed.), *The Measurement of Economic and Social Performance*, pp. 233–338.

Christensen, L. R., Cummings, D. and Jorgenson, D. W. (1981) 'Relative Productivity Levels, 1947–1973', *European Economic Review*, vol. 16, no. 1, May, pp. 61–94.

Denison, E. F. (1967) *Why Growth Rates Differ* (Washington, DC: The Brookings Institution).

Denison, E. F. (1974) *Accounting for United States Economic Growth* (Washington, DC: The Brookings Institution).

Dougherty, C. (1992) 'A Comparison of Productivity and Economic Growth in the G-7 Countries', Doctoral dissertation, Harvard University.

Dougherty, C. and Jorgenson, D. W. (1996) 'International Comparisons of the Sources of Economic Growth', *American Economic Review*, vol. 86, no. 2 (May), pp. 25–9.

Dougherty, C. and Jorgenson, D. W. (1997) 'There Is No Silver Bullet: Investment and Growth in the G7', *National Institute Economic Review*, no. 162 (October), pp. 57–74.

Douglas, P. H. (1948) 'Are There Laws of Production?', *American Economic Review*, vol. 38, no. 1 (March), pp. 1–41.

Englander, A. S. and Gurney, A. (1994) 'OECD Productivity Growth: Medium-Term Trends', *OECD Economic Studies*, vol. 22 (Spring), pp. 111–30.

Fraumeni, B. M. (1997) 'The Measurement of Depreciation in the U.S. National Income and Wealth Accounts', *Survey of Current Business*, vol. 77, no. 7 (July), pp. 7–23.

Gilbert, M. and Kravis, I. B. (1954) *An International Comparison of National Products and the Purchasing Power of Currencies* (Paris: OEEC).

Gilbert, M. Beckerman, W., Edelman, J., Marris S., Stuvel, G. and Teichert, M. (1958) *Comparative National Products and Price Levels* (Paris: OEEC).

Goldsmith, R. (1955–6) *A Study of Saving in the United States*, 3 vols (Princeton, NJ: Princeton University Press).

Goldsmith, R. (1962) *The National Wealth of the United States in the Postwar Period* (New York: National Bureau of Economic Research).

Gordon, R. J. (1990) *The Measurement of Durable Goods Prices* (University of Chicago Press).

Griliches, Z. (1960) 'Measuring Inputs in Agriculture: A Critical Survey', *Journal of Farm Economics*, vol. 40, no. 5 (December), pp. 1398–427.

Griliches, Z. (1973) 'Research Expenditures and Growth Accounting', in B. Williams (ed.), *Science and Technology in Economic Growth*, London: Macmillan, pp. 59–95.

Griliches, Z. (1992) 'The Search for R&D Spillovers', *Scandinavian Journal of Economics*, vol. 94, Supplement, pp. 29–47.

Griliches, Z. (1995) 'R&D and Productivity: Econometric Results and Measurement Issues', in P. Stoneman (ed.), *Handbook of the Economics of Innovation and Technological Change* (Oxford: Basil Blackwell), pp. 52–89.

Grossman, G. M. and Helpman, E. (1991) *Innovation and Growth* (Cambridge, Mass.: MIT Press).

Grossman, G. M. and Helpman, E. (1994) 'Endogenous Innovation in the Theory of Growth', *Journal of Economic Perspectives*, vol. 8, no. 1 (Winter), pp. 23–44.

Hall, B. H. (1993) 'Industrial Research in the 1980s: Did the Rate of Return Fall?', *Brookings Papers on Economic Activity: Macroeconomics*, vol. 2, pp. 289–331.

Hall, R. E. (1971) 'The Measurement of Quality Change from Vintage Price Data', in Z. Griliches (ed.), *Price Indexes and Quality Change* (Cambridge, Mass.: Harvard University Press), pp. 240–71.

Hall, R. E. and Jorgenson, D. W. (1967) 'Tax Policy and Investment Behavior', *American Economic Review*, vol. 57, no. 3 (June), pp. 391–414.

Hall, R. E. and Jorgenson, D. W. (1969) 'Tax Policy and Investment Behavior: Reply and Further Results', *American Economic Review*, vol. 59, no. 3 (June), pp. 388–401.

Hall, R. E. and Jorgenson, D. W. (1971) 'Applications of the Theory of Optimal Capital Accumulation', in G. Fromm (ed.), *Tax Incentives and Capital Spending* (Amsterdam, North-Holland), pp. 9–60.

Hall, R. E. and Jones, C. I. (1997) 'Levels of Economic Activity Across Countries,' *American Economic Review*, vol. 87, no. 2, (May), pp. 173–7.

Ho, M. S. and Jorgenson, D. W. (1998) 'The Quality of the U.S. Work Force, 1948–95', Harvard University, Department of Economics.

Hulten, C. R. and Wykoff, F. C. (1982) 'The Measurement of Economic Depreciation', in C. R. Hulten (ed.), *Depreciation, Inflation and the Taxation of Income from Capital*, pp. 81–125.

Inter-Secretariat Working Group on National Accounts (1993) *System of National Accounts 1993* (New York, United Nations), pp. 379–406.

Islam, N. (1995) 'Growth Empirics', *Quarterly Journal of Economics*, vol. 110, no. 4, (November), pp. 1127–70.

Jorgenson, D. W. (1963) 'Capital Theory and Investment Behavior', *American Economic Review*, vol. 53, no. 2 (May), pp. 247–59.

Jorgenson, D. W. (1966) 'The Embodiment Hypothesis', *Journal of Political Economy*, vol. 74, no. 1, (February), pp. 1–17.

Jorgenson, D. W. (1967) 'The Theory of Investment Behavior', in R. Ferber (ed.), *Determinants of Investment Behavior* (New York: Columbia University Press), pp. 247–59.

Jorgenson, D. W. (1973) 'The Economic Theory of Replacement and Depreciation', in W. Sellekaerts (ed.), *Econometrics and Economic Theory* (New York: Macmillan), pp. 189–221.

Jorgenson, D. W. (1990) 'Productivity and Economic Growth', in E. R. Berndt and J. Triplett (eds), *Fifty Years of Economic Measurement* (University of Chicago Press), pp. 19–118.

Jorgenson, D. W. (1996) 'Empirical Studies of Depreciation', *Economic Inquiry*, vol. 34, no. 1 (January), pp. 24–42.

Jorgenson, D. W. and Fraumeni, B. M. (1989) 'The Accumulation of Human and Nonhuman Capital, 1948–1984', in R. E. Lipsey, and H. S. Tice (eds), *The Measurement of Savings, Investment, and Wealth* (University of Chicago Press), pp. 227–82.

Jorgenson, D. W. and Fraumeni, B. M. (1992a) 'Investment in Education and U.S. Economic Growth', *Scandinavian Journal of Economics*, vol. 94, Supplement, pp. 51–70.

Jorgenson, D. W. and Fraumeni, B. M. (1992b) 'The Output of the Education Sector', in Z. Griliches (ed.), *Output Measurement in the Services Sector* (University of Chicago Press), pp. 303–38.

Jorgenson, D. W. and Griliches Z. (1967) 'The Explanation of Productivity Change', *Review of Economic Studies* vol. 34, no. 99 (July), pp. 249–80.

Jorgenson, D. W., Gollop, F. M. and Fraumeni, B. M. (1987) *Productivity and U.S. Economic Growth* (Cambridge, Mass.: Harvard University Press).

Kravis, I. B., Heston, A. and Summers R. (1978) *International Comparisons of Real Product and Purchasing Power* (Baltimore, Md.: Johns Hopkins University Press).

Kuznets, S. (1961) *Capital in the American Economy* (Princeton, NJ: Princeton University Press).

Kuznets, S. (1971) *Economic Growth of Nations* (Cambridge, Mass.: Harvard University Press).

Lau, L. J. (1996) 'The Sources of Long-Term Economic Growth: Observations from the Experience of Developed and Developing Countries', in R. Landau, T. Taylor, and G. Wright (eds), *The Mosaic of Economic Growth* (Palo Alto, Calif.: Stanford University Press), pp. 63–91.

Levine, R. and Renelt, D. (1992) 'A Sensitivity Analysis of Cross-Country Regressions', *American Economic Review*, vol. 82, no. 4 (September), pp. 942–63.

Lucas, R. E. (1988) 'On the Mechanics of Economic Development', *Journal of Monetary Economics*, vol. 22, no. 1 (July). pp. 2–42.

Machlup, F. (1962) *The Production and Distribution of Knowledge in the United States* (Princeton, NS: Princeton University Press).

Maddison, A. (1982) *Phases of Capitalist Development* (Oxford University Press).

Maddison, A. (1991) *Dynamic Forces in Capitalist Development* (Oxford University Press).

Maddison, A. (1995) *Monitoring the World Economy* (Paris: Organization for Economic Cooperation and Development).

Mankiw, N. G., Romer, D. and Weil, D. (1992) 'A Contribution to the Empirics of Economic Growth', *Quarterly Journal of Economics*, vol. 107, no. 2 (May) pp. 407–37.

Mincer, J. (1974) *Schooling, Experience, and Earnings* (New York: Columbia University Press).

Nordhaus, W. D. and Tobin, J. (1972) *Is Growth Obsolete?* (New York: National Bureau of Economic Research); reprinted 1973 in M. Moss (ed.), *The Measurement of Economic and Social Performance* (New York: Columbia University Press), pp. 509–32.

Pieper, P. E. (1989) 'Construction Price Statistics Revisited', in D. W. Jorgenson and R. Landau (eds), *Technology and Capital Formation* (Cambridge Mass.: MIT Press), pp. 293–330.

Pieper, P. E. (1990) 'The Measurement of Construction Prices: Retrospect and Prospect', in E. R. Berndt and J. Triplett (eds), *Fifty Years of Economic Measurement* (University of Chicago Press), pp. 239–68.

Romer, P. (1986), 'Increasing Returns and Long-Run Growth', *Journal of Political Economy*, Vol. 94, No. 5, October, pp. 1002–1037.

Romer, P. (1987) 'Crazy Explanations for the Productivity Slowdown', in S. Fischer (ed.), *NBER Macroeconomics Annual* (Cambridge, Mass.: MIT Press), pp. 163–201.

Romer, P. (1990) 'Endogenous Technological Change', *Journal of Political Economy*, vol. 98, no. 5, pt 2 (October), pp. S71–S102.

Romer, P. (1994) 'The Origins of Endogenous Growth', *Journal of Economic Perspectives*, vol. 8, no. 1 (Winter), pp. 3–20.

Samuelson, P. A. (1961) 'The Evaluation of "Social Income": Capital Formation and Wealth', in F. A. Lutz and D. C. Hague (eds), *The Theory of Capital* (London: Macmillan), pp. 32–57.

Schultz, T. W. (1961) 'Investment in Human Capital', *American Economic Review*, vol. 51, no. 1 (March), pp. 1–17.

Solow, R. (1956) 'A contribution to the Theory of Economic Growth', *Quarterly Journal of Economics*, vol. 70, no. 1, February, pp. 65–94.

Solow, R. M. (1957) 'Technical Change and the Aggregate Production Function', *Review of Economics and Statistics*, vol. 39, no. 3 (August), pp. 312–20.

Solow, M. (1960) 'Investment and Technical Progress', in K. J. Arrow, S. Karlin and P. Suppes (eds), *Mathematical Methods in the Social Sciences, 1959* (Palo Alto, Calif.: Standford University Press), pp. 89–104.

Solow, M. (1970, revised 1992) *Growth Theory*, (New York: Oxford University Press).

Stone, R. (1992) 'The Accounts of Society', in K.-G. Maler (ed.), *Nobel Lectures: Economic Sciences, 1981–1990* (Singapore: World Scientific), pp. 115–139.

Summers, R. and Heston A. (1984) 'Improved International Comparisons of Real Product and its Composition: 1950–1980', *Review of Income and Wealth*, series 30, no. 1, March, pp. 1–25.

Summers, R. and Heston A. (1988) 'A New Set of International Comparisons of Real Product and Price Levels: Estimates for 130 Countries, 1950–1985', *Review of Income and Wealth*, series 34, no. 1, March, pp. 19–26.

Summers, R. and Heston, A. (1991) 'The Penn World Table (Mark 5): An Expanded Set of International Comparisons, 1950–1988', *Quarterly Journal of Economics*, vol. 106, no. 2 (May), pp. 327–68.

Summers, R., Kravis, I. B. and Heston, A. (1980) 'International Comparisons of Real Product and Its Composition, 1950–77', *Review of Income and Wealth*, series 26, no. 1, (March), pp. 19–66.

Tinbergen, J. (1959) 'On the Theory of Trend Movements', in J. Tinbergen, *Selected Papers*, (Amsterdam: North-Holland), 1959, pp. 182–221 (trans. from 'Zur Theorie der Langfristigen Wirtschaftsentwicklung', *Weltwirtschaftliches Archiv*, Band 55, Nu. 1 (1942), pp. 511–49.

Triplett, J. (1996) 'Measuring the Capital Stock: A Review of Concepts and Data Needs', *Economic Inquiry*, vol. 34, no. 1, January, pp. 36–40.

United Nations (1968) *A System of National Accounts* (New York: United Nations).

World Bank (1994) *World Development Report 1993* (Washington, DC: World Bank).

Comments

Reiner König

Dale Jorgenson's principal concern is the search for a new consensus model for the classical subject of economic growth – that is, the search for an academic framework that is both empirically meaningful and theoretically well-founded. The attempt to reconcile these two methodologies is undoubtedly praiseworthy as the rapid increase in new theoretical approaches and empirical evidence in this field have produced a very heterogeneous picture so far. According to Jorgenson, the path to 'fruitful coexistence' is routed via growth accounting – an approach he has applied for decades, has developed further with remarkable energy and carried to a high art.

The research results addressed by Jorgenson yield the central hypothesis that the traditional growth paradigm is by no means obsolete. Rather, it has to be reinterpreted in the light of an augmented concept of capital. This 'trick' consists, on the one hand, in a greater differentiation of tangible assets and, on the other particularly in the inclusion of human capital. Jorgenson disaggregates both types of input (labour and capital) much more and measures them more carefully than others do (for example, Kuznets). Such an augmented model has already been derived theoretically and tested with remarkable success – for example, in the well-known study by Mankiw, *et al.* (1992).

The notion that the creation of jobs is basically only a sub-category of the investment activity of enterprises and is therefore driven by the rate of return indicates the significant and proper idea of this research approach. The same applies to the various substitution processes that occur, in particular, between unskilled labour and capital, and to the partly substitutional and partly complementary relationship between unskilled and skilled labour. In my opinion, therefore, the Jorgenson approach makes a major contribution towards achieving a better understanding of macroeconomic developments.

It would, however, be presumptuous of me to try to do justice to Jorgenson's comprehensive research work with these brief remarks. All that I can do, therefore, is to supplement his work by pointing out certain 'system-immanent' aspects and economic policy implications. A detailed critical appraisal would lie outside the bounds of my competence.

On the whole, the approach chosen by Jorgenson results in a marked increase in the measured contribution of labour input to economic growth, so that productivity declines in importance. This is true at least in the USA, and to a certain degree also in Japan. In particular, around a fifth of US growth is attributed to the qualitative improvement in labour input in the past; it would therefore appear that in the USA, a 'knowledge-based society' is a reality of considerable significance.

However, in a study on the G7 countries by Dougherty and Jorgenson (1997) these findings do not hold equally for the European countries. Thus over 50 per cent of the growth in output per capita in Germany, France and Italy between 1960 and 1989 is still attributed to technical progress. It is true that this proportion declined in the period after 1973. Nevertheless, classic productivity gains still appear to play a greater role in Europe than in the USA, whereas the quality of the labour force, and hence investment in human capital, contribute very little to growth.

However, in interpreting such studies one should always bear in mind that the empirical results almost inevitably depend on the indicator used for human capital. For example, the data-intensive approaches used by Jorgenson include a variety of individual factors such as gender, educational attainment and employment status. However, one is often tempted to list further potential explanatory candidates almost on an *ad hoc* basis. In Germany's case, for example, one could refer to the special feature known as the 'dual training' system,[1] which has established itself as an important factor in the vocational training field. Naturally, the explanatory power of a hypothesis can often be increased by adding variables. But here, econometricians often come up against the problem of multicollinearity. That is one reason why the economically important phenomenon of the spill-overs of respective determinants is very hard to capture empirically.

In addition, cross-sectional analyses at the level of national economies quickly give rise to the question of whether educational systems are qualitatively comparable. To circumvent these problems, one alternative is to use an input indicator for the stock of human capital, such as expenditure on education and training. According to the data published by the OECD for the year 1993, the USA invests a comparatively high amount in human capital in relation to GDP. Germany is at the upper end of the middle segment, whereas Japan's spending on education relative to GDP is low. This fact could help to modify the international productivity story a little. But comparisons are still similarly far from simple when spending on education is used as a proxy variable. Furthermore, Arrow's learning-by-doing, which is so important in many areas, and which also represents a significant form of human capital, cannot be captured adequately by either approach. But it is unquestionably evident that hardly any convincing statistics are available at present for the group of factors subsumed under human capital.

Even if the data set is taken into consideration, the consensus suggested by Jorgenson is still not perfect, at least from a European point of view. Quite a high proportion of growth still falls like 'manna from heaven'. To overcome this problem, the consensus model should, as Jorgenson has already hinted, include the spill-over effects of innovation processes that are generally associated with technological change. Today there is a broad agreement that these effects are of great significance for the dynamics of growth. But technological change, and the technical knowledge that triggers it, have many dimensions. As an example, the stock of scientists also needs to be taken into account. However, in this context too we should be wary of *ad hoc* explanations. Even so, particular attention should be devoted to the role of R&D, as has already been emphasized in a number of theoretical models of endogenous growth.

Moreover, a number of empirical studies already exist in which the growth accounting framework is extended to include the accumulated spending on R&D as an input factor. In order to assess its contribution to output growth the ratio of R&D spending to GDP is usually included in an aggregate production function along with the traditional inputs. The coefficient of R&D spending provides an estimate of the social rate of return to R&D. It turns out that the rate of return to R&D is uniformly high in the aforementioned studies. In a study by Coe and Helpman (1993) it exceeds 100 per cent in some cases, which seems improbable. This implausible outcome may be caused, on the one hand, by the interdependency between productivity growth and spending on R&D but, on the other hand, the data on R&D expenditure are often of a poor quality. It is likely that this situation will not change much in the near future.

What consequences has the augmented consensus model had for economic policy? First, the principle that investment is of crucial importance to the future capacity of an economy continues to apply. Without disregarding the benefit of tangible investments, intangible investments will gain importance. Extending the knowledge base and making effective use of the knowledge potential are more than ever the key to enlarging the production potential of economies. Nor is there any change in the fundamental insight that saving and investment imply forgoing current consumption. Hence, the prime requirements and the litmus test of a good supply policy is still to encourage the process of accumulation, to prevent everything that obstructs technological change, and to create a beneficial framework for investment activity in the broader sense. The intangible investments category underlines that, as this type of capital spending normally relates to investments that take a long time to mature and that tie up capital for a lengthy period.

In Europe the important role of further training and retraining has certainly been recognised. Thus high priority has been assigned to acquiring professional qualifications within the framework of an active labour market policy, in order to combat unemployment. However, at times when public authorities are subject to stringent budget constraints, the implementation of this theoretically sensible approach often encounters limits in practice. Another consideration is that not only the number of trainees or the amount of spending on training are relevant *per se*. The most important criterion is the quality of the training. Good training depends above all on how and, in particular, on what kind of, knowledge is being imparted. Add to this, in order to be successful in the labour market, the required knowledge definitely has to be combined with personal initiative and individual effort. Work ethic and what is known as the 'secondary virtues' are undoubtedly important factors in this respect. But it is very hard for the government to promote such 'meta-economic' growth factors. Furthermore, they are not susceptible to empirical research.

However, the consequences for the labour market resulting from developments towards a knowledge-based economy are multi faceted. The trend towards a service and high-tech society is characterized by a rising share of highly skilled employees in those segments, which means that the demand for unskilled labour is declining. In the past – according to a study by Nickell and Bell (1996) – these structural shifts were associated with a rise in unemployment in Germany and France of only around one-fifth. But there are manpower projections that indicate that the number of unskilled employees in the economy as a whole in Germany could decline by half up to the year 2010; hence the present share of unskilled labour of about 20 per cent would fall to 10 per cent. But the extent of this decrease appears to be a little exaggerated, as technological change is not triggered solely by individuals in the knowledge-intensive professions. A complementary link exists in that employees with a lower level of formal education are also needed for the implementation of the change. In addition, many service enterprises make use of capital goods which have to be supplied by the manufacturing industry. Nevertheless, the tendency towards a decreasing share of low-skilled workers in overall employment cannot be rejected.

According to the laws of the market, a lower demand for unskilled labour should be reflected in the wage structure. In reality, however, that is countered by insufficient downward flexibility of wages and insufficient sectoral and qualification-specific wage differentiation in Europe, which means that unskilled workers may be forced increasingly into unemployment in this process. Unemployment, and especially the proportion of long-term unemployed who, while they often have some vocational training in formal terms, have an ever-decreasing stock of human capital, is already relatively high in continental Europe. Yet, given wage inflexibility in the lower segments, problems in the labour market could intensify further, and the possibility of social tensions cannot be ruled out.

In terms of economic policy, the high level of unemployment among low-skilled workers in continental Europe requires special attention. Innovative solutions are required to overcome the problem, in two respects. First, with reference of the level of qualification. Which suggests a need to increase the range of retraining facilities available, but which primarily demands a system of vocational training that is geared closely to the changing requirements of the labour market. Second, a particularly important role needs to be played by wage negotiators and by the pay structure. Only then can low-qualified individuals also participate in the improved growth prospects of a knowledge-based economy.

Note

1. Under the dual training system, young people receive practical vocational training at a firm on a contractual basis, accompanied by a course of theoretical instruction at a state institution geared to their intended vocation. The combined training package normally lasts three years.

References

Coe, D. T. and Helpman, E. (1993) 'International R&D Spillovers', NBER Working Paper No. 4444.

Dougherty, C. and Jorgenson, D. W. (1997) 'There is No Silver Bullet: Investment and Growth in the G7', *National Institute Economic Review*, vol. 162 (October), pp. 57–74.

Nickell, S. and Bell, B. (1996) 'Changes in the Distribution of Wages and Unemployment in OECD Countries', *American Economic Review, Papers and Proceedings*, vol. 86 (May), pp. 302–8.

9
The Japanese Economy in a World of Knowledge-based Growth

Charles I. Jones

Introduction

At least since the time of Solow (1956) and Swan (1956), economists have understood that growth in multifactor productivity is essential to sustained growth in per capita income. The question asked in modern growth theory is, basically, 'Where does this multifactor productivity growth come from?' The growth literature contains many answers to this question, ranging from learning-by-doing (Arrow, 1962a) to human capital accumulation (Lucas, 1988) to externalities to public capital. An additional possibility, however, is that productivity growth results from the discovery of new ideas. This is the possibility that is examined in detail in this chapter.

The recent examination of idea-based growth models in the growth literature is influenced tremendously by the work of Romer (1986, 1990). Romer himself is careful to give credit to a large body of earlier work that includes Arrow (1962b), Phelps (1966), Shell (1966), Nordhaus (1969) and others. And much important work has extended Romer's contributions, including Grossman and Helpman (1991), and Aghion and Howitt (1992). More widely, work on idea-based economic growth encompasses a wide range of research, far too broad to review here.[1]

This chapter presents an overview of knowledge-based growth, both at a conceptual level and through the presentation and calibration of a simple growth model. The second section reviews the important insights that arise when we think of growth as resulting from the creation of new ideas. Issues such as increasing returns to scale, knowledge spill-overs and externalities, imperfect competition and property rights are the focus of our attention. The third section outlines a simple model of knowledge-based growth to examine these issues more formally. The increasing returns to scale associated with the non-rivalry (or infinite expansibility) of ideas is shown to be an essential feature of ideas-based growth. We see not only that growth in per capita income results from growth in the stock of ideas, but also that the growth in the stock of ideas results from growth in the world's research efforts.

The global nature of idea-based growth is important from the demand side as well. The fact that entrepreneurs such as Bill Gates can sell their creations in a large world market raises the return to research and stimulates research activity throughout the world.

The fourth section provides a simple quantitative look at the idea-based growth model. We see not only that research effort in the G5 countries (France, Germany, Japan, the UK, and the USA) has been growing since the early 1960s, but also that research intensity – the fraction of the G5 population engaged in research – has also been growing. Japan is an important component of this growth, comprising about 15 per cent of G5 research activity in 1965, and more than 25 per cent in 1990.

A simple experiment at the end of the chapter emphasizes the importance of research effort and the potential magnitude of the gains, both social and private, from research activity. While measurement problems make precise interpretation difficult, the exercise suggests that a modest shift of labour into research in Japan that costs about 1/30th of a per cent of Japanese GDP could raise G5 GDP by about 1 per cent in the long run. This number is perhaps too large to be believed, but it is suggestive that large returns to research can be obtained if we can simply figure out the best way to capture them.

Knowledge-based growth

What is an idea? In ideas-based growth models, an idea is typically defined as the 'instructions' for transforming basic raw materials in an economy such as labour or capital into either a new kind of good, a better version of an existing good, or a larger quantity of existing goods. The nature of these instructions is often not important. What matters is that the economy can now use a given collection of raw materials to produce a higher quantity of (quality-adjusted) goods and greater utility.

The economics of ideas

My feeling is that the most important insight of the idea-based growth literature can be summarized very concisely by the following relationships:

$$Ideas \rightarrow Non\text{-}rivalrous \rightarrow IRS \rightarrow Imperfect\ competition \qquad (9.1)$$

Each of these links will be examined in turn.

The first link indicates that a fundamental property of ideas is that they are non-rivalrous. Recall that a good is rivalrous if one person's use of the good diminishes or eliminates the potential for someone else to use the good simultaneously. Most goods that we think of are rivalrous: an plane seat on a particular flight at a particular time, a unit of computer processing power, or a live performance of Beethoven's Fifty Symphony by the Tokyo Philharmonic Orchestra.

In contrast, ideas are not like most other economic goods. They are non-rivalrous in that one person's use of an idea does not in any way diminish the usefulness of the idea to someone else simultaneously. Examples include the fundamental theorem of calculus, the just-in-time inventory method, and the sequence of musical notes that make up the Fifth Symphony. If you are sitting in the front row, centre seat, for a performance of the symphony it means that I cannot also be sitting there, but there is no technological limitation that precludes several different orchestras from performing the symphony simultaneously. The instructions for performing the symphony are non-rivalrous. Drawing on a letter written by Thomas Jefferson in 1813 brought to his attention by Paul David (1993), Quah (1996) uses the term 'infinite expansibility' in place of non-rivalry: once an idea is created, it can be expanded infinitely to any scale of production.

The second link in Equation (9.1) states that the non-rivalrous nature of ideas implies that production of goods in the economy is characterized by increasing returns to scale. Let Y be the quantity of output (or GDP) produced by an economy, let A represent the level of knowledge in the economy, and let X represent a vector of rivalrous inputs that are used to produce output, such as capital and labour. We might relate inputs and outputs using a production function, such as:

$$Y = F(A, X) \tag{9.2}$$

The standard replication argument says that in order to double the output produced in this fashion, we simply duplicate every rivalrous input. We build an identical factory and hire an identical number of workers, and we obtain twice the output. This argument is used to justify an assumption of constant returns to scale in X. That is, for any number $\lambda > 1$, $F(A, \lambda X) = \lambda Y$.

But what happens if we also double the stock of knowledge in the economy? Provided the marginal product of knowledge is always positive, it is easy to see that $F(\lambda A, \lambda X) > \lambda Y$. If we double both knowledge and all rivalrous inputs, we shall more than double output. Production is characterized by increasing returns to scale. Notice that non-rivalry or infinite expansibility of ideas is essential to this argument. One can double output simply by building a new factory and duplicating the number of workers, because the instructions for producing the output do not need to be reproduced or reinvented. The instructions can be used at any scale of production once they have been created.

For example, consider the production of the compact disc (CD) player by Sony. Producing the very first CD player required an enormous research investment. One might think of the invention as the discovery of the precise instructions for assembling a CD player. After the invention, subsequent units could be produced much more cheaply because the instructions did not need to be reinvented. This is the hallmark of increasing returns to scale.

The final link in Equation (9.1) connects increasing returns to scale and imperfect competition. It is well known that, in the presence of increasing returns to scale, all factors cannot be paid their marginal products; firms would make negative profits under these circumstances. From a modelling standpoint, there are two ways to handle increasing returns. We can assume that the increasing returns are entirely external and maintain perfect competition. This is the case in the Arrow (1962) learning-by-doing story, or in Shell (1966), where ideas are thought of not only as non-rivalrous, but also as non-excludable – that is, as pure public goods. However, in part because of the patent system and in part because of trade secrets, inventors seem to be able to capture some part of the value of a new idea. For either of these reasons, an inventor may have, at least temporarily, some market power. This suggests the second way of handling increasing returns: imperfect competition.

The importance of imperfect competition in the economics of ideas has long been understood. If Sony is required to sell CD players at marginal cost, there will be no way to recoup the large fixed cost that is incurred in order to invent the CD player in the first place. Some *ex-post* market power allows Sony to earn quasi-rents that make the invention worthwhile.

Some policy implications

From the previous section, it is clear that the economics of ideas is very different from the economics of wheat, for example, or other traditional, rivalrous goods. Ideas are different in that they are non-rivalrous, which leads to increasing returns and imperfect competition. And ideas are different in that they are only partially excludable. Issues related to property rights and spill-overs naturally arise. The individual or organization that creates a new idea may not be fully compensated on the margin for the social value of the idea. This may occur both because of the direct benefits of the idea to consumers, but also because future researchers benefit from the knowledge created by current researchers (the 'standing on shoulders' effect alluded to by Isaac Newton).

A large body of research reviewed by Griliches (1992) and Nadiri (1993), among others, generally finds that the social rates of return to research are appreciably greater than the private rate of return. Jones and Williams (1998) argue that the difference between these rates of return indicates that firms may underinvest in research by at least a factor of two, with much larger factors possible.

This raises the very interesting but very difficult question of what is to be done. The patent system is one policy response that grants monopoly power to an inventor for a limited period of time in order to allow the inventor to capture some of the social value that is created. But this system is far from perfect. Patents are in effect for only a short period of time, they require costly adjudication by the legal system for their scope to be defined, they can be 'invented around', and they slow the adoption and diffusion of the idea because the price of the good is kept above marginal cost. Kremer (1996) proposes a novel mechanism through which the government purchases some patents from the private sector and then places them in the public domain. The purchase price could be set to reflect the social value of the innovation, if that can be determined. An example Paul Romer, has provided is the polymerase chain reaction (PCR). Biotech researchers in private as well as in university and government settings use the PCR technique extensively, but at a price that is much higher than the underlying marginal cost. It might make sense for both the US and Japanese governments to purchase a licence covering all current and future domestic use of the idea and then allow researchers to use it without paying an additional fee.

More generally, it is important to recognize that the patent system and the way in which a government attempts to line up private and social returns to research are essentially ideas themselves. And there is no reason to think that the best ideas have already been discovered and implemented.

A simple model

This section presents a simple model of idea-based growth to illustrate some of the themes highlighted above, as well as some of the important results developed in the idea-based growth literature.[2] It is helpful to view the model as a toy experiment, like one a chemist might set up in a laboratory. We shall build a miniature economy populated with simple economic agents and endowed with simple production possibilities. At the appropriate time, we shall flip the 'on' switch and then watch the toy economy to see how it behaves. Key parameters in the model will be picked so as to match some elements of the data for Japan, the USA, and other advanced economies, so that when we conduct experiments with the toy model, they may have some relevance for the way economic growth works in the world today.

The economic environment

Suppose our toy model consists of a number of separate 'countries' or economies, all of which are basically similar. Each economy produces a consumption/capital good that is identical to that produced in other countries. Each economy also produces ideas that are shared across economies. This sharing of ideas is the only way the different economies interact.

The first piece of the economic environment in this model is a production technology for an output/consumption good. We assume that some quantity Y of this good is produced by combining capital K and labour L_Y with the available stock of knowledge A:

$$Y = A^\sigma K^\alpha L_Y^{1-\alpha} \tag{9.3}$$

where $\sigma > 0$ and $0 < \alpha < 1$ are parameters of the production function. This kind of production function can be motivated in a number of different ways. In particular, it is worth noting that it emerges from a Romer (1990) style arrangement, in which output is produced by combining labour and an expanding range of intermediate capital goods, where A indicates the range of goods for which designs have been invented. Notice that the production function exhibits constant returns to scale to the rivalrous inputs K and L_Y, and therefore increasing returns to scale to the inputs and technology together. As discussed above, this critical feature of the model results from the fact that the non-rivalrous stock of knowledge A can be used at any scale of production without having to be reproduced.

The next part of the economic environment describes how the various inputs are themselves 'produced'. For capital and labour, we follow the standard arrangement of Solow (1956). Capital is simply the accumulation of forgone consumption:

$$\dot{K} = s_K Y - dK, \; k_0 > 0 \tag{9.4}$$

where $0 < s_K < 1$ is the saving/investment rate in the economy and $d > 0$ is a parameter measuring the rate of depreciation of capital.

One can easily allow utility-maximizing agents to choose a time path for the saving rate s_K. Alternatively, one can follow Solow (1956) and take the allocative decisions to be given exogenously. This is the method pursued here. We shall assume that s_K (as well as other allocative decisions) are simply exogenous parameters of the model. Looking ahead, it also greatly simplifies the analysis to assume that the fraction of the population who work as researchers to produce new ideas is given exogenously. In this simple model, we shall not undertake the very important analysis of the economic incentives that lead individuals to produce ideas. We only pause here to note that such analysis is one of the main contributions of recent work on economic growth.

Let L be the total quantity of labour in a particular economy, and assume that it grows exogenously over time at rate $n > 0$:

$$L = L_0 \, e^{nt}, \; L_0 > 0 \tag{9.5}$$

Every economy in this toy world will have the same rate of population growth.

In addition to producing output, labour in each economy can also be used to produce new ideas or new knowledge. However, unlike the production of goods, the production of ideas occurs at the 'world' level. This way of modelling ideas is motivated by the simple but important fact that ideas used in any particular economy are invented throughout the world. Singapore does not grow simply because of ideas invented by Singaporeans. Rather, Singapore benefits from ideas created in Japan, the USA and so on. Once this consideration is introduced, issues of technology transfer and the diffusion of ideas become extremely important. In the simple model analyzed here, we finesse this issue by assuming instantaneous diffusion of knowledge. As soon as a new idea is invented, it becomes useful in every economy in the world. This is clearly a weakness of the model, but there are already enough things going on that it is a convenient simplification to make at the moment.

Let A represent the total stock of ideas discovered in the world. Then, $\dot{A}$ represents the number of new ideas invented at a given point in time. We assume that new ideas are produced according to:

$$\dot{A} = \bar{\delta} R \qquad (9.6)$$

where R is the total number of researchers throughout the world looking for new ideas and $\bar{\delta}$ measures the number of new ideas that can be produced by a single unit of research effort. We assume that the economy begins at time 0 with some stock of ideas $A_0 > 0$ already given.

While individual researchers, who are small relative to the aggregate, might take $\bar{\delta}$ as given, one can imagine that the productivity of research might depend on characteristics of the economy. For example, the productivity of research may depend on the number of ideas discovered in the past – that is, $\bar{\delta} = \delta A^{\phi}$. A value of $\phi > 0$ would indicate that ideas discovered in the past raise the productivity of current research effort. Such positive 'knowledge spillovers' probably characterize at least some ideas, such as the discovery of calculus or the semiconductor. On the other hand, it is also possible that ϕ is negative. For example, suppose that the best ideas are discovered first and then it is increasingly difficult to find a truly original and useful idea. This case might correspond to what has been called 'fishing out': in a fixed pool of fish, as more fish are caught it becomes harder and harder to catch a new fish. Finally, one could also imagine that the knowledge spill-overs and fishing out concern offset, in which case one might want to consider $\phi = 0$ so that the productivity of research is simply some constant $\delta > 0$.

Another consideration in the production of ideas is the possibility of duplicative research. If we double the number of researchers looking for new ideas at a given point in time, shall we in expectation double the number of new ideas that get created? Perhaps not. This congestion effect can be included in the model by supposing that it is R^{λ} that enters the production function, where $0 < \lambda \leq 1$ potentially captures the duplication effect. Therefore, we replace Equation (9.6) with:

$$\dot{A} = \delta R^{\lambda} A^{\phi} \qquad (9.7)$$

We use the notation L_A to represent a particular economy's stock of researchers, so that R is simply the sum of L_A across countries. The resource constraint for any particular economy is:

$$L_Y + L_A = L \qquad (9.8)$$

Finally, we assume that a constant fraction of the labour force works in research:

$$L_A = s_A L \tag{9.9}$$

and therefore $L/_Y = (1 - s_A) L$.

The balanced growth path

Given this arrangement, one can show that the economy will converge over time to a balanced growth path – that is, a situation in which all variables are growing at constant exponential rates. This is the situation that we shall focus upon.

Along a balanced growth path, it is easy to show that the following relationships hold:

$$g_y = g_k = \frac{\sigma}{1-\alpha} g_A \tag{9.10}$$

where g_x denotes the exponential growth rate of some placeholder variable x along a balanced-growth path, and lower case letters correspond to the 'per capita' version of the upper case letters. For example, $y \equiv Y/L$ denotes output per capita. The first equality in this equation comes from the capital accumulation equation ($\dot{K}/K$ is constant only if Y/K is constant). The second equality comes from log-differentiating the production function.

Equation (9.10) illustrates the Solow (1956) result that long-run growth in per capita income results from growth in productivity. Here, however, productivity is related to the stock of ideas, and per capita income grows in the long run only if the stock of ideas that can be used in the economy grows. Therefore, we have:

Result 1 Long-run growth in per capita income occurs because the stock of ideas (or knowledge) in the economy grows in the long run.

What, then, determines the growth rate of ideas along a balanced growth path? To answer this question, rewrite Equation (9.7) as:

$$\frac{\dot{A}}{A} = \delta \frac{R^\lambda}{A^{1-\phi}} \tag{9.11}$$

By definition, $\dot{A}/A$ will be constant along a balanced growth path. But this will be the case only if the numerator and denominator on the right-hand-side of Equation (9.11) grow at the same rate. Therefore,

$$g_A = \frac{\lambda}{1-\phi} g_R \tag{9.12}$$

That is, the growth rate of the stock of ideas is proportional to the growth rate of the number of researchers.

Combining this last equation with Equation (9.10), we find that:

$$g_y = \gamma g_R \tag{9.13}$$

where $\gamma \equiv \frac{\sigma}{1-\alpha} \frac{\lambda}{1-\phi}$. This gives us our second main result:

Result 2   Long-run growth in the stock of ideas and therefore in per capita income is proportional to the long-run growth rate of the world's stock of researchers.

The intuition for this result is straightforward. Researchers produce ideas, and growth in the stock of ideas requires growth in the number of researchers. A simple example illustrates the point. Consider the case in which $\lambda = 1$ and $\phi = 0$. Therefore, the productivity of research is constant. Suppose that each researcher produces one new idea every period. If the number of researchers is constant, then the stock of ideas will rise over time, but at a declining rate: for example, if there are ten new ideas each period and the economy begins with a stock of a hundred ideas, then the growth rate will be very high initially, but will decline as the stock of ideas accumulates. If each researcher produces one new idea, then clearly sustained growth in the stock of ideas will require sustained growth in the effective number of researchers.

One can also solve this model for the (growing) level of per capita income along a balanced growth path. The first part of this argument is exactly like that in Solow (1956). From the capital accumulation equation, Equation (9.4), one can easily see that the capital–output ratio along a balanced growth path is equal to $s_K/(n + g_y + d)$. Substituting this into the production function, one finds:

$$y^*(t) = \left(\frac{s_k}{n + g_y + d}\right)^{\frac{\alpha}{1-\alpha}} A^*(t)^{\frac{\sigma}{1-\alpha}} \tag{9.14}$$

where the time index t is explicitly included to indicate which variables are changing over time, and the superscript * indicates a value along a balanced growth path.

Notice that log-differentiating this relationship gives (part of) Equation (9.10): output per worker along the balanced growth path is proportional to the stock of ideas raised to some power.

The value of $A^*(t)$ can be found by rewriting Equation (9.11). Notice that this equation implies that:

$$A^*(t) = \left(\frac{\delta}{g_A}\right)^{\frac{1}{1-\phi}} R(t)^{\frac{\lambda}{1-\phi}} \tag{9.15}$$

That is, the stock of ideas along a balanced growth path is proportional to the number of researchers (raised to some power).

Combining these last two equations, we have the solution for the level of output per capita along a balanced growth path:

$$y^*(t) = \left(\frac{s_k}{n + g_y + d}\right)^{\frac{\alpha}{1-\alpha}} \left(\frac{\delta}{g_A}\right)^{\frac{\gamma}{\lambda}} R(t)^\gamma \tag{9.16}$$

where $\gamma \equiv \frac{\sigma}{1-\alpha} \frac{\lambda}{1-\phi}$. This gives us our third main result:

Result 3 The level of output per capita along a balanced growth path is proportional to the world's effective number of researchers, raised to the power γ.

As above, the number of researchers determines the number of ideas, and the number of ideas determines the level of per capita income.

Relating the model to data

In this section, we consider how the simple toy model outlined above can help us to interpret various facts observed about the advanced countries of the world.

The world's effective research stock

Based on the results given so far, a critical determinant of economic growth is the world's effective research stock. Economies grow because of growth in the stock of ideas, and this stock grows because of growth in R. The question then is, why does R grow over time?

There are at least three sources of growth in R. First, the number of (world) researchers can grow simply because the population of the world is growing. Second, the number of researchers can grow because of a rising research intensity – a rise in the fraction of the population that searches for new ideas. Finally, the effective number of researchers may grow if the quality of the researchers grows – for example, because of human capital accumulation.

As a historical matter, all three of these sources appear to be relevant. The first two are quite easy to document. Figure 9.1 shows the rise in population and researchers for the G5 countries of France, (West) Germany, Japan, the UK, and the USA. For present purposes, these aggregates will represent the 'world' research effort. This is likely to be a conservative judgement, since one suspects that an increasing number of countries are now capable of conducting frontier research.

One sees in the figure two things. First, there has been a basic rise in the population of the G5 countries, at an average rate of 0.8 per cent per year during the period 1965 to 1991. This means that more people are available to conduct research, which should serve as a source of research and idea growth. Second, there has been an even larger rise in the number of researchers in the

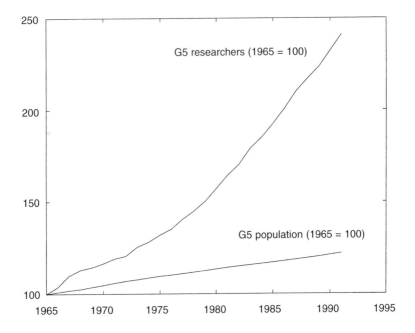

Figure 9.1   Researchers and population in the G5 countries
Sources: Research data, National Science Board (1993, 1996). The data are spliced together at the
year 1979 and log-linearly interpolated for some countries. Population data from Penn World
Tables, Version 5.6, Summers and Heston (1991).

G5 countries. The series plotted is the number of scientists and engineers
engaged in R&D, according to the US National Science Foundation.[3] The
number of researchers has grown at an average annual rate of 3.4 per cent over
the 1965 to 1991 period, increasing by a factor of nearly two-and-a-half.

The implication of these two facts is a rise in research intensity in the G5
countries, defined as the fraction of the population who work as researchers.
This implication is illustrated in Figure 9.2. Research intensity rises from
slightly less than two-tenths of one per cent of the population in 1965 to
slightly less than four-tenths of one per cent in 1991, roughly doubling.

This observation is quite striking and is consistent with the popular notion
that the importance of 'knowledge' and ideas is rising. It is interesting to
speculate on the causes of the rise in research intensity. Jones (1997) proposes
that the increased openness and development of the world economy is one
likely source: the scale of the market over which an innovator can spread the
fixed cost of research is much larger today than it was in the early 1970s, and is
likely to be even larger in the future. Transportation and communication costs

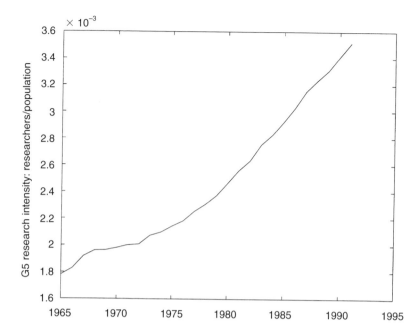

Figure 9.2 Research intensity in the G5 countries
Source: See notes to Figure 9.1.

are lower, barriers to international trade have fallen, and the fraction of the world's population that has an income greater than the poverty line has risen. These changes raise the return to research and could explain the rise in research intensity.

Growth in the world's stock of researchers, R, can then easily explain the growth in the world's stock of ideas, which underlies growth in per capita income.

The magnitude of long-run level effects

In the long-run, a country's growth rate is determined by the rate of growth of the world's stock of ideas. Therefore, in this model, all countries share the same long-run growth rate. This is not to say that differences in policies are not important, however. Differences in policies translate into differences in the level of income across countries. As one simple example of this, the USA and Malawi grew at nearly identical rates over the period 1960 to 1990. The enormous differences in policies and institutions between these two countries is reflected in the fact that per capita income in Malawi is only about 3 per cent of that in the USA.

These differences are reflected explicitly in Equation (9.16), reproduced here:

$$y^*(t) = \left(\frac{s_K}{n + g_y + d}\right)^{\frac{\alpha}{1-\alpha}} \left(\frac{\delta}{g_A}\right)^{\frac{\gamma}{\lambda}} R(t)^\gamma \qquad (9.17)$$

While income levels are proportional to the world's effective stock of researchers, the factor of proportionality depends on country-specific variables. In this simple model, the main country-specific variable is the investment rate in physical capital, but in more general models, investment in human capital and barriers to technology transfer will presumably matter as well.

Although the model predicts that all countries will share the same long-run growth rate, this does not mean that countries cannot grow at different rates for long periods of time, such as decades. In the model, such growth differences are understood as transition dynamics. Consider a country that begins on a balanced growth path with a low investment rate (or with low human capital investment and high barriers to technology transfer). According to the equation above, the country will therefore have a low income level. If this country undergoes a reform which raises its investment rate, its long-run income level will rise. In the medium term, the country's growth rate will be faster than the rate implied by the world stock of ideas as the country transits to its higher income level.

This is merely the result of simple transition dynamics like that in the standard Solow (1956) model: countries grow more rapidly the further they are below their steady-state balanced-growth path. As they approach the balanced-growth path, the growth rate declines to the long-run growth rate, determined as above by the growth rate of world research effort.

One might naturally inquire as to the magnitude of the long-run level effects. For example, if a country raises its investment rate, by how much does its level of income along the balanced growth path rise in the long run? Or, more pertinent to the R&D spirit of the model, if a country raises its own research intensity, what is the effect on the long-run level of income?

The first of these questions is straightforward to answer, so we begin by considering the investment rate. According to Equation (9.17), the elasticity of per capita income along a balanced growth path with respect to the investment rate is $\alpha/(1 - \alpha)$. With perfect competition, α corresponds to the capital share of income (and even in many models with imperfect competition it can be computed as one minus labour's share of income), so it is conventional to pick a value of $\alpha = 1/3$. This means that the elasticity is 1/2, so it is the square root of the investment rate that affects the level of income in Equation (9.17): doubling the investment rate will, in the long-run, result in the level of income being higher by a factor of $\sqrt{2}$, or about 40 per cent higher than what it would otherwise have been.

To conduct the same exercise for a country's own research effort is slightly more complicated because it is *world* research effort rather than an individual country's effort that matters in the long run. For this exercise, we shall be more specific and focus on an increase in Japanese research intensity.

If research intensity is measured simply as the number of scientists and engineers engaged in R&D (as above), then:

$$R = L_A + \bar{L}_A \qquad (9.18)$$

where L_A will denote the number of researchers in Japan and $\bar{L}_A$ will denote the number of researchers in the rest of the world. (This 'overbar' notation will continue to be used to denote the rest of the world.) With some algebraic manipulation, this equation can be rewritten as:

$$R = (s_A l + \bar{s}_A \bar{l}) L^w \qquad (9.19)$$

where s_A denotes the fraction of a country's population that works in research and l denotes the fraction of the G5 population that lives in a particular country. L^w stands for the G5 population as a whole. Therefore, this equation simply says that G5 research intensity R/L^w is a weighted average of Japan's research intensity and the rest of the G5's research intensity, where the weights reflect population shares.

In this simple model, a rise in Japanese research intensity will raise the number of researchers in the world and therefore raise the number of new ideas that get produced. To determine the magnitude of the effect, however, we need to know several things. First, from equation (9.17), we need to know the elasticity γ in order to translate the rise in research intensity into a rise in income. Second, we need to know the elements in Equation (9.19) so that we can determine by how much world research intensity is raised.

Recall that γ is a function of four parameters in the model; in particular, it is equal to $\frac{\sigma}{1-\alpha} \frac{\lambda}{1-\phi}$. It is very difficult to obtain values for each of these parameters individually. However, also recall that γ multiplied by the growth rate of the research stock is equal to the growth rate of per capita income in the long run. Based on recent data on US growth, and using a measure of the growth rate of research effort, Jones (1997) calculates a rough value for γ that is about 1/3. This is the value we will use.

The elements of Equation (9.19) are reported in Table 9.1, together with some additional statistics. Japan's share of the G5 population is about 22 per cent, while its share of the G5 research effort is 25 per cent. This difference reflects the fact that research intensity S_A in Japan is 0.34 per cent, slightly higher than the average of 0.31 per cent in the other G5 countries. Another interesting statistic in this table is the 59 per cent of patents in the USA granted to the G5 countries originate in the USA. The remainder, the bulk of which are Japanese, originate from foreign research efforts. This emphasizes the importance of a global perspective in understanding the contribution of idea-based growth.[4]

Table 9.1   Data on the G5 economies (percentages)

	Shares of the G5			Research intensity S_A, 1987
	Population 1990	Researchers 1987	US patents 1990	
Japan	22	25	24	0.34
Rest of G5	78	75	76	0.31
USA	46	53	59	0.36
W. Germany	12	10	9	0.27
France	10	6	4	0.20
UK	10	6	3	0.24

Sources: Data from National Science Board (1993) and Penn World Tables, Mark 5.6, Summers and Heston (1991).

Now consider the following experiment. Suppose we raise Japanese research intensity from 0.34 per cent to 0.39 per cent – that is, by 5 percentage points, or about 15 per cent of its level in 1987. Because Japan's population is only 22 per cent of the G5 total, this raises G5 research intensity by only about 1 percentage point, from 0.32 per cent to 0.33 per cent.

This means that G5 research intensity rises by about 3 per cent. Now recall that the elasticity of balanced-growth-path income with respect to research, the parameter γ, is about 1/3. This means that the net effect on Japan (and the entire G5) in the long run is a rise in balanced-growth-path income by about 1 per cent.

Is this a big number or a small number? For this purpose, it is helpful to measure the shift in labour in units of GDP instead of bodies. We are moving 0.05 per cent of Japan's labour force. To get a cost, we multiply by the total wage bill in Japan, which is about 2/3 of Japan's GDP (recall, we are assuming $\alpha = 1/3$). Therefore, the cost of this experiment is about 0.05* 2/3 = 0.033 per cent of Japan's GDP each period. In exchange, we get (eventually) a 1 per cent higher G5 GDP each period, or perhaps even a 1 per cent higher *world* GDP. With such calculations, it is not hard to see why economists generally find large social returns to R&D![5]

An important qualification of this calculation is that it hinges on the magnitude of research effort being measured correctly. If research effort is mismeasured by a factor of ten, so that, for example, 3.2 per cent of the G5 population works in research instead of 0.32 per cent, then the cost of this improvement will be mismeasured by a factor of ten as well. Of course, the calculated gain is so large as to appear to be robust to even an order of magnitude mismeasurement, but one needs to recognize this degree of uncertainty in the calculation.

Along these lines, one might wonder if it is plausible to think that less than one per cent of the population is essentially responsible for creating the ideas that underlie all economic growth. On the one hand, this seems extraordinarily low. Any time someone creates a new business, one might think of this as a contribution to knowledge. The creation of the Big Mac by McDonald's was a very valuable idea that probably did not show up in the research statistics. On the other hand, one can also think of key individuals whose creations have been extremely valuable, such as Isaac Newton, Thomas Edison, and Kyota Sugimoto, the inventor of the Japanese typewriter.

A very important question to ask is how much of this increase would be captured by Japan's researchers (which is relevant as to whether or not they will undertake this change by themselves) and by Japan's economy as a whole. For this latter question, a natural minimum estimate would be 1 per cent of Japan's own GDP, so even the *domestic* social return to research seems very high.

A final question to ask in this environment is how long it takes to reach the long run. The answer is that it depends on the detailed parameterization of the simple model. Growth rates can (obviously) either be very high for a short period of time or not very high for a longer period of time. With a relatively low social discount rate, the differences along this front are relatively unimportant.

Conclusion

Economic growth has resulted in enormous increases in standards of living since the late nineteenth century. According to Maddison (1995), US per capita income was higher at the end of the 1990s by a factor of ten than in 1870; and Japanese per capita income is higher by a factor of twenty six. If the prices indices that are used to compute these ratios overstate inflation by 1 per cent per year on average, then US income would have risen by a factor of thirty-five and Japanese income by a factor of ninety. Understanding these extraordinary changes is clearly one of the most important problems in economics.

Research on economic growth since the Second World War points to the importance of knowledge and ideas as the source of these enormous improvements in income. Economic growth occurs as we discover newer and better ways to use the resources at our disposal. A central source of the growth in ideas that underlies the growth in per capita income is the increase in the number of researchers throughout the world. In the G5 countries alone, there are nearly two and a half times more researchers in 1991 than there were in 1965. And this rise is surely augmented by the increase in researchers made possible by the increased development of economies outside the G5.

The continued growth and development of the world economy suggests that the market for new ideas continues to expand. In particular, the rapid growth of China and India, which between them hold 40 per cent of the world's population, represents an enormous potential source of research and demand for the products of innovation.

Simple calculations, as well as detailed studies, suggest that the social returns to research, both domestically and world wide, are enormous, and potentially much larger than the private returns. This wedge suggests that private agents may not have appropriate incentives to engage in the search for new ideas. One implication is that the search for new institutions and arrangements to encourage the creation of new ideas could be one of the most socially valuable activities around.

Notes

1. A more detailed review can be found in Jones (1998), among other places.
2. The model is largely taken from Jones (1995, 1998).
3. There are enormous difficulties in measurement in this respect. Who really counts as a researcher? And are researchers counted in the same way across countries? These issues are ignored here.
4. A more detailed analysis of this last statistic can be found in Eaton and Kortum (1994).
5. One must be careful in evaluating this statement. While it is possible to calculate the social return to R&D from the production possibilities of the model and observations on allocations, one must also say something about the private rate of return in order to determine whether or not there is too little research. This requires an analysis of the market economy. Still, most of the evidence supports the claim that social rates of return to research are much greater than private rates of return.

References

Aghion, P. and Howitt, P. (1992) 'A Model of Growth through Creative Destruction', *Econometrica*, vol. 60 (March), pp. 323–51.

Arrow, K. J. (1962a) 'The Economic Implications of Learning by Doing', *Review of Economic Studies*, vol. 29 (June), pp. 153–73.

Arrow, K. J. (1962b) 'Economic Welfare and the Allocation of Resources for Invention', in R. R. Nelson (ed.), *The Rate and Direction of Inventive Activity* (Princeton, NJ: Princeton University Press.

David, P. A. (1993) 'Knowledge, Property, and the System Dynamics of Technological Change', *Proceedings of the World Bank Annual Conference on Development Economics, 1992*, pp. 215–48.

Eaton, J. and Kortum, S. S. (1994) 'International Patenting and Technology Diffusion', Mimeo, Boston University.

Griliches, Z. (1992) 'The Search for R&D Spillovers', *Scandinavian Journal of Economics*, vol. 94, pp. 29–47.

Grossman, G. M. and Helpman, E. (1991) *Innovation and Growth in the Global Economy* (Cambridge, Mass.: MIT Press).

Jones, C. I. (1995) 'R&D-Based Models of Economic Growth', *Journal of Political Economy*, vol. 103 (August), pp. 759–84.

Jones, C. I. (1997) 'The Upcoming Slowdown in U.S. Economic Growth', NBER Working Paper No. 6284.

Jones, C. I. (1998) *Introduction to Economic Growth* (New York: W. W. Norton).

Jones, C. I. and Williams, J. C. (1998) 'Measuring the Social Return to R&D', *Quarterly Journal of Economics*, November, vol. 113, pp. 1119–35.

Kremer, M. (1996) 'A Mechanism for Encouraging Innovation', MIT Working Paper.

Lucas, R. E. (1988) 'On the Mechanics of Economic Development', *Journal of Monetary Economics*, vol. 22, pp. 3–42.

Maddison, A. (1995) *Monitoring the World Economy 1820–1992* (Paris: Organization for Economic Cooperation and Development).

Nadiri, M. I. (1993) 'Innovations and Technological Spillovers', NBER Working Paper No. 4423.

National Science Board (1993) *Science & Engineering Indicators – 1993* (Washington, DC: US Government Printing Office).

National Science Board (1996) *Science & Engineering Indicators – 1996* (Washington, DC: US Government Printing Office).

Nordhaus, W. D. (1969) 'An Economic Theory of Technological Change', *American Economic Association Papers and Proceedings*, vol. 59 (May), pp. 18–28.

Phelps, E. S. (1966) 'Models of Technical Progress and the Golden Rule of Research', *Review of Economic Studies*, vol. 33 (April), pp. 133–45.

Quah, D. T. (1996) 'The Invisible Hand and the Weightless Economy', Mimeo LSE Economics Department.

Romer, P. M. (1986) 'Increasing Returns and Long-Run Growth', *Journal of Political Economy*, vol. 94 (October), pp. 1002–37.

Romer, P. M. (1990) 'Endogenous Technological Change', *Journal of Political Economy*, vol. 98 (October), pp. S71–S102.

Shell, K. (1966) 'Toward a Theory of Inventive Activity and Capital Accumulation', *American Economic Association Papers and Proceedings*, vol. 56, pp. 62–8.

Solow, R. M. (1956) 'A Contribution to the Theory of Economic Growth', *Quarterly Journal of Economics*, vol. 70 (February), pp. 65–94.

Summers, R. and Heston, A. (1991) 'The Penn World Table (Mark 5): An Expanded Set of International Comparisons: 1950–1988', *Quarterly Journal of Economics*, vol. 106 (May), pp. 327–68.

Swan, T. W. (1956) 'Economic Growth and Capital Accumulation', *The Economic Record*, Vol. 32 (November), pp. 334–61.

Comments

Lex Hoogduin

Before commenting on the chapter by Dr Jones, I have to acknowledge that I am not an expert in growth theory, old or new. My comments should be interpreted as those of an economist with an interest in the subject, but not active in this field of research. I only hope that at least some of my comments are useful to the author.

The basic claim made in the chapter is that the strong economic growth since the late 1800s is primarily associated with the creation and global diffusion of new ideas. A small model is presented to illustrate that a relatively small number of research activities can induce large gains in welfare, and that a relatively modest shift of the labour force to research activities in Japan can represent a high-yield investment.

The proposition that economic growth is associated with the creation and diffusion of ideas is simple and appealing. Theory has to make abstractions. It cannot analyze everything at once. My basic question in relation to this chapter is, however, whether or not the model is too simple for what the author intends to show? Does it not leave out certain things that should be included? One might argue that a research strategy that starts off from the simplest possible basis can, indeed, be very fruitful. I acknowledge this general point. Let me therefore explain why I do not feel fully at ease with this strategy in this chapter as it stands. I have based my stance on both empirical and more theoretical considerations.

Let me turn first to the empirical argument. Dr Jones uses a calibrated version of his model to provide information about Japan, about the real world. What caught my attention, however, is that, in calibrating the model, he does not examine whether this model can replicate the actual economic growth performance of recent decades in Japan and other industrial countries, although he includes a reference to a paper on the USA. My suggestion, therefore, would be to extend the fourth section of the chapter (relating the model to data) or add a new section exploring whether the actual growth process can be explained reasonably well by the model for plausible values of the parameters.

It might be argued that the model intends to explain neither more nor less than the association between the production of ideas and economic growth since the late 1800s. However, I believe that it is important to assess the robustness of the small model over slightly shorter periods. One could, for example, use the same period (1965–98), that is used to examine the development of research intensity.

I am particularly interested in an analysis of the period from 1965 to late 1990s because I am not sure whether the model is indeed capable of providing a reasonable explanation of economic growth over this period. I have not performed a formal test, but have conducted some eyeball econometrics and applied my knowledge on growth over recent decades. As far as I am aware, growth has slowed since the early 1970s, both within the above-mentioned period and in comparison with the previous period. The figures and graphs in the chapter, if anything, appear to suggest that research intensity has accelerated or has shown a relatively constant rate of growth. In any event, I do not envisage a decrease in research intensity. I am referring to Figures 9.1 and 9.2 on pages 262 and 263. However, as mentioned above, this is only eyeball econometrics, so I may be wrong. Another, more forward-looking, way of formulating the question is to ask whether or not the analysis in the chapter supports the pessimistic views presented by Professor Jorgensen, or whether it provides grounds for increased optimism.

A further reason for my interest in a more fully elaborated calibration over this period, which is effectively a reformulation of my previous point, is that productivity growth has slowed over recent decades (that is, the so-called productivity puzzle, which was discussed in earlier chapters) despite the apparent increase in research activity. Perhaps this simply reflects measurement problems but, irrespective of the explanation offered, the chapter could benefit from a more detailed analysis of the correspondence between the facts and the model.

I should also like to suggest a rather more theoretical reason for raising the issue of whether or not the model makes too many abstractions. In essence, the chapter argues that economic growth is the result of providing sufficient research resources, although the precise relationship between research intensity and growth depends on a number of parameters. In the interests of fairness and to avoid any misunderstanding, Dr Jones acknowledges that factors other than merely increasing the number of researchers are important. He does not favour mono-causality, but applies a certain research strategy. However, by focusing on the quantity of resources, he at least creates the impression that this is a key factor, perhaps even *the* decisive one. In my view, this is debatable, and it would seem useful to break down the chain from the conception of an idea to its impact on growth into more components, in order to be able to identify the most important elements of the chain. I am interested in Dr Jones' view on this matter and should like to ask him whether he thinks that his analysis could usefully be extended to factors that explain the relationship between research input and the commercial application of research output, and to the factors that determine the diffusion of new commercial ideas? Would it, in his opinion, be a worthwhile follow-up to this chapter to assess the relative importance of different factors. Alternatively, are more historical case studies likely to prove more fruitful?

Finally, I should like to turn to some more detailed remarks or questions. Can we really take it for granted, in spite of the trend towards globalization, that research resources will soon be available to all, or are there still important factors hampering the diffusion of knowledge? As regards the calculation of the costs inherent in research: is Dr Jones not underestimating those costs by taking labour costs alone? What about the costs of other inputs?

I would like to conclude with a remark on the estimates of the return on a higher research intensity in Japan. The high returns do indeed appear too good to be true. One wonders why such highly profitable investment opportunities would remain unexploited if they existed. If it were due solely to the generally beneficial character of research, one would surely advocate an analysis of the reasons why governments do not promote this more than they do. It would apparently imply that the political process is highly inefficient. This underlines how interesting it would be to incorporate details on the production of research into the chapter. This is, of course, no criticism of the chapter itself, but merely a suggestion to extend the scope of the analysis.

Comments

Shin-ichi Fukuda

This chapter provides a very interesting overview of knowledge-based growth and its global nature, on which the author has made significant contributions in his previous studies. Although the presented model is simple, I think it captures the essential features of knowledge-based growth and derives various important implications. However, it seems that various restrictive assumptions of the model might have derived very large social returns to R&D in its calibration, particularly at the world level. Thus I shall mainly comment on the assumptions that the chapter imposed for its analytical simplicity. I have five comments.

The first comment is on the assumption of instantaneous diffusion of knowledge, especially the production of ideas at the 'world' level. Needless to say, this is not a realistic assumption, at least in the short run. The assumption may be fine in the long run, which is the time-span the chapter focuses on. However, even in the long run, international technological diffusion will be more limited than domestic diffusion. For example, the chapter mentioned Kremer's mechanism for encouraging innovation. The basic idea of this mechanism design is that the governement purchases some patents from the private sector and then places them in the public domain. The mechanism may work well in encouraging domestic technological diffusion. But, unless ideal international policy co-ordination is possible, it is less likely that it works well in encouraging international technological diffusion. When governments have more difficulty in encouraging international technological diffusion, the assumption of the model will overestimate welfare gains from the creation of knowledge at the world level.

The second comment is on the assumption of no international mobility of labour and capital. This assumption may be justifiable for the international mobility of low- or middle-income workers. But, the assumption may be less realistic for the mobility of high-income researchers and physical capital stock, at least in the long run. In particular, when there exist increasing returns to scale in country-specific production functions, international factor mobility may have different implications for the balanced growth path of each country. For example, suppose that the international mobility of researchers is

273

completely free, and that there exist increasing returns to scale in the R&D sector of each country, then, as long as successful researchers can obtain some temporal monopoly rents, we shall have a concentration of researchers in one country in the long-run equilibrium. Under these circumstances, it is no clearer whether knowledge-based growth really brings the same long-run growth rate of national income for all countries.

The third comment is on the assumption of a one-sector model. Although the model is standard, the one-sector model tends to neglect the role of international trade as an engine of growth. In particular, in considering the economic growth of postwar Japan, the assumption is slightly strange, because the role of exports through comparative advantage was very important. When comparative advantage allows international trade, the country no longer needs technological progress in all sectors. This indicates that even if international technological diffusion is large, foreign R&D activities for some specific sector may not help domestic economic growth when the country does not have the comparative advantage in that sector. This argument is probably more important for developing countries and less important for industrial countries, because intra-industry trade is more significant among industrial countries. However, even in international trade among industrial countries, inter-industry trade is not negligible. Therefore, even if we focus only on economic growth in industrial countries, the assumption of a one-sector model may overestimate the effects of international technological spill-overs.

The fourth comment is on types of R&D activity. Although the author considered only one type of R&D activity, in reality R&D activities have several stages. They are usually classified into three types: 'basic researches', where a direct practical application is not sought; 'applied researches', where a practical application is sought; and 'development', which uses available knowledge obtained as a result of basic and applied research. The effects of technological spill-overs will differ depending on the type of R&D activities. For example, the fundamental theorem of calculus that was innovated by basic researches will be more easily learned than, for example, the vehicle manufacturer Toyota's just-in-time inventory method that is classified into applied researches. Thus it will be important to classify the types of R&D activity to obtain more accurate estimates on the effects of international technological spill-overs.[1]

My final comment is on the interaction of knowledge-based growth with other sources of economic growth such as learning-by-doing and human capital accumulation. As was mentioned in the chapter's introduction, the importance of these sources has been stressed by a large number of previous studies. How do these sources of economic growth interact with each other? In order to estimate the effects of technological spill-overs more accurately, it is important to consider the interaction of knowledge-based growth with the other sources of economic growth. In particular, when we look at the cost composition of R&D expenditure, labour costs continue to hold the highest share. This implies that the estimated effects of technologiecal spill-overs may not be accurate unless we allow for the difference in human capital accumulation among countries.

Note

1. It has often been pointed out that Japan is superior to other industrial countries in much applied research, but not in basic research. This indicates that Japan enjoyed the effects of international technological spill-overs of basic research in developing its applied research, but also that Japan's applied research had relatively smaller spill-over effects on the applied research levels of other countries.

10
Wage and Job Trends in the US Labour Market: An Assessment

Marvin H. Kosters

Introduction

Developments in the US labour market attracted a great deal of popular discussion and research attention during the 1980s and 1990s. One of the most prominent themes in domestic discussions of the US labour market was the idea that strong employment growth has been deeply flawed by stagnant or declining wages and growing wage inequality.[1] During a period in which most labour market trends have been extraordinarily favourable, the prevalence of commentary emphasizing unfavourable implications for workers and their families shows noteworthy disagreement about labour market facts, and differences in their interpretation.

The strength of employment growth in the US economy has been recognized widely. During the 1970s and 1980s, jobs were created in sufficient numbers to absorb the abnormally large influx of workers represented by the entry of the 'baby boom' generation into the workforce. Moreover, the proportion of the working age population in the labour force increased, and the unemployment rate fell below 5 per cent in 1997 – a level lower than had seemed sustainable since the 1960s. These trends look particularly good compared with experiences in European countries, where employment growth, particularly in the private sector, has been extremely weak. It has been observed that a major reason for the larger increase in employment in the US is the more rapid growth in the population and the workforce than in Europe. This observation is valid, but the contrast can perhaps best be viewed as underscoring the magnitude of the US job-creation achievement instead of detracting from it.

When the 'US model' is described as an example of successful job creation, those who take a critical view often argue that many of the 'new' jobs are 'poor' jobs. That is, pay levels for new jobs are said to be low, especially for people without professional skills. Critics also point to the increase in wage inequality that occurred. Criticisms along these line have made it easier to dismiss the US record of job growth as being seriously flawed, and to regard deterioration in job quality and increased inequality as too high a price to pay for strong employment growth. To set the stage for more detailed discussion, the first part of this chapter is devoted to a broad description and interpretation of what has happened to the level of average wages and to wage inequality in the US labour market.

The view that the economy relies increasingly heavily on a highly skilled and educated workforce to manage the production and distribution of technologically sophisticated goods and services is another prominent theme in discussions of the US labour market performance. In the current economic and labour market environment, workers are sometimes characterized as being increasingly vulnerable to changing production requirements. The rapid pace of change has implications for the kinds of skill that workers need to develop, how much flexibility they need to assume to enable them to change jobs and adapt to new work, how job security and satisfaction are affected, and how wage-setting is influenced by a more dynamic and competitive economic environment. To address these questions, I discuss recent evidence on job stability and analyses of the underlying sources of changes in the US labour market.

The rise in the value that the labour market has placed on workers with more sophisticated skills raises questions about the adequacy of education and skill development policies for upgrading workers' qualifications. The corresponding decline in the relative wages of the less skilled, in turn, raises the issue of whether policies can be developed that could help them to earn a middle-class living. Policies to address these specific concerns should, of course, be considered in the context of the need to maintain a broad policy and institutional environment that encourages job creation and economic growth. The extraordinarily favourable general performance of the US economy in the late 1990s, with regard to both unemployment and inflation, raises questions about whether it can be attributed to traditional and perhaps temporary sources, or whether a new, more skill-intensive and knowledge-based economy may be bringing about changes in productivity and labour market performance that can be expected to persist.

US labour market performance

Wage levels

In popular discussion, the average worker is often described as falling behind. The real wages of the average worker have sometimes been characterized as declining to levels that prevailed in the 1960s. This view of workers' pay levels is contradicted by the most comprehensive information that is available on workers' productivity and pay. Several different kinds of measure of what workers are paid are available.[2] Two of the most commonly cited conventional measures are charted in Figure 10.1. It is clear from this figure that these data

278

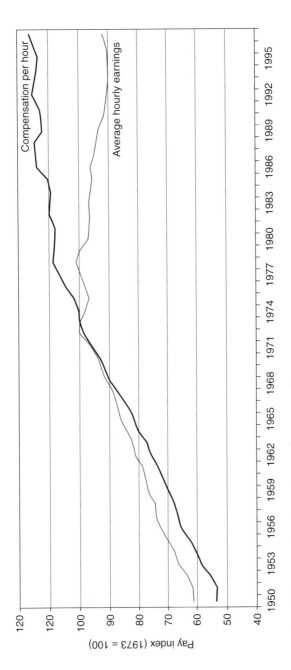

Figure 10.1 Real average hourly earnings and compensation
Notes: Compensation per hour includes wages and salaries of employees plus benefits (employers' contributions for social insurance and private benefit plans). It covers the non-farm business sector. Average hourly earnings does not include non-wage benefits. It covers production and non-supervisory workers in the private, non-farm sector of the economy. Both measures are adjusted for inflation using CPI-U-X1.
Source: Kosters, AEI, February 1998.

can be used to tell quite different stories about how the average worker has fared. One measure suggests that workers are about 15 per cent better off than they were in 1973, while the other suggests that real wages declined by about 10 per cent to the level of the late 1960s. One reason for the discrepancy is the difference between these two measures in the extent to which they include all components of the total compensation that workers receive. Another is the difference in the comprehensiveness of their coverage of all workers. To interpret what these and related measures of workers' pay mean for trends in the average worker's well-being, it is necessary to consider some of the most significant relevant differences between these measures.

Compensation per hour is much more inclusive than average hourly earnings in terms of the components of workers' pay that are included. Average hourly earnings does not include non-cash benefits, and some cash wage payments such as bonuses, commissions, and irregular incentive payments, are also excluded. Compensation per hour, on the other hand, includes not only all cash wage payments, but also costs such as employers' contributions for social insurance and the costs of providing health plans and private retirement programmes. The cost of providing some non-wage benefits, such as health insurance plans, has increased more rapidly over the years than have wages, and these costs have accounted for a growing share of total compensation.

Compositional shifts

Differences in the characteristics of workers whose pay is reflected in these measures are also important. The average hourly earnings measure covers only production and non-supervisory workers, while compensation per hour covers all workers in the non-farm business sector. The first important point about production and non-supervisory workers is that workers in this category are less skilled than average. As is clear in the discussion of the distribution of wages, less-skilled workers have received smaller wage increases than have more-skilled workers since the late 1970s. This difference in the size of wage increases is illustrated by data charted in Figure 10.2 on the average wages of hourly workers – workers paid by the hour – compared with salaried workers. Real wages of workers paid by the hour have declined since the late 1970s, in contrast to the pay of salaried workers. Workers paid by the hour are not entirely equivalent to production and non-supervisory workers, but in practice there is apparently a great deal of overlap.

A feature of production and non-supervisory workers that has received very little attention is the lack of stability in the definition of which workers are included. The composition of workers in this category was apparently shifted away from workers with the highest wages in the group, especially during the early 1980s. To explain this shift, it should first be noted that the only reason it is necessary for employers to distinguish between production and non-supervisory workers and other workers is for the purpose of reporting the

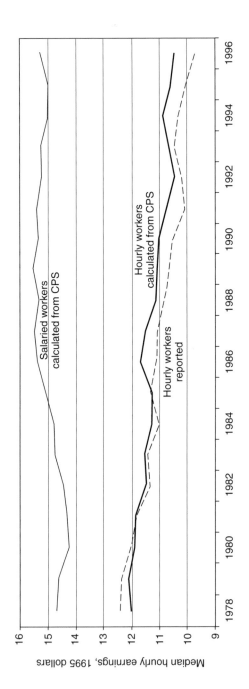

Figure 10.2 Real median hourly earnings, hourly versus salaried employees

Notes: Real median hourly earnings are median average hourly earnings for workers age 25–54 in the Earner Study sample of the Population Survey. Workers must have the following characteristics: (a) the longest job in the reporting year was not farm, self-emp and unincorporated, or without pay; (b) workers reported having been employed full-time in the reporting year; and (c) workers must have reported working for more than 13 weeks in the reporting year. Hourly earnings as calculated from the CPS are derived by dividing in wage and salary by total weeks worked in the reporting year to derive average weekly earnings, then dividing average weekly earnings average hours worked per week in the reporting year. Reported hourly earnings for hourly workers is self-reported. Medians are deflated by CPI-U-X1.

Source: Kosters AEI, February 1998.

wages, hours and employment data from which the average hourly earnings figures are computed. Payroll records do need to be kept, however, for workers who are not exempt from overtime requirements, a category of workers that is in turn closely comparable with workers paid by the hour. Failure to adjust upwards the wage test component of the administrative regulations used to distinguish between exempt and non-exempt workers after the late 1970s meant that it became much easier for workers with some supervisory responsibilities to pass the wage-test hurdle in the early 1980s, thereby reducing average wages for the workers who remained in the lower-paid, production and non-supervisory category.[3]

The decline in the real value of the wage test was very pronounced in the late 1970s and early 1980s, as shown in Figure 10.3, and to the extent that this has shifted the composition of the sample, the decline helped to pull down the real average hourly earnings measure charted in the same figure. This erosion in the real level of the wage test produces a distorted measure of wages for the typical worker remaining in the non-exempt group. It would have the effect of reducing measured average real wages of non-exempt workers, even if there were no decline in the wage of any individual worker. Thus, in addition to its limitations because of the components of pay that it fails to include, and the below-average skills of workers in this group, real average hourly earnings of production and non-supervisory workers is not reliable as a measure of the trend in the level of wages for the typical worker because of changes in the composition of the workers covered.

Price measurement

The long-term trend in the level of real compensation depends largely on productivity growth, but real compensation is also influenced by short-term departures from measured productivity growth. Real wages could fall short of productivity growth if, for example, payments to labour were increasing less rapidly than payments to capital and other inputs, and real wage increases could exceed productivity growth if payments to labour were increasing at the expense of other payments. To see whether labour is sharing fully in productivity growth, however, it is necessary to measure real wages by using the same set of prices as those used to measure the real output that is used to compute growth in productivity. That is, wages need to be adjusted for inflation using the prices of output that workers produce, and not the prices for a market basket that workers consume. Labour and other inputs need to be paid out of the real value of the output they are used to produce. As shown in Figure 10.4, the two measures of prices have diverged in recent years, and this divergence is the main reason why real wage increases measured on the basis of consumer prices for their consumption market basket have fallen short of productivity growth. Most of the divergence disappears when prices of domestically-produced current output are used to adjust for inflation,

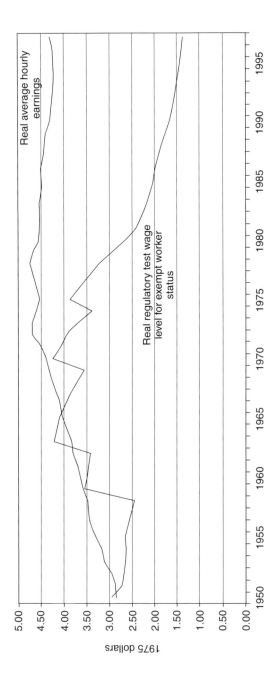

Figure 10.3 Real average hourly earnings and regulatory test wage for exempt status

Notes: Real average hourly earnings cover production and non-supervisory workers in the private, non-farm sector of the economy. The regulatory test wage for exempt worker status is the 'long-test' wage for administrative classification of workers as exempt from the minimum wage and overtime provisions of the Fair Labor Standards Act. Both measures are adjusted for inflation using CPI-U-X1.

Source: Kosters, AEI, March 1998.

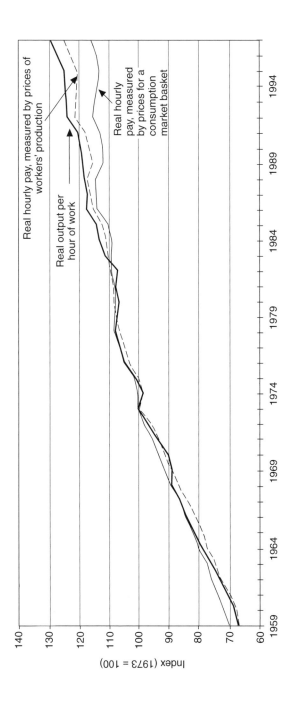

Figure 10.4 Workers' productivity and pay, non-farm business sector

Notes: Real output per hour is adjusted for inflation using the Implicit Price Deflator for the non-farm business sector for the economy; this price Index is also used to measure workers' pay in terms of the prices for this production. To obtain real hourly pay in terms of its consumption value, nominal wages are deflated by CPI-U-X1. Compensation per hour is used as the basis for both measures of real hourly pay.

Source: Kosters, AEI, February 1998.

however, and the difference that remains mainly reflects the dilution of measured private-sector productivity gains because they need to be spread to public sector wages and the rise in the profit share during the current strong and sustained cyclical expansion.

A great deal of attention has also been focused recently on the adequacy of the Consumer Price Index (CPI) itself as a measure of the prices consumers pay for a market basket of goods and services.[4] Issues that have been addressed include the extent to which changes in the index are an accurate reflection of changes in the real material well-being of consumers. Careful examination of many of the procedures that have been used to collect and assemble the price data has revealed significant opportunities for making technical improvements. Improvements of this kind can be made without addressing the more difficult conceptual issues such as whether compensation for price increases would leave consumers no better off than if the previous pattern of prices and products prevailed, or whose well-being should be measured.

Several important technical improvements in the methodology for the CPI were introduced during the late 1990s. When a change in the way the costs of owner-occupied housing were measured in the CPI was introduced in 1983, data were developed to take this major change into account. A special measure, CPI-U-X1, is often used to measure levels of real well-being over time, because it uses a method that is consistent over time. It is appropriate to apply the same reasoning to recent improvements in methods and procedures, by taking these changes into account. If these recent changes were not taken into account, there would be an apparent decline in inflation and a corresponding rise in real wage growth that would be attributable solely to changes in the way prices are measured.

To take into account recent changes in methods and procedures for measuring prices, I have reduced the price index used to compute real wages by half a percentage point per year. An adjustment of this size is supported by research on the impact of the new procedures, although questions can be raised about the most appropriate path for adjusting the CPI over time.[5] I have applied the adjustment from 1978 to 1997 because this corresponds closely to the period between the introduction and subsequent elimination of the most important source of bias that was removed by recent changes. The data charted in Figure 10.5 reflect this adjustment in prices. These adjusted data show continuing increases in both real average compensation per hour and in hourly wages and salaries, with average wages up more than 20 per cent since 1973, and compensation up by almost 30 per cent. The trends these data show are consistent with measures of productivity growth and other comprehensive measures of wages and compensation.[6] Although increases since the early 1970s have not been as large as during the 1950s and 1960s, the improvement they show is quite different from the commonly expressed view of stagnation or widespread decline in real wages for the typical worker.

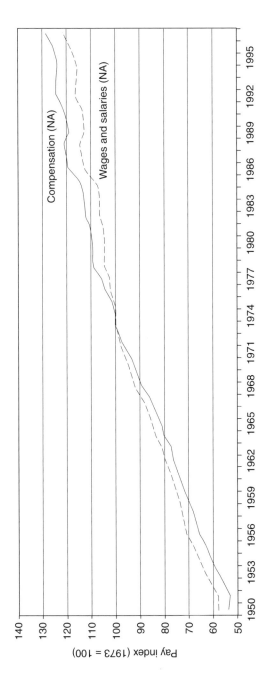

Figure 10.5 Adjusted measures of real wages and compensation, comparisons from 1973.

Notes: Compensation (NA) includes wages and salaries, plus benefits, for the non-farm business sector, and wages and salaries (NA) uses National Income and Product Accounts data to remove the growth of non-wage benefits from compensation per hour. In addition to adjustment for inflation using CPI-U-X1, a further adjustment is made to the price index of one-half of a percentage point per year, beginning in 1978, to take into account changes in methodology and procedures used by the Bureau of Labor Statistics.

Source: Kosters, AEI, March 1998.

The distribution of wages

If the average level of real wages is up, what about wage inequality? Most measures of the distribution of wages show a substantial increase in wage inequality in the US labour market that began at some point in the 1970s. Some of the questions raised by this widening of wage inequality include: what caused the wider wage disparity? Are any systematic patterns shown by the increase in wage inequality? What are the economic effects of increased wage inequality? What forces might limit or reverse the widening of wage inequality? What are the likely social and political consequences of greater wage inequality? All these questions have received attention.

Inequality and skills

In some popular discussions, a rise in wage inequality is described as resulting from 'those who were already well off grabbing most of the gains', with the major role implicitly assigned to greed. Some discussions point to policy changes as a source of increased inequality, and others see 'the poor getting poorer and the rich, richer' as a normal state of affairs in the absence of vigorous efforts by government policies to counter this trend.[7] Other commentaries stressing the need for well-developed skills come closer to the mark, and this is evident from comparisons of data on wage trends for workers with different levels of education.

The data charted in Figure 10.6 provide a simple and straightforward indicator of how much the spread of the distribution of wages has widened. By themselves, these data do not provide any clues about why wages became more widely dispersed. And although this measure of the gap between wages at the 20th and 80th percentiles compares only two positions in the overall wage distribution, since wage inequality has in fact widened quite evenly across the distribution, this simple measure sketches out a picture of what happened to wage inequality that is quite valid.

We can begin to gain an insight into the underlying sources of the rise in wage inequality by examining the trend of wage differences between workers with different schooling levels. Data on the ratio of wages of college graduates to high school graduates' wages are charted in Figure 10.7. According to these data, the college wage premium declined from the late 1960s to the late 1970s, after which it began a substantial rise that continued into the 1990s. In 1978, the average wage of a college graduate was 25 per cent higher than for a high-school-level worker; but by 1996 the college graduate was earning about 50 per cent more. One point that should be noted about these changes is that about half of the increase in the college wage premium since the late 1970s represents a recovery from an unusually low level of the college wage premium around that time. Another point is that there are at least some tentative signs that the college wage premium may recently have stabilized, or even perhaps declined.

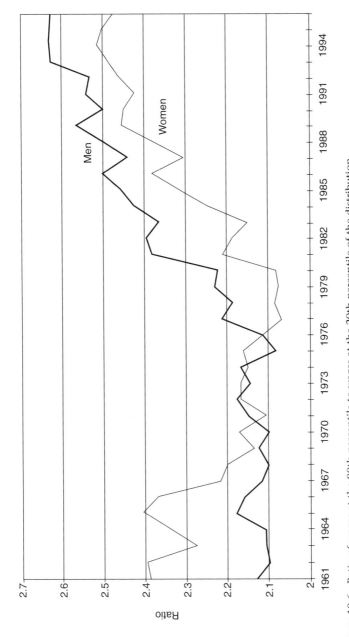

Figure 10.6 Ratio of wages at the 80th percentile to wages at the 20th percentile of the distribution
Source: Kosters, AEI, February 1998.

288

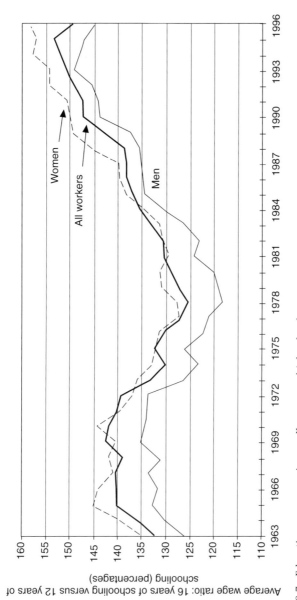

Figure 10.7 Education wage premium: college versus high school

Note: Average wages were computed for the middle 80 per cent of hourly wages for each group (the top and bottom 10 per cent were excluded).

Source: Kosters, AEI, January 1998.

Schooling is one way that workers develop skills; learning through work experience on the job is another. If the schooling wage premium increased because the labour market placed a higher value on workers with more skills, then the wage premium for additional work experience would also be expected to rise. The work experience wage premium has risen since the late 1970s, although the timing of changes in wage premiums seems to reflect changes in both demand and supply. The rise in skill premiums at a time when the skills of the workforce were substantially upgraded implies that skill demands were rising. On the supply side, the big influx of young, college-educated members of the baby boom generation into the workforce in the 1970s was followed by a gradual slowdown in the growth of the share of the workforce accounted for by college graduates. The gradual ageing of the workforce that has resulted is associated with the accumulation of more work experience for the average worker.

Because one of the largest components of the cost of getting a college education is the earnings that are forgone while attending an educational establishment instead of working, the rise in the college wage premium strengthened incentives for college-level schooling. The striking rise in the college enrolment rate in parallel with the rise in the college wage premium charted in Figure 10.8 illustrates the effect of higher rewards for investment in human capital. During much of the 1970s, less than 50 per cent of young people were undertaking educational courses during the autumn following their graduation from high school, but by the 1990s more than 60 per cent of recent high school graduates were enrolled in post-secondary schools. A larger proportion of youth obtaining additional schooling immediately after graduating from high school is only one dimension of such increases in investment, of course. Other dimensions include part-time schooling while working, going back to education full-time after working for a time, and taking advantage of more training provided by employers. A larger proportion of youth with college-level credentials results in a large proportion who are able to earn college-level wages. In addition, the increase in the relative supply of college-level workers stimulated by higher economic rewards is a self-correcting force that limits the extent to which schooling wage premiums and wage inequality continue to widen. Some of the most recent data suggest that wage premiums for schooling may have stabilized or perhaps declined slightly.

Socio-political implications

Economic effects on earnings levels, labour force attachment and skill development incentives are, of course, not the only effects of wage inequality with which we should be concerned. Some commentators have expressed concerns that wider differences in average wages for workers with different schooling levels have given rise to a 'two-tier labour market', with workers having schooling beyond high-school level being able to earn a middle-class

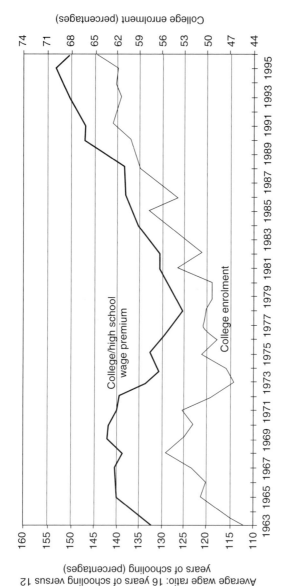

Figure 10.8 College enrolment and college wage premium

Notes: Enrolment figures are the percentage of high school graduates aged 16–24 who were enrolled in college in the October following graduation. Average wages were computed for the middle 80 per cent of hourly wages for full-time workers age 25–54 (the top and bottom 10 per cent were excluded). Wages of workers with 16 years of schooling are compared with those with 12 years of schooling.

Source: Kosters, AEI, March 1998.

income, while those with only high-school credentials or less cannot.[8] It has also been suggested that wider wage differences are socially and politically divisive, because workers whose wages are lower will see themselves as having less in common with other workers and citizens who have higher wages or salaries. The significance of these concerns is difficult to evaluate, but it is useful to look at relevant data to get some insight into how sharply divided wages are for workers with different educational credentials.

One way to assess the degree of separation between workers with different levels of schooling is to look at measures of overlap between distributions. The extent of overlap is affected by what happens to both changes in the gap in average wages between different groups, and changes in dispersion within schooling groups. Both measures have widened since the late 1970s, mainly because years of schooling is an important measure, but only a crude and incomplete measure, of workers' skills. It is possible to look at the degree of overlap between distributions in various ways, and I present some simple comparisons of wages for high school and college graduates in Figure 10.9.[9] These comparisons trace the position in the high-school wage distribution of the median wage for college graduates since 1963.

The location of the college median in relation to high-school wage distribution declined from the late 1960s to the late 1970s. That is, the degree of overlap increased when the wage gap narrowed. Since the late 1970s, the degree of overlap has reduced as the wage gap has widened. By 1996, about 77 per cent of high-school graduates earned less than the median wage for college graduates. Conversely, almost one in four high school graduates earned more than the college median. The gap between average wages of college and high-school-level workers was considerably wider in the mid-1990s than during the 1960s. It is worth nothing, however, that the measure of the degree of overlap reported in Figure 10.9 shows that these two wage distributions have recently been no more sharply divided than in the 1960s. Consequently, it is not clear that workers with different schooling credentials now have significantly less in common than previously, and recent developments in the labour market may not necessarily pose a more serious threat to social or political cohesiveness.

Focusing only on averages for two major schooling categories masks a great deal of diversity within each group. Moreover, the workforce can be further differentiated by more detailed schooling categories, occupational and skill specialities, and work experience. Smoothed wage distributions for high-school and college graduates are charted in Figure 10.10, along with median wages for three other schooling categories. High-school and college graduates account for more than 50 per cent of the adult, full-time workforce. Almost another 30 per cent is accounted for by workers with some college education, to reach a total of about 80 per cent of the workforce. Workers without high-school credentials and those with advanced degrees each account for only about 10 per cent. Differences between median wages of workers in each schooling category are certainly evident in these data, but the amount of

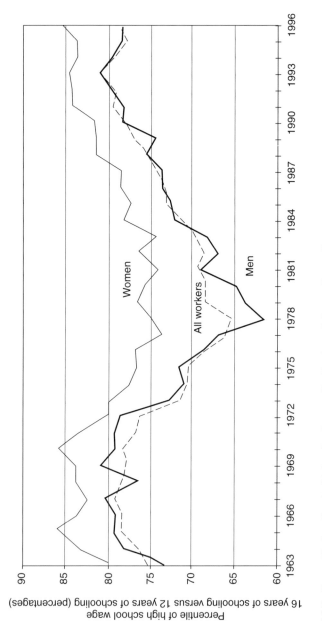

Figure 10.9 Percentile location in high school wage distribution of the median college wage

Note: Percentile location in the wage distribution for high-school-level workers of the median wage for college level workers.

Source: Kosters, AEI, January 1998.

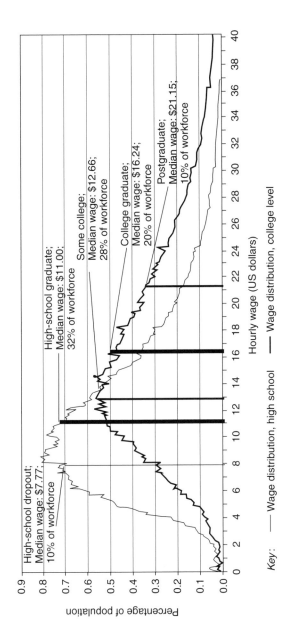

Figure 10.10 Wage distributions by education, full-time workers aged 25–54, 1996

Notes: Histograms calculated on $0.10 increments in wage levels. Histograms have been smoothed using a symmetric moving average filter with a width equal to ± 20% of the wage level.

Source: Kosters, AEI, January 1998.

overlap in the distributions is also striking. The wage data describe a continuum across the social and economic scales; there is no great divide based on differences in schooling credentials.

Job security, wages and labour market performance

Job stability and worker insecurity

Whether jobs have become less stable and workers more insecure has come to public attention in several contexts. Serious doubt has sometimes been expressed about whether long-term employment with a single employer is a realistic prospect for most workers, and in particular whether long-term or lifetime jobs have become much less common in the USA than in the past. It has also been noted that the proportion of employment consisting of temporary and contract jobs has increased, which some contend has reduced workers' job security and loyalty to employers. A great deal of publicity has also been given in recent years to corporate downsizing, in part because plans for major reductions in employment are now more likely than previously to be announced in advance to comply with legislation requiring advance notice, but perhaps for other reasons as well.[10] Finally, wage acceleration that has been more modest than anticipated in view of increasingly tight labour markets and low unemployment in 1997 and 1998 has raised questions about whether workers' concerns about losing their jobs, with the reduction in pay that this could entail, might be keeping workers from pressing harder for pay increases.

A great deal of recent research has been carried out to try to ferret out facts about job stability. The issue can be explored at several levels. Has job tenure declined in recent years? If it has declined, is this undesirable? Have workers' perceptions changed markedly, irrespective of actual job loss experience? The first of these questions is easiest to address by examining the data.

The information on job tenure that is available is essentially of two kinds: data on the length of time workers have been on their current job; and data on the incidence of job loss. What do these data show? I conclude that job tenure remained essentially unchanged during the 1980s, but that it may have declined slightly by the mid-1990s. However, the decline, if any, was quite small, and most indicators of job stability remain well within the range of experience since the 1950s.

Estimated job retention rates over four-year periods for the workforce as a whole were in the order of 55 per cent, and estimates of the maximum size of a change from the mid-1980s to the early 1990s were only about one percentage point.[11] The changes from 1979 to 1996 in the proportions of employed workers who had been in their job for ten years (from 0.41 to 0.35) or twenty years (from 0.25 to 0.21) were more noticeable, but sensitive to factors such as end points for measurements. For example, from 1983 to 1993 (the next longest span for which these data are available), the proportion of people who had their jobs for ten years declined by only 0.01 with no change at all for workers with twenty years in their jobs.[12] Estimates of rates of job loss over three-year periods derived from surveys of worker displacement showed a decline from about 0.13 to 0.11 from 1983 to 1995, but the lowest rate (0.09) was registered for 1989.[13] These data show that any changes that may have occurred were very small.

We should be cautious about placing too much reliance on these data as measures of change. One reason for caution is the kinds of adjustment that need to be made to take into account small differences over time in the questions that were asked in different surveys. Another reason is that cyclical conditions were different when the surveys took place. Adjustments to take into account rounding and heaping in the survey responses introduce still another reason for caution. Whether adjustments should be made to take into account differences in age and other demographic characteristics, or whether primary attention should instead be focused on broad job aggregates is another issue. In many instances, the direction of estimated effects is affected by choices about what adjustments are most appropriate. Although the evidence, taken as a whole, seems to point to the possibility of a small reduction in job stability from the 1980s to the 1990s, any change that may have occurred, as I pointed out above, has been very small.[14]

A somewhat different but related dimension of work experience has sometimes received attention by proponents of the view that the quality of jobs has deteriorated. Temporary, contract and part-time work have often been criticized in this context. The subject of part-time work is not very relevant to job security issues in my judgement, because there has been little change in its incidence and the implications for wages of part-time work are often exaggerated.[15] It is clear, however, that there has been a pronounced increase in temporary work. The implications of the growth of temporary work on workers' perceptions of job security should be assessed in terms of two features that seem to point in opposite directions. It may be that workers who are employed in temporary jobs are less secure about maintaining their employment than others. For the workforce as a whole, however, the availability of temporary work may be viewed as a significant new labour market institution that can be used to earn income while looking for a more permanent job, and perhaps as an activity that can itself contribute to finding a good job match. That is, the availability of temporary employment in the event of job loss may assuage concerns among workers about losing their jobs among those employed in long-term jobs more than it heightens concerns of those in temporary jobs, and on balance enhances confidence that some kind of more-or-less suitable work is always available.[16]

The other main sources of information on job security experience and perceptions are the monthly employment and unemployment data collected in the Current Population Survey (CPS) and attitudinal surveys. A review of

CPS data shows no unusual patterns for the incidence of job loss, although duration of unemployment has recently been on the high side. Workers also appear to be somewhat more reluctant of leave their jobs than has been typical during tight labour markets. Although some reports based on special-purpose surveys seem to show an unusual degree of worker insecurity in view of labour market conditions, the large, well-established attitudinal surveys, such as relevant parts of the surveys of consumer confidence conducted by the Survey Research Center at the University of Michigan, and the Conference Board, do not seem to show any atypical cyclical behaviour. Taken together, the evidence provides little basis for concluding that workers feel sufficiently less secure in their jobs and that they are more reluctant to press for higher pay than might normally be expected under contemporary labour market conditions.

Sources of changes in the structure of wages

Changes that took place in recent decades – changes in technology, in workers' skills, in the wage structure, and in global trade – have stimulated a great deal of research intended to develop and improve insights into the sources of these changes. With regard to analysis of the dramatic rise in the wage premium for skills since the late 1970s, three kinds of sources have been identified: supply; demand; and the institutional and regulatory environment. Among institutional and regulatory changes, those that have received the most attention are policies such as the minimum wage that could have had a direct regulatory impact on the distribution of wages; trends like the decline in the extent of unionization that could affect wages for particular groups; and the introduction of more competition into transportation and communication markets by extensive deregulation.

As is widely recognized, the real value of the minimum wage has declined since the 1970s in relation to average wages. The likely implication of this decline for employment and for the distribution of wages is mitigated, however, by the less-well-known expansion of coverage by minimum-wage requirements to sectors with wages that were previously much lower than the wages in covered sectors. The minimum wage, at levels that prevailed in the mid-1990s, probably on balance has a smaller impact on the wage distribution now than in the 1970s. Nevertheless, there is general agreement that a decline in the real level of the minimum wage could have made only a small contribution to wage inequality, because the direct quantitative contribution it could make is very small and because the widening spread of wages is not concentrated in the lower part of the wage distribution, but instead extends across the entire spread of distribution.[17]

The decline in unionization among the US labour force is another factor in the environment that could have contributed to increased wage inequality. Some research points toward the possibility that lower unionization might have increased wage inequality, but questions remain about whether the decline in unionization is largely a result of broader economic trends that have influenced industry and occupational patterns.[18] Certainly, the downward trend in unionization began long before wage inequality began to increase. After reaching a peak of more than 25 per cent of the workforce in the 1950s, unionization gradually declined to reach about half that rate in 1997, and in the private sector the decline has been much steeper.

A trend toward stronger competition in US markets for products and services has almost certainly influenced the competitiveness of the labour market as well. One source of this trend has been extensive deregulation in the transportation and communications sectors. Increased competition in the automobile and steel industries did not come about from deregulation, but from the development of strong competition from abroad that was only partially offset by efforts to protect domestic producers. Changes in competitive conditions in product markets seem to have contributed more to competition in the labour market, and to the changes in the structure of wages that resulted, than to changes in labour market regulation.

The supply and demand framework that economists generally use to analyze economic changes is applicable to the labour market as well. Research indicates that changes in relative supplies of labour with different schooling levels have influenced the timing and magnitude of changes in relative wages. This research also shows that changes in the structure of wages cannot be accounted for by changes in supply alone.[19] Demand shifts were also evidently at work.

Attention has been focused on two sources of changes in demand: international trade and technological change. The idea of trade as a cause of increased wage inequality comes readily to mind as a presumptive consequence of low-wage competition from abroad, especially for production of goods that do not rely heavily on highly skilled workers. A sophisticated body of theory lends support to trade as a possible source of downward pressure on the relative wages of less-skilled workers. Although it has been argued that trade has made an important contribution to increased wage inequality, most economists apparently hold the view that only a relatively small share of the increase in the skill premium could be attributable to increased competition from low-wage countries.[20]

Partly through a process of elimination, some degree of consensus has emerged among economists that a major role should be assigned to skill-biased technological change to explain the increase in the wage premium that employers are willing to pay for workers with better skills. Evidence in support of the view that technology is the main source of the increase in wage inequality is, by and large, indirect. Research on the relationship between wages and computer usage constitutes perhaps the most direct evidence.[21] However, a great deal of indirect evidence from research using a variety of methods and approaches points to an important role for technology.[22]

Although much attention has been focused on whether technological change has recently had a significant skill bias, and whether this bias has

Table 10.1   Employment shares by schooling categories, 1940–95 (percentages)

Year	High-school dropouts	High-school graduates	Some college	College graduates
1940	68.7	19.0	6.3	6.0
1950	58.5	24.3	9.5	7.7
1960	50.0	27.4	12.5	10.1
1970	36.1	34.1	16.4	13.4
1980	21.4	35.8	23.6	19.2
1990	12.0	33.3	30.8	24.0
1995	9.7	34.0	30.1	26.2

Note: Data are from decennial census, except for those of 1995, which are based on the Current Population Survey.
Source: Adapted from Autor *et al.* (1997), Appendix table A1.

become more pronounced, there is really no question about its direction and significance over the long term. The impressive upgrading of the education levels of the US workforce that has been taking place for more than half a century is shown in Table 10.1. In the absence of a significant bias towards making more effective use of workers with additional schooling, a big decline in the economic return to schooling would be expected instead of stability, and in recent years, expansion of the schooling wage premium.

In view of the presumed role of skill-biased technological change, is it reasonable to suppose that nothing can be identified on the horizon that might lead to stabilization or reversal of the recent rise in wage inequality? The increase in the proportion of young people who are investing in additional schooling that has already been noted should be viewed as an important qualification. But in addition, judgements about what can reasonably be expected in the future depend on ideas that are often implicit in thinking about causal relationships. A model that attempts to reconcile US experience in recent years that combines a sharp decline in the price of investment goods (computers), a slowdown in productivity growth (beginning in the early 1970s), and an expansion of the skill premium for wages, has been developed by Greenwood (1997) for example. He uses the model to examine recent trends and relate them to earlier historical experience. This analysis suggests that strong gains in productivity growth will be realized in the future, and that further downward pressure on the relative wages of the least skilled workers will be relieved as new technologies mature. This and other models should receive consideration as alternatives to approaches that simply project a continuation of trends in the recent past.

What kinds of policies should be pursued to facilitate constructive changes and reduce adverse impacts on particular groups and sectors? The first step in considering this question is, perhaps, to identify the main problems that need to be alleviated. In my view, assuring a minimum, decent level of living for families of adults who are willing and able to work should be the main concern. In view of all the many economic and policy forces that put that goal in jeopardy at one time or another for workers of all kinds, primary reliance on general policies to support incomes seems more appropriate than special programmes for workers presumed to be affected mainly by changes in trade, technology or other disturbances. In addition, it may be appropriate to try to speed up adjustments, even those adjustments that are already under way in response to stronger incentives, such as more investment in schooling.

Policies to stimulate more investment in workers' skills seems to be one of the most obvious approaches to facilitating adjustment. Questions about education include whether increased emphasis should be placed at lower or higher levels of schooling, as well as whether policy changes should originate at the Federal level or at state or local levels. It seems clear, however, on the basis of decades of experience in the USA and many empirical studies that federally-sponsored efforts to provide training to workers outside regular institutional schooling channels have not been very successful.[23] If further subsidies for post-secondary schooling and training are desirable, extensive reliance should be placed on the diverse opportunities that are available, from community colleges to major research universities.[24] Improving the quality of schooling at all levels is, of course, an appealing goal, and while there is no shortage of ideas about how this might be done, the evidence provides little assurance that devoting more financial resources to schooling at elementary and secondary levels would have much effect.

Contemporary labour market performance

The unemployment rate declined below 5 per cent by the middle of 1997. The increase in jobs during the year that followed exceeded growth in the working age population by about half a million workers, driving the proportion of the working-age population with jobs to a record high of above 64 per cent. The proportion of people in the labour force with jobs was higher than in earlier cyclical peaks, the pace of job creation was higher than is sustainable over the long term, and instances in which firms experienced difficulties attracting workers with the requisite skills were frequently reported. Yet, the size of wage increases was rising only modestly, increases in total hourly labour costs were small, and labour costs per unit of output were quite stable as a result of at least a temporary revival of productivity growth. Under these circumstances, despite labour market conditions that were extraordinarily tight, price inflation gradually subsided. This unexpectedly favourable combination of low unemployment and declining inflation was a puzzle that raised questions about its causes and whether they were temporary or permanent.[25]

Although no consensus emerged about causes, a number of possible contributing factors have been suggested. Some involve price behaviour, others relate to labour costs, and still others are based on structural or market changes. Explanations based on prices usually point to the deceleration in prices of imports and of health services, and the striking decline in computer prices. The deceleration or decline in all these prices was generally viewed as likely to be, at least in part, temporary. However, the changes in methodology for constructing prices indexes that were recently introduced can be expected to be a more durable source of smaller measured price increases.

There was little acceleration in the rate of increase in labour costs despite tight labour markets. Price behaviour probably contributed to the limited acceleration in wage increases in at least two ways. First, the difficulties that firms experienced in passing on cost increases reduced their willingness to allow labour costs to rise, and declining inflation has increased the acceptability to workers of small nominal wage increases. Second, smaller increases in health care costs are translated quite directly into smaller increases in this component of total costs. It should be recognized, of course, that it is the *total* cost of labour, including non-wage benefits such as health plans, that is presumably critical for business firms. However, trends in the costs of health plans often become evident only after a lag, particularly for firms that self-insure, and it is uncertain how long a lower health cost trend will persist. These circumstances produced a combination of some acceleration in the wage component of labour costs, and smaller than projected increases in the total cost of labour.

The changes discussed so far should probably be regarded as being temporary and subject to reversal, with the result that conditions could change rapidly to bring about price and employment performance more comparable with earlier experience. It is possible, however, that changes in regulatory and institutional arrangements might make a more lasting contribution to improved performance. Stronger competition from international trade and extensive deregulation of the transportation and communications sectors of the economy may increase resistance to labour and other cost increases. Increased competition in capital markets, through a more active market for corporate control, for example, could be having a more general impact on the discipline that firms exercise to keep cost increases under control and to cut costs when feasible. On the labour market side, the extraordinary growth in jobs in the temporary help services sector may be making a noticeable contribution in enabling the economy to run at a lower unemployment rate without overheating.[26]

Increased competitiveness in markets for goods and services, in the capital market, and in the labour market, could result in less job security for workers. The evidence does not suggest that job tenure of the average worker declined very much, and the incidence of job loss seems, if anything, less concentrated among particular groups, such as construction and manufacturing production workers. Unemployment data suggest that the likelihood of being recalled to the same job has declined, and that layoff more frequently entails finding a new job instead. Finding a new job may also more frequently include acceptance of at least a temporary reduction in pay, although there is no evidence that such a change has occurred. Workers could perhaps have become more fearful of losing their jobs, as has been suggested by data from some specialized surveys.[27] In view of the small size of changes in job stability and the uncertainty about how these changes should be interpreted, however, it seems quite unlikely that workers' worries about their jobs has produced a reluctance to press for wage increases, which could be a significant source of wage restraint under contemporary labour market conditions.

Why wage and price behaviour was so subdued during the late 1990s years of tight markets remains a major puzzle. Some of the sources of better-than-expected performance are most probably temporary. There are also reasons to believe that stronger competition has contributed to more timely and thoroughgoing adjustments to changes in conditions, including pervasive shifts in the structure of wages. New technology has almost certainly contributed to a stronger demand for skilled workers, but important linkages between the technology, skill demands and achievement of better employment and inflation performance have not been established. Indeed, the widespread upgrading of skill requirements in recent years that has been associated with the increased emphasis on knowledge and information-based production requirements could, if anything, have the opposite effect if these developments increase the difficulties that less-skilled workers experience in finding suitable jobs.

Notes

1. For discussions that are representative of conventional views see, for example, Uchitelle (1998), Auerbach and Belous (1998), and Bollier (1998).
2. The most important measures of the level and distribution of workers' pay are discussed in Kosters (1998).
3. The administrative tests for exemption from the minimum wage and overtime provisions of the Fair Labor Standards Act involve both a duties test and a wage test. To be classified as exempt, it is necessary for an employee to meet the requirements of the duties test for supervisory responsibilities and independent exercise of discretion and, in addition, the employee's pay must exceed levels set by the regulations. There are two levels specified for the wage test, with somewhat less stringent duties requirements specified for employees that meet the higher wage test level. Because the increase in wage test levels that was scheduled for implementation in 1980 was postponed indefinitely, the erosion of the real level of the wage test since the late 1970s has made the wage test essentially irrelevant in recent years for establishing the exempt and non-exempt status of employees.
4. See Boskin *et al.* (1996).
5. This is a conservative estimate based largely on estimates developed by the Bureau of Labor Statistics (1997). See also Council of Economic Advisers (1998, table 2–4).
6. Information on wages and compensation from the Employment Cost Index, for example, shows similar trends; see Kosters (1998).
7. For an influential treatment of these issues, see Phillips (1990).
8. Reich (1991) and Thurow (1996).
9. Wage data are presented in this way in Pierce and Welch (1996, figure 4.2, p. 56).

10. For examples of high-profile commentary along these lines see, for example, *New York Times* (1996) and Barlett and Steele (1996).
11. Neumark *et al.* (1997, table 3).
12. Farber (1997, table 1).
13. Farber (1998).
14. Gottschalk and Moffitt (1998) review earlier studies, and the new evidence they present shows no deterioration in job stability or related conditions associated with job change in the USA. Jaeger and Stevens (July 1998) also analyze evidence from different data sources. This conclusion is also corroborated by evidence from studies of job stability in the UK and Italy cited in *The Economist* (1998, p. 76).
15. Kosters and McCullough (1994).
16. Kosters (1997).
17. Bound and Johnson (1991).
18. For a careful analysis of effects of labour unions, see Freeman (1993).
19. For an excellent general, formal treatment of this question, see Murphy and Welch (1991).
20. Some selections from an extensive and rapidly growing body of literature on this subject are: Bhagwati (1994), Wood (1994), Burtless (1995), Borjas *et al.* (1997).
21. Krueger (1993).
22. Much of this research is referenced and summarized in Autor *et al.* (1997).
23. See LaLonde (1995); Orr *et al.* (1996); Friedlander *et al.* (1997); and O'Neill and O'Neill (1997).
24. For discussions of the likely effects of policies intended to expand post-secondary schooling, see Heckman *et al.* (1998), and Kosters (1999).
25. For contemporary commentary on these issues, see, for example, Council of Economic Advisers (1998) and Congressional Budget Office (1998).
26. Although average daily temporary employment of some 2.5 million workers may seem small in relation to about 130 million employed workers, it looms much larger in relation to 6.5 million unemployed.
27. Alan Greenspan, Chairman of the Federal Reserve Board of Governors, cited data from one of these surveys, for example, in his Humphrey-Hawkins Testimony on 26 February 1997.

References

Auerbach, J. A. and Belous, R. S. (eds) (1998) *The Inequality Paradox: Growth of Income Disparity* (Washington, DC: National Policy Association).

Autor, D. H., Katz, L. F. and Krueger, A. B. (1997) 'Computing Inequality: Have Computers Changed the Labor Market?', National Bureau of Economic Research Working Paper No. 5956 (March).

Barlett, D. L. and Steele, J. B. (1996) *America: What Went Wrong?* (Kansas City, Mo.: Andrews and McMeel).

Bhagwati, J. and Kosters, M. H. (eds) (1994) *Trade and Wages: Leveling Wages Down?* (Washington, DC: AEI Press).

Bollier, D. (1998) *Work and Future Society: Where Are the Economy and Technology Taking Us?* (Washington, DC: Aspen Institute).

Borjas, G. J., Freeman, R. B. and Katz, L. F. (1997) 'How Much Do Immigration and Trade Affect Labor Market Outcomes?', *Brookings Papers on Economic Activity*, no. 1.

Boskin, M., Dulberger, E., Gordon, R., Griliches, Z. and Jorgenson, D. (1996) 'Toward a More Accurate Measure of the Cost of Living', Final Report of the Boskin Commission to the Finance Committee, United States Senate (Washington, DC: GPO).

Bound, J. and Johnson, G. (1991) 'Wages in the United States during the 1980s and Beyond', in M. H. Kosters (ed.), *Workers and their Wages: Changing Patterns in the United States* (Washington, DC: AEI Press).

Bureau of Labor Statistics (1997) 'The Consumer Price Index, Current Methods and Procedures, and Methodological issues and Improvements', Mimeo, US Bureau of Labor Statistics.

Burtless, G. (1995) 'International Trade and the Rise in Earnings Inequality'. *Journal of Economic Literature* (June).

Congressional Budget Office (1998) *Economic and Budget Outlook: Fiscal Years 1999–2008* (Washington DC: GPO).

Council of Economic Advisers (1998) 'Expected Effects on Changes in the CPI and Real GDP of CPI Methodological Changes', *Economic Report of the President* (Washington, DC: GPO), p. 80, table 2–4.

Economist (1998) 21 February, p. 76.

Farber, H. S. (1997) 'Trends in Long Term Employment in the United States, 1979–96', Working Paper No. 384, Industrial Relations Section, Princeton University (July), table 1.

Farber, H. S. (1998) 'Has the Rate of Job Loss Increased in the Nineties?', Working Paper No. 394, Industrial Relations Section, Princeton University (January).

Freeman, R. B. (1993) 'How Much Has De-Unionization Contributed to the Rise in Male Earnings Inequality?', in S. Danziger and P. Gottschalk (eds), *Uneven Tides* (New York: Russell Sage Foundation).

Friedlander, D., Greenberg, D. H. and Robins, P. K. (1997) 'Evaluating Government Training Programs for the Economically Disadvantaged', *Journal of Economic Literature* (December).

Gottschalk, P. and Moffitt, R. (1999) 'Changes in Job Instability and Insecurity Using Monthly Survey Data', *Journal of Labor Economics*, vol. 17(4), S91–126.

Greenwood, J. (1997) *The Third Industrial Revolution: Technology, Productivity, and Income Inequality* (Washington, DC: AEI Press).

Heckman, J. J., Lochner, L. and Taber, C. (1998) 'General Equilibrium Treatment Effects: A Study of Tuition Policy', National Bureau of Economic Research Working Paper No. 6426 (February).

Jaeger, D. A. and Stevens, A. H. (1998) 'Is Job Stability in the United States Falling? Reconciling Trends in the Current Population Survey and the Panel Study of Income Dynamics', National Bureau of Economic Research Working Paper No. 6650 (July).

Kosters, M. H. (1995) 'Part-Time Pay', *Journal of Labor Research*, xvi, no. 3 (Summer).

Kosters, M. H. (1997) 'New Employment Relationships and the Labor Market', *Journal of Labor Research*, vol. xvii, no. 4 (Fall).

Kosters, M. H. (1998) *Wage Levels and Inequality: Measuring and Interpreting the Trends* (Washington, DC: American Enterprise Institute).

Kosters, M. H. (ed.) (1999) *Financing College Tuition* (Washington, DC: AEI Press).

Kosters, M. H. and McCullough, D. (1994) 'Does Part-Time Work Pay?', *American Enterprise* (November/December).

Krueger, A. B. (1993) 'How Computers Have Changed the Wage Structure: Evidence from Micro Data', *Quarterly Journal of Economics* (February).

LaLonde, R. J. (1995) 'The Promise of Public Sector-Sponsored Training Programs', *The Journal of Economic Perspectives*, vol. 9, no. 2 (Spring).

Murphy, K. M. and Welch, F. (1991) 'The Role of International Trade in Wage Differentials', in M. H. Kosters (ed.), *Workers and Their Wages: Changing Patterns in the United States* (Washington, DC: AEI Press).

Neumark, D., Polsky, D. and Hansen, D. (1997) 'Has Job Stability Declined Yet? New Evidence for the 1990s', National Bureau of Economic Research Working Paper No. 6330 (December), table 3.

New York Times (1996) *The Downsizing of America* (New York: Times Books).

O'Neill, D. M. and O'Neill, J. E. (1997) *Lessons for Welfare Reform: An Analysis of the AFDC Caseload and Past Welfare-to-Work Programs* (Kalamazoo, MI: W. E. Upjohn Institute).

Orr, L. L., Bloom, H. S., Bell, S. H., Doolittle, F., Lin, W. and Cave, G. (1996) *Does Training for the Disadvantaged Work? Evidence from the National JTPA Study* (Washington, DC: The Urban Institute).

Phillips, K. (1990) *The Politics of Rich and Poor: Wealth and the American Electorate in the Reagan Aftermath* (New York: Random House).

Pierce, B. and Welch, F. (1996) 'Changes in the Structure of Wages', in E. A. Hanushek and D. W. Jorgenson (eds), *Improving America's Schools: The Role of Incentives* (Washington, DC: National Research Council, National Academy of Sciences), p. 56, fig. 4.2.

Reich, R. B. (1991) *The Work of Nations: Preparing Ourselves for 21st Century Capitalism* (New York: Alfred A. Knopf).

Thurow. L. (1996) *The Future of Capitalism* (New York: William Morrow).

Uchitelle, L. (1998) 'America's Treadmill Economy', *New York Times*, 8 March, section 3.

Wood, A. (1994) *North–South Trade, Employment, and Inequality: Changing Fortunes in a Skill-Driven World* (New York: Oxford University Press).

Comments

Palle S. Andersen

Let me start by complimenting Mr Kosters on a very interesting, wide-ranging and well-balanced chapter. It is also a chapter with which I find myself in total agreement, so in my comments I shall mainly try to complement Mr Kosters' work with some international comparisons, relate the four issues discussed in the chapter to the topics of the Bank of Japan conference and pose a few specific questions along the way.

Real wages, real compensation, labour productivity and functional income shares

In commenting on this issue, I shall use Figure C10.1 showing comparative changes in five of the major countries. The US developments are similar to those shown in Mr Kosters' paper, although the data sources are not the same. I have relied exclusively on OECD national accounts and labour force data to make the developments more comparable across countries.

Starting with the average growth of real wages and salaries respectively, and real compensation per employee, we see that in most countries real compensation has grown more rapidly than real wages and salaries. There are two sources of this difference. First, non-wage labour costs have grown faster than wage costs. Second, the prices of what employees produce (the GDP deflator) have grown less fast than the prices of what employees buy (consumption deflator). Note, however, some interesting differences between the five countries. In Japan and Canada we see a picture very similar to that of the USA, with real compensation exceeding the growth of real wages and salaries. In contrast, in the UK real compensation has grown less fast than have real wages and salaries, mainly reflecting efforts to reduce social security contributions. In Germany, similar efforts have helped to reduce the growth of real compensation, though it is still slightly higher than that of real wages and salaries.

Let me also note that the graph is not representative of what we observed in the USA during the mid-1990s, when non-wage labour costs slowed

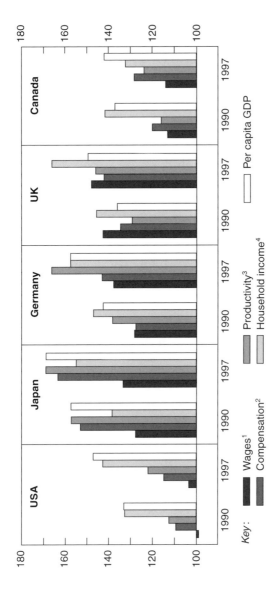

Figure C10.1 Alternative measures of per capita real income and output (1973 = 100).
Notes: 1. Wages and salaries per employee (whole economy), deflated by the consumption deflator; 2. Per employee, deflated by the GDP deflator; 3. Ratio of GDP to total employment; 4 Per capita household disposable income, deflated by the consumption deflator.
Sources: OECD Economic Outlook and national data.

significantly relative to real wages, and helped to dampen the growth of total compensation. In this context, it would be interesting to know if there is a trade-off between increases in, respectively, non-wage labour costs and wages. In other words, do employees push for higher wages in periods when the growth of various non-wage benefits is falling?

Let me now turn to the differential growth rates of respectively real compensation and labour productivity. It is well known that when the growth of labour productivity exceeds that of real compensation, the capital income share tends to increase. From this identity it appears that the capital income share has fallen in Canada, whereas it has been largely stable since 1973 in Japan and the UK. For the USA we observe a slight increase in the capital income share, which was somewhat more pronounced in the 1990s. This is even more evident in Germany, where there the profit share of the private business sector increased from 34.5 per cent to 39 per cent during 1993–7.

Given the subject of the Bank of Japan conference, it is relevant to ask whether technological innovation, combined with lower relative prices of capital goods and the removal of capital account restrictions, may have influenced the distribution of income between capital and labour. I think they have. However, because these various changes have increased the mobility of capital relative to that of labour, it is also necessary to take account of institutional factors as they have a major impact on the adaptability of labour markets. Let me illustrate this by looking more specifically at the developments in the USA and Germany:

(i) As discussed in Mr Kosters' paper, the US labour market is very flexible and adaptable, and this has allowed the unemployment rate to fall below most measures of the NAIRU without leading to higher inflation. Moreover, employment growth has been very fast, so that the growth of capital per employed worker in the private business sector averaged only 1.7 per cent during the 1990s. Moreover, because of the high employment growth, the rise in the capital income share has been smaller than in Germany;

(ii) In Germany, by contrast, the labour market is much less flexible and, driven by a rise in the price of labour relative to that of capital, investment has been mainly of a capital-deepening nature. Hence, employment has largely stagnated and the average growth of capital per worker employed was more than twice that of the USA during the 1990s. This, in turn, has led to a marked acceleration of labour productivity growth and, with the high rate of unemployment moderating wage claims, a marked improvement in capital income, as noted above.

A more rigorous analysis of developments in the USA and Germany would obviously have to include a number of other factors as well as a model that allows various hypotheses to be tested.[1] However, the above comparison serves to illustrate that the impact of new technologies is not confined to productivity growth but may, depending on institutional factors, also include the distribution of factor income.

As time is short, I shall not go through the rest of the Figure C10.1, except to note one phenomenon that has some bearing on the discussion of wage dispersions. As the graph shows, the growth of real per capita household income in the USA exceeds that of labour productivity by a considerable margin. A similar, albeit less pronounced, development can be observed for the UK and Canada, whereas in Japan and Germany the growth of real per capita household income has been less than labour productivity gains. In part, these differences can be attributed to the fact that we are now using a different income concept, which is also influenced by changes in taxes and transfers. However, a key factor has been the employment performance of the USA compared with, for example, Germany and Japan. This has led to a marked rise in the proportion of the working population so that the increase in real per capita disposable income, to a large extent, reflects more income earners per household. Against the background of a widening wage dispersion (see below) this development is worth highlighting as it implies that the increase in the inequality of wages has only in part, or not at all, been accompanied by a more unequal distribution of household income.

Changes in wage dispersions

The increase in the skill premiums in the USA and the resulting widening of wage differentials has been a widely debated issue. It is also an important part of Mr Kosters' chapter and he adds an interesting angle to the debate with his overlapping wage distributions in Figure 10.9 and 10.10.

The unique position of the USA is also evident from Table C.10.1 on selected labour indicators. Indeed, in several countries, wage dispersions have been fairly stable, or even narrowed. In this context, three questions have been posed. Can the rise in skill premiums be attributed to technological developments biased in favour of skilled workers? How do institutional factors affect the adjustment of labour markets to such changes? What are the consequences for social equity?

With respect to the first question, a number of authors have concluded that biased technological changes have played a major role. However, most have come to this conclusion by default, as other possible influences on wage dispersions were found to be very small or statistically insignificant. Recently, some micro-based studies have appeared with more direct measures of technological changes. But the results are still preliminary and spread over a wide range.

As to the second and third questions, most of the debate has been shaped by two models with very different characteristics: a US model, emphasising efficiency and flexibility; and a European model, with institutions aimed at preserving social equity as a main feature. According to the US model, wage differentials would adjust flexibly to changes in the relative demand for skilled and unskilled workers and unemployment would remain low. In the European model, by contrast, the institutional factors would 'freeze' the wage structure and changes in relative demand would appear mainly as rising unemployment for unskilled workers. Although helpful, the models do not tell the whole story. In the USA, the widening of wage distribution has not led to a smooth absorption of low-skilled workers. Indeed, many low-skilled workers seem to have left the labour force rather than accept a low-paying job. In Europe, there has been a rise in unskilled unemployment, as the model would predict. However, the rise is not significantly larger than for skilled workers. Moreover, some countries (Denmark, Ireland and the Netherlands, for example) have succeeded in reducing unemployment without any noticeable change in wage dispersions.

All in all, and without having a rigorous proof, I would argue that since technological changes are of global nature, the differences across countries in their apparent impact on relative wages can be attributed mainly to differences in labour market institutions. In other words, in the US model, the biased nature of the technological changes has contributed to a widening of wage dispersion. In Europe, by contrast, institutional factors prevent such a widening, and biases in the new technologies are reflected as higher unemployment.

Influence of foreign trade and other external factors

A number of the empirical studies, including some of those referred to briefly above, have attempted to identify possible effects of trade with emerging market countries on the distribution of employment and wages. The current consensus seems to be that such trade has had only a small effect on the relative demand for skilled and unskilled workers, except in certain sectors and in regions bordering on low-wage countries.

However, to assess the potential impact of external factors on labour markets, we need to go beyond trade and consider migration, outsourcing and, in particular, foreign direct investment (FDI). For the USA, there is some evidence that immigration has had a slightly depressing effect on unskilled wages, and there are also some studies which have found significant effects of outsourcing. As to FDI, recent years have witnessed a marked rise in, and a growing role for, multinational enterprises in foreign trade. Much of this increase can be attributed to new technologies and a resulting fall in communication costs, which have enabled multinationals to arbitrage on cost differentials and thus create new and more efficient ways of organizing production on a global level. In theory, this is also one channel by which new technologies can enhance total factor productivity, but I have not yet seen any empirical evidence to confirm this. Given the focus on minimizing overall costs, the rise in FDI might also have contributed to the skill premium. However, on this point, most empirical studies indicate only marginal effects.

Recent changes in the US labour market

Again, I find myself in total agreement with Mr Kosters' analysis, and have only two supplementary points. As Table C10.1 shows, part-time and temporary workers now account for sizeable proportions of total employment, and the proportions have increased significantly in recent years. As regards part-time workers, the USA is close to the OECD average but well behind the Netherlands, where the rise in part-time work has played a significant role in raising the overall participation rate, as well as in reducing unemployment. Although the number of temporary workers in the USA is large in relation to the number of unemployed, it is very low when measured relative to total employment. In this regard, Spain is the front-runner, as temporary work contracts there have been used as a means of circumventing very high layoff costs.

Has the NAIRU fallen in the USA? I think the jury is still out and I shall merely refer to Figure C10.2, which, in a very compact way, may throw some additional light on the issue. The graph attempts to identify possible changes in the behaviour of employees by looking at changes in real unit labour costs (or the share of wages in total income) relative to the rate of unemployment. For example, for the UK, it appears that wage behaviour has moderated, as the change in real unit labour costs associated with a given rate of unemployment is below the historical trend. In Germany, by contrast, employees or their unions appear to have become more aggressive, suggesting that the fall in real unit labour costs can be attributed entirely to the historically high rate of unemployment. The graph for the USA, is (unfortunately) consistent with the consensus view – that is, no firm evidence of a change in the NAIRU.

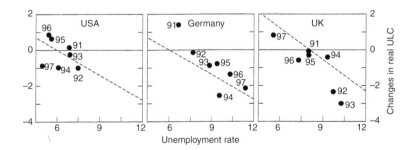

Figure C10.2   Unemployment rate and changes in real unit labour costs (percentages)
Notes: Unit labour costs in the business sector deflated by the GDP deflator. Historical relationship between unemployment and changes in real labour costs estimated over 1980–97
Sources: Bank of England 'Inflation Report' (February 1998); *OECD Economic Outlook* and national data.

Table C10.1 Selected labour market characteristics and indicators

Countries	Total unemployment[1] 1997	Structural unemployment[2] 1996	Long-term unemployment[2] 1997	Labour costs[3] 1997	Tax wedge[4] 1994	Net replacement rate[5] 1994	Dispersion of earnings[6] 1980s	1990s	Part-time workers[7] 1997	Temporary workers[7] 1994	Hours worked[8] 1997[11]	Minimum wage[9] 1997	Activity rate[10] 1995	Public employment[11]
USA	4.9	5.6	8.7	66 (39)	24.8	16	3.25	4.35	13.2	2.2	1 966	36.1	73.5	14.0
Japan	2.4	2.7	21.8	73 (71)	16.3	45	3.00	3.00	21.8	10.4	1 890	46.8	70.0	6.0
Germany	11.4	9.6	47.8	100 (82)	39.5	54	2.69	2.32	15.0	10.3	1 574	n.a.	63.5	15.6
France	12.4	9.7	41.2	67 (93)	41.3	55	3.26	3.28	15.5	11.0	1 656	68.7	58.8	24.8
Italy	12.3	10.6	57.0	62 (103)	47.2	19	2.64	2.80	12.4	7.3	1 682	n.a.	50.5	16.1
UK	6.9	7.0	38.6	60 (40)	31.1	51	2.79	3.38	23.1	6.5	1 731	45.0	70.8	14.4
Canada	9.2	8.5	12.5	61 (38)	21.4	47	4.00	4.20	19.0	8.8	1 732	38.2	67.9	19.6
Australia	8.6	8.5	30.8	58 (38)	22.4	31	2.84	2.92	26.2	23.5	1 866	n.a.	66.3	19.9
Austria	6.2	5.4	28.7	81 (98)	35.3	26	3.45	3.66	10.8	n.a.	n.a.	n.a.	67.2	22.5
Belgium	12.7	10.6	60.5	83 (92)	44.6	59	2.39	2.25	17.4	11.0	n.a.	59.9	57.0	19.2
Denmark	7.6	9.0	27.2	82 (25)	36.8	81	2.14	2.17	17.9	12.0	1 525	n.a.	75.4	30.7
Finland	14.5	15.4	31.1	80 (82)	39.4	59	2.46	2.38	7.5	13.5	1 763	n.a.	63.6	25.2
Ireland	10.2	12.8	57.0	51 (40)	31.6	37	n.a.	n.a.	16.7	9.4	n.a.	n.a.	56.1	13.4
The Netherlands	5.6	6.3	49.1	76 (77)	42.5	69	2.51	2.59	29.1	10.9	1 397	58.1	67.5	12.1
New Zealand	6.7	6.0	19.5	n.a.	24.3	34	2.89	3.04	22.7	n.a.	1 838	52.8	65.4	18.0[12]
Norway	4.1	5.1	12.8	88 (49)	32.5	62	2.06	1.98	21.2	8.0	1 399	n.a.	77.3	30.6
Spain	20.8	20.9	55.5	52 (82)	33.7	49	n.a.	n.a.	7.9	33.7	1 809	40.6	49.0	15.2
Sweden	8.0	6.7	29.6	82 (70)	46.8	67	2.04	2.13	14.2	13.5	1 552	n.a.	70.7	31.3
Switzerland	5.2	3.1	28.5	89 (52)	23.8	62	2.72	2.72	25.4	n.a.	1 643	n.a.	78.1	13.9

Notes: 1. As percentages of total labour force; 2. Persons without a job for larger than 12 months, in percentages of total unemployment; 3. Total labour costs per hour in manufacturing–indices, Western Germany = 100; figures in brackets indicate the ratio of non-wage labour costs to wages, in percentages; 4. Income taxes and social security contributions in percentages of gross labour costs; 5. Post-tax unemployment benefits (including various social benefits) in percentages of post-tax wage, averages for 2 income levels, 3 duration categories and 3 types of families; for Austria, gross replacement rate; 6. Ratio of upper limit of earnings in 9th decile to upper limit of earnings in 1st decile. 7. As percentages of total employment; 8. Average annual hours worked per person employed; 9. Legislative minimum wage as a percentage of average wage in manufacturing; for the United Kingdom, the figure refers to the minimum wage as of July 1998; 10. Employment as percentages of population of working age; 11. 1994 for Italy; and 1995 for Denmark, the Netherlands and Switzerland; 12. 1985.

Sources: OECD Economic Outlook, June 1998; OECD Employment Outlook, July 1998; OECD Implementing the OECD Jobs Strategy, Member Countries' Experience, 1997; and Institute of the German Economy IW-Trends, 2/1998.

Note

1. See J. O. Blanchard (1997) 'The Medium Run', *Brookings Papers on Economic Activity*, pp. 89–141 (Washington, DC: Brookings Institution), which tests the hypothesis that the shift to capital income in Germany and a number of other European countries could reflect technological innovations (or implementations) that are biased against labour.

Part V

Monetary Policy under the Irreversible Trend of a Knowledge-based Economy

11
Monetary Policy in the Age of Information Technology*

Robert J. Gordon

> The invention of the seminconductor transistor set in motion a technological revolution that is arguably even more impressive and pervasive than that of the Great Industrial Revolution of the last century. (Flamm, 1997, p. 1)

Introduction

Much of the contribution of information technology (IT) and its implications for monetary policy involve controversial issues, but there can be no controversy about the growing importance of IT as a share of total economic activity and a source of lower inflation. If there were a single indicator of inflation, and if the effect of IT on that inflation indicator could be measured unambiguously, then the implications of IT for monetary policy would be relatively straightforward. IT would improve the inflation – unemployment trade-off and would lower the NAIRU.

Since the companion chapter to this one (Chapter 12 by James Stock) has as its main focus the recent decline in the NAIRU for the USA, only a short preliminary section is devoted to that topic here. We ask in that section how much IT could have contributed to the decline in the NAIRU. And we relate the effect of IT on the NAIRU to two earlier strands of analysis of monetary policy: namely, the optimal reaction of policy-makers to supply shocks, and the case for a monetary policy that targets nominal GDP growth.

Monetary policy and productivity growth

Instead of focusing on the reduction in the NAIRU – the first major channel by which IT alters the environment in which monetary policy operates, the main

* This research is supported by the National Bureau of Economic Research. Any opinions expressed here are those of the author and not of the National Bureau of Economic Research. I am grateful to James Stock for helpful discussions and to Tominori Ishikawa for research assistance.

topic of this chapter will be the second major channel – the effects of IT on productivity growth. If the inflation – unemployment trade-off and its reactions to IT are well understood, one might argue that the monetary policy-makers could close their eyes to the pace of productivity growth. In this view, 'only the NAIRU matters'.

In what context would it make sense for monetary policy-makers to be interested in productivity growth? First, as Stock's work in Chapter 12 shows, estimation of the NAIRU is subject to substantial uncertainty. Central bankers may react by preferring a two-pronged approach, in which they try to estimate not just the NAIRU but also the growth rate of 'natural' or 'potential' output – that is, the growth rate of the economy consistent with steady inflation. Clearly, an understanding of productivity growth is directly relevant for the estimation of potential output growth, which often proceeds by adding together an estimate of future productivity growth and that of the growth rate of future potential hours of work.

Second, monetary policy-makers may attempt to cope with the uncertainty surrounding estimates of the NAIRU by examining the behaviour of alternative price and wage indexes and the NAIRU estimates that are the byproducts of several types of price and wage measures.[1] For example, in late 1997 and during 1998 the major US inflation rate indexes (GDP deflator, consumption deflator, and the CPI) exhibited substantial decelerations despite record low levels of the actual unemployment rate. However, several wage indexes have exhibited accelerations, and the NAIRU estimates corresponding to these wage indexes are considerably higher than for the price indexes.[2] Clearly, monetary policy-makers have a strong motivation to understand why price and wage indexes are diverging. One interpretation is that different forces are influencing prices and wages, at least temporarily, and that the growing wedge between price and wage growth will be resolved by a squeeze on profits. Another interpretation is that a marked acceleration in real wage growth is consistent with the acceleration of productivity growth that occurred in the US data in 1996–8.

Thus it seems that productivity is important after all. The 1996–8 acceleration of productivity growth to an annual average of 2 per cent, after twenty-five years of growth averaging only 1 per cent, might be the harbinger of a revival of productivity growth.[3] Set against this optimistic view is a pessimistic interpretation in which the 1996–8 experience simply made up for the period 1992–5, in which productivity growth was virtually zero. The pessimists view 1996–8 as a temporary 'blip' in a dismal story in which US business productivity has grown at a meagre rate of just 1.2 per cent whether one looks back to the mid-1980s, or beyond. Despite this lack of progress, productivity growth should have revived because of measurement improvements in the Consumer Price Index (CPI) which have had the effect of reducing measured inflation relative to true inflation, and raising measured productivity growth relative to true productivity growth.

The contradiction between the deceleration of price indexes and acceleration of wage indexes, and the ambiguous behaviour of productivity growth in the later 1990s suggests that central bankers should welcome an investigation of the interconnections between IT and aggregate productivity growth. No one has better stated the puzzling nature of these interconnections than Nobel-prize winner Robert M. Solow.

The 'Solow paradox'

It has been more than a decade since Robert M. Solow (1987) came up with his lovely quip, 'You can see the computer age everywhere but in the productivity statistics.' The prevailing reaction to Solow's paradox has been 'Well, computers are indeed everywhere, so there must be something wrong with the productivity statistics.' The idea that the contribution of computers to output is inherently difficult to measure and has been understated systematically can be classified as the first solution to the Solow paradox.[4]

A second possible solution to the paradox has been suggested by the important work of Oliner and Sichel (1994), and Sichel (1997), who criticize Solow's basic premise by arguing that 'the computers are *not* everywhere.' Specifically, computers and related peripherals represent only about 2 per cent of the nation's capital stock. Further, this tiny share is not likely to increase appreciably, as so much of investment in computers is chewed up by depreciation and obsolescence of relatively young hardware and software. Only if the return from computers were to increase dramatically in the future would their contribution to productivity growth accelerate.

A third explanation has been proposed by David (1990) and others. David argues by analogy with the invention of the electric motor around 1880; the payoff of the electric motor in creating an acceleration of productivity growth in US manufacturing did not become apparent in the statistics until the interval 1913–29. This analogy would seem to imply that it may take a full generation before systems of production are changed to take full advantage of IT.

There is a fourth possible solution to the Solow paradox. Computers may be pervasive, but they have not created a revival of productivity growth because there is something unique about computers. According to this interpretation, the David (1990) analogy with electric motors fails, because there is no comparison between the rate of decline in computer prices over the history of the computer age since the early 1950s, and the rate of decline in the prices of electric motors in the early twentieth century. As a result of this drastic decline in prices, computers have been subject to diminishing marginal returns and diminishing marginal utility much sooner and to a much greater extent than have electric motors.

This chapter takes a closer look at the first interpretation, that the contribution of computers is understated through a systematic tendency of the official data to understate the contribution of computers to output and productivity growth. An important new source of data, released in 1997,[5] allows us to pinpoint exactly where the productivity slowdown has occurred, how much is in industries where productivity is hard to measure, and how much shifts in the composition of the nation's output can explain the slowdown.

Plan of the chapter

The chapter's second section offers a brief review of IT's impact on inflation in the context of the literature on supply shocks and nominal GDP targeting. The third section examines the facts that lie behind the Solow paradox, including the path of multifactor productivity (MFP) growth since the late 1800s for the entire US economy and the path of labour productivity growth since the Second World War. Next, we examine the industrial composition of productivity growth and the productivity slowdown at the level of individual two-digit industries, using the newly released data. Our point of departure is Griliches' Presidential Address, which demonstrates that the composition of output has shifted toward those industries where output is relatively hard to measure, and so measurement errors may have contributed to the slowdown even if measurement has become no worse at the level of individual industries. We find that the industries suffering the most severe productivity growth slowdowns include not just those where output is hard to measure, but also a number where output is relatively *easy* to measure, and we find no tendency for computer-intensive industries to exhibit larger productivity growth slowdowns.

Monetary policy, IT and the NAIRU

In the US national income accounts, the price deflator of computers declined at a rate of 35–40 per cent per annum in 1996–7. Expenditure on narrowly-defined computer hardware in recent years has increased rapidly as a share of GDP and of business investment, not just in real terms but also in nominal terms, and computer hardware is the tip of an iceberg of IT that also includes software, peripheral equipment and telecommunications equipment.

Putting together the rapid decline of computer prices and the increasing share of IT, there can be no doubt that IT is holding down the rate of inflation in both an arithmetical and substantive sense. Narrowly-defined computer hardware is currently contributing to a reduction of US inflation at an annual rate of almost 0.5 per cent per year, and this number would climb towards 1 per cent per year if a broader definition of IT, including telecommunications equipment, were used.[6] Thus the first implication of IT for monetary policy is obvious: the growing importance of IT operates as a beneficial supply shock, similar to the impact of a sharp drop in the price of oil, and with the opposite impact of a sharp increase in the price of oil such as those that occurred in 1973–5 and 1979–81. The economy's trade-off schedule between inflation and unemployment is shifted downwards, as is its NAIRU. This allows monetary policy-makers to choose lower inflation with the same unemployment rate, lower unemployment with the same inflation rate, or lower rates of both unemployment and inflation.[7]

The central bank cannot make the actual unemployment rate differ from the NAIRU in the long run, but it can maintain a stable rate of inflation if it succeeds in setting the actual unemployment rate equal to the NAIRU. If, instead of maintaining a stable rate of inflation, the central bank desires to reduce the inflation rate towards zero or some other target, it needs to keep the actual unemployment rate above the NAIRU. Either way, whether the goal is steady inflation or lower inflation, the Fed needs to know the value of the NAIRU and little else. By this interpretation, all that the central bank cares about is the econometric estimation of the time-varying NAIRU, as pioneered by Stock in his work with Watson and Staiger (1997a, 1997b), and extended in my own work (Gordon, 1997a, 1997b), and by Stock and Watson (1998) and Stock (1998).

Computer prices as a beneficial supply shock

The oil shocks of 1973–5 and 1979–81 appeared at the time to be permanent – lasting more than a few years, but ultimately proved to be temporary, since the real price of oil declined in several stages after 1981 until in the late 1990s it was no higher than at the time of the first 1973 shock. The beneficial supply shock created by computer prices in the 1990s would appear to be permanent, since there is no reason for computer prices to reverse their historical decline and begin to rise in real terms.

If the real price of computers declined for ever at a steady rate, and if the share of computers in nominal GDP was fixed at some level, then the effect of computers on inflation in the GDP deflator would be easy to calculate. In the example provided above, computers subtract 0.5 per cent at an annual rate from aggregate inflation. However, with a fixed rate of computer deflation and a fixed share of computers in total expenditures, the 0.5 per cent downward impact on inflation would remain fixed. If the economy was operating below the NAIRU and as a result inflation in the non-computer part of the economy was accelerating, the mere existence of computer price deflation would not prevent aggregate inflation from accelerating if the downward impact of computers on inflation was fixed at 0.5 per cent, or some other number, as hypothesized above. Under these conditions, with a fixed share and fixed deflation rate, computers would not reduce the NAIRU. For computers to matter for monetary policy, their downward impact must increase from year to year, either because their share in nominal spending increases and/or because the rate of deflation in computer prices increases.

An increase in the downward impact of computer prices on the US rate of inflation is exactly what happened in 1996 and 1997, and this contributed to an improvement in the policy environment faced by the Federal Reserve

Board. Figure 11.1 displays the 1995–7 increase in the share of nominal computer hardware expenditure, both in GDP and in personal consumption expenditure.[8] Figure 11.2 shows the 1995–7 acceleration in the rate of deflation for computers in GDP and in personal consumption expenditure, respectively. Taken together, the impact of computers in reducing the rate of change of the GDP deflator is shown in Figure 11.3.[9]

My explanation for the coexistence of low inflation and low unemployment in the 1996–8 period relies not just on the beneficial supply shock supplied by computers, but also on the beneficial effects of a deceleration in the rate of medical care inflation as well as measurement improvements that have reduced the measured rate of inflation relative to the true rate of inflation. Figure 11.4 contrasts the official GDP deflator with an alternative GDP deflator that is 'stripped' of computer and medical care expenditures as well as the impact of the measurement improvements.

Finally, Figure 11.5 contrasts the time-varying NAIRU, estimated by the same technique as in Staiger *et al.* (1997a, 1997b) and Gordon (1997a, 1997b), for both the official and 'stripped' GDP deflator. It appears that the three elements that are stripped out of the official GDP deflator – computer spending, medical care spending and measurement improvements – explain all the decline in the NAIRU in the 1990s. Of this difference between the two NAIRUs corresponding to the official and stripped GDP deflators, computers contribute roughly a third.

Beneficial supply shocks and nominal GDP targeting

Nominal GDP targeting is a particular type of monetary rule that implicitly applies equal weights to deviations of inflation and real GDP growth from target rates.[10] As I showed in my contributions to the first Bank of Japan monetary conference (Gordon, 1985), a nominal GDP targeting rule leads to instability unless the targeting regime commences when the economy is operating with its unemployment rate at the NAIRU (that is, the unemployment gap is zero), and when the target growth rate of nominal GDP is set at the inherited rate of inertial inflation (corrected for any temporary supply shocks) plus the growth rate of potential real GDP.[11]

The impact of computers on a central bank that has implemented a nominal GDP targeting regime is likely to be minor. If the nominal share of computer spending increases slowly by a tenth of a percentage point per year or less, as seems to be suggested by Figure 11.1, and if the rate of computer deflation is relatively steady at 25–40 per cent per year, then in a given year computers have the effect of reducing the inflation rate by three to four hundredths of a percentage point as compared to the previous year.[12] This impact is trivial compared to the effect of oil prices, import prices, and even measurement changes, which in some recent years have reduced the inflation rate by as much as one or two tenths of a percentage point.

If the central bank sets a nominal GDP target and maintains the actual rate of nominal GDP growth successfully at that target, and if the economy starts

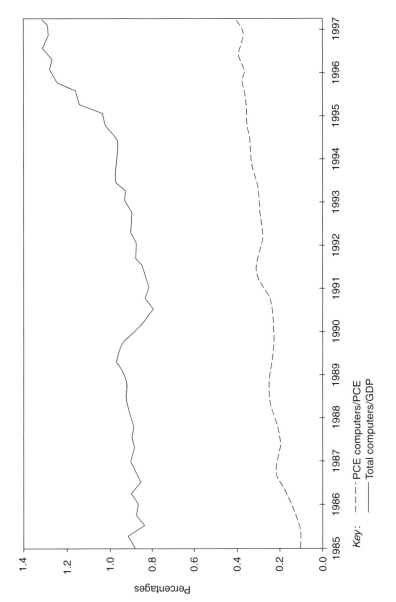

Figure 11.1 Share of computers in PCE and GDP

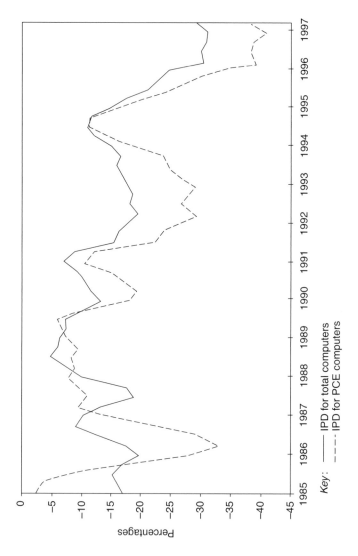

Figure 11.2 Implicit price deflators for computers

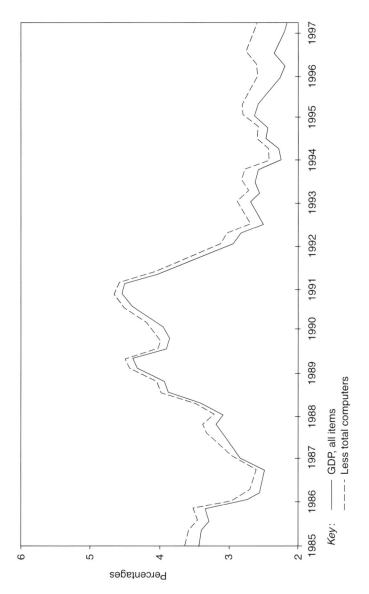

Figure 11.3 GDP deflator-based alternative measures of inflation exclusion: total computers

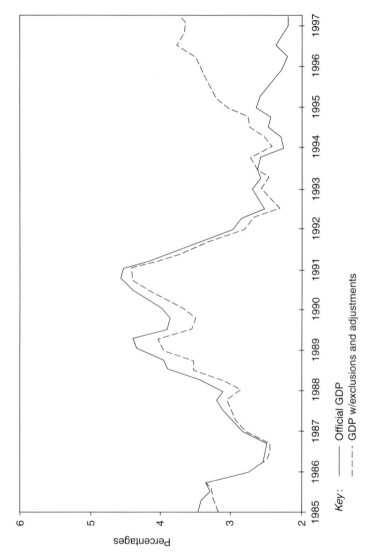

Figure 11.4 GDP deflator-based alternative measures of inflation

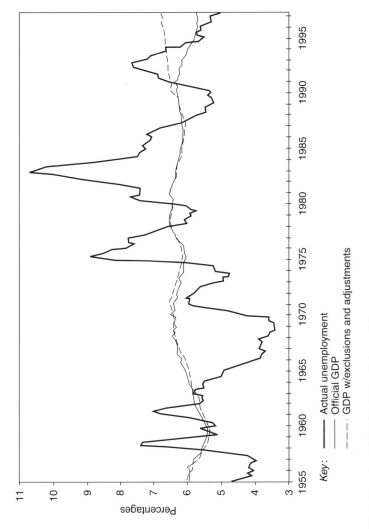

Figure 11.5 GDP deflator-based TV-NAIRUs, std dev = 0.2

the nominal GDP targeting regime with a zero unemployment gap, then any beneficial supply shock will reduce the inflation rate and increase the rate of real GDP growth. Whether this creates a positive GDP gap depends on whether the rate of potential GDP growth increases *pari passu* with real GDP growth. If the beneficial supply shock takes the form of measurement improvements in price indexes, then real GDP and potential real GDP will accelerate by the same amount. But there is no assurance that an increased share of computers in total GDP will generate a corresponding increase in productivity. Thus the key issue for monetary policy in formulating the proper response to an increasing share of computer prices in GDP comes back to the basic topic of this Chapter. Has the computer revolution, or more generally the IT revolution, created an acceleration of productivity growth? If not, why not?

Basic facts regarding computers and productivity growth

The unhappy facts supporting Solow's paradox are presented first in Table 11.1, which displays the growth rates of output, labour input, capital input and MFP for selected intervals dating back to 1870. The years chosen for the intervals are those when the economy was operating in a neutral cyclical position – that is, at its NAIRU, and the final year of 1996 is the most recent year for which official data on MFP are available. The upper half of the table displays intervals spanning one to three business cycles, while the bottom half displays averages over longer intervals of 43, 51, and 32 years, respectively.

It is important to observe that the growth rates of input and of MFP in Table 11.1 are based on a homogenous concept – that is, of straight quantities of aggregate labour and capital input with no adjustment for the shifting composition of labour (among age, sex, and education categories) and of capital (between structures and equipment, and among types of equipment with different service lives – for example, furniture versus computers). Thus the MFP growth rate in Table 11.1 for 1988–96 is more optimistic than the official MFP statistics published by the Bureau of Labor Statistics (BLS). For example, in place of the 1988–96 MFP growth rate of 0.79 per cent, which does not take account of changes in labour and capital composition, the equivalent BLS figure for MFP growth is a mere 0.12 per cent.

This historical record shows the phenomenon I previously (Gordon, 1999) called 'one big wave,' an acceleration of MFP growth that peaked in 1928–50, followed by a deceleration to 1964. In my own research I have questioned a particular aspect of these data, namely the extremely slow growth in capital input recorded for the 1928–50 interval, and my results reduce MFP growth during that interval and slightly increase MFP growth in the following two intervals, spanning 1950–72. But my results do not change the record of slow MFP growth after 1964 that, according to the BLS version, can be almost entirely accounted for by shifts in the composition of labour and capital with virtually nothing left over for 'true' MFP growth.

Table 11.1 Annual percentage growth rates of output, inputs and MFP for non-farm, non-housing business GDP, 1870–1996

Years	Output	Labour	Capital	MFP
Medium-term trend				
1870–91	4.41	3.56	4.48	0.39
1891–1913	4.43	2.92	3.85	1.14
1913–28	3.11	1.42	2.21	1.42
1928–50	2.75	0.91	0.74	1.90
1950–64	3.50	1.41	2.89	1.47
1964–72	3.63	1.82	4.08	0.89
1972–9	2.99	2.38	3.46	0.16
1979–88	2.55	1.09	3.35	0.59
1988–96	2.74	1.74	2.26	0.79
Long-term trend				
1870–1913	4.42	3.24	4.16	0.77
1913–64	3.06	1.20	1.76	1.64
1964–96	2.97	1.74	3.25	0.61

Sources: Based on data from Kendrick (1961) for 1870–1929, and BEA for 1929–96.

The basic data on US aggregate productivity performance are published quarterly by the BLS and refer to output per hour or average labour productivity (ALP), and not to MFP. The record for selected postwar intervals is provided in Table 11.2, which extends to 1997. Business sector ALP has grown in the late 1990s and since the late 1980s at the slowest rates of the postwar period, with no sign of a revival. The BLS provides further information for three sub-aggregates, durable and non-durable manufacturing and the

Table 11.2 Productivity growth, 1949–97

	1949–60	1960–72	1972–78	1978–87	1987–93	1993–97
BLS output per hour in Business Sector						
Total (76% of GDP)	3.24	3.25	1.84	1.13	1.05	1.05
1. Manufacturing (17%)	1.85	3.23	2.63	2.59	2.13	3.45
(a) Durable (9%)	1.43	3.64	2.33	3.02	2.97	4.43
(b) Nondurable (8%)	2.79	2.94	2.93	1.89	1.16	2.04
2. Non-manufacturing (59%)	3.63	3.26	1.61	0.71	0.74	0.36
3. Non-financial corporate sector (52%)	–	2.53	1.51	0.58	1.05	2.00
4. Financial and Noncorporate Sector (24%)	–	3.59	1.99	1.38	1.05	0.58

Note: Data on lines 3 and 4 are available only through 1997:Q3.

non-financial corporate sector. Productivity growth in the late 1990s was much faster in these sub-aggregates than for the total economy, which means that it must have been much worse in the omitted residual.

While the residual sectors are not published by the BLS, on the grounds that methodologies are inconsistent, they can be calculated trivially. As we shall see, the caution by the BLS is unnecessary, because exactly the same conclusions emerge when the consistent data set compiled by the US Bureau of Economic Analayis (BEA) is used, and this allows the calculation of ALP growth for nearly fifty additional two-digit industries. As shown in Table 11.2, productivity growth outside of manufacturing slowed significantly in the 1990s (line 2), further deepening the computer paradox, since that is where most of the computers are located. As ALP growth accelerated in the non-financial corporate sector (line 3), it decelerated commensurately in the financial and non-corporate sectors (line 4).

Productivity by two-digit industry

The BEA has published gross product originating (that is, real value added) by industry (GPO) data to the end of 1996. The GPO data can be converted into labour's average product (ALP) by dividing through by hours worked in each industry.[13] At the time of writing, real GPO data using the current improved methodology are published only back to 1977, but Table 11.3 treads where the BEA will not, by comparing post-1977 data with the published pre-1977 data.[14]

Table 11.3 arranges the data in the same order as the BEA original tables, except that it converts the private economy into the private business sector (for comparability with the standard BLS aggregate series). To save space, the two-digit manufacturing industries are not shown separately, except for the two crucially important industries where the production of computers and related machinery is concentrated: 'Industrial machinery' and 'Electronic and other electrical equipment'. The table exhibits annual growth rates of ALP on each line for the intervals 1948–67, 1967–77 and 1977–96, and calculates a slowdown rate between the last period and the first. Shown in the final column is the share of each sector in nominal 1992 GDP.

Allowing for differences in time intervals, Table 11.3 echoes the BLS conclusion in Table 11.2 that manufacturing has exhibited no productivity slowdown and that durables has performed better than non-durables. However, the sterling achievement of durables is almost entirely attributable to the one-third of durable output located in the machinery and electronic sectors. Omitting these, as shown on the next line, what we shall call 'net durables' exhibits a sharp productivity slowdown which is worse than that in many of the service industries. Table 11.3 contains numerous other interesting contrasts. Of all the industries shown, the productivity champion for 1977–96 was the rail transportation industry, beating even machinery and electronics. There was a productivity explosion in non-depository institutions, and

Table 11.3 Productivity growth by industry

	1948–67	1967–77	1977–96	Slowdown 1977–96 vs 48–67	Share in 1992 GDP
GDP	2.10	1.28	0.85	-1.25	100.00
Private Business[a]	2.21	1.23	0.90	-1.32	74.08
Agriculture, forestry and fishing	3.87	0.12	2.80	-1.07	1.80
Mining	4.89	-2.61	2.56	-2.33	1.48
Construction	1.92	-2.63	-0.96	-2.88	3.68
Manufacturing	2.63	2.81	2.86	0.23	17.03
Durable goods	2.31	2.35	3.32	1.01	9.18
Industrial machinery, electronic and other electrical equipment[b]	2.09	3.29	7.36	5.27	3.32
'Net' durable goods	2.47	1.96	0.65	-1.82	5.86
Non-durable goods	2.99	3.56	2.26	-0.73	7.85
Transportation	1.97	2.78	0.38	-1.59	3.09
Rail transportation	4.48	2.28	8.84	4.38	0.35
Local and inter-urban passenger transit	-3.59	-0.22	-1.20	2.39	0.17
Trucking and warehousing	3.82	3.57	-1.71	-5.54	1.32
Water transportation	0.95	5.54	0.00	-0.95	0.16
Transportation by air	7.11	1.75	1.15	-5.96	0.69
Pipelines, except natural gas	9.40	3.93	0.14	-9.25	0.08
Transportation services	-1.33	0.12	-0.10	1.23	0.31
Communications	5.21	4.69	3.56	-1.65	2.58
Telephone and telegraph	5.98	4.18	4.55	-1.43	2.08
Radio and television	1.39	2.41	-2.30	-3.69	0.50
Electricity gas and sanitary services	6.08	3.33	1.25	-4.83	2.80
Wholesale trade	3.01	2.24	3.09	0.08	6.51
Retail trade	1.69	0.89	1.07	-0.62	8.72

Table 11.3 (continued)

	1948–67	1967–77	1977–96	Slowdown 1977–96 vs 48–67	Share in 1992 GDP
Finance, Insurance (excludes Real estate)	0.24	0.96	0.55	0.31	6.61
Depository institutions^c	0.03	0.21	-1.19	-1.21	3.20
Non-depository institutions^d	-0.26	0.34	4.81	5.07	0.45
Security and commodity brokers	0.11	0.14	4.31	4.20	0.79
Insurance carriers	0.75	2.28	0.86	0.11	1.34
Insurance agents, brokers, and service, electronic and other electric equipment	0.36	-0.08	-0.60	-0.96	0.63
Holding and other investment offices	-0.23	0.08	-0.19	0.04	0.20
Services except household services	0.95	0.51	-0.86	-1.81	19.07
Hotels and other lodging places	0.93	0.56	0.02	-0.90	0.82
Personal services	1.86	0.90	-1.28	-3.14	0.66
Business services	-0.39	-0.16	0.50	0.88	3.51
Auto repair, services and parking	3.39	1.60	-1.51	-4.90	0.82
Miscellaneous repair services	-0.12	0.16	-1.47	-1.35	0.28
Motion pictures	-0.74	0.85	0.42	1.15	0.32
Amusement and recreation services	1.40	-0.35	-0.13	-1.53	0.77
Health services	0.99	0.04	-1.81	-2.79	5.91
Legal services	0.23	-2.01	-2.13	-2.36	1.44
Educational services	-0.03	0.19	-0.64	-0.62	0.74
Social services and membership orgs	0.21	0.20	-0.01	-0.22	1.21
Other services^e	0.38	0.08	0.09	-0.30	2.60
Sectors excluded from private business sector:					
Real estate	4.78	-0.37	0.72	-4.06	11.77
Services: private households	0.42	0.78	0.58	0.16	0.16
Government: Federal, state, local	0.19	0.36	0.37	0.19	13.99

Table 11.3 (*continued*)

Notes: (a) Private business is equal to the NIPA private sector minus real estate and private household services. These exclusions are listed separately at the end of the table.

(b) 'Industrial machinery' was ratio-linked to the earlier definition 'Machinery, except electrical', in 1987. Similarly, 'Electronic and other electrical equipment' was ratio linked in 1987 to the earlier definition 'Electric and electronic equipment'.

(c) 'Depository institutions' was ratio-linked in 1987 to the earlier definition 'Banking'.

(d) 'Non-depository institutions' was ratio-linked in 1987 to the earlier definition 'Credit agencies other than banks'.

(e) 'Other services' was ratio-linked in 1987 to the earlier definition 'Miscellaneous professional services'.

Gross product originating by industry is currently published by the BEA only for 1977–96. Estimates are not published for years prior to 1977 because the methodology previously developed to develop estimates for those years has been discarded and is inconsistent with the data for 1977 to date. In this table all growth rates are calculated separately for the old and new data, and readers should be cautioned that growth rates for 1948–77 are based on a different methodology than for 1977–96.

Sources: Gross product originating, 1987–96, is in Lum and Yuskavage (1997). For 1977–87, the source was *Survey of Current Business*, August 1996, p. 153, and for a few industries with definitions that changed in 1987 was *Survey of Current Business*, May 1993, p. 53. All GPO data for 1948–77 are taken from the *National Income and Product Accounts of the U.S., 1929–82, Statistical Tables*, September 1986, table 6.2. Persons engaged for 1996 were obtained from the NIPA revisions in the *Survey of Current Business*, August 1997. For 1977 and 1987, the source was the NIPA, vol. 2, 1959–88, September 1992, and for earlier years was the *NIPA 1929–82* cited above. Hours worked are provided in the NIPA only for one-digit industries and were obtained for two-digit industries by assuming that hours per employee across two-digit industries within any one-digit industry were identical.

security and commodity brokers, suggesting that BEA has dropped its previous practice of extrapolating output in these industries on the basis of labour input.

The slowdown culprits

Table 11.4 provides a rearrangement of the Table 11.3 data with thirty-six industry groups ranked by the size of the slowdown, from the largest slowdown to the largest acceleration. The table lists both the magnitude of the slowdown and the absolute magnitude of ALP growth during 1977–96; the ALP growth rates for 1948–67 and 1967–77 are not repeated. The groups listed are mutually exclusive: that is, manufacturing is divided into three groups (machinery and electronics, 'net' durables, and non-durables) but the total for manufacturing is not listed separately. Similarly, the totals for such categories as transportation, finance/insurance and services are not listed separately.

Two other pieces of information are listed in Table 11.4. Each of the thirty-six industry groups is 'rated' on the criterion of accuracy of measurement, from category A which represents the most accurate, to category D, representing the least accurate. Definitions of the four categories are provided in the notes to Table 11.6 on page 000 below. This measurement classification goes well beyond the cruder distinction introduced by Griliches (1994), who grouped the whole of agriculture, mining, manufacturing, transportation, communications and public utilities into an easier-to-measure category, and the remaining industries (construction, trade, FIRE (Finance, Insurance, Real Estate), and services) into a harder-to-measure category. Our finer-grained categories reflect the fact that within the finance, insurance and service sectors, various industries may differ in their intrinsic difficulty of measurement. For example, personal services (such as barber's shops and beauty parlours) are rated in the 'A' category; the product changes little over decades, there are few if any unmeasured product attributes, and there has never been a suggestion that the underlying Consumer Price Indexes for haircuts or beauty treatments contain a bias. Further, the rapid productivity growth in BEA measures of productivity for non-depository institutions and securities brokers since 1977, contrasted with negative productivity growth for depository institutions, suggests that the BEA may be capturing the growth in transactions per employee in the former groups with less error than in the latter group.

The second additional piece of information shown is the growth in ALP as measured by the BLS industry productivity programme. The BLS measures are based on a gross output concept rather than the BEA's value-added concept, and thus might be expected to differ. Published BLS employment weights are used to aggregate the individual BLS indexes for particular industries – for example, beauty parlours, bakeries, coal mining, brick and structural clay tiles and so on, into categories corresponding to the BEA measures.

The overall productivity growth slowdown for the private business sector in the BEA data for 1977–96 compared with 1948–67 is 1.32 per cent per year, as

Table 11.4 Productivity slowdown culprits

Measurement category in order		Slowdown 1977–96 versus 1948–67	Growth in Output/Hour BEA 1977–96	BLS 1979–95	Share in 1992 GDP
Industry					
1. Pipelines, except natural gas	A	-9.25	0.14	1.22	0.08
2. Transportation by air	A	-5.96	1.15	2.28	0.69
3. Trucking and warehousing[a]	B	-5.54	-1.71	2.70	1.32
4. Auto repair, services and parking	C	-4.90	-1.51	0.67	0.82
5. Electricity, gas and sanitary services	A	-4.83	1.25	2.21	2.80
6. Radio and television	D	-3.69	-2.30		0.50
7. Personal services[b]	A	-3.14	-1.28	0.58	0.66
8. Construction	C	-2.88	-0.96		3.68
9. Health services	D	-2.79	-1.81		5.91
10. Legal services	C	-2.36	-2.13		1.44
11. Mining	A	-2.33	2.56	2.42	1.48
12. 'Net' durable goods	B	-1.82	0.65	1.93	5.86
13. Amusement and recreation services	D	-1.53	-0.13		0.77
14. Telephone and telegraph	B	-1.43	4.55	5.28	2.08
15. Miscellaneous repair services	A	-1.35	-1.47		0.28
Private Business Sector		-1.32	0.90		74.08
16. Depository institutions	D	-1.21	-1.19	2.74	3.20
17. Agriculture	A	-1.07	2.80		1.80
18. Insurance agents	D	-0.96	-0.60		0.63
19. Water transportation	A	-0.95	0.00		0.16
20. Hotels and other lodging places	C	-0.90	0.02	0.24	0.82
21. Non-durable manufacturing	B	-0.73	2.26	2.52	7.85

Table 11.4 (continued)

Measurement category in order		Slowdown 1977–96 versus 1948–67	Growth in Output/Hour BEA 1977–96	BLS 1979–95	Share in 1992 GDP
22. Retail trade	C	-0.62	1.07	0.90	8.72
23. Educational services	D	-0.62	-0.64		0.74
24. Other services	D	-0.30	0.09		2.60
25. Social services and membership organizations	C	-0.22	-0.01		1.21
26. Holding and other investment offices	D	0.04	-0.19		0.20
27. Wholesale trade	C	0.08	3.09		6.51
28. Insurance carriers	C	0.11	0.86		1.34
29. Business services	D	0.88	0.50		3.51
30. Motion pictures	C	1.15	0.42		0.32
31. Transportation services	D	1.23	-0.10		0.31
32. Local and inter-urban passenger transit	A	2.39	-1.20		0.17
33. Security and commodity brokers	B	4.20	4.31		0.79
34. Rail transportation	A	4.38	8.84	7.31	0.35
35. Non-depository institutions	B	5.07	4.81		0.45
36. Industrial amchinery and equipment; Electronic and other electrical equipment	B	5.27	7.36	2.19	3.32

Notes: (a) BLS trucking excludes warehousing and local trucking and is available only through 1989.
(b) BLS personal services refers to the aggregate of two categories, (i) laundry, cleaning and garment services; and (ii) beauty and barbers' shops.
Slowdown, BEA ALP growth, and 1992 share are all copied from Table 11.2. BLS ALP growth from *Productivity by Industry 1995*, USDL 97–132, 23 April, 1997. All BLS sub-industries are aggregated into industries that correspond to BEA definitions, using 1995 employment weights provided in the BLS release.
BLS ALP growth is available for numerous industries in durable and non-durable manufacturing. These will be aggregated and included in the next version of this table.

shown on the second line of Table 11.3. Thus all industries ranked 1–15 in Table 11.4 have greater-than-average slowdowns, while the remaining industries ranked 16–36 experienced either a smaller slowdown than average or a productivity growth acceleration (hence there is a dividing line drawn after the industry ranked 15th). This ranking contains some familiar culprits, including construction, health services and mining. But there are some unfamiliar culprits as well, including telephone/telegraph and, perhaps most surprisingly, 'net' durable goods – that is, the two-thirds of durable goods' production excluding industrial machinery and electronic/electrical goods.

Clearly, the ranking of industries by the extent of the slowdown cuts across the categories of measurement accuracy, whether in Griliches' original dichotomy or our more finely-tuned categorization. Some of the largest slowdowns occurred in industries where output is particularly easy to measure – for example, pipelines, air transportation, utilities and mining. But some of the largest accelerations also occurred in industries where output is relatively easy to measure, including railways.

Conflicts in the official data

The BEA and BLS productivity data are not directly comparable; the concepts are different (value-added compared to gross output), the time periods are slightly different, and in some cases the industry definitions do not match exactly.[15] Nevertheless, it is intriguing to note a tendency for the BLS productivity growth rates for 1979–95 to exceed those of the corresponding BEA growth rates for 1977–96, sometimes by substantial amounts. As shown in Table 11.5, the difference between the weighted average growth rates of output per hour for the BLS and BEA data depends heavily on whether the industrial and electronic machinery industries are included. The BLS and BEA data for these industries are clearly not comparable, as the BLS does not cover the computer industry which, through the BEA's use of a hedonic price deflator for computers, contributes much of the outstanding performance of this pair of industries in the BEA data.

Excluding this pair, the BLS growth rates exceed those of the BEA by a weighted average of 0.93 per cent, and 1.06 per cent for non-manufacturing. Stated another way, the BLS growth rates are double those of the BEA growth rates for comparable industries. The discrepancy between the BLS and BEA growth rates applies not just to the industries that are ranked as harder to measure, but also to those that are ranked as being easier to measure. This finding questions the utility of the Griliches distinction, since the BLS–BEA discrepancies suggest that measurement difficulties may plague the easier-to-measure sectors as much as the harder-to-measure ones.

The BLS–BEA differences may usefully indicate the potential range of measurement errors, but there is no presumption that one of the indexes is more accurate than the other. For example, my study of the transportation sector (Gordon, 1992, pp. 374–82) concluded that the BLS measure was

Table 11.5 Annual growth rates BEA and BLS output per hour, alternative industry aggregates, weighted by BEA 1992 nominal output

	Growth in output hour			*Share in 1992 GDP*
	BEA	*BLS*		
	1977–96	*1979–95*	*BLS–BEA*	*GDP*
All industries covered by BLS, using BEA weight	1.69	2.11	0.42	40.05
All industries excluding industrial machinery and equipment; electornic/electrical equipment	1.18	2.11	0.92	36.73
All non-manufacturing industries	0.95	2.01	1.06	23.02

Source: Computed from Table 11.4.

superior for air transportation, but the BEA measure was preferable for trucking and warehousing. Thus, until detailed industry-by-industry comparisons are made and explained, and until these comparisons are extended further back into the early years of the postwar period, we cannot conclude that these measurement differences help to explain the productivity slowdown, but the possibility exists.

The shifting composition of economic activity

Since the early and pioneering study of the productivity slowdown by Nordhaus (1972), a familiar hypothesis has been that the slowdown could have been partly or largely caused by the shifting composition of economic activity. So far, our ALP growth rate for the private business aggregate in the BEA data has been based on the published total output measured in constant 1982 dollars (1948–77) or constant 1992 dollars (1977–96). However, these aggregates differ from the conceptually preferable chain-weighted or Törnqvist indexes, with weights based on shifting nominal output shares.

The first two lines of Table 11.6 contrast the productivity growth rates published by the BEA with a 'quasi-Törnqvist' which, rather than shifting weights each year, bases the aggregation within a time interval on the average of the nominal output shares for the first and last year of each interval. Thus the growth rate of ALP for 1948–67 is aggregated from the thirty-six component sub-industries (those listed in Table 11.4), using an average of 1948 and 1967 nominal shares, and similarly for 1967–77 and 1977–96. The use of the quasi-Törnqvist weights boosts productivity growth in all periods without changing the magnitude of the slowdown appreciably. Some of the reasons for the higher growth rates are obvious. For example, prior to 1977, the weights on manufacturing were uniformly higher than in recession-racked 1982. Further, Tornqvist weights are higher in the earlier years for other sectors

Table 11.6 BEA productivity growth, alternative weights and by measurement category

	1948–67	1967–77	1977–96	Slowdown 1977–96 versus 1948–67	Share in 1992 GDP
Alternative weights for private business GDP					74.08
As published,					
1982 constant dollars for 1948–77;					
1992 constant dollars for 1977–96	2.21	1.23	0.90	–1.32	
Quasi-Tornqvist	2.57	1.46	1.33	–1.24	
All periods with 1948–67 average nominal share	2.57	1.48	1.80	–0.77	
All periods with 1977–96 average nominal share	2.25	1.30	1.33	–0.92	
All periods with 1948 average nominal share	2.82	1.64	2.00	–0.82	
All periods with 1996 average nominal share	2.06	1.21	1.16	–0.90	
Private business GDP by measurement category,					
weights within categories as published					
Category A (most accurate)	4.62	1.12	1.74	–2.87	8.47
Category B	2.89	2.94	2.52	–0.37	21.67
Category C	1.92	0.51	0.92	–1.00	23.52
Category D (least accurate)	0.41	0.24	–0.69	–1.10	19.71
Addendum: Categories A and B	3.38	2.43	2.30	–1.08	30.14

Notes: Measurement categories are defined as follows:

A Based on quantitative measures of output or deflation with no known reason for bias.

B Based on quantitative measures of output or deflation subject to possible bias for quality change; unmeasured product attributes largely absent.

C Based primarily on deflation which may be subject to bias for quality change; unmeasured product attributes relatively minor.

D Based primarily on deflation which may be subject to bias for quality change; unmeasured product attributes may be substantial.

with relatively higher productivity growth – for example, agriculture. In the later 1990s, the use of the average of 1977 and 1996 weights, rather than the BEA's 1992 weights, reduces the importance of industries having negative productivity growth, such as medical care.

How much of the slowdown was caused by a shift in composition towards industries that have had relatively slow ALP growth rates throughout the postwar period? We can answer this question by using weights fixed at the beginning of the period, or at the end of the period. With fixed 1948–67 weights, the slowdown drops from –1.24 per cent to –0.77 per cent, and with fixed 1977–96 weights to –0.92 per cent. Averaging these two alternative measures of the fixed-weight slowdown, we conclude that exactly a third of the slowdown in the quasi-Tornqvist indexes can be accounted for by a shift to slower-growing sectors – for example, from agriculture and manufacturing to services. The remaining two-thirds of the slowdown is caused by a deceleration of ALP growth within individual industries which, as we saw in Table 11.4, affects twenty-five of the thirty-six industries listed.

The bottom section of Table 11.5 aggregates the ALP growth rates and slowdown measures by measurement category. Somewhat surprisingly, the largest slowdown occurred in the category where productivity is easiest to measure. However, if categories A and B are aggregated, as on the last line of the table, we conclude that the slowdown has been uniform across categories. Productivity growth has always been fastest in the categories that are the easiest to measure, and slowest in those categories that are hardest to measure.

I emerge from this exercise with a different slant than emerged from Griliches (1994), at least as I understand it. I took him to be saying that 'things are OK with reasonably robust productivity growth and negligible slowdowns in the easier-to-measure sectors and are not OK in the harder-to-measure sectors where most of the slowdown has occurred, hence mismeasurement may have become more important'. My conclusion is that things are not OK in the easier-to-measure sectors, which have experienced the same order-of-magnitude slowdown as the harder-to-measure sectors. There is no correlation of the slowdown with difficulty of measurement, just a shift in the composition of output to sectors that have always had poor productivity growth performance, back in the 'golden age' as well as in the late 1990s.

Price measurement and the productivity paradox

There remains the possibility that inflation is overstated more in the hard-to-measure categories C and D than in the easier-to-measure categories A and B. Assuming that current-dollar spending is correctly measured, then any overstatement of inflation would correspond to an understatement of output and productivity growth. Let us assume that in the 1990s the hard-to-measure sectors have inflation that is understated by 1.5 per cent per year, while the easier-to-measure sectors have inflation that is understated by 0.5 per cent per year. In the context of the Boskin Commission report (Boskin *et al.*, 1996), this amounts to assuming that quality change and new product bias is zero in the easier-to-measure categories and proceeds at a rate of 1 per cent per year in the harder-to-measure categories.[16] Since categories C and D comprised 38 per cent of private business GDP in 1948, and 59 per cent in 1992, these assumptions imply that inflation was overstated by 0.9 per cent in 1948 and 1.1 per cent in 1992, while productivity growth was understated by the same amount.[17] Thus this particular form of the mismeasurement hypothesis would explain 0.2 per cent of the productivity growth slowdown, somewhat less than the 0.3 per cent explained by the shifting shares hypothesis in Table 11.6.

In a related exercise, Steindel (1997) takes a narrower definition of the hard-to-measure sectors, including financial and business services, medical care, and educational and charitable expenses. He makes two alternative assumptions about price mismeasurement in these sectors, (i) that their prices rise at the same rate as other products (instead of faster); and (ii) that their prices rise 2 per cent more slowly than as published. He calculates that assumption (i) boosts productivity growth by 0.2 per cent for 1960–73 and 0.4 per cent for 1974–96, explaining 0.2 per cent of the slowdown, the same amount as our alternative calculation above. Assumption (ii) boosts productivity growth by 0.3 per cent for 1960–73, and 0.4 per cent for 1974–96, explaining only 0.1 per cent of the slowdown. Despite the differing approaches and assumptions of these exercises, they all arrive at the same conclusion. The hypothesis that inflation is mismeasured more in a sub-set of hard-to-measure sectors cannot plausibly explain more than a small fraction of the overall post-1973 productivity growth slowdown.

All of this investigation of the productivity data is motivated by the first proposed resolution of the Solow paradox, that computers are not in the productivity statistics because the benefits of computers have been mismeasured. We have concluded that the productivity slowdown is pervasive across industries that are both intensive and non-intensive in computer use. It is also pervasive across industries where output is relatively easy and relatively hard to measure. Thus it is hard to make a case that the output of computers is being missed systematically in the output and productivity statistics.

Waiting for Godot

As the years go by without a productivity payoff from computers commensurate with their cost, journalists have become more frenetic in proclaiming that we are in the midst of a true revolution: 'Computers may be the most profound technology since steam power ignited the Industrial Revolution.'[18] There is a 'waiting for Godot' quality to the anticipation generated as productivity growth continues to languish while computer investment continues to surge. Those who wait for Godot appeal to David's (1990) electricity analogy, arguing that as twenty-five years elapsed between the invention of electricity and the beginning of its transformation of farm, home and factory, so it is reasonable also to expect such a delayed impact of computers. Yet, if anything is clear, it is that however unimportant computers are today in generating productivity growth, we can be sure that at the margin it was *more* important a decade ago and will be *less* important a decade hence, simply because continuing exponential declines in the cost of computer power reduce the marginal product of computer power – that is, push incremental increases in computer power into lower and lower productivity uses.

Since Gary Becker's seminal article (Becker, 1965) on the economics of time, household production has been viewed as an activity that combines market goods and time. The fixed supply of time to any individual creates the fundamental limitation on the ability of exponential growth in computer speed and memory to create commensurate increases in output and productivity. In performing the two activities that were revolutionized by the personal computer – namely, text manipulation (word processing) and mathematical calculation (spreadsheets) – I cannot type or think any faster than I did with my first 1983 personal computer that contained one-fiftieth of the memory and operated at one-thirtieth of the speed of my present model. The capital stock with which I work has increased by a factor of at least fifteen, according to the hedonic price methodology used by the BEA in the US national accounts, yet my productivity has hardly budged, apart occasionally benefiting for a few seconds when I can jump from the beginning to the end of a 50-page paper much faster than in 1983.[19] As a result, there has been an exponential rate of decline in my output-to-capital ratio, and an equally sharp decline in the marginal productivity of computer capital.

The pervasiveness of diminishing returns

There is nothing unique about the applicability of diminishing returns to the computer hardware and software industries. Numerous industries have run into barriers to steady growth in productivity, most notably the airline industry when jet aircraft reached natural barriers of size and speed, and the electric utility industry when turbogenerator/boiler sets reached natural barriers of temperature and pressure. The apparent dearth of productivity growth in the construction and home maintenance industry reflects the fact that portable electric power tools could only be invented once and have been subject to only marginal improvements in recent decades. The retailing industry has been subject to diminishing returns for years. In the decade up to 1996, retailing square feet per capita increased by 31 per cent, leading to reduced real sales per square foot and per employee.

Diminishing returns has significant implications for measurement. Unless weights are changed continuously to reflect the ever-falling marginal value of computer speed and memory, it is likely that official accounts will overstate the growth rate of computer investment and capital input relative to final non-computer output. If so, then measures of MFP that subtract the overstated capital input series will provide an even more dismal view of the payoff from computers than the labour productivity series examined in Tables 11.2 to 11.6 above. While the BEA's new chain-weighted output indexes avoid previous conceptual errors, some analysts compute the contribution of computers to output growth and inflation in a way that greatly exaggerates the role of computers.[20]

Continuity from mainframes to personal computers

The diminishing returns argument provides the definitive answer to the David (1990) 'delay' hypothesis. The reason that electric motors and consumer appliances took time to diffuse is that initially they were very expensive and did not work very well. But the personal computer worked reliably from the beginning, provided its main benefits early on, and encountered relatively soon not just diminishing returns but the pervasiveness of face-to-face technology in the service sector that limits the ability of super-fast computers to replace labour input in a significant way.

The David (1990) 'delay' hypothesis encounters another obstacle. Personal computers are only a secondary step in the evolution of computer technology that began with the first commercial mainframe computer (the UNIVAC I in 1951). Price indexes complied by Chow (1967), Gordon (1990, ch. 6), Berndt and Griliches (1993) and Flamm (1997), show that steady price declines at geometric rates of 25–35 per cent have characterized both the mainframe and personal computer industries since the beginning.[21] Many of the industries that are the heaviest users of computer technology – for example, airlines, banks and insurance companies – began in the 1960s and 1970s with mainframe technology and still perform the most computation-intensive activities on mainframes, often using PCs only as smart terminals to access the mainframe database. In this sense, computers have been around for more than forty years, not just a decade or so, and the 'waiting for Godot' hypothesis of David and others loses further credibility.

Conclusion

The point of departure for this chapter is the justified concern of central bankers that the information technology (IT) revolution may have fundamentally changed the environment in which monetary policy is conducted. We find that IT in general, and computers in particular, have acted, at least in the USA, as a beneficial supply shock that has improved the inflation–unemployment trade-off, particularly in the mid-1990s. If the share of computers in nominal spending and the rate of decline of computer prices is constant, then the existence of computers will reduce inflation by a fixed amount but will not change the unemployment rate below which the inflation rate in the non-computer part of the economy will accelerate – that is, under these conditions the existence of computers does not reduce the NAIRU. Instead, the NAIRU is reduced when there is an increase in the nominal share of computer spending, and when the rate of decline of computer prices accelerates; both of these events occurred in the mid-1990s and contributed to the decline of the US NAIRU during that period.

More profound issues are raised for monetary policy by the apparent failure of IT to boost the rate of multifactor productivity (MFP) growth or of average labour productivity (ALP) growth in the USA during the 1990s. The framework for our study of computers and productivity growth is the famous Solow computer paradox, that computers are everywhere except in the productivity statistics. We organized our investigation by four different approaches to resolving the Solow paradox – that official measures of productivity miss the contribution of computers; that computers are too small a part of the capital stock to have a major impact; that the benefits of computers for productivity have been delayed and are awaiting us in the future; and finally, the hypothesis that diminishing returns contradict the delay hypothesis and make the greatest benefit from computers almost surely in the past rather than the future.

Our review of the productivity data shows that MFP growth has been much lower since 1964 than previously, and that there was no acceleration of ALP growth in 1988–98 compared with 1973–88. Our analysis of industry data shows that there is a huge variation in the extent of the post-1972 productivity growth slowdown across industries, suggesting the futility of any attempt to explain the slowdown by a single overarching explanation. Perhaps the greatest surprise of the investigation is that productivity growth in durable manufacturing, far from being the star sector of the economy, has in fact been very poor once the industries producing computers are excluded, and that the greatest achievement of computers seems to have been in reproducing more computers.

The productivity slowdown has occurred at roughly the same magnitude across industries with widely differing degrees of difficulty in output measurement. The statistical investigation concludes that roughly a third of the slowdown has been caused by a shift in the composition of industrial output towards those sectors where productivity grew relatively slowly, both before and after the advent of the slowdown, regardless of whether output in those sectors is relatively easy to measure or relatively hard to measure.

The negative view of computers and the IT revolution taken in this chapter does not deny that computers have produced benefits for firms, and consumer surplus for households. Some industries, particularly in manufacturing, have not experienced a productivity slowdown at all, and the IT revolution may be partly, or largely, responsible for these success stories. Computers have produced many useful new services or attributes of services, from automated teller machines, to cash-management accounts or to frequent-flyer pro-grammes, although most of these innovations were made possible by mainframe computers, not personal computers, and the benefits from mainframes reach back more than forty years, not just over the period from the early 1980s, in which the information technology revolution is claimed to have occurred. In the end my conclusion is that the productivity slowdown is real, and that diminishing returns places the most productive contribution of the computer in the past. My conclusion stands in sharp contrast to the widespread view that we have a 'new economy' dominated by the revolutionary implications of the information age.

Notes

1. By definition, the NAIRU is the rate of unemployment that is consistent with steady, non-accelerating inflation for some price index. There is a different NAIRU for each price index, e.g., the GDP deflator, personal consumption deflator, and CPI. There is also a different NAIRU for each concept of unit labor cost growth, e.g., the growth rate of a wage index minus the growth rate in actual or potential productivity. NAIRU estimates for several U. S. wage indexes are provided in Gordon (1997b).
2. Gordon (1997b) estimates that the wage–NAIRU was as high as 6 per cent in mid-1997.
3. Private business output per hour grew at an average annual rate of 2.04 per cent for the twelve-quarter period between 1995:Q4 and 1998:Q4.
4. The first three proposed explanations of the Solow paradox correspond to those in Allen (1997), while the fourth is contributed here for the first time. Allen's review of the first (mismeasurement) hypothesis largely consists of a summary of Baily and Gordon (1988). Triplett (1998) parses the explanations of the Solow paradox into seven and explores briefly that is also the main theme of this paper; that the contribution of computers to productivity growth is inherently limited and subject to diminishing returns.
5. The new source of data was the long-awaited updating of data on gross product originating by two-digit industry contained in the article by Lum and Yuskavage (1997).
6. The current nominal share of producer and consumer computer hardware spending in US nominal GDP is about 1.4 per cent, which multiplied by a rate of price decline of about 35 per cent per year contributes to reducing the rate of change of the GDP deflator by 0.49 percentage points per annum.
7. The theory of monetary policy reactions in the presence of supply shocks was introduced by Gordon (1975) and Phelps (1978), and these two contributions were subsequently synthesized by Gordon (1984).
8. The upper line is the nominal share of computers purchased both as producers' durable equipment and as personal consumption expenditure as a share of nominal GDP; the lower line is the share of consumption computers as a share of nominal personal consumption expenditure.
9. The contribution of computers to reducing inflation is computed on a chain-weighted basis by subtracting the chain-weighted nominal share of computers in GDP multiplied by the rate of computer price deflation in the GDP deflator. This yields a chain-weighted price deflator for non-computer GDP. An alternative method, to subtract both nominal and real computer spending from nominal and real GDP, introduces base-year bias and greatly exaggerates the difference made by excluding computers.
10. In the USA, where the unemployment gap (the actual unemployment rate minus the NAIRU) fluctuates by about half as much as the output gap (the percentage log ratio

of actual to potential GDP), a nominal GDP target implicitly places a weight of 2/3 on deviations of the inflation rate from target, and 1/3 on the unemployment gap.

11. For a more recent treatment of nominal GDP targeting and references, both to Gordon (1985) and more recent literature, see Hall and Mankiw (1994).

12. If in 1996 the share of computers in GDP is 0.01, and the rate of computer deflation is -0.35, the impact on the GDP deflator is -0.0035. If the next year the computer share increases to 0.11, and the rate of computer deflation stays the same, the impact on the GDP deflator rises to -0.00385, a difference of 0.00035, or 3.5 hundredths of a percentage point.

13. As described in the notes to Table 11.3, the BEA publishes hours data only at the one-digit level. The exercise carried out here requires the assumption that hours per employee in each two digit industry within a one-digit industry are identical to the one-digit industry average.

14. The BEA no longer publishes pre-1977 data because of numerous changes in methodology that were introduced with its current data for the year 1977 and later.

15. Both the BEA and BLS data are available annually. However, to save space, recent BLS releases have presented growth rates over relatively long intervals rather than annual levels for each industry. In preparing Table 11.4, I have taken the short cut of using the published BLS growth rates for the interval shown (1979–95) rather than locating the underlying annual data and calculating growth rates for the same period as shown in Table 11.4 for the BEA data for 1977–96.

16. These numbers reflect the assumption that the upward bias of inflation in the easier-to-measure categories is limited to upper-level, lower-level and outlet substitution bias, determined to be 0.5 per cent per year in 1995–6 by Boskin *et al.* (1996). Quality and new product bias was determined to be 0.6 per cent by the Boskin Commission report, and this is allocated as 1 per cent per year in the harder-to-measure sectors and zero per cent per year in the easier-to-measure sectors.

17. The share of categories C and D in GDP are shown in Table 11.6. Corresponding data for 1948 are obtained from the sources underlying Tables 11.3 and 11.4.

18. Mandel (1994, p. 23), quoted by Sichel (1997, p. 1).

19. A price index that declines at 25 per cent per year for fifteen years reaches a level of 2.4 in 1998 on a base of 1983 = 100. This implies that my present $1000 1998-model computer represents $42 300 at 1983 prices, of seqithe times the $2500 that I spent in 1983 on my computer net of peripherals.

20. In particular, in the years after the 1992 base year, the computer contribution will be greatly overstated if nominal and real expenditure on computers are subtracted from nominal and real GDP (or any lesser aggregate). See Note 10 above.

21. The transition from mainframes to personal computers for many activities created a sharp decline in price along the transition path that has apparently not been measured by any of the numerous hedonic regression studies of computer prices, which have focused exclusively on mainframes or PCs, but not both together.

References

Allen, D. S. (1997) 'Where's the Productivity Growth from the Information Technology Revolution?', *Review, Federal Reserve Bank of St Louis* (March/April), pp. 15–25.

Baily, M. N. and Gordon, R. J. (1988) 'The Productivity Slowdown, Measurement Issues, and the Explosion of Computer Power', *Brookings Papers on Economic Activity*, vol. 19, no. 2, pp. 347–420.

Becker, G. S. (1965) 'A Theory of the Allocation of Time', *Economic Journal*, vol. 75 (September), pp. 493–517.

Berndt, E. R. and Griliches, Z. (1993) 'Price Indexes for Micro Computers: An Exploratory Study', in M. Foss, M. Manser and A. Young, (eds), *Price Measurements and Their Uses*, Studies in Income and Wealth, vol. 57 (University of Chicago Press for NBER), pp. 63–93.

Boskin, M. J., Dulberger, E. R., Gordon, R. J., Griliches, Z. and Jorgenson, D. W. (1996) 'Toward a More Accurate Measure of the Cost of Living. Final Report to the Senate Finance Committee of the Advisory Commission to Study the Consumer Price Index'. (4 December)

Bureau of Economic Analysis, 'Survey of Current Business', various issues, Washington, DC.

Bureau of Economic Analysis, 'National Income and Product Accounts', various versions, Washington, DC.

Bureau of Labor Statistics, 'Productivity and Costs', various issues. Washington, DC.

Bureau of Labor Statistics (1997), 'Productivity by Industry 1995', Washington, DC.

Chow, G. C. (1967) 'Technological Change and the Demand for Computers', *American Economic Review*, vol. 57 (December), pp. 1117–30.

David, P. A. (1990) 'The Dynamo and the Computer: An Historical Perspective on the Modern Productivity Paradox', *American Economic Review, Papers and Proceedings*, vol. 80 (May), pp. 355–61.

Flamm, K. (1997) 'More for Less: The Economic Impact of Semiconductors', Semiconductor Industry Association (December).

Gordon, R. J. (1975) 'Alternative Responses of Policy to External Supply Shocks', *Brookings Papers on Economic Activity*, 6 (no. 1), 183–206.

Gordon, R. J. (1984) 'Supply Shocks and Monetary Policy Revisited', *American Economic Review Papers and Proceedings*, vol. 4 (May), pp. 38–43.

Gordon, R. J. (1985) 'The Conduct of Monetary Policy', in A. Ando, H. Eguchi, R. Farmer and Y. Suzuki (eds), *Monetary Policy in Our Times* (Cambridge, Mass.: MIT Press), pp. 45–81.

Gordon, R. J. (1990) *The Measurement of Durable Goods Prices* (University of Chicago Press for NBER).

Gordon, R. J. (1992) 'Productivity in the Transportation Sector', in Z. Griliches (ed.), *Output Measurement in the Service Sectors* (University of Chicago for NBER), pp. 371–427.

Gordon, R. J. (1997a) 'The Time-Varying NAIRU and its Implications for Economic Policy', *Journal of Economic Perspectives*, vol. 11 (February), pp. 11–32.

Gordon, R. J. (1997b) 'Price, Wage, and Unemployment Dynamics in the Recent Experience of the United States', Working paper, Northwestern University (November).

Gordon, R. J. (1999) 'American Economic Growth since 1870: One Big Wave?', *American Economic Review, Papers and Proceedings*, vol. 89 (May), pp. 123–28.

Griliches, Z. (1994) 'Productivity, R & D, and the Data Constraint', *American Economic Review*, vol. 84 (March), pp. 1–23.

Hall, R. E. and Mankiw, N. G. (1994) 'Nominal Income Targeting', in N. G. Mankiw (ed.), *Monetary Policy* (University of Chicago Press for NBER), pp. 71–93.

Kendrick, J. (1961) *Productivity Trends in the United States*, National Bureau of Economic Research (Princeton: Princeton University Press).

Lum, S. K. S. and Yuskavage, R. E. (1997) 'Gross Product by Industry, 1947–96', *Survey of Current Business* (November), pp. 20–35.

Mandel, M. J. (1994) 'The Digital Juggernaut', *Business Week*, 18 May.

Mokyr, J. and Sten, R. (1997) 'Science, Health, and Household Technology: The Effect of the Pasteur Revolution on Consumer Demand', in Bresnahan and Gordon (1997), *The Economics of New Goods* (University of Chicago Press), pp. 143–200.

Nordhaus, W. D. (1972) 'The Recent Productivity Slowdown', *Brookings Papers on Economic Activity*, vol. 3, No. 3, pp. 493–536.

Oliner, S. D. and Sichel, D. E. (1994) 'Computers and Output Growth Revisited: How Big Is the Puzzle?', *Brookings Papers on Economic Activity*, vol. 25, no. 2, pp. 273–317.

Phelps, E. S. (1978) 'Commodity-Supply Shock and Full-Employment Monetary Policy', *Journal of Money, Credit, and Banking* (May), pp. 206–21.

Staiger, D. Stock, J. H. and Watson, M. W. (1997a) 'The NAIRU, Unemployment, and Monetary Policy', *Journal of Economic Perspectives*, vol. 11 (Winter), pp. 33–51.

Stauger, D., Stock, J. H. and Watson, M. W. (1997b) 'How Precise Are Estimates of the Natural Rate of Unemployment?', in C. Romer and D. Romer, (eds), *Reducing Inflation: Motivation and Strategy* (University of Chicago Press for NBER), pp. 195–242.

Sichel, D. E. (1997) *The Computer Revolution: An Economic Perspective* (Washington, DC: the Brookings Institution).

Solow, R. M. (1987) 'We'd Better Watch Out', *New York Times Book Review*, 12 July, p. 36.

Steindel C. (1997) 'Measuring Economic Activity and Economic Welfare: What Are We Missing?', Federal Reserve Bank of New York, Research Paper No. 9732 (October).

Stock, J. H. and Watson, M. W. (1998) 'Median Unbiased Estimation of Coefficient Variance in a Time Varying Parameter Model', *Journal of the American Statistical Association*, vol. 93, pp. 349–58.

Triplett, J. E. (1998) 'The Solow Productivity Paradox: What Computers Do to Productivity?', Paper presented to the American Economics Association meetings, 4 January.

12
Monetary Policy in a Changing Economy: Indicators, Rules and the Shift Towards Intangible Output*

James H. Stock

Introduction

The trend towards production, in which knowledge and intellectual activity play an increasingly important role, and in which output is often intangible, holds the possibility of changing the speed and nature of many aspects of microeconomic activity. These range from having an increasingly decentralized workforce, to increasing consumer and worker access to information, or to reducing transactions costs in markets. Such broad changes arguably could alter the relationship between economic indicators and overall economic activity, both because these shifts exacerbate the challenges of measuring productivity and inflation, and because they introduce structural changes that could affect timing and correlations between macroeconomic time series.

This chapter considers the effects of the trend towards knowledge-based production on indicators that are used in forming monetary policy, and the resulting implications for the conduct of monetary policy. At a general level, monetary policy is conducted using many indicators, formal and informal. Some of these measure demand pressure; most prominently, they include the gap between the unemployment rate and the natural rate of unemployment, as measured by the non-accelerating inflation rate of unemployment (NAIRU), and the GDP gap (the gap between real GDP and potential GDP). Other indicators focus on supply shocks, such as price inflation for imported commodities. One would expect that, to a greater or lesser degree, the relationship of all these indicators to economic activity,

---

* The author thanks Robert Shimer for kindly providing his demographically adjusted unemployment data; Robert Gordon, Takatoshi Ito, Michael Moskow, Georg Rich, Glenn Rudebusch, John Taylor and Mark Watson for helpful comments and discussions; and Noah Weisberger for research assistance. The research requested here is part of a larger research programme with Mark Watson at Princeton University.

and thus their value to monetary policy authorities, would change with underlying shifts in the structure of the economy.

In the USA, the recent low rates of unemployment has put one of these indicators, the gap between the unemployment rate and the NAIRU, at the centre of policy discussions. This chapter therefore addresses two questions. First, are recent changes in the NAIRU in the USA and in some other developed economies related to the world-wide trend towards knowledge-based production? Second, what are the implications of these changes, and of uncertainty about an evolving economy more generally, for the conduct of monetary policy? These questions are addressed in three steps.

First, evidence on the NAIRU in the major economies in North America and Europe is examined. Several studies, including Staiger *et al.* (1997a, 1997b), Gordon (1997), and the Council of Economic Advisers (1998), have concluded that there is evidence that the NAIRU has recently fallen in the USA. The analysis here follows these papers and estimates time-varying NAIRUs by specifying the NAIRU as an unobserved stochastic process that is inferred from a Phillips-type relationship. Some technical innovations, described in the second section, are used to estimate new quarterly time-varying NAIRU series for the USA. Formal estimation of the NAIRU for other countries is not undertaken. However, informal evidence on trends in the natural rate of unemployment is discussed for Canada and the major European economies.

Second, the relationship between these time-varying NAIRUs and measures of knowledge-based production is examined empirically. This is difficult because of the paucity of time-series data documenting this shift. However, several proxies are suggested for the USA (specifically, shifts in the shares of employment and income of various service sectors and a time-series on the returns to education) that permit some empirical analysis. While there is some evidence of a link between changes in the NAIRU in the USA and these proxies for knowledge-based production, the weight of the evidence is that the shift towards knowledge-based production does not appear to be a proximate or primary cause of changes in the NAIRU, and in particular of the declines in the NAIRU over the 1990s.

Finally, implications are drawn for the conduct of monetary policy. The evidence is consistent with the view that both the relationship between the unemployment rate and inflation, and that between interest rates and the unemployment rate have evolved over the past several decades, although it is difficult to pinpoint the source of these changes. This raises the broader question of how to conduct monetary policy when the economy is evolving but the direction of that evolution is difficult to predict. To make the discussion concrete, this question is addressed using a modification of a model developed by Rudebusch and Svensson (1998) to study monetary policy rules. The results are surprising. In the presence of evolving parameters, and thus of uncertainty about the current values of the parameters, robust policy rules tend to be somewhat more aggressive than they would be were the parameters constant and known. In this model, at least, taking an aggressive policy stand guards against the possibility that policy is less effective than one would think, based on the point estimates of the model.

Time-varying estimates of the NAIRU: methodology

The definition of the NAIRU as the rate of unemployment that leads to a constant rate of price inflation provides a concrete framework in which the NAIRU can be estimated econometrically. This framework, from Gordon (1982), is based on a Phillips-type relationship in which changes in rates of inflation are determined by the unemployment rate, inertial effects (lagged changes in inflation), and supply shocks or other special factors. This framework constitutes the standard method for estimation of the NAIRU, (see Congressional Budget Office, 1994; and Fuhrer, 1995). Specifically, the NAIRU is implicitly defined by the time-series regression:

$$\Delta \pi_t = \beta(L)(u_{t-1} - \bar{u}_{t-1}) + \delta(L)\Delta \pi_{t-1} + \gamma(L)X_t + \epsilon)_t \qquad (12.1)$$

where π_t is the rate of inflation, u_t is the unemployment rate, X_t is a vector of supply shock variables, L is the lag operator, $\bar{u}_t$ is the NAIRU at date t, and ϵ_t is a serially uncorrelated disturbance with mean zero and variance σ^2\epsilon. It is assumed in this literature and here that, after controlling suitably for supply shocks, ϵ_t is uncorrelated with the regressors. One justification for this is viewing Equation (12.1) as a reduced form relationship within which the unemployment gap, u_t-$\bar{u}_t$, is predetermined but not strictly exogenous.

In the standard formulation, the NAIRU is assumed to be constant – that is, $\bar{u}_t = u$. However, to examine the possibility that the NAIRU has changed over time and that these changes are related to knowledge-based production, this framework has been modified to include a time-varying NAIRU. Following King *et al.* (1995), Staiger *et al.* (1997a) and Gordon (1997), NAIRU is modelled as an unobserved variable that follows a random walk:

$$\bar{u}_t = \bar{u}_{t-1} + \eta_t, E\eta_t = 0, \text{ var}(\eta_t) = \tau^2 \qquad (12.2)$$

where the disturbance η_t is serially uncorrelated and is uncorrelated with ϵ_t. When $\tau^2 = 0$, the NAIRU is constant; positive values of τ^2 permit movements in the NAIRU.

Estimation of the parameters of Equations (12.1) and (12.2) presents some technical difficulties, and the approach adopted here differs from that previously used in the literature in two main ways. The first difference concerns parameter estimation. The model as written constitutes a state space model that is linear in variables but non-linear in the parameters, with Equation (12.1) being the measurement equation and Equation (12.2) the state equation. In principle, the fixed parameters of the model ($\beta(L)$, $\delta(L)$,

$\gamma(L)$, τ^2, σ_ϵ^2) can be jointly estimated by maximum likelihood in which the non-linear restrictions across the parameters are imposed. The main difficulty with this approach, however, is that when the true value of τ^2 is small, the maximum likelihood estimator suffers from considerable finite-sample bias. This bias is related to the so-called 'pile-up' problem in the estimation of a moving average coefficient when the true moving average root is nearly unity (see Stock, 1994 for a discussion of the MA unit root case), and a similar pile-up problem exists here in which the MLE takes on the value $\tau^2 = 0$ with high probability even when the true value of τ^2 is positive. Thus Staiger *et al.* (1997b) and Gordon (1997) imposed values of τ^2 rather than estimating τ^2.

Here, I take advantage of recent theoretical developments in Stock and Watson (1998) to construct median unbiased estimates of τ^2 and confidence intervals for τ^2. These are then used to guide subsequent estimation. The method in Stock and Watson (1998) entails constructing confidence intervals for τ^2 by inverting certain tests for parameter stability using the method of confidence belts. They show that, asymptotically, confidence intervals thus constructed have the correct coverage rate under the nesting $\tau = 0(1/T)$ (this is the neighbourhood in which these tests have non-trivial asymptotic power). Because an equal-tailed confidence interval with 0 per cent coverage is a median-unbiased estimator of τ, (and thus of τ^2, this method provides both interval and point estimates.

This procedure can be implemented using a variety of break tests. The specific break test used here is the Wald statistic version of the Quandt (1960) likelihood ratio (QLR) test. This is the maximal value of the Wald regression test of no change in the regression coefficients (or a subset thereof), over a range T_1, ..., T_2, where T_1 and T_2 are chosen to exclu inital and final 15 per cent of the observations. At a risk of some confusion, this will be referred to below as the QLR statistic, even though it is computed in Wald form. Monte Carlo results and theory show that this maximal Wald statistic behaves in a very similar way to the Andrews – Ploberger (1994) test statistic, and has somewhat better size and power properties than the mean Wald statistic (see Stock and Watson, 1996; 1998). Results were also computed for the Andrews–Ploberger (1994) and mean Wald statistic, and the results were similar to those obtained using the QLR statistic.

The second technical innovation involves a simpler strategy for the estimation of the remaining fixed parameters, ($\beta(L)$, $\delta(L)$, $\gamma(L)$, τ^2), Given an estimate of τ^2, these parameters can be estimated by maximum likelihood using the Kalman filter. However, this is computationally cumbersome and the asymptotic theory in Stock and Watson (1998) provides a simpler approach. When $\tau = 0(1/T)$, Equation (12.1) can be rewritten:

$$\Delta\pi_t = \mu_t + \beta(L)u_{t-1} + \delta(L)\Delta\pi_{t-1} + \gamma(L)X_t + \tilde{\epsilon}_t \qquad (12.3)$$

where $\tilde{\epsilon}_t = \epsilon_t + O_p(1/T)$ and $\mu_t = \beta(1)\bar{u}_{t-1}$, so $\mu_t = \mu_{t-1}$ where $+ \tilde{\eta}_t$, where $\tilde{\eta}_t = \beta(1)\eta_t$. Stock and Watson (1998) showed that, if $\delta(L) = 0$, then $\beta(L)$, $\gamma(L)$ and σ_ϵ^2 are efficiently estimated by ordinary least squares regression of $\delta\pi_t$ on a constant and u_{t-1}, X_t, and their lags as called for in Equation (12.1). It can further be shown that, for $\delta(L) \neq 0$, the least squares estimates of $\delta(L)$, $\beta(L)$, $\gamma(L)$ and σ_ϵ^2 are $T^{\frac{1}{2}}$-consistent. Based on this result, these parameters are here estimated by OLS.

Given these parameter estimates, $\bar{u}_t$ is estimated using the Kalman smoother in the linear state space model in Equation (12.2) and (12.3). Estimated signal extraction variances for $\bar{u}_t$ are computed using standard Kalman smoother formula. Note that these variances incorporate only uncertainty about $\bar{u}_t$, given the data and the parameters, and do not incorporate uncertainty about the parameters.

Time-varying estimates of the NAIRU

Results for the USA

Time-varying NAIRU specifications for the USA were estimated using quarterly data from 1961:1 to 1997:3, with earlier observations used for initial conditions. Inflation is measured by the annualized growth rate of the consumer price index (CPI). The supply shock variables are those used in Staiger *et al.* (1997a, 1997b), specifically Gordon's (1982) variable representing the imposition and elimination of the Nixon wage and price controls (entered contemporaneously) and a variable measuring the log of the ratio of the food and energy prices to the CPI. Five measures of the unemployment rate are used: the total civilian unemployment rate, aged 16 and over; the unemployment rate for married men with a spouse present; the unemployment rate of males, ages 25–54; the unemployment rate for males, ages 35–44; and Shimer's (1998) demographically adjusted unemployment rate. Shimer's adjustments correct for the changing demographics of the US labour force and thus help to control for the implied shifts in labour force attachment (and the associated changes in the NAIRU) as the baby boom ages. Time varying NAIRUs were also estimated for other inflation measures (the chained GDP deflator, the chained personal consumption expenditure deflator, and the CPI excluding food and energy). Although the precision of the estimates of the NAIRU depends appreciably on which inflation series is used, the point estimates do not. Because the focus of this part of the chapter is on understanding the relationship between changes in the NAIRU and knowledge-based production, this means that little is lost by restricting attention to results based on the CPI.

Estimation and testing results are summarized in Table 12.1. Consistent with other results in the literature, the formal statistical evidence that the US NAIRU has changed over time is mixed.

This is mainly a consequence of the imprecision with which the NAIRU is estimated. While the NAIRU might have changed over this sample, the standard framework for its estimation provides such imprecise estimates that it is difficult to distinguish statistically significant movements in the NAIRU. Similarly, the median unbiased estimates of τ are all small – zero, in fact, for three of the five unemployment rate series. At the same time, these results are consistent with the NAIRU exhibiting moderately large movements; the 90 per cent confidence intervals contain values of τ up to approximately 0.10. This upper end corresponds to quarterly standard deviations of the movements in τ of approximately 0.1 percentage points, which in turn corresponds to a standard deviation of decadal changes in the NAIRU of 0.6 percentage points.

Because using the small or zero point estimates of τ would result in NAIRUs that are constant or essentially so, for the purposes of this chapter it is of greater interest to maintain the possibility that the NAIRU might have been changing over time, and to extract the associated time-varying NAIRUs. We therefore adopt the value $\tau = 0.1$, which corresponds approximately to the upper end of the 90 per cent confidence intervals for τ in Table 12.1.

Estimated time-varying NAIRUs (based on $\tau = 0.1$) for three of the five unemployment rate series, extracted using the Kalman smoother, along with one standard deviation signal extraction error band and the associated unemployment rate, are plotted in Figures 12.1 to 12.3. Although the levels of the NAIRU depend on the unemployment rate series, the general time-series pattern of the time-varying NAIRUs does not. All the NAIRUs increased over the 1960s, peaked around 1980, and showed, a marked decline during the 1990s. All the NAIRUs also have large signal extraction errors, so that most of the actual values of the unemployment rate fall within a single standard deviation band.

Evolution of the unemployment rate in Canada and Europe

It would be of interest to have reliable estimates of time-varying NAIRUs for other G7 countries, since these could provide further insights into the relationship between information technology and the evolution of the NAIRU. However, there are several impediments to obtaining such estimates. Comparably defined data are not available across all these countries at a quarterly level for the long spans needed to estimate the coefficients accurately. Each country has, to a certain extent, its own unique set of supply shocks and institutional histories, and proper estimation of the NAIRU requires proper specification of these shocks and institutional nuances. Most importantly, some question whether the Phillips curve, as discussed so far, is appropriate for all the G7 countries. Certainly, the experience of persistently high unemployment rates in the 1980s and 1990s in some European countries suggests that the time-varying component of any NAIRU for those countries would need to be large. For these reasons, formal estimates of the NAIRU are

Table 12.1 Time-varying NAIRU models: USA, 1961:1–1997:3 (dependent variable: change in CPI inflation)

Unemployment variable	Total	Marr Male	Male 25–54	Male 35–44	Dem. adj.
R^{-2}	0.391	0.367	0.362	0.424	0.398
$\hat{\beta}$ (1) (std error)	−0.226	−0.284	−0.196	−0.212	−0.257
	(0.080)	(0.098)	(0.068)	(0.070)	(0.079)
QLR statistics testing constancy of:					
intercept	2.41	1.88	3.76	3.27	3.18
intercept and β (1)	3.52	6.81	6.08	6.33	4.42
Median-unbiased estimate of τ	0.0	0.0	0.021	0.006	0.0
90 per cent confidence interval for τ	(0,0.119)	(0,0.092)	(0,0.181)	(0,0.159)	(0,0.154)

Notes: All specifications include four lags each of unemployment and changes in inflation, the contemporaneous value of Gordon's (1982) Nixon wage and price control series, and a single lag of the relative price of food and energy as discussed in the text. The QLR test is significant at the: [+]10%; *5%; **1% level.

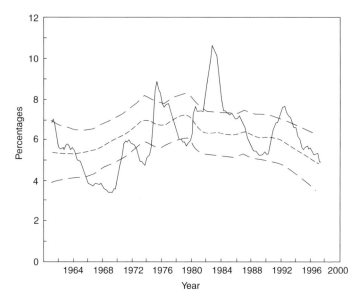

Figure 12.1   Total unemployment (solid line), time-varying NAIRU (dashed line), and standard deviation bands for the NAIRU, USA, 1961:1–1997:3

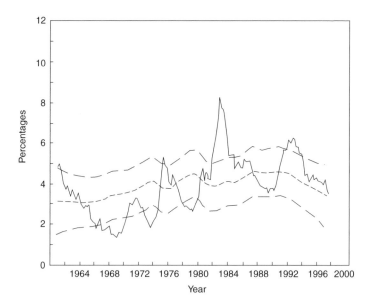

Figure 12.2   Male unemployment, ages 35–44 (solid line), time-varying NAIRU (dashed line), and standard deviation bands for the NAIRU, 1961:1–1997:3

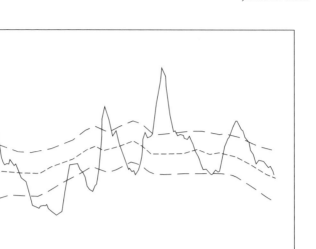

Figure 12.3 Demographically adjusted unemployment (solid line), time-varying NAIRU (dashed line), and standard deviation bands for the NAIRU, 1961:1–1997:3

not presented here for other G7 countries. Rather, some informal evidence is provided on trends in the natural rates of unemployment for these countries.

Table 12.2 contains evidence on the recent behaviour of the rates of inflation and unemployment in the G7 countries, excluding Japan. (Japan is omitted because the slowdown and dropping rates of inflation of the 1990s make historical comparisons difficult.) During the 1990s, each of these countries experience periods of approximately constant rates of inflation; these periods, and the associated changes in the annual rate of inflation, are listed in the first two numerical columns of the table. Because the rate of inflation was approximately constant over this multi-year period, the average unemployment rate over this period provides a crude estimate of the NAIRU in these countries (note, however, that this estimate does not control for supply shocks). Evidently, the NAIRUs for these countries vary considerably, with Canada, France, Italy and the UK having the highest estimates, and Germany and the USA the lowest. Comparison with the 15-year average unemployment rate over 1960–74 suggests that for all these countries except the USA, the NAIRU has risen substantially. Of course, this corresponds to the so-called problem of hysterisis in European unemployment rates. European unemployment rates have generally remained high since the end of the 1980s, so this suggests that the NAIRU for France, Italy and the UK has remained approximately constant since then, while the Canadian NAIRU arguably has

Table 12.2   Inflation and unemployment in Europe and North America: 1990s
compared to 1960s and early 1970s

Country	Period	Change in inflation (%)	Average unemployment (%)	Average unemployment rate, 1960–74 (%)
Canada	1993–6	–0.3	10.2	5.1
France	1993–6	–0.1	12.1	2.1
Italy	1993–6	–0.3	11.4	3.3
UK	1992–5	–0.3	9.8	2.9
Germany	1991–3	0.3	4.9	0.7
USA	1993–6	0.0	6.0	5.0

Notes: Entries in the column 'Change in inflation', are the change in the annual rate of inflation over the indicated period in preceding column, and entries in the 'Average unemployment' column are the average annual rates of unemployment over the same period. The right-hand 1 column provides the average annual rate of unemployment over the 15-year comparison period 1960–74.

risen during that time. Historical comparisons for Germany are less appropriate, because of German unification.

With these estimates of time varying NAIRUs in hand, I now turn to the question of whether variations in the NAIRU are related to shifts in production towards knowledge-based and intangible output.

Are the changes in the NAIRU related to shifts toward intangible output?

Many explanations have been put forward for the trends in the NAIRUs is evident in Figures 12.1 to 12.3, especially the decline in the US NAIRU during the 1990s. Some of these explanations involve the increasing international-ization of product markets. According to this argument, firms face additional foreign competition, which leads to price restraint, so that prices do not increase as quickly when demand increases. Other explanations focus on labour markets. Because firms are increasingly mobile, according to this view workers fear that the firm will move production overseas if the workers press wage demands aggressively. Other explanations focus on demographics: as the baby boom ages, an increasing share of the workforce has a higher job attachment so, all else being equal, the natural rate of unemployment will rise.

Another set of explanations involves technology and the shift towards knowledge-based production. Employment arrangements at knowledge-based firms seem to differ from those in traditional manufacturing, with greater turnover, possibly reflecting a greater importance of general human capital rather than firm specific human capital. To the extent that general human capital is increasingly important, training costs are reduced and search times could be shorter. Additionally, to the extent that production can be based on telecommuting rather than physical presence at the worksite, then the range of employment opportunities for unemployed workers in knowledge-based industries is increased (the transaction cost of taking a new job at a distant location is decreased). At the same time, this results in a larger pool of potential workers, so local labour supply restrictions are less binding, which could serve to moderate wage increases. Finally, the amount of employment through temporary employment agencies has been increasing, at least in the USA, and improved information technology arguably facilitates job-matching through these agencies. These considerations all suggest that shifts towards knowledge-based production could reduce the natural rate of unemployment, which would be reflected in a decline in the NAIRU.

In this section, I focus on the final set of these explanations – the link between changes in the NAIRU and knowledge-based production. Because many aspects of knowledge-based production are new, only a limited amount of long time-series data is available for this purpose. I therefore focus on two sets of proxies for knowledge-based production in the USA. The first set focuses on the rising importance of the service sector, in which much knowledge-based output is produced, and in particular on relatively skill-intensive service sectors. In particular, four proxies are examined: the share of total income produced in the service sector; the share of total employment in the service sector; the share of total employment in business services; and the share of total employment in finance, insurance and real estate.

The second measure is annual time-series data on the returns to an additional year of education. The datum for a given year is the coefficient on years of education in an ordinary least squares regression of log wages on years of education and a standard list of socioeconomic control variables, estimated using the March Current Population Survey (these regressions contain between 24 000 and 120 000 observations, depending on the year). Because of data availability, this series starts in 1979, and because of a change in the survey measurement of the years of education in 1992, it ends in 1991. This series was taken from Abdul-Hadi (1997).

These series are plotted in Figures 12.4 to 12.8. Also plotted in these graphs are adjusted time-varying NAIRUs for the five unemployment rate series for the USA. To facilitate comparisons, these NAIRUs have been adjusted (rescaled and shifted) so that they are on the same basis as the NAIRU for the total unemployment rate; the parameters for the rescaling and shifting were taken from a regression of the particular unemployment rate – for example, the married male unemployment rate, on the total unemployment rate.

It is evident from inspection of Figures 12.4 to 12.8 that the five proxies for knowledge-based production and the time-varying NAIRUs have different trending properties. Generally speaking, these proxies all increase, whereas the NAIRUs increased in the 1970s and declined in the late 1980s and early 1990s. In terms of overall trends, the sharpest increases in the returns to education and in the importance of services in the economy have similar timing to the recent decline in the NAIRU. However, all these proxies were increasing for a

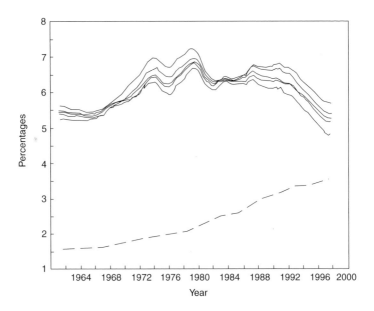

Figure 12.4   Time-varying NAIRUs for the USA (solid lines) and the rescaled income share of all services (dashed line, divided by 10), quarterly

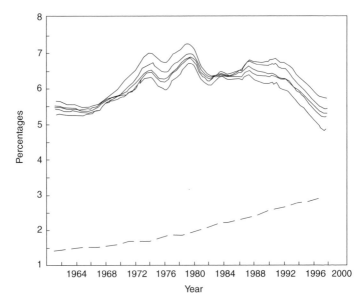

Figure 12.5   Time-varying NAIRUs for the USA (solid lines) and the share of employment in all services (dashed line, divided by 10), quarterly

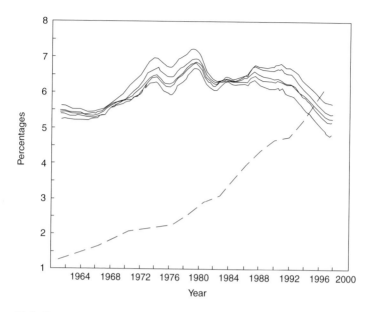

Figure 12.6 Time-varying NAIRUs for the USA (solid lines) and the share of employment in business services (dashed line), quarterly

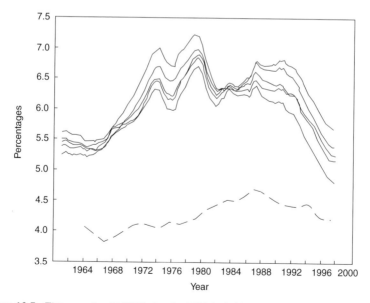

Figure 12.7 Time-varying NAIRUs for the USA (solid lines) and the share of employment in finance, insurance and real estate (dashed line), quarterly

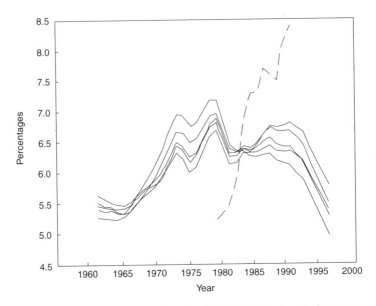

Figure 12.8 Time-varying NAIRUs for the USA (solid lines) and the return to an additional year of education (dashed line), annual

considerable length of time prior to the recent declines. Although data on computer usage itself is not analyzed, the same trending features would presumably be found there, with the trend towards computerization occuring over many years, and the decline in the NAIRU being a more recent phenomenon.

Formal statistical analysis of these relationship is challenging because of the slowly moving trends in these series and the fact that the TV NAIRU is itself an estimated series. None the less, it is useful to look at some cross-correlations, which are presented in Table 12.3 for the services shares (no such results are presented for the returns to education because there are only thirteen observations in that series). Changes in the shares of services (execpt for employment in finance, insurance and real estate) are negatively correlated with future declines in the NAIRU, although in many cases these correlations are not statistically significant.

Information that is arguably more useful is obtained by asking whether changes in the shares of services helps to predict changes in the NAIRU, given past changes in the NAIRU. This can be examined by Granger causality tests, the p-values of which are reported in Table 12.3. Two of the four measures of shares of services predict changes in the NAIRU at the 10 per cent significance level, one of which (the employment share of business services) is significant at the 5 per cent level.

Table 12.3   Correlations between time-varying NAIRU (total unemployment) and measures of service sector growth, USA

	Income share, services	Employment share of: Total services	Business services	FIRE
Cross-correlations at lag:				
0	–0.12	–0.43	–0.34	0.07
1	–0.17	–0.42	–0.39	0.05
2	–0.13	–0.36	–0.41	0.04
3	–0.18	–0.34	–0.46	0.03
4	–0.13	–0.30	–0.47	0.04
5	–0.15	–0.23	–0.41	0.07
6	–0.10	–0.13	–0.38	0.07
7	–0.09	–0.10	–0.37	0.08
8	–0.05	–0.12	–0.34	0.09
9	–0.06	–0.13	–0.33	0.05
10	–0.13	–0.15	–0.30	0.02
11	–0.08	–0.09	–0.26	0.04
12	–0.05	–0.05	–0.22	0.07
Granger-causality *p*-value	.078	.456	.031	.986
No. of observations	141	141	141	129

Notes: All statistics pertain to changes in the TVP–NAIRU estimate (total unemployment) and changes in the service sector share variable given at the top of each column. For the Granger-causality regressions, the dependent variable is the change in the TVP–NAIRU estimate, and four lags of both variables and a constant were included in the regression. Standard errors for the correlations are approximately .08.

Finally, it is useful to contrast these trends with the evidence on international trends in the NAIRU. The trend towards knowledge-based production has been present in all developed economies, so one would expect it to have a similar effect on the evolution of their NAIRUs. However, the recent behaviour of the natural rate of unemployment differs sharply across G7 countries. For continential Europe, the NAIRU increased sharply during the 1970s and 1980s, and there was no sign of a decline in the 1990s. The natural rate also seems to have been approximately flat since the late 1980s in the UK. However, the Canadian experience is similar to that of the USA. Thus, an attribution of these trends to shifts towards information technology would need to explain why this shift causes an increase in the NAIRU in Europe but a drop in the NAIRU in North America.

Overall, these results provide a mixed view of the link between increased knowledge-based production and changes in the NAIRU. In terms of timing, the declines in the NAIRU in the USA are recent, but the trend towards the increasing importance of services, the increasing returns to education, and increasing knowledge-based production has been with us for at least since the 1970s. Moreover, different developed countries have different trends in the natural rate, yet if increasing knowledge-based production is an important source of these changes one would expect to see similar behaviour of NAIRUs internationally. An examination of shorter-run links for the USA (Table 12.3) shows that increases in the share of services tend to be associated with future drops in the NAIRU. However, the ability of these changes to predict changes in the NAIRU is limited to one or two series. In summary, there is evidence that the NAIRU has been changing in G7 countries, but the evidence examined here suggests that these changes are not driven primarily by the trend towards knowledge-based production.

Before concluding this section, I turn briefly to another of the proposed explanations for the recent decline in the NAIRU in the USA – the ageing of the workforce (Shimer, 1998). According to this argument, the natural rate of total unemployment would decline as workers in the baby-boom grow older, because older workers have greater labour force attachment. It is true that the NAIRU based on the prime-aged male unemployment rate, for example, is lower than that for the overall workforce, and varies less than the NAIRU for total unemployment. However, the time-varying NAIRU for married males, males ages 25–54, males ages 35–44, and the demographically adjusted unemployment rate is qualitatively similar to the NAIRU for overall unemployment. Once these five estimated time-varying NAIRUs are placed on the same scale by regression adjustment, as is done in Figures 12.4 to 12.8, they are similar, indeed, and in particular all show a decline in the NAIRU in the late 1990s. This graphical look at the data suggests that demographic changes, while important for many aspects of the macroeconomy and labour markets, play a minor role in the historical evolution of the NAIRU in the USA.

Monetary policy in the presence of model instability

The evidence in the previous sections suggests that the NAIRU has changed over time in the G7 countries. This section turns to the question of the conduct of monetary policy in the presence of the uncertainty that is caused by such changes.

The topic of policy rules under uncertainty has been subjected to considerable study. On a formal level, this literature has focused typically on the problem of optimal control when the model parameters are unknown and when the decision-maker is able to place a prior distribution over the unknown parameters. In a static context with linear models and quadratic loss, the resulting optimal policy rules are based on parameter values that are shrunk towards zero (Brainard, 1967). In a dynamic context, optimal dynamic policy typically involves some deliberate experimentation to learn about the parameter values; see Wieland (1996, 1997).

A drawback of this standard decision theoretic approach is that it requires policy-makers to specify prior distributions over parameters. Given the complexity of the models used in the conduct of monetary policy, this is entirely unrealistic. This section therefore pursues an approach that does not require priors and in this sense is better suited to generalization to actual policy-making problems. The specific approach here is adopted from the literature on robust control, and is based on finding minimax rules – that is, policy rules that minimize the maximum risk over some specified subset of the parameter space.

To illustrate this approach, and the importance of parameter evolution more generally, I consider a simple two-equation model taken from Rudebusch and Svensson (1998), estimated on quarterly US data. Their model consists of a Phillips-type equation linking inflation to a demand measure, and of an equation linking the demand measure to monetary policy as measured by the *ex-post* real federal funds rate. Three modifications of their model are made here. First, their demand measure is the output gap; to be consistent with the emphasis so far on the NAIRU, this is replaced here by the unemployment gap (the unemployment rate less the NAIRU). Second, their Phillips equation does not control for any supply shocks; for consistency with the previous sections, I include the two supply shock measures that were used above to estimate the NAIRU models for the USA (the Nixon price controls and the relative price of food and energy). Third, I allow for some of the key parameters to vary over time.

The modified Rudebusch–Svensson model is

$$\Delta\pi_t = \alpha_\pi(L)\Delta\pi_{t-1} + \alpha_{y,t}(u_t - \bar{u}_t) + \gamma'X_t + \epsilon_{1t} \quad (12.4)$$

$$u_t = \mu_t + \beta_u(L)u_{t-1} - \beta_{r,t}(\bar{i}_{t-1} - \bar{\pi}_{t-1}) + \epsilon_{2t} \quad (12.5)$$

where $\alpha_\pi(L)$ is a third-order lag polynomial, $\beta_u(L)$ is second-order, $\bar{i}_t$ is the four-quarter moving average of the Federal Funds rate (so $\bar{i}_t = (\bar{i}_t + i_{t-1} + i_{t-2} + i_{t-3})/4$), $\bar{\pi}_t$ is the four-quarter moving average of inflation, and X_t are the supply shock proxy variables. Rudebusch and Svensson (1998) provide motivation for studying this model. For the purposes here it suffices to view these as two reduced-form equations that describe the evolution of unemployment and inflation.

Following Rudebusch and Svensson, the policy-maker is assumed to have quadratic loss (L_t) involving annual average inflation, the unemployment gap, and changes in the norminal interest rate:

$$L_t = \bar{\pi}_t^2 + a_u(u_t - \bar{u}_t)^2 + a_i(i_t - i_{t-1})^2 \quad (12.6)$$

The loss function parameters are set to a_u = and a_i = 8.

The model in Equations (12.4) and (12.5) involves two sets of time-varying parameters, an intercept drift ($\bar{u}_t$ and μ_t) and time varitation in the slope coefficients $\alpha_{y,t}$ and $\beta_{r,t}$. Under quadratic loss, the optimal rule given all the slope coefficients does not involve the intercepts. I therefore focus on the time-varying slope coefficients, which are modelled as

$$\alpha_{y,t} = \alpha_{y,t-1} + \eta_{1,t} \tag{12.7a}$$

$$\beta_{r,t} = \beta_{r,t-1} + \eta_{2,t} \tag{12.7b}$$

where $\eta_t = (\eta_{1,t} \ \eta_{2,t})'$ serially uncorrelated, uncorrelated with ϵ_t, and has covariance matrix Σ.

The econometric methodology described in the second section to estimate the time-varying NAIRU models was used to used to estimate the complete model in Equations (2.4), (12.5) and (12.7). Estimation was performed equation by equation using US quarterly data from 1961:1 to 1997:3, with earlier observations for initial conditions. Time-varying parameters were estimated for the four intercept and slope coefficients. For the optimal control calculations below, to focus attention on the role of evolution of the two slope coefficients in Equation (12.7), all other coefficients are treated as being constant and known.

To discuss optimal policy, one must specify a class of policy rules. One approach is to derive model-specific optimal policies in the standard way specified in optimal control theory. For the purposes of this illustration, however, the results are more transparent if attention is restricted to a simple class of policy rules. There is, in fact, a large literature on simple rules for monetary policy; see the papers in Taylor (1998) for a summary. Again, I follow Rudebusch and Svensson and consider policy within the context of a parameterized rule of the type considered by Taylor (1993):

$$i_t = g_\pi \bar{\pi}_{t-1} - g_u(u_{t-1} - \bar{u}_t) \tag{12.8}$$

The original Taylor rule (Taylor, 1993) is expressed not in terms of the unemployment gap but in terms of the output gap, and is $i_t = 1.5\,\pi_{t-1} + 0.5 y_t^{\text{gap}}$, where y_t^{gap} is the relative gap between actual GDP and potential GDP in percentage points. This rule can be converted to one based on the unemployment gap using Okun's law. With an Okun's law coefficient of 2.5, the coefficient on the output gap corresponds to a coefficient on the unemployment gap of 1.25. It will be convenient to refer to this rule, $i_t = 1.5\bar{\pi}_{t-1} - 1.25(u_{t-1} - \bar{u}_t)$, as the unemployment-based Taylor rule.

Based on these estimated parameters and loss functions, two calculations were performed. The first provides a calibration of whether the estimated time variation is significant from an economic perspective. This calculation addresses the counterfactual question: suppose the estimated time-varying slope coefficients, along with the other model coefficients, had in fact been known historically. What would have been the time path of the optimal Taylor-type rule coefficients?

The answer to this question is given by the two time series of coefficients, g_π and g_u plotted in Figure 12.9. Although the optimal (counterfactual)

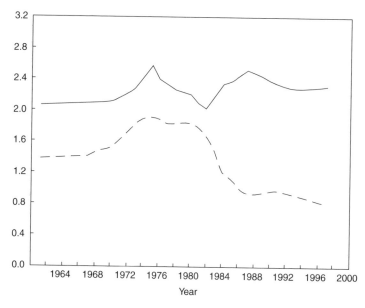

Figure 12.9 Optimized Taylor-type rule parameters, g_π (solid line) and g_μ (dashed lines) for counterfactual, time-varying, historically optimal policies within modified Rudebusch–Svensson model

coefficient on inflation is relatively constant, the coefficient on unemployment varies considerably over this period. At the end of the sample, the coefficient on inflation is 2.3 and the coefficient on the unemployment gap is 0.8. Thus, for these coefficients, the optimal central bank rule reacts somewhat more strongly to inflation than under the Taylor rule (g_π = 2.3 versus 1.5 for the Taylor rule) but somewhat less strongly to the unemployment gap than under the Taylor rule (g_u = 0.8 versus 1.25 for the unemployment-based Taylor rule). While not being identical, these coefficients are broadly in keeping with those of the Taylor rule. According to these calculations, the optimal counterfactual rule would react less to an increase in unemployment in the late 1990s than in the early 1980s.

Of course, in real time, the parameters are unknown, both because of econometric (sampling) uncertainty and because the model changes over time. What is the optimal policy for a central bank in this model, faced with such uncertainty? Here, I focus on the second of these sources of uncertainty, which reflects the recognition that the economy is changing over time, but the nature of that change is incompletely understood.

To compute the optimal control rule under this uncertainty, suppose that the central bank is concerned about minimizing loss in a worst-case scenario – that is, that the central bank is interested in following a minimax policy. This policy will be a robust control rule in the sense that it guards against worst-case outcomes. To calculate this rule, it is necessary to have a measure of the uncertainty associated with the time evolution of the model. This is provided by the Kalman filter estimate of the time-varying coefficients and of the signal extraction error covariance matrix. For specificity, these are computed for the final quarter in the sample, 1997:3, and the minimax rule is computed by considering parameters that fall in a one standard deviation confidence ellipse around the Kalman smoother point estimate of the time-varying slope coefficients for 1997:3.

The resulting minimax robust policy for 1997:3 has coefficients of $g_\pi = 3.4$ and $g_u = 1.5$. These coefficients are both larger than the optimal coefficients for 1997:3 in the absence of uncertainty, portrayed in Figure 12.9. The coefficient on unemployment is approximately the same as the corresponding coefficient in the unemployment-based Taylor rule. However, the coefficient on inflation in the robust rule is more than twice the Taylor rule coefficient on inflation.

Evidently, the minimax robust rule is more aggressive than the rule that ignores parameter uncertainty, in the sense that the reaction to an increase in the unemployment rate or in inflation is more vigorous. Initially this might seem surprising from the perspective of Brainard-type calculations, in which uncertainty induces less vigorous responses. Under the minimax policy, however, the policy-maker is guarding against parameter values that include those in which policy has very little effect. In that circumstance, an aggressive response is called for; if this induces overshooting, as it will if the response to policy is larger than for the worst-case parameters, the overshooting can be subsequently, counteracted. The not result is that the disadvantages of a too-vigorous policy, in the case that policy is effective, are outweighed by the advantages of an aggressive response, in the case that it is not.

Discussion and conclusions

There are many reasons for the evolution of the NAIRU in developed economies since the 1960s. Recently, a possible source of this evolution has been the shift to an information economy and the growing importance of computers. The analysis of the fourth section, which uses shares of employment and the return to education to proxy for the trend towards an information economy, suggests that this trend is not a proximate or primary cause of the shifts in the NAIRU that have been seen in the past few years. It is difficult to obtain long time-series that measure accurately the trends towards knowledge-based production, and using different proxies might yield different conclusions. What the foregoing analysis indicates, however, is that because many changes in the economy affect these series, because the trends are long-term, and because these series are, in any event, measured with considerable noise, it is difficult to isolate statistically the role of any one of the factors.

The fact that the source of these shifts is not readily apparent underscores the importance of examining monetary policy that is robust to changes in the underlying economy, whatever their source. The main finding from the fifth section was that the amount of parameter variation estimated in a small macroeconomic model for the USA is economically important, and that different policies result when this time variation is taken into account. The robust rules that emerge suggest that a monetary authority facing uncertainty about how the economy is evolving should be willing to pursue policies that are somewhat more aggressive than might be indicated by simple point estimates of their models. A more aggressive stance against inflation or, for that matter, against deflation, guards against the possibility that monetary policy is less effective than the point estimates suggest. It should be emphasized that this conclusion was reached after making many simplificat-ions: the modified Rudebusch–Svensson (1989) model is linear and small, time variation was admitted only for a subset of the parameters, quadratic loss was used, and estimation uncertainty was ignored. An important research question is whether these qualitative conclusions hold up when these simplifications are relaxed.

This chapter has focused on the NAIRU and on models involving the unemployment rate. However, if the role of unemployment as an economic indicator is changing, there is a premium on finding other indicators that have more stable links to economic activity. Of the indicators not studied here, some seem likely to be particularly susceptible to measurement problems induced by the shift to knowledge-based production; these include the GDP gap, because of the difficulties in measuring productivity and thus in measuring potential GDP. On the other hand, there are some real quantity indicators, the measurement of which is largely unaffected by the trend towards knowledge-based production. An example of such an indicator is housing starts, which for the USA has proved to be a useful demand proxy for forecasting inflation (Stock and Watson, 1997b). One avenue of further research suggested is refining the list of such indicators and assessing the stability of their relation to overall economic activity and to measures of monetary policy.

References

Abdul-Hadi, S. (1997) 'The Determinants of U.S. Wage Rates, 1979–1995', Undergraduate paper, Harvard University and the National Bureau of Economic Research.

Andrews, D. W. K. and Ploberger, W. (1994) 'Optimal Tests When a Nuisance Parameter is Present Only Under the Alternative', *Econometrica*, vol. 62, pp. 1383–414.

Brainard, W. (1967) 'Uncertainty and the Effectiveness of Policy', *American Economic Review*, vol. 57, pp. 411–25.

Congressional Budget Office (1994) 'Reestimating the NAIRU', *The Economic and Budget Outlook*, August 1994.

Council of Economic Advisers (1998) *Economic Report of the President* (Washington, DC: US Government Printing Office).

Fuhrer, J. C. (1995) 'The Phillips Curve is Alive and Well', *New England Economic Review of the Federal Reserve Bank of Boston* (March/April), pp. 41–56.

Gordon, R. J. (1982) 'Price Inertia and Ineffectiveness in the United States', *Journal of Political Economy*, vol. 90, pp. 1087–117.

Gordon, R. J. (1997) 'The Time-Varying NAIRU and its Implications for Economic Policy', *Journal of Economic Perspectives*, vol. 11, pp. 11–32.

King, R. G., Stock, H. and Watson, M. W. (1995) 'Temporal Instability of the Unemploymen–inflation Relationship', *Economic Perspectives of the Federal Reserve Bank of Chicago* (May/June), pp. 2–12.

McFadden (eds), *Handbook of Econometrics, vol. IV* (Amsterdam: Elsevier), pp. 2740–843.

Quandt, R. E. (1960) 'Tests of the Hypothesis that a Linear Regression System Obeys Two Separate Regimes', *Journal of the American Statistical Association*, vol. 55, pp. 324–30.

Rudebusch, G. D. and Svensson, L. E. O. (1998) 'Policy Rules for Inflation Targeting', in J. Taylor (ed.), *Policy Rules for Inflation Targeting* (University of Chicago Press for the NBER).

Shimer, R. (1998) 'Why Is the U.S. Unemployment Rate So Much Lower', *NBER Macroeconomic Annual 1998*.

Staiger, D., Stock, J. H. and Watson, M. W. (1997a) 'The NAIRU, Unemployment, and Monetary Policy', *Journal of Economic Perspectives*, vol. 11, pp. 33–51.

Staiger, D., Stock, J. H. and Watson, M. W. (1997b) 'How Precise are Estimates of the Natural Rate of Unemployment?', in C. Romer and D. Romer (eds), *Reducing Inflation: Motivation and Strategy* (University of Chicago Press for the NBER), pp. 195–242.

Stock, J. H. (1994) 'Unit Roots, Structural Breaks, and Trends', ch. 46 in R. Engle and D. McFadden (eds), *Handbook of Econometrics, vol. IV* (Amsterdam: Elsevier), pp. 2740–843.

Stock, J. H. and Watson, M. W. (1996) 'Evidence on Structural Instability in Macroeconomic Time Series Relations', *Journal of Business and Economic Statistics*, vol. 14, no. 1, pp. 11–30.

Stock, J. H. and Watson, M. W. (1998) 'Median Unbiased Estimation of Coefficient Variance in a Time Varying Parameter Model', *Journal of the American Statistical Association*, vol. 93, pp. 349–58.

Taylor, J. B. (1993) 'Discretion versus Policy Rules in Practice', *Carnegie–Rochester Conference Series on Public Policy*, vol. 39, pp. 195–214.

Taylor, J. B. (ed.) (1998) *Policy Rules for Inflation Targeting* (University of Chicago Press for the NBER).

Wieland, V. (1996) 'Monetary Policy, Parameter Uncertainty and Optimal Learning', MS, Board of Governors of the Federal Reserve System.

Wieland, V. (1997) 'Monetary Policy and Uncertainty about the Natural Unemployment Rate', MS, Board of Governors of the Federal Reserve System.

Comments

Michael H. Moskow

Introduction

The theme of the Bank of Japan conference was a very important one for monetary policy globally. How should monetary policy by conducted in a world of knowledge-based growth, quality change and uncertain measurement? In the USA, the Federal Reserve's monetary policy objectives are to foster maximum sustainable economic growth and low inflation. In order to achieve these goals, at a minimum, policy-makers need to have useful estimates of the economy's growth potential, an assessment of the factors that may be changing this potential growth rate, and the relationship between inflation and these possibly changing growth factors.

I found the chapters by Bob Gordon and Jim Stock to be very interesting and helpful, and I must say they are useful reminders of how difficult a central banker's job is. My comments are organized in the following way. First, I'll discuss Stock's analysis of the NAIRU and how those estimates compare with research at the Federal Reserve Bank of Chicago. Second, I'll comment on Gordon's chapter and some alternative interpretations of the information technology revolution. Third, I would like to return to Stock's discussion of robust monetary policy in the face of parameter uncertainty, which has also been discussed by John Taylor.

Stock's chapter

In the first part of Stock's chapter, he discusses a method for estimating the non-accelerating inflation rate of unemployment, the NAIRU. The NAIRU is defined as the rate of unemployment that leads to a constant rate of price inflation. If this theory is accurate, and if monetary authorities know the value of the NAIRU relative to the given period's unemployment rate, this knowledge would be useful for hitting an inflation objective.

The estimation methods here are more advanced than those in two earlier papers by Stock and his co-authors that I know of (a 1996 NBER conference I attended where Staiger, Stock and Watson presented related results on the NAIRU; and a 1995 Federal Reserve Bank of Chicago Economic Perspectives article by Stock, Mark Watson and Robert King). But as Stock said, a basic result from this research is that a large degree of uncertainty surrounds our knowledge of the NAIRU. For example, glancing at the estimated NAIRU in

Figure 12.1 on page 354 for total unemployment from 1961–97, I am left with the impression that the NAIRU varies somewhat over time. The standard error bands and statistical tests, however, cannot reject the hypothesis that the NAIRU is constant over this period. Nevertheless, I agree with Stock's decision to consider the time-varying estimates. If this theory is useful for policy-making, I shall take seriously the fact that the NAIRU moves around somewhat over time. But what are the factors that account for this variation?

Stock's paper investigates the correlations between the NAIRU estimates and several proxies for the shift towards knowledge-based production. These proxies are the share of income in services; the share of employment in services; business services; and finance, insurance and real estate. At best, the evidence seems mixed that time-variation in the NAIRU is caused by trend movements towards knowledge-based production. (See Stock's assessment on page 366–7.)

I want to pursue this issue further in a slightly different context. In his 1968 Presidential address to the American Economic Association, Milton Friedman defined the natural rate of unemployment in two complementary ways. One explicitly defines the NAIRU in terms of inflation. This approach is used by Stock and Gordon. The other definition is that the natural rate of unemployment is the rate of unemployment that the economy would grind out on its own over time. This latter definition does not make any explicit references to the rate of inflation. I want to describe briefly our efforts at the Federal Reserve Bank of Chicago to estimate a natural rate of unemployment that is consistent with this alternative definition. Then I shall relate this alternative measure back to the theme of the conference. This analysis is based on research conducted by Rissman (1997).

The natural rate of unemployment reflects factors that contribute to frictional and structural unemployment, but not cyclical unemployment. Rissman's analysis starts by dividing industry employment movements into two parts: a cyclical component and an industry component. The cycle variable is unobserved, but estimated from the similar way in which it influences each industry over time. The industry component is an idiosyncratic part of employment movement, and is unrelated to the business cycle component. Rissman assumes that large amounts of dispersion in these idiosyncratic industry components for any given time period are associated with a high degree of labour reallocation across sectors and industries. In this scenario, the natural rate rises when this reallocation activity is high (and the activity is not caused by the common business cycle component). This analysis is a refinement of David Lilien's (1982) research on sectoral dispersion and structural unemployment.

In many ways, the qualitative movements in Rissman's natural rate of unemployment are similar to Stock's estimates. Like Stock's estimates in Figure 12.1 for total unemployment, Rissman's natural rate generally rises through the 1960s and into the mid-1970s. Both measures display a double-hump in the mid-1970s and early 1980s (although the timing is not identical). Both measures generally fell from the early 1980s to the late 1990s, although Rissman's measure increased briefly in the early 1990s mainly because of idiosyncratic government employment shocks which seem to have been related to reduced military spending. On the other hand, Rissman's natural rate is often one to one-and-a-half percentage points higher than Stock's estimates. And Stock's measure is smoother than Rissman's. In any event, it appears that these two measures are capturing similar economic phenomena, but with sufficiently interesting differences to warrant considering both measures.

With Rissman's concept of the natural rate, there are two ways that the natural rate can change over time that are related to the theme of this volume. First, if the idiosyncratic industry shocks become less volatile over time, then Rissman's dispersion measure will fall over time. Hence, structural reallocation and the natural rate will fall. Now why might this be the case? I am going to be speculative here. Perhaps information technology is making inventory controls more efficient. Fewer stock-outs and less excess inventory building could mean more stable employment within a sector. Similarly, production methods have undoubtedly improved somewhat because of IT. In any event, Rissman's estimated idiosyncratic manufacturing shocks have been substantially smaller since the mid-1980s compared with the 1970s and early 1980s. This accounts for a substantial fall in the natural rate over this period.

Second, if the employment shares are increasing over time in industries with comparatively low idiosyncratic shock variances, then the weighted average dispersion measure will fall. In fact, the services and finance, insurance and real estate sectors have relatively low volatility, and Stock's figures show a rising share of employment in these sectors which would imply a lower natural rate in Rissman's model.

So, in this model of a time-varying natural rate, growth in information technology and knowledge-based production could account for some reductions in the natural rate over time. The very rough evidence that I have sketched suggests that smaller idiosyncratic shocks have played a larger role than slowly shifting employment shares. In this sense, Stock's weak evidence is compatible with Rissman's analysis. Although the results are not definitive, both Stock's and Rissman's models give weak support to the hypothesis that the natural rate has declined because of fundamental changes in the labour market.

Gordon's chapter

Now let me turn to Gordon's chapter. The focus of this is the relationship between IT and productivity growth. To the extent that higher productivity can support a lower NAIRU, this is related to Stock's analysis. The impression we get from Gordon's interesting and provocative paper is that investment in IT is not leading to higher productivity growth.

The first step in Gordon's analysis is an examination of evidence on productivity growth. From the perspective of proponents of the 'new economy', the persistent slowdown in measured productivity growth since the early 1970s appears to present a problem. Gordon's analysis of productivity is aimed at deflating the case that the official government data systematically understate the contribution of IT to productivity growth. Here, I think Gordon is quite convincing.

Let us assume that Gordon is correct and that the productivity growth slowdown is indeed genuine and not a figment of measurement error. What does this say about the prospects for a 'new economy'? Gordon's view is that the slowdown is in fact a reflection of a fundamental problem with computers, specifically, and IT more broadly. His thesis is argued in four parts.

First, compared to other eras of great technological change – such as electricity, electric motors, the internal combustion engine, petrochemicals and plastics – the development of computers and related information technology is not very significant. Second, Gordon argues that there are fundamental limits on what computers can do, so that large sectors of the economy, much as services, cannot take advantage of them. Third, in Gordon's assessment, the best uses of IT have already been implemented and future uses will have much lower payoff than previous uses. Finally, Gordon views a large percentage of current uses of IT to be wasteful, and that far from contributing to productivity growth, IT in many instances substracts from it.

Taken together, these points make the case that the observed productivity slowdown is in large part caused by over-investment in IT, and that we should not ever expect any substantial productivity gains from IT. Gordon's discussion of these issues represents a healthy challenge to conventional wisdom, and therefore is welcomed. However, since his views are largely based on anecdote and opinion, it is difficult to judge their validity. If his thesis were the only reasonable interpretation of the productivity slowdown in the face of seemingly rapid advancements in IT and their widespread implementation, it would be a cause for great concern. Fortunately, it is not.

What I have in mind here is the so-called delayed implementation hypothesis advanced by David in Chapter 3 and a related set of arguments developed by Jeremy Greenwood (1996), the University of Rochester, and his co-author Mehmet Yorukoglu (1996) that I will discuss.

Both David and Greenwood look back in history to other episodes in which great technological advances occurred. Interestingly, these episodes have many things in common with recent experience in the USA. Consider Greenwood's analysis of the Industrial Revolutions in Britain and the USA. These years were marked by (i) an initial slowdown in productivity growth; (ii) an initial rise in income inequality; and (iii) dramatic drops in the prices of new capital equipment associated with the underlying technological innovations. These facts are consistent with what we have seen in the USA since the mid-1970s.

What connects these observations? Greenwood and Yorukoglu develop a formal economic model with several key ingredients. First, technological progress is embodied in new equipment whose cost of production falls continuously through time. Second, firms face a learning curve when they adopt a new technology. Third, firms can travel down their learning curves faster only if they hire skilled labour. The basic idea is that it takes time for firms to work out the best uses of new technology, and that many mistakes will be made in the process. However, the best uses will eventually be found, and productivity will rise. Moreover, when the best uses of new technology have been found, skilled labour will become less necessary, and wage inequality should be expected to decline.

One of the interesting results to come out of the work by Greenwood and Yorukoglu is that there are very long lags between the initial introduction of new technology and subsequent productivity gains. In their model it takes about twenty years before productivity growth surpasses its old level, and forty years for the level of productivity to cross its old trend line, the path that productivity would have travelled along if it had continued at its old growth rate. Another interesting result from their analysis is that in the initial stages of the introduction of the new technology, the stock market is predicted to boom.

I do not want this discussion to mean that we should ignore Gordon's points and adopt the David–Greenwood view. But there are other reasonable explanations for why measured productivity has slowed in the face of tremendous investments in new technology. In the end, we shall have to wait for many years before one view or another is proved correct (or perhaps some other, entirely different, explanation will emerge.) The David–Greenwood view and the Gordon view are virtually irrefutable without many more years of data.

Ultimately, I am left with the impression that we know very little about what is really going on. We are uncertain about which economy we are in.

Monetary policy under uncertainty

How should monetary policy be conducted when policy-makers are uncertain about their model of the economy? This leads me to the final section of Stock's and Taylor's chapters. The intuition from Brainard's analysis of this question is that policy makers should respond cautiously. When Stock and others have considered this question in a different context, they find that policy-makers should respond aggressively to many uncertain situations. (This is a fast-growing field of analysis that is called robust control theory.) I think the intuition goes something like this: suppose that inflation is expected to increase over the next year, but the policy-maker is uncertain whether a 100 basis point tightening will have a negligible effect or a super-contractionary effect. Brainard-style caution might suggest tightening by 100 basis points or less, and then wait to see if the policy move had a small effect or a stringent effect. The robust control intuition is that policy-makers should move more aggressively, by 300 basis points, say. If the negligible effect is relevant, this action will move inflation closer to the desired level. If the super-contractionary effect is active, all is well, because now the monetary authority knows it can quickly shift gears back to an easier stance. And because policy is very effective, this will quickly become a reasonably controlled situation. There is a sense in which this is really a *cautious* policy prescription, even though it would not be recognized that way by its effects on the policy instrument.

I think a potential shortcoming of the robust control analysis here is the simplicity of the economic example. Volatile monetary policy actions can confuse financial markets and individual planners. These actions have potential costs that are not fully accounted for in this analysis. Reversing the policy course as rapidly as the robust control policy dictates may have additional negative effects on the economy that are not accounted for in these experiments. I am not sure this is the case; I suspect that many policy-makers place some credence on this possibility. But having read this chapter and recognizing my own uncertainty about how the economy changes over time, I have learnt something: I am not quite sure what the *cautious* course of action is. There is a temptation to equate *caution* with small movements in the *monetary policy instrument*. But, in fact, equating *caution* with small movements in the *policy goal variables* may require accepting larger movements in the policy instrument. This is an interesting idea and I am glad that more research is being directed towards it.

Conclusion

In conclusion, the Stock and Gordon chapters are interesting and thought-provoking. They both suggest a high degree of uncertainty about the true nature of the economy. This uncertainty is unlikely to be resolved within a time-frame that allows monetary policy to ignore its many potential consequences. We are thus left with the task of formulating monetary policy in an uncertain world – something that we have done in the past and are certain to do in the future.

References

Brainard, W. (1967) 'Uncertainty and the Effectiveness of Policy,' *American Economic Review*, vol. 57, pp. 411–25.

Greenwood, J. (1996) 'The Third Industrial Revolution', Working Paper, No. 435 Rochester Center for Economic Research (prepared for the American Enterprise Institute).

Greenwood, J. and Yorukoglu, M. (1996) '1974', Working paper No. 429 (Rochester Center for Economic Research).

King, R., Stock, J. and Watson, M. (1995) 'Temporal Instability of the Unemployment–Inflation Relationship', *Economic Perspectives, Federal Reserve Bank of Chicago* (May/June), pp. 2–12.

Lilien, D. (1982) 'Sectoral Shifts and Cyclical Unemployment', *Journal of Political Economy*, vol. 90, pp. 777–93.

Rissman, E. (1997) 'Measuring Labor Market Turbulence', *Economic Perspectives, Federal Reserve Bank of Chicago* (May/June), pp. 2–14.

Rissman, E. (1998) 'Estimates of the Natural Rate of Unemployment', Unpublished MS, Federal Reserve Bank of Chicago.

Staiger, D., Stock, J. and Watson, M. (1996) 'How Precise Are Estimates of the Natural Rate of Unemployment?', in C. Romer and D. Romer (eds), *Reducing Inflation: Motivation and Strategy* (University of Chicago Press for the NBER), pp. 195–242.

Comments

Takatoshi Ito

Great reversal of the unemployment rate

The low unemployment rate has been one of the hallmarks of the Japanese economy for decades. Moreover, the unemployment rate in Japan has been insensitive to business cycles, so the Phillips curve has been found to be near vertical. However, this all changed in the 1990s.

It appears that the unemployment rate in Japan will become higher than that of the USA for the first time in (postwar) history, barring unexpected, sudden shocks to either economy. The unemployment rates in the two countries have been very close since April 1998. The US unemployment rate was 4.3 per cent in April, while in Japan it was 4.1 per cent. See Figure C12.1 for the monthly movements of the unemployment rate in 1997 and 1998.

Figure C12.2 shows the long time-series of the unemployment rates of the two countries. The Japanese unemployment rate shows a trend increase, without visible business-cycle fluctuations. In contrast, the US unemployment rate shows large-amplitude fluctuating. Figure C12.3 shows the Phillips curves for both countries for 1968–83. Except for one year (1973), when Japan experienced high inflation (23 per cent), Japan's inflation range from 2 per cent to 12 per cent while the unemployment rate was typically below 3 per cent (except for 1998). The US unemployment rate never went below 3 per cent. The Japanese plots suggest a very steep, if not vertical, Phillips curve, while the US plots suggest a downward-sloping Phillips curve. Figure C12.4 shows a similar graph for more recent years. Since both countries succeeded in taming inflation, the graph, which keeps the same scale as Figure C12.3 for comparison purpose, suggest that the plots all seem to be clustered. Still, the Japanese clusters and the US clusters are quite separate. Figure C12.5 rescaled Figure C12.4, so that the Phillips curves are more distinct. The US economy in 1995 is quite different from that in the preceding decade. In the case of Japan, the inflation rate is near zero, and the unemployment rate is creeping up. Suddenly the Japanese Phillips curve looks horizontal instead of vertical.

Why the US-economy is doing so well

Since the low US unemployment rate in 1998 was not accompanied by any increase in CPI inflation, a shift in the NAIRU (or a shift in the Phillips curve) is suspected. Professor Stock's chapter gives an answer by estimating a time-

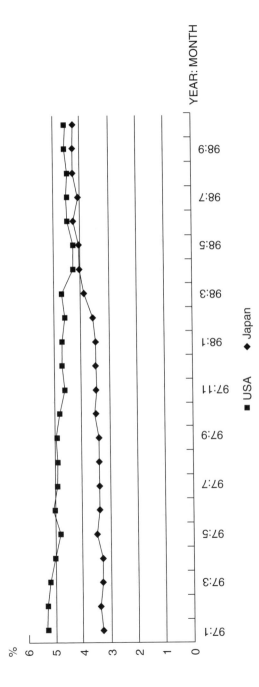

Figure C12.1 Unemployment rate: USA compared to Japan, monthly

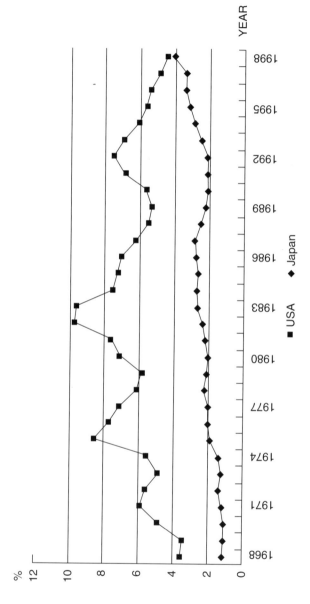

Figure C12.2 Unemployment rate: USA compared to Japan, annual

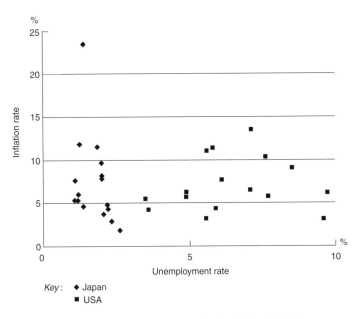

Figure C12.3   Phillips curve: Japan compared with the USA, 1968–83

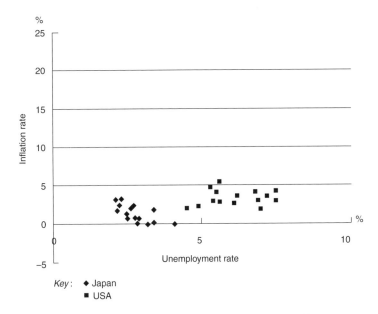

Figure C12.4   Phillips curve: Japan compared with the USA, 1984–98

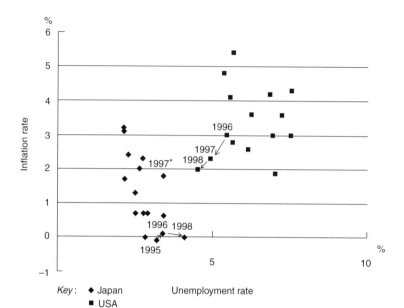

Figure C12.5   Phillips curve: Japan compared with the USA, 1984–98
Note: *Consumption tax increase (April 97)

varying NAIRU model. The NAIRU has been evolving over time and indeed coming down over several recent years, but the chapter does not indicate what factors explain these. Apparently, the employment shares of industries that are considered to benefit from information technology (IT) do not show any correlation with the movement of TV–NAIRU.

The coexistence of rapid growth, which lowers unemployment, and low unemployment suggests a positive supply shock or large TFP growth. IT is suspected as being at the root of this phenomenon. However, Professor Gordon's chapter is rather sceptical about this explanation. According to him, it may be the case that computer are not used to enhance productivity (say, by producing more automobiles given the same amount of labour and capital input) but widely abused for fun (for example, more computer games).

The purpose of my comments is to argue that an international perspective adds more mystery to the drama of waiting for Godot (as David put it).

Why is the Japanese economy doing so badly? – Differential effects of the IT revolution

Suppose for the moment that IT is a principal reason for the combination of low inflation and low unemployment in the USA. Why wouldn't Japan, one of the leading IT nations with extremely maths-orientated students, benefit from IT?

There are five reasons why IT may have increased productivity in the USA but not in Japan. First, the USA is good at developing software, while Japan is good at producing hardware. It is the software that was to contribute to intangible output and TFP growth. This explains the stark contrast. Second, although students are highly trained in maths, they learn it in the wrong way (by calculation and memorization, but not innovation). Third, Japan, in fact, may be a backward nation as far as the usage of IT technology is concerned: measured per capita, IT indicators are low in Japan.

The number of personal computers in homes is low, because there is no space to put them in small Japanese houses. The number who have internet access from home is low because phone calls are charged by the minute (the measured call system) and the internet thus becomes very expensive to use. Cable television (CATV) accessibility is quite low, because the Ministry of Post and Telecommunications is cool towards it. Computers are not taught properly in elementary and secondary schools, because the Ministry of Education has not encouraged this. For technology-related products, a key is how the government wisely got itself involved. Of course, the government has to see how the market is evolving, but remaining detached is impossible. The government is responsible for regulating (wisely) radio frequencies, telecommunications, CATV operation, and digital money.

Fourth, the IT revolution obviously favours professionals. Many workers in Japan are not professionals but rather are firm-specific skilled workers. Fifth, the IT revolution requires labour mobility to increase its effectiveness. The lifetime employment practice of Japanese workers hampers labour mobility in Japan. Those who become redundant because of computers and other IT revolutions cannot be removed from companies, so labour costs bring down company performance.

Why is the Japanese economy doing so badly? – Nothing to do with the IT revolution

An alternative explanation for contrasting macro performances in the USA and Japan is that macro performances in both countries have nothing to do with IT. Professor Gordon is right about the USA, and Japanese performance is a result of the bursting economic bubble (that is, asset deflation and the reverse wealth effect), a mistake in bank supervision, and a mistake in fiscal policy (1997).

Evidence from employment statistics

Workers by sector reveal that the most booming sectors in the 1990s in Japan were the construction industry and services (see Table C12.1). The number of

Table C12.1 Japanese employment by industrial sectors

Growth rates over specified periods	All	Agri	Construction	Manufacturing	Transport telecom, gas, water	Wholesale, retail finance, real estate	Services	Government employees
1980–85	1.0	-2.6	-0.7	1.2	-0.3	1.3	3.2	0.0
1985–90	1.5	-2.3	2.1	0.7	1.5	1.7	3.5	-0.4
1990–95	0.7	-3.7	2.4	-0.7	1.8	0.4	2.4	2.3
1995–97	0.8	-2.3	1.6	-0.5	0.4	0.5	2.6	-0.7

construction workers increased because of various public spending packages in the 1990s. It is least the relevant to the IT revolution. The service sector is an aggregate of various industries, some of them IT-related and some not. It is not clear from this table whether Japan is in the midst of an IT revolution.

If workers are divided by their types of work (see Table C12.2), it is clear that professional employees are increasing. This is partial evidence of an IT revolution, but unskilled and clerical support staff are also increasing. Again, it is unclear from the composition of workers whether Japan is experiencing an IT revolution.

The implication for monetary policy

Implications of the presence or absence of an IT revolution for monetary policy are unclear. Professor Taylor (Chapter 2 of this volume) mentioned that decision-making becomes more difficult because targets are hard to analyze (price indices), the meaning of instruments may change (payment system), and the relationship from instruments to targets becomes uncertain. I share this view.

Professor Taylor also mentioned that there is a possibility that decision-making may become easier because information processing is easier. He gave an example of solving a rational expectations macro model for simulation exercises. However, we should know that the private sector also benefits from this, and do similar exercises to predict policy response functions. The Lucas critique becomes more plausible. So, it is less clear whether the ease of simulation would benefit policy-makers, unless ease of simulation on the part of the private sector is taken into account in public sector simulation, and that in turn is taken into account in the private sector, and so on.

It is easy to say that a more robust monetary policy is sought. Professor Stock argues that it means that more risks (experimentation?) should be taken.

Table C12.2 Composition of workers in Japan

	1980	1990	1997
Number of workers total (thousand)	553.6	624.9	655.7
Professional (%)	7.9	11.0	12.6
Managerial (%)	4.0	3.8	3.4
Clerical (%)	16.7	18.5	19.4
Sales (%)	14.4	15.0	14.3
Maintenance/guard (%)	9.0	8.6	9.7
Agriculture/forestry (%)	10.3	7.2	5.3
Transport/telecom (%)	4.5	3.7	3.7
Manufacturing/Construction (%)	29.9	27.2	26.0
Unskilled (%)	3.0	4.4	5.0

Professor Meltzer (Chapter 1 of this volume), if I read him correctly, argues that a traditional steady hand (in terms of monetary aggregate) is desirable, because the relationship between monetary aggregate and real activity is remarkably stable, in the long run.

It seems to me that in a world of uncertainty (both in structure and relationships), benefits from learning-by-doing (both successes and failures) increase. As long as the central bank is accountable, some experimentation, (rather than doing nothing) may be desirable.

To avoid misunderstanding, experimentation means taking an initiative in new fields, such as electronic money and other revolutions in financial markets, but not with respect to monetary policy. What I mean here is that the central bank has to make it clear what is its final target, its operational target, and the behavioural 'rule'. Policy instruments have to be credible. Reputation must be 'earned' rather than by announcement. It should avoid discretionary 'trembling hands'. Experimentation does not mean changing policy every month.

The NAIRU may be shifting in Japan, for both temporal (business cycle) and structural (demise of Japanese lifetime employment, and *keiretsu* relationships) reasons. Is the Japanese potential growth rate lower now than it was in the 1975–89 period? It is not clear how the Bank of Japan could separate these effects. This is related, but not so strongly, to the question of whether Japan is benefiting from the IT revolution at all.

The Japanese monetary and fiscal authorities are facing more difficult questions, such as how to avoid deflation and how to deal with the non-performing loans problem, decisively, in the coming months. Looking for effects of the IT revolution may come later, when the economy recovers from recession.

Concluding remarks

For those who believe that US performance is a result of the IT revolution, the miserable performance of the Japanese economy in the 1990s needs an explanation. For those who are waiting for Godot, the Japanese macro situation is irrelevant.

What is happening is true. But, depending on who is speaking, accounts of events are different. It seems to me that the drama being played out in front of us is not 'Waiting for Godot' but 'Rashomon' – a similar event can be described differently by different observers.

Comments

Georg Rich

Chapter 11 by Robert J. Gordon

Robert Gordon, as usual, presented a very interesting chapter, from which a great deal can be learned. The question of how the advance of IT has affected consumer prices, the NAIRU and potential output is of considerable concern to central banks. Gordon focuses on the relationship between the computer revolution and productivity growth. He provides a breakdown of productivity growth by individual industries down to the two-digit level. His data shed new light on the reasons for the productivity slowdown. He demonstrates that the decline in productivity growth is not limited to the service sector; it also shows up in manufacturing, notably in industries producing easy-to-measure output. Moreover, Gordon finds that shifts in the composition of output from manufacturing to services explain only a third of the decline in productivity growth over the postwar period. He attributes these findings to the serious limitations of computers, which reduce greatly their significance as instruments for boosting productivity.

Gordon mentions several reasons why monetary policy-makers should be interested in productivity growth. I fully agree with Gordon that productivity is a concept that central banks cannot ignore. The Swiss National Bank (SNB) certainly pays attention to the questions raised in Gordon's chapter. We attempt to manage money growth with the aim of (i) maintaining price stability, and (ii) allowing the Swiss economy to exploit its growth potential. Of course, this approach requires reasonably reliable estimates of potential output.

As to Gordon's analysis of productivity growth, his otherwise comprehensive study ignores an issue that appears to assume increasing importance in Europe and other parts of the world. A significant share of aggregate investment is designed to reduce or avoid damage to the environment. It allows firms to introduce new production techniques and new products meeting environment standards set by governments. This type of investment frequently does not raise measured output, but none the less enhances welfare. Thus, the slowdown in measured productivity growth need not imply that growth in the average person's welfare has also declined.

Chapter 12 by James H. Stock

In his stimulating chapter, Stock finds that the NAIRU in all the G7 countries has tended to change over time. He is unable to uncover much of a relationship between the estimated movements in the NAIRU and various measures of knowledge-based production. Therefore, Stock's results cast doubt on the notion that the IT revolution has acted as a driving force behind recent changes in the NAIRU.

While I find Stock's empirical research illuminating, I am less convinced by his analysis of optimum central-bank feedback rules in the presence of uncertainty about the parameters of a structural model incorporating a time-varying NAIRU. Stock concludes that uncertainty about the structural parameters calls for an aggressive central-bank response to random shocks. His result is at variance with Brainard's (1967) classic – and intuitive – postulate of a slow response in the face of uncertainty. I believe that Stock's result is attributable to two unrealistic features of his analysis.

First, according to his Equations (12.4) and (12.5), a change in the real rate of interest begins to affect the unemployment rate (u) and the first difference in the inflation rate ($\Delta\pi$) after one quarter. Once two quarters have elapsed, half of the real interest rate effect has passed through to u and $\Delta\pi$. Thus, the central bank is able to elicit a relatively quick response in the two variables, allowing it to estimate the size of the α_y and β_r parameters after a short period of time. Considering these short policy lags, the central bank has ample time to adjust its policy course if it realizes that its aggressive response was inappropriate. However, in the world I know, policy lags tend to be much longer than those appearing in Stock's chapter.

Second, the uncertainties central banks face are not limited to the structural parameters of the model and the transitory, or permanent, nature of the shocks hitting the economy. Central banks are usually even uncertain about the true model describing the transmission of monetary policy impulses and other shocks. If central banks are unsure about the true model, new questions arise, which remain open in Stock's chapter: do Equations (12.4) and (12.5) capture the essence of the transmission process? Is the NAIRU a useful concept to begin with? I doubt that central banks confronted with these tricky questions should react aggressively to random shocks.

John B. Taylor (Chapter 2)

The discussion of optimal feedback rules naturally leads to Taylor's interesting discussion of recent innovations in monetary policy research. He is certainly correct in arguing that the policy simulations made possible by recent advances in IT are of great help to central banks. Nevertheless, we should recognize the limitations of this strand of research. Consider Table 2.1 in Taylor's chapter. Central banks following Taylor's feedback rules are able to reduce the standard deviation of inflation to an average of slightly more than 2 per cent. It should be emphasized that this is not a brilliant outcome. In the cases of Germany and Switzerland, for example, inflation has averaged roughly 3 per cent since the mid-1970s. Had the Bundesbank and SNB achieved this average by following Taylor's feedback rules, the (quarterly) inflation rates would have varied within a 95 per cent confidence range of slightly less than –1 per cent and slightly more than +7 per cent. The actual performance of the Bundesbank and the SNB were at least as good, if not better, than the outcome of Taylor's feedback rules.[1] However, the SNB would not claim that its performance since the 1970s was wholly satisfactory, even though it achieved a lower average inflation rate than most other central banks. Clearly, Taylor's feedback rules would be of little help in improving the SNB's performance. Following these rules, the SNB could avoid big policy mistakes, but would be unlikely to be able to achieve better outcomes than in the past.

Nevertheless, the SNB regularly monitors, among other indicators, an interest rate series derived from one of Taylor's feedback rules. This should not be construed as implying that the SNB in fact adheres to such a rule. The SNB's approach differs from Taylor's feedback rules in at least two respects. First, the SNB has always attached a low weight to the actual inflation rate in setting monetary policy. Instead, it has stressed the need for a forward-looking policy approach. Second, for this reason, the SNB has focused its attention on indicators that provide useful information on future price movements. In Switzerland, monetary aggregates have played a particularly useful role as leading indicators of inflation.

Allan H. Meltzer (Chapter 1)

The IT revolution has led to a massive increase in the quantity of data available to policy-makers, as well as the general public. Considering the easy access to masses of information, one might expect the quality of monetary policy also to have increased. However, Meltzer doubts that the IT revolution is helping central banks to improve their policy performance. In his view, easy access to enormous quantities of data need not imply that the quality of information is also increasing. On the contrary, central banks seem to be confronted with a deterioration in the quality of data crucial for the conduct of monetary policy. The measurement problems associated with output, the price level, the NAIRU and other variables are a good case in point. Moreover, historical experience suggests that poor data have not prevented central banks from pursuing good monetary policies.

According to Meltzer, central banks may circumvent the difficulties arising from imprecise data by focusing their attention on the relationship between monetary velocity and long-term interest rates. Money and interest rate statistics are less affected by measurement problems than other variables.

Meltzer also presents impressive empirical evidence of a stable long-run relationship between the monetary base velocity and long-turn rates of interest in the USA, Germany and Japan. As a representative of a central bank that still pays attention to money, of course I like Meltzer's findings. It is possible that many central banks have gone too far in playing down the role of money. Nevertheless, Meltzer's analysis raises two questions.

First, as indicated by Meltzer's estimates, in all the three countries, and notably in Germany and Japan, serious instabilities in the relationship between velocity and interest rates did arise from time to time. While there may be plausible *ex-post* explanations for these instabilities, central banks relying on the velocity–interest relationship as a policy guide would still face considerable uncertainty about the appropriate policy course, because such *ex-post* knowledge would probably be of limited use in forecasting future changes in velocity.

Second, interest-induced velocity movements complicate the central banks' task of setting monetary policy even if the velocity functions are otherwise stable. Such movements introduce substantial play in the link between base-money growth and the central banks' ultimate target variables. In the presence of interest-induced velocity movements, steady expansion in the money supply, as originally proposed by monetarist economists, is unlikely to be an optimum policy strategy. Instead, central banks should adjust money growth to major shocks hitting the economy. This raises other, widely-debated, questions. Should central banks exercise discretion in varying money growth, by monitoring additional, and possibly imprecise, policy indicators? Or should they adjust money growth on the strength of a policy rule – for example, by the rule proposed by Meltzer (1987)? Thus, Meltzer's analysis is inexorably linked with the old rules-versus-discretion debate.

Note

1. Interestingly enough, actual movements in German and in Swiss money market rates since 1980 are reasonably well described by analogous series derived from one of Taylor's feedback rules (Rich, 1999, figs 5 and 6).

References

Brainard, W. (1967) 'Uncertainty and the Effectiveness of Policy', *American Economic Review*, vol. 57 (May), pp. 411–25.

Meltzer, A. (1987) 'Limits of Short-Run Stabilization Policy', *Economic Inquiry*, vol. 25 (January), pp. 1–14.

Rich, G. (1999) 'Inflation and Money Stock Targets: Is There Really a Difference?', Unpublished MS, Swiss National Bank.

Part VI
Concluding Comments

13
Information Technology and the Financial Environment of Central Banking: Summary Comments

Peter M. Garber

I want to take seriously the title of the conference, held in June 1998, upon which this book is based, and which contains the concepts of monetary policy and knowledge-based growth. Here knowledge-based growth seems to mean developments in information technology (IT), and uncertain measurements of growth because of qualitative changes in computing and communications. The chapters of the book, based on the conference papers, have raised many important issues. For example, what are the output benefits from a major innovation, and when in the cycle of implementation of an innovation do those benefits occur? What is the nature of property rights in knowledge-based goods; and how should property rights be allocated? How does research and development activity increase production? How does the measurement of economic activity and the price level go off track in the face of these innovations? What are the sources of long-term growth; and what forecasts can we make of long-term growth? What determines the real wages that we measure and the evolution of the size and distribution of real wages across the labour force?

In general, these are questions that concern the real economy, particularly issues of long-term real growth. We know that monetary policy has little impact in this domain, except to the extent that it maintains a relatively stable nominal environment. Therefore, it was difficult for the authors to connect their results directly to monetary policy. Of course, these questions are of interest to policy-markers in general. Specifically, regulatory authorities might adjust operations to implement various innovations to foster their maximum effect on long-term growth. Also, tax and fiscal policies will have to be set to be consistent with altered perceptions of growth potential. The monetary authority might try to cajole the fiscal authority to adjust policy to be consistent with a stable, nominal environment over the long run.

The chapters in this book come closest to monetary policy through the mismeasurement issue. Monetary policy is based on information available to the monetary authorities; if the background economic information available is flawed then we can expect incorrect decisions. In particular, if monetary policy is targeted at stabilizing inflation or the price level, it is useful to refine the inflation concept to the extent that it is overstated. Of course, monetary authorities recognize that the price level does tend to be overstated because of technological innovations and new products. Indeed, a guess of the magnitude of overstatement can be made, adjusting the goal accordingly. When there is movement of 'actual' inflation around that rule of thumb, it is beneficial to have better information, as Stock pointed out in Chapter 12.

That is the point at which the information revolution seems to plug into monetary policy, at least according to the authors of this volume – that is, through the statistical department of the central bank. In addition, if a more finely tuned policy is implemented through the kind of NAIRU vision that was discussed during the conference, it is useful to have better information to distinguish changing growth-rate trends from transitory shifts in activity.

However, the general view is that these connections to monetary policy are tenuous. There is a general lack of attempts by the authors to derive monetary policy implications from their results. This is not a criticism of the contributions themselves: these chapters stand alone in their own fields, but it does indicate that it is difficult to make the connection. The exception, of course, is the discussion centred on implications for monetary policy through the NAIRU vision.

This view of monetary policy and of central bank policy in general is a very narrow one in that it restricts the monetary policy implications of the information revolution to to the statistical dimension. Specifically, the most basic goal of a central bank is financial stability. Usually, a central bank exists in an environment of relatively stable financial institutions and markets; and it can therefore implement its other goals without paying too much attention to financial stability. But if the financial system becomes unstable, then all other goals are quickly dropped, and the financial system is supported. The operational methods of some central banks may be driven by the NAIRU view – that is, attempting to trade-off inflation against unemployment rates or against activity levels. Most central banks implement an exchange rate policy as a primary goal, given financial stability. Many central banks have dropped the belief that they can fine-tune very well and have shifted to price level stability as a goal.

The discussion throughout the book has been centred on the USA and US data. Federal Reserve Policy during the late 1990s has been implemented in a very benign period. Previous to that, however, there was a period of financial instability, which jostled the Federal Reserve's macro-policy goals. Interest rates were kept quite low for too long a time in the early 1990s in order to pump profit and capital back into the banking system, which had been denuded of capital during the problems of the 1980s.

Most central banks in the world have been seriously damaged by financial markets in the 1990s, which have thrown off track macro-policies that central banks attempted to implement. In particular, those central banks (and this includes those in Europe, Asia and Latin America) that had aimed at exchange-rate stability were attacked by financial markets and forced to raise interest rates dramatically for long periods of time. Central banks could be attacked in such magnitude because the world's speculative capital could be leveraged and thrown against any individual central bank in massive amounts, making it almost impossible for a central bank to defend itself.

The rubric for such integrated massing of capital across borders is 'globalization'. Whenever a sentence is seen that analyzes the sources of globalization, the second part of the sentence always talks about the reduction in computation costs and the revolution in communications. Both taken together mean that markets can come together, carry out a tremendous number of financial transactions, guided by modern risk-control methods, and overwhelm almost any central bank.

Therefore, I would like to aim my comment at the direct impact of information technology on the environment in which central banks work – as opposed to its impact on the real productivity of the economy, which everyone here has agreed only tangentially relates to the business of central banking. I would like to use two ideas as the focus of this discussion, one that arose in John Taylor's discussion (Chapter 2) and one from Paul David (Chapter 3).

Taylor argued that information technology changes have an important impact on central banks through their research departments' refined ability to offer advice to senior officials. Research departments can now compute large-scale problems of a much more refined nature than was possible before, and produce rational expectations solutions. There was some discussion that in a tug-of-war between central-bank and private-sector research departments, the private-sector research departments could overwhelm the central banks. Having seen how private-sector research departments work, I do not think so. Central-bank research departments would have the superior weapons.

Nevertheless, I would like to extend that vision to the rest of the departments of the central banks, and to use David's discussion of how innovations are implemented and effect important production increases. David argued that innovations have very important production effects when productive institutions adapt their organization to them. Bill Dewald and Allen Meltzer mentioned that information technology has been used and adopted to its maximum extent in the financial system, so we would expect the principle expounded by David to be most relevant in this industry.

The financial system is a business of information; and financial institutions, particularly those in the wholesale market, have become completely connected to computer networks. On the trading floors of financial institutions there is now very little space that is not crammed with computers and communications equipment. People who deal in these markets cannot talk to a client or customer without first turning in to their Bloomberg screen to check the latest transactions. Dealers have to talk to the traders to see who is doing the latest deals and what the explanations for these deals are. When people in this business go on the road, they are armed to the teeth – more heavily armed than any modern-day soldier – with the most up-to-date laptops and cell-phones and travelling Bloombergs.

Central banks are not the research department but the business end of the financial system. The financial system itself has been completely reorganized on the basis of this technology, and probably the most reorganised of all the industries that use information technology. This reorganization is the basis of the globalization of the financial system and the obsolescence of traditional financial institutions. Indeed, this sudden obsolescence is one reason that we see so many financial crises breaking out. There is no exit strategy for the 'walking dead' institutions that have no reason to exist in the current world, and are therefore constrained to survive by doubling up debts and losing heavily.

There has therefore been an increase in financial-sector instability, the aspect of the environment to which central banks are most fundamentally sensitive. Central banks have been pried away from their serene ability to confine themselves to picking the inflation–unemployment combination they want, rather being forced to act in ever-increasing emergencies to support their financial systems. That is the agenda now on the table for central banks, a direct result of the information technology revolution.

Inside the restructured financial system, emphasis has shifted among different activities. For instance, there is much less relationship lending – long-term relationships between banking systems or banks and final customers. The financial sector is trading-orientated because the marginal cost of trading is almost zero. Inside these institutions there has been a rise in the power of certain departments, such as relative-value departments. Relative-value activity is often referred to as arbitrage, but it is worked on a scale at which it taxes the liquidity assumptions upon which the arbitrage is based, so in effect it is risk arbitrage or regulatory arbitrage. In part, it is there to invent products to circumvent prudential regulation; and this is another reason that banking systems, especially those that are less supervised, have found themselves in serious trouble. It is not too far off the mark to infer that relative value departments consist of hundreds of physicists. The end of the Cold War released the physicists from nuclear weapons development and made them unemployed for a few years, but they have now been picked up by investment banks to do relative-value work.

Again, this activity increases the volatility in the environment in which central banks work. With the exception of a few central banks – those in the pre-eminent financial centres – central banks have not adapted as rapidly their own internal structure to this revolution. In particular, we have had a suggestion that the statistics departments of central banks might adjust their price level calculations to the IT revolution. This is an effort to repair data that have been undermined through the effects of IT on the real economy. More generally, the effect of the IT revolution on the financial system has undermined much of the data that central banks use to effect or assess policy. Specifically, the meaning of balance of payments capital accounts data has been confounded by the existence of computer-driven financial innovations that hide the true positions of the participants in the financial sector. The meaning of foreign direct investment measures can be completely undermined. We regard foreign direct investment as a very stable form of investment, but in general much of what is classified as foreign direct investment nowadays is really undertaken by foreigners only as a hedge against derivative products that pass on the equity risk to a domestic resident. What is long-term stable investment, and what is really only short-term hot money, is not evident anymore from the data.

So the statistics departments of central banks have generally to be revamped to absorb this lesson. They have to understand how the financial system works to degrade our ability to interpret financial statistics. Bank supervision has generally been slow moving in crisis after crisis, notably in Asia, and specifically in Japan. After the problems of the 1980s, bank supervision in the USA was reorganized, but its success has been during a boom. Yet, it remains to be seen whether these innovations in banking supervision will prevent a banking problem in the USA when the downturn comes.

In maintaining pegged exchange regimes, foreign exchange departments in central banks have operated with defensive strategies that have been made obsolete by the computer-driven trading and hedging operations in financial markets. For example, during the 1992 ERM crisis, central banks suffered from the illusion that interest rate defence would force speculators to buy into the currency. Quite the contrary, the defensive rise in interest rates awakened various computers programmed to do dynamic hedging in currency options, and the logic of the hedging operation was to sell the weak currency. Central banks were surprised at the avalanche of sales that fell on them when the interest rate was increased. They were also surprised because they did not realize how big the markets had become, and how much could be thrown at them in these computer-driven transactions.

I was in a trading room in the late 1990s here in Tokyo – just before the co-ordinated intervention occurred – and there was a moment where the yen was at 146 per dollar. Suddenly, a trade occurred at 143, and that woke up everybody in the room. The currency strategist instantly received a Bloomberg e-mail message from a customer in New York asking 'What's going on here?' Immediately, the currency strategist relayed the message across the room to a sales person, who replied 'I think a big trading company sold the yen and now it needs to cover, so it's strictly a technical issue.' The strategist typed this message to both the customer *and* to his entire address book and added that they should not worry about this technical move. The message instantly went out to a hundred clients, and all this happened in a matter of seconds. Those hundred clients also have their own e-mail lists, so the message went quickly to an exponentially growing list of recipients around the world. Then the sales person who had said 'I think it's a trading company' got an e-mail that said 'Don't worry, this is a Japanese trading company selling dollars in order to cover' and the salesman said 'I was right!'

This story illustrates how powerful the information flow is in the financial system. I would like to counterpoise this against what I know happened in the International Monetary Fund (IMF) during the Mexican crisis. At the time of the Mexican crisis, there were only two Bloomberg screens in the IMF. One was in the investment office for the pension fund, so that the pension fund manager could have proper information for tracking investments. The other one happened to be in the capital markets group in the Research Department. Up-to-date information coming into the Fund on how the Mexican crisis was evolving was therefore not flowing through the area departments or senior management. Rather, it was the relatively isolated capital markets group that controlled much of the information flow. Senior management and the area departments were making decisions in a partial information vacuum.

Central banks are closer to the markets because of their interventions, but in many cases the central banks themselves are not very well equipped. In addition, information may not flow well within the central banks. Senior management in some central banks often consider it to be demeaning to type e-mails. Information flows are typically hierarchical rather than horizontal, as they are in the market, so information can flow slowly in central banks. Normally, in a benign financial environment, this is not a problem, because the central bank need not hurry in going about its business of implementing macroeconomic policy. In a disturbed financial environment, however, a central bank cannot afford to be slow, so getting connected to computer networks is an institutional change along the lines of Paul David that has to be implemented before central banks can catch up with the changed financial environment.

The conclusion of the book's contributions is that the knowledge-based revolution, particularly in IT, has little directly to do with monetary policy as currently practised. We may need a little twist here in the inflation measurement, and a little tweak there in the real output measure, but nothing fundamental has to be changed in the paradigm behind the operations of the central bank. However, the central bank works through the financial system. The changes wrought by the IT revolution have radically altered the central bank's operational environment, and this has narrowed the scope of the central bank in implementing standard monetary policy.

Part VII
Background Paper

14

The Impact of Information Technology and Implications for Monetary Policy

*Tetsuya Inoue**

Introduction

Our modern economy is currently confronting an irreversible trend towards increasingly conceptual and intangible forms of economic resources. We can find examples of this trend everywhere in our economy: factories are introducing computer-aided design (CAD) and computer-aided manufacturing (CAM); most offices are using computers to manage inventories and human resources; and increasingly households are becoming connected to the Internet and owing mobile phones. Since such changes are spreading throughout our economy, we might say that we are in the third industrial revolution, following the first industrial revolution, when machine production by steam engines began, and the second industrial revolution, when electric power and chemical engineering appeared.

The major force that is propelling this movement is, of course, the rapid innovation in information technology (IT). It has been a stylized fact in the fields of economic growth theory and economic history that the innovation is the engine of economic growth. As with the steam engine and electric power, innovations in IT are expected to change all areas of economic activity, including investment, consumption, employment and production, and to bring about a great improvement in economic performance. In this process, a firm that introduces new technologies in IT will benefit from improvements in efficiency such as decreasing its costs of production, and rapid and more accurate decision-making. Since more and more firms pursuing these benefits will introduce new technologies and use improved goods and services as inputs, the improvement in economic efficiency will spread to the whole economy. We also find that the effects of network externalities and increasing

* I would like to thank Professor Masahiro Kuroda (Keio University), Professor Yukinobu Kitamura (Hitotsubashi University), Tooru Ohmori (Bank of Japan), and Hitoshi Mio (Bank of Japan) for their helpful comments.

returns to scale have played major roles here. These changes, taken as a whole, will improve macroeconomic performance by promoting new industries, gaining efficiency in the allocation of productive resources, and the increased accumulation of human capital.

There has been a persistent doubt, however, among academic economists and policy-makers that we have not yet obtained the fruits of this trend towards innovation in IT. This line of argument first appeared in the discussion concerning the productivity slowdown, and has long been drawing the attention of academic economists. These analyses can be categorized into the following two hypotheses. The first seeks the cause of this productivity slowdown in the existence of measurement errors in economic statistics representing prices and quantities. In other words, we may suspect that the current system of economic statistics either does not cover new goods and services, and/or it does not measure correctly quality changes in existing goods and services. The second hypothesis seeks the cause of the slowdown in the adjustment costs of introducing new technology. As for this hypothesis, the meaning of the term 'adjustment costs' is very broad; it not only contains the cost of instalment of physical equipment, but also the costs of complementary innovations, the training of labour, scrapping old equipment, and moving capital from declining industries. It should be emphasized that these hypotheses are not mutually contradictory.

We shall show, with the help of theoretical models and empirical results provided by academic economists, the trajectories and mechanisms through which innovations in IT have an impact on the economy. At the microeconomic level, switching costs from existing technologies and network externalities may play important roles in delaying the propagation of new technologies. In addition to the aggregation effects of such externalities, the costs of moving capital to growing industries and of retraining labour will hamper the macroeconomic performance as a whole. Mismeasurements in economic statistics may prevent firms and households from making optimal decisions, since these firms and households will not be able to observe accurately the changes in relative prices.

Since innovations in IT may be changing economic performance in many aspects, it is surely an important task to discuss optimal monetary policy in such changing economies. Because we do not yet have enough theoretical discussions or empirical studies available, we shall confine ourselves to suggesting a list of issues for future discussion on how we can improve efficiency in conducting monetary policy, by focusing on the effects of the evolution of the price mechanism.

The main discussion in this chapter can be summarized as follows. In the first half of the chapter we review in detail the discussions relating to the IT paradox. We discuss two major hypotheses which may explain the reasons for the IT paradox: (i) measurement errors in economic statistics; and (ii) a broad range of adjustment costs for the introduction of new technology. Regarding the latter hypothesis, we also review the lessons from the studies of past industrial revolutions. We identify that we should be much more careful about the effects of mismeasurement, and not only of price indexes, since such errors may cause serious problems when one tries to observe economic relations. We also see that a time lag between the introduction of new technology and the observation of its fruits can be explained by the effects of such adjustment costs at both microeconomic and macroeconomic levels. The costs are incurred, for example, by installing capital equipment, network externalities, retraining labour, and moving capital between industries. As for the implications for investment or consumption of information itself, which can be regarded as another major aspect of current innovation in IT, we have only limited insights so far. Since it is very important to know the effects of current innovation on the formation of expectations or on asymmetries of information, especially in financial markets, we expect further investigation in this area.

In the second half of the chapter we present the issues which concern the relationship between the effects of innovations in IT and the optimal way of conducting monetary policy, by focusing on the price mechanism. If the measurement errors in price indexes become serious through the various effects of innovations in IT, such as intangible quality changes, they may to some extent incur damage to the credibility of monetary policy. For example, central banks may not be able to conduct a targeting policy for either the inflation rate or the GDP growth rate, since it will be quite difficult to observe the achievement of such a policy. Thus we again identify the importance of the investigation of measurement errors in economic statistics. Under the standard framework of the Phillips Curve or NAIRU, the effects of innovations in IT can be regarded as 'supply shocks'. Since such shocks bring about a low unemployment rate without raising the inflation rate, we do not need to accommodate them by using monetary policy. However, when we take into consideration the costs of inefficiency caused by the possibility that fluctuations exist in the general price level, or nominal rigidities in our economy, we should be more careful about this conclusion of non-accommodation.

The IT paradox and its hypotheses

The productivity slowdown and IT paradox

In the USA after the Second World War, the growth of GDP accelerated, in spite of bearish forecasts for the postwar economy. In this long-lasting boom, total factor productivity (TFP) and labour productivity also showed dramatic increases. As Abramovitz and David (1996) and Freeman and Soete (1997) show, there had not been such an acceleration in productivity growth since the first Industrial Revolution. Moreover, the situation was similar in most of the developed economies in Europe and Asia. But the trend of rising productivity disappeared after the early 1970s. The most dramatic change was identified in the USA, where the growth rate of productivity fell below 1 per cent per year compared with the previous rate of 3 per cent (see Table 14.1). This phenomenon was first analyzed systematically by Nordhaus (1972); he argued that the most important reason is the shift of the US economy towards/ service industries with low productivity. Even in the 1980s, the paradox was alive and well, although there was a small improvement in the growth rate of productivity.

Baily and Gordon (1988) brought a new line of analyses and empirical findings to this stagnant situation. They reconsidered the paradox by analyzing the effects of an already rapid increase in IT investment, and presented the 'IT paradox'. The term 'IT paradox' refers to the situation where a rapid increase in IT investment does not cause an equivalent acceleration of productivity growth. As Griliches (1994) and Van Ark and Pilat (1993) later showed, the IT paradox has also been shown to be true in some of the other developed economies (see Table 14.1). Even in the 1990s, when the continuous growth of IT investment can be seen, the paradox is current in the sense that the growth rate of productivity has not reached the level of the 1960s.[1] In the years of the IT paradox, there have been many research papers tackling the issues in this area.

We shall now review the discussion of the above two hypotheses in turn.[2]

Measurement errors in economic statistics

The first hypothesis deals with the problems caused by measurement errors in economic statistics. We may suspect that the current system of economic statistics cannot accurately measure the value of IT-related goods and services, and thus mis-estimates the value of production and value added of the firms that use such goods and services as intermediate inputs. As a result, we may also have inaccurate measurement of GDP as well. I shall discuss in detail this hypothesis in two parts: (i) problems in the area of economic activities where the measurement of economic statistics is inaccurate; and (ii) problems in the area of economic activities that economic statistics do not cover at all.

Measurement error of price

The most important problem of measurement error in economic statistics is, of course, mismeasurement of price. Since we see the improvements in the quality of existing goods and services, thanks to IT, firms and consumers frequently switch their demands to such improved goods and services. We may suspect that such changes of quality are not reflected accurately in calculating a price index, which may bring about the mismeasurement of GDP and value added.

Following Nordhaus (1972), we have a literature of analyses regarding mismeasurement of price. For example, Gordon (1990) suggested that a price index of durable goods consumption had an upward bias of 3 per cent.

Table 14.1 Total factor productivity in selected OECD countries (Average annual growth rate, percent)

Year/Country	United States	Japan	Canada	Switzerland	West Germany	France	Great Britain
1961–65	2.25	6.21	2.56	2.72	3.21	3.64	1.85
1966–70	1.01	6.85	1.85	2.64	2.67	3.26	3.00
1971–75	0.50	2.05	1.59	0.30	2.48	2.39	2.02
1976–80	0.41	1.11	0.76	1.32	1.56	2.19	0.90
1981–85	0.62	1.53	1.18	0.41	1.38	1.91	1.75
1986–90	0.52	2.11	0.15	1.91	2.10	1.46	1.06
1991–92	0.56	1.54	-0.29	0.25	2.11	-0.02	0.58

Source: Summary from Diewert and Fox (1997).

Shiratsuka (1995) on automobile prices in Japan; Berndt and Griliches (1993) on PCs; Dulburger (1993) on semiconductors; and Brown and Greenstein (1995) on mainframe computers all showed that the prices of consumer durables and capital goods were subject to serious mismeasurement. In addition, Gordon and Griliches (1997) and Kozicki (1997) pointed out that imperfect competition and product life-cycles of goods make the situation even worse.

It is in the area of services where the problem of mismeasurement is most serious. We may be aware that most of the impact of IT on economic activities is realized through quality improvements and the introduction of new services in corporate-service industries. However, as for the case of services, it may be quite difficult to make adjustments for quality changes, because they are intangible. In addition, we may not be able to find a 'representative' price, because the way such services are transacted is so flexible that there may be a large range of different prices depending on a variety of transactions. We may regard such a variety of services as being mutually heterogeneous. The seriousness of this problem is confirmed by many empirical studies; for example, Baily and Gordon (1988) analyzed four of the industries within which serious mismeasurement has occurred (Finance and insurance, Construction, Retail, and Transportation), three of which belong to the category of 'service industry'. Or you may remember the empirical studies on the adjustment of quality changes in consumer services such as housing, telephones, transportation, medical care, and entertainment quoted by Boskin (1996). Slifman and Corrado (1996) also suggest that outsourcing corporate services to small firms in the 1990s have be aggravated the problems of coverage of economic statistics. Thus, taking into consideration both such mismeasurements in service industries and the simultaneously increasing share of service production, we may have a hypothesis to explain the IT paradox. In fact, this hypothesis is suggested for the case of the USA by empirical studies conducted by Darby (1992), Griliches (1994), Kozicki (1997), Nordhaus (1997) and Nakamura (1997).[3] The increasing share of services is also found in productive resources. For example, Stewert (1997) shows that about 70 per cent of inputs in automobile manufacturing is 'intangible'. Wynne and Sigalla (1996) estimates that upward bias by substitution effect in price indexes of intermediate inputs is 0.3 per cent. Therefore, measurement error of price has also worsened the estimation of the value of intermediate inputs, which results in mismeasurement of value added.[4]

Coverage to new goods and services

We also suspect that the current system of economic statistics does not cover the new goods and services developed with IT. Slifman and Corrado (1996) also suggest that the new and growing corporate services industry is seriously under-recorded by economic statistics. We should note that Meltzer (1997) estimated that the value of computer software reached 150 per cent of that of hardware, but at the same time, it has not been hardy measured accurately. This situation is also true in most of the developed countries; as for Japan, Mizoguchi (1996) showed that the estimated value of IT service production between 1974 and 1993 ranged from 120 per cent to 170 per cent of the value recorded by official statistics.

In relation to this problem of coverage, we suspect that some kinds of economic activity may have been categorized improperly. A typical example is computer software. If computer software is used for several years in a firm for designing its products or for accounting, it clearly possesses the characteristics of a capital good, just like a machining centre or a truck. But, in the system of national accounts (SNA), by which most countries calculate GDP, computer software has been regarded as an intermediate input for production despite the above characteristics. Such improper treatment of software has distorted the value of GDP in the years when such software produces service inputs for its user. That is, in the year in which a firm buys an item of software, the value of GDP is underestimated, since the value of the software is calculated as an intermediate input despite the fact that it should be regarded as an investment. In contrast, in the years when the software is used for production activities, the value of GDP is overestimated, because the value of the depreciation of the software is missed under the current SNA. In addition, it should be noted that such improper treatment leads us to mismeasure the value of capital stock, which will result in mismeasurement of total factor productivity (TFP).

Countermeasures for mismeasurement

Although we have a literature analyzing the problems of mismeasurement of economic statistics, we have few effective and practical proposals for solving such problems other than the geometrical average, which is known to be an effective measure for controlling the substitution effects in the calculation of price indexes, and is infact used in many countries.

For example, the hedonic approach has been suggested as a measure for quality adjustments in price. Many analyses, including Boskin (1996), regard this approach as being almost the only effective measure with a theoretical background. We, however, know that in both the USA and Japan, this approach is applied to only a few of the products in price indexes.[5] As for the reasons, we will have to solve theoretical problems such as how to avoid being arbitrary in selecting characteristics, or how to understand the relationship between the index theory and 'Lancaster's theory'. In addition, almost every government's statistical agency claims that a relatively large cost is involved in collecting data for regression on 'characteristics'. On the other hand, it has been shown that substitution effects can be controlled by introducing the geometrical mean into our calculation of a price index. Boskin (1996) shows, however, that the magnitude of such substitution effects in consumption is not as large as those of quality changes. Wynne and Sigalla (1996) also suggest that its impact may be small on intermediate inputs as well. Thus we may conclude that we do not yet have a decisively effective countermeasure to correct the measurement error of a price index.

For a broader coverage of new goods and services, as Boskin (1996) points out, there may be no short cut other than the immediate incorporation of new goods and services into economic statistics. This kind of countermeasure might be difficult, considering the additional cost of statistics production and the additional burden on reporters. As for the problem of categorization, we may advance by adopting the new system of national accounts (93SNA), since computer software can properly be categorized as productive capital in this new system. We should note, however, that there must be an accurate measure of software production and transactions so that such a new system may work adequately. Here, we shall face the same problem as above: such characteristics as the existence of small firms and the large variety of transactions will make estimating difficult. So this area of problems too, we do not yet have very effective countermeasures so far.

Adjustment cost – lessons from the industrial revolutions

As we saw in the Introduction, the second hypothesis seeks its cause in the adjustment costs of introducing new technologies. According to this hypothesis, the cost refers not only to the adjustment cost of installing physical equipment, but also to the cost of complementary investment, such as developing computer programs for flexible manufacturing systems and retraining labour. It also includes the cost of reallocation of productive resources from declining industries to the growing new industry of IT. Since economic historians emphasize the effects of such adjustment costs in the past industrial revolutions, we shall start the discussion of this hypothesis by reviewing such analyses by economic historians.

Time lags of introduction of new technology

Many economic historians, including Crafts, David and Freeman, provided many implications from their studies of past industrial revolutions. Among such implications, the point they most emphasize is that it took many years from the innovations of key technologies for each industrial revolution, before we observed the economic impact of those innovations. David (1994) and Freeman and Soete (1997) show that only 5 per cent of factories and 3 per cent of households in the USA introduced electric power in 1889, eight years after the first power station in New York had been built. And it took another twenty years before 50 per cent of factories introduced electricity. If we parallel the situation at the start of the twenty-first century with this historic fact, we might have to wait for a time to enjoy the fruits of IT innovation, although it is not so clear when the latest industrial revolution started (see Figure 14.1). It can indeed be argued that the time lag will be much shorter, since the speed of innovations in IT is much faster than those in past revolutions.[6] Therefore, we

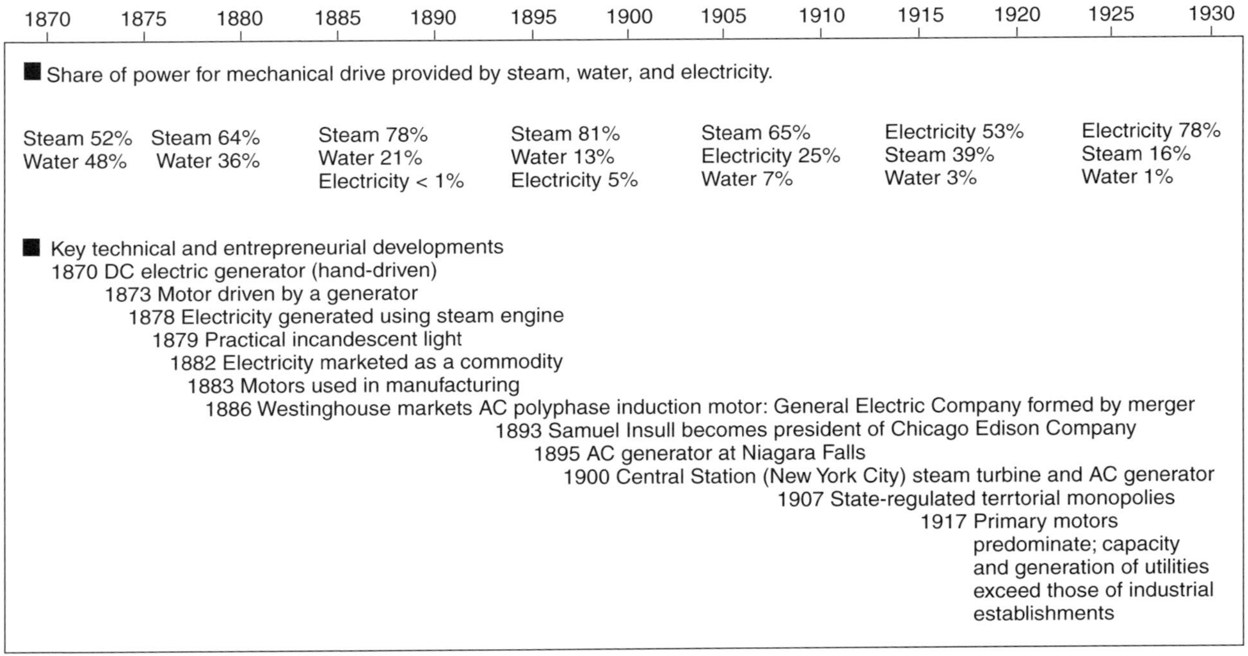

1870 1875 1880 1885 1890 1895 1900 1905 1910 1915 1920 1925 1930

■ Share of power for mechanical drive provided by steam, water, and electricity.

Steam 52%	Steam 64%	Steam 78%	Steam 81%	Steam 65%	Electricity 53%	Electricity 78%
Water 48%	Water 36%	Water 21%	Water 13%	Electricity 25%	Steam 39%	Steam 16%
		Electricity < 1%	Electricity 5%	Water 7%	Water 3%	Water 1%

■ Key technical and entrepreneurial developments
1870 DC electric generator (hand-driven)
1873 Motor driven by a generator
1878 Electricity generated using steam engine
1879 Practical incandescent light
1882 Electricity marketed as a commodity
1883 Motors used in manufacturing
1886 Westinghouse markets AC polyphase induction motor: General Electric Company formed by merger
1893 Samuel Insull becomes president of Chicago Edison Company
1895 AC generator at Niagara Falls
1900 Central Station (New York City) steam turbine and AC generator
1907 State-regulated territorial monopolies
1917 Primary motors predominate; capacity and generation of utilities exceed those of industrial establishments

Figure 14.1 Major developments and share of electricity
Source: Summary from Devine (1983).

review in detail the discussion of the implications obtained from studies of past industrial revolutions.

Some important characteristics of the introduction of new technologies

The introduction and propagation of new technology by the market mechanism. First, I would like to insist that most of the new technologies have been introduced and propagated by market forces. National laboratories and universities indeed played an important role in the development of basic technologies, or in the creation of demands related to military power or to the exploration of universe, especially in chemistry in the second revolution, or in supercomputers and communications in the latest 'revolution'. But, at the stage of innovation when such new technologies are being refined for commercial use, the major forces promoting innovations in IT have arisen from profit-maximizing enterprises with the help of demands from utility-maximizing consumers. If we focus on the role of market mechanisms, some important characteristics can be pointed out, as below.

Commercialization of research and development (R&D) activities is one of the most important characteristics of the current industrial revolution. Although, R&D activities had already begun in the electrical equipment industry and the chemicals industry in the second industrial revolution, we find such activities in almost all the kinds of industries on a much larger scales in the current 'revolution' (see Figure 14.2). The importance of R&D activities is emphasized by Crafts (1996) and Freeman and Soete (1997), by suggesting that one of the reasons for the differences in GDP growth rates between the first and the second revolutions lies in the fact that R&D activity was not performed systematically in the 'first' industrial revolution. In order to

Innovations	Firm	Year
Single crystal growing	Western Electric	1950
Integrated circuit (IC)	Signetics	1962
Light-emitting diodes	Texas instruments	1964
Beam lead	Western Electric	1964
Charge-coupled device (CCD)	Fairchild	1969
Static random-access memory (SRAM)	Intel	1969
Dynamic random-access memory (DRAM)	Intel	1971
Microprocessor	Intel	1972

Figure 14.2   Major innovations in semiconductors
Source: Summary from Dosi (1981).

promote costly innovations that have the characteristics of externalities such as non-excludability and non-rivalry, most of our economic societies have a system of intellectual property rights. As Klenow (1996) emphasizes, such a system has also played an important role in accelerating R&D activities. We may understand that while most basic research is carried out by national laboratories and universities, most of the innovations are established by commercial R&D. Risk of innovation consists of commercial risk as well as technology risk. Considering that some technology risks are controlled at the stage of basic research, commercial risk may be most important for each firm in its R&D activities. Some famous stories suggest that controlling commercial risk is sometimes a very hard task for entrepreneurs. Freeman and Soete (1997) reports that the legal section of Bell Laboratories at first declined to file the patent for the laser, since they could not imagine the usefulness of lasers for communications. Or, according to Rosenberg (1996), at the beginning of the 1950s, an executive of IBM was bearish in forecasting the sales of computers, since he believed that just a few computers would satisfy the whole world's needs. Another example given by Rosenberg (1996) is that, at the end of nineteenth century, no one was interested in buying the patent for the production of telephones which was on sale for only a hundred thousand dollars. Thus, these interesting examples illustrate that the difficulty of controlling commercial risks may delay the realization of the efforts of R&D activities.

Commercial risk is much more difficult to control, because of the existence of various kinds of externality. Here, imperfect competition also performs an important role. With – or even without – a system of intellectual property rights, innovations are advanced by imperfect competition, because each innovation is born in a particular enterprise and is commercialized through the production of heterogeneous goods or services. As a result, strategic actions by respective firms may play an important role in deciding aggregate economic performance. We shall show that such intentions by firms under externalities and/or imperfect competition may delay the introduction and propagation of new technology.

A system of new technology. The next point we would like to emphasize is that it is the whole system of new technologies, and not a single innovation, that has had a major impact on macroeconomic performance. For example, in the second industrial revolution, the propagation of electric power was not realized by the innovation of the dynamo itself. As David (1990) shows, by a series of complementary innovations such as the electric light bulb and many kinds of mechanical equipment, electrical technology gradually permeated factories of every kind, as well as private households. He also insists that even the structural change in a factory to allow for the optimal use of electric power should be included as a component of the system of technology.[7] In addition, Freeman and Soete (1997) suggest that the appearance of large and bureaucratic firms, helped by telephones and steel-framed skyscrapers, was an important component of the innovations in the previous industrial revolution.

Thus, complementary innovations are of the utmost importance for the propagation of key technologies throughout our economy. Since most of these complementary innovations are themselves pursued by the R&D activities of private firms, the time for such necessary innovations may be one of the primary sources of the time lag before we are able to observe the fruits of new technologies. David (1990) and Kitamura (1997) emphasize that, in the situation at the start of the twenty-first century, it may be necessary to take into account not only the innovation of the computer itself, but also the reorganization of the company system or the changes in consumers' lifestyles.

One more important implication can be drawn from this line of argument. Even in the course of an industrial revolution, the existing system of capital equipment is never replaced all at once by a new one. Each firm will decide the optimal timing for such replacements by comparing the costs of scrapping the existing equipment and the benefits expected from the new technology. Thus the existence of switching costs may in some cases delay the propagation of new technology. David (1990) emphasizes this effect of switching costs by showing that the industries introducing electricity in the early years of the earlier industrial revolution were the newly-developing industries such as petrochemicals and special steels, which suffered no switching costs at all. As we shall see below, in this period when more and more firms are gradually introducing new technology, the trajectory of macroeconomics performance may show some interesting characteristics.

Changes in relative prices.   The last point that we should note is that economic historians report that economy-wide changes of relative prices occurred in the first two Industrial Revolutions. Such changes of relative prices can be regarded as the inevitable results from of the application of economy of scale in the textiles in the first Industrial Revolution, and steel, chemical, and machinery in the second Industrial Revolution. For example, Freeman and Soete (1997) shows that a dramatic fall in the relative price of steel made it economically feasible to build skyscrapers and large network of railroads, and to make automobiles (Table 14.2). As for our current Innovation, Sichel (1997) shows the price of computer services has been falling at a rate of 7% annually after adjusting for quality changes, and emphasizes that this rapid change in relative price is almost comparable to those of telephones and railways in the years of their rapid propagation as shown by Gordon (1990) (Table 14.3).

A change of relative price brings about substitution of demands by consumers and firms. By these effects, marginal productivity or the profit

Table 14.2 Relative prices of steel rails in the United States

Year	Steel rails, US$ per ton	Consumer price Index
1870	107	38
1875	69	33
1880	68	29
1885	29	27
1890	32	27
1893	26	27
1895	24	25
1898	18	25
1910	28	28
1920	54	60
1930	43	50

Source: Freeman and Soete (1997).

Table 14.3 Prices of computing services, electricity, rail transit, and airline transit, various periods

Item	Period of coverage	Observed price change (percent, annual rate)	GDP or GNP defaltor (percent, annual rate)	Real price change (percent, annual rate)
Computing services	1987–1993	–4.4	3.5	–7.9
Electricity	1899–1948	–4.5	2.5	–7.0
Rail transit	1850–1890	–2.7	0.0	–2.7
Airline transit	1935–1948	0.2	5.0	–4.8

Source: Sichel (1997).

rate of a supplier firm will be changed, which may result in the reallocation of productive resources. We, however, need to spend time and cost for this reallocation of productive resources. As we have already discussed, re-training labor and scrapping existing capital equipment will burden us with such costs. Or you may recall the discussions of 'irreversibility of investments' by V. Ramey and A. Abel.[8] We may regard that these time and costs are the alternative sources of the time lag already discussed.

Another implication of the changes in relative prices is that the IT paradox may be more serious than it appears. Greenwood *et al.* (1997) show empirically that the price of capital equipment has fallen at an average rate of 3 per cent per year from 1954 to 1990. This finding indicates that the growth rate of capital inputs may have been undervalued in calculating TFP, with the result that the growth rate of TFP has been overestimated.

The introduction of new technology and its impact on the economy

Having reviewed the implications of two mutually complementary hypotheses, we can now proceed to discuss the mechanisms and impact of IT innovation on existing theoretical models and empirical results.

The impact of new technology

To begin the discussion we review the effects of innovation in IT within the standard framework of economics. A firm introducing new technology in IT seeks to improve efficiency in production – for example, by decreasing its costs of production and rendering its decision-making more efficient. If these results are realized, the relative price of its goods or services may fall, and their quality may be improved. In addition, new goods and services may be developed with the new technology. Firms other than those introducing new technology may also benefit from such improvements, since they use the new products as capital equipment or intermediate inputs. In addition, the effects of network externalities and increasing returns to scale can also be expected. As a result of these effects, the aggregate supply curve will shift to the right. At the same time, the aggregate demand curve will shift to the right, reflecting increased demands for goods and services in IT from increasing numbers of firms and households. Thus we have economic growth without accelerating inflation by extending the production activities of the IT industries. In such an expansion of the economy, we may gain from the efficiency of resource allocation and accumulation of human capital at the macroeconomic level.

We need to check the effects of externalities of IT. In the literature of new growth theory, Romer (1988) and Barro (1990), for example, present growth models with externalities of government expenditure.[9] In fact, Muniagurria (1995) shows growth models with three kinds of productive resources (capital, human capital and technology), and shows the possibility of increasing returns to scale at the macroeconomic level by assuming no depreciation of technology.

If increasing returns to scale exist, there will be some special characteristics such as a discrepancy in economic growth rates, as Fukuda (1997) shows. However, we should note that recent empirical results of the macroeconomic level are mixed.[10] Some academic economists of the Real Business Cycle school, including Hall (1988) and Cabarello and Lyons (1992), suggest that we have increasing returns to scale at the macroeconomic level. On the other hand, a series of analyses by Aiyagari (1994), Burnside (1996), and Basu and Fernald (1997a, 1997b) deny such results by taking into consideration of the effects of imperfect competition, the actual utilization rate, and the accurate valuation of intermediate inputs. These results themselves may not be relevant here, since most of them use the data set by Jorgenson *et al.* (1987) which covers the period up to the middle of the

1980s. In spite of this obsolescence, this line of argument has some important implications. First, in order to estimate macroeconomics performance, it is necessary to measure accurately the value of intermediate inputs as well as that of capital equipment. If there are measurement errors for intermediate inputs, we may fail to judge whether the economy shows increasing returns to scale or not. Second, according to the results achieved by the opponents of increasing returns to scale, TFP may even have been overestimated in these years. Although their analyses say little about the growth rate of TFP, they may further deepen the IT paradox.[11]

The situation is much the same for externalities. At the microeconomic level, we have some evidence of the effects of externalities from IT; see, for example, Greenstein *et al.* (1997). But at the macroeconomic level, we have few empirical results in spite of the rich accumulation of theoretical models. One of the reasons may be the difficulty in identifying ways of propagation of the new technology itself. Some academic economists have begun to tackle this difficult problem by analyzing huge amounts of information on patent registration and citation from the USA. From their results, we have some interesting insights in this area. Eaton and Kortum (1996) show that the effects of the international transfer of technology by patent citation are enhanced by the level of human capital accumulation in the host country. Jaffe and Trajtenberg (1996) also suggest that patents registered by corporate firms are more frequently cited than those registered by national laboratories and universities. However, as Griliches (1994) warns, before we can discuss the mechanism of propagation of technology by using these results, we should be clear about the relationship between the contents of a patent and its fruits, and the stability of the relationship. As for the studies using parent information, we may be at the stage of accumulating empirical results to formulate some stylized facts.[12]

Adjustment costs of the introduction of new technology

Although new technology may be able to improve economic performance through various mechanisms, it may not be easy to see the results in such a short time. As lessons from past industrial revolutions suggest, various kinds of adjustment costs may have roles in delaying the propagation of new technology. In this section, we discuss the effects of such adjustment costs by using existing theoretical models and empirical results.

Adjustment costs at the microeconomic level

In a market economy, for each firm, it is uncertain about the aggregate results of introducing new technology, because the results themselves will be the effects of the decision-making by each firm. In addition, the standard of technologies may be changed more frequently because of the increasing productivity of R&D activities, as is clear from recent developments in the operating systems of PCs. In this situation, the switching cost is a very important factor each firm needs to take into account when deciding the optimal timing of converting technologies. Bresnahan and Greenstein (1996) illustrate the consequences of switching costs for converting computer systems in a firm: not only the cost of replacement hardware, but also the costs of developing new software, retraining staff in the information system department, and changing the ways of using computers at the end-user level.

When a switching cost exists, we have the lock-in effect of the so-called *de facto* standards as Farrel and Saloner (1986), or Klemperer (1987a, 1987b) show. Moreover, Farrel and Shapiro (1988) insist that such effects may be strengthened when suppliers are able to control the value of switching costs. However, we should not be in a hurry to judge that the switching cost will always prevent the introduction of new technology. For example, Stein (1997) discusses the effects of switching costs in the framework of 'creative destruction'. 'Creative destruction' was an idea first explored by Schumpeter (1934); it refers to the phenomenon in which the endogenous introduction of new goods and services, or new ways of production, continually destroys the old ones. He assumes that the switching cost for buyers is increasing over time by learning-by-doing, and that innovations outside the market benefit potential suppliers. Under such assumptions, the longer the incumbent supplier dominates this market, the more probably it will continue to dominate it; on the other hand, once a new entry has occurred, the more frequently such a conversion will occur again.[13,14]

By focusing on the idea that technological systems have played a major role in previous industrial revolutions, we can present some new implications as well. In the present industrial revolution, we have a system of computers and communication networks. Milgrom and Roberts (1990) illustrate that, by connecting computers via communication networks, a firm can improve its efficiency in production with the integration of CAD and FMS (Flexible Manufacturing System), or in its white-collar office with computerized control of its inventories and funds. Since we can observe a dramatic increase in investment in communications in recent years (see Figure 14.3), these effects will have a big impact on business activities as a whole.

As will be clear from the above discussion, network externality plays a major role in the present industrial revolution. Network externalities, as discussed by Katz and Shapiro (1985) are the externalities by which each buyer or user will be benefited from the increase in their number. This line of argument is, of course, applicable to the analysis of the actions of firms, by focusing on their demand for goods and services in the form of capital equipment and intermediate inputs. Then the effect of externalities may be regarded as the increase in marginal productivity of such inputs. We can say that the effects of network externalities are positive for economic performance, if the full compatibility is satisfied by all the users of the system. In the example given by Milgrom and Roberts (1990), a firm will benefit if more retailers or banks are connected to such a network.

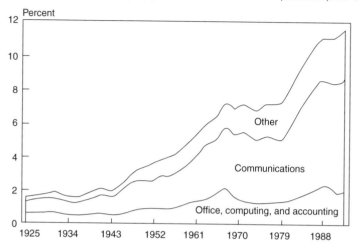

[1] Information processing equipment as a share of the net capital stock (1925–93)

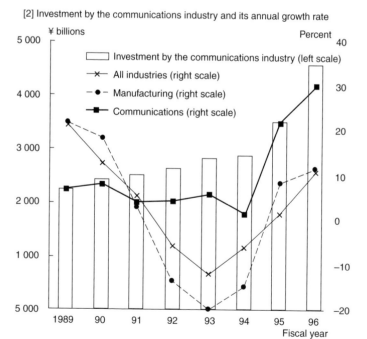

[2] Investment by the communications industry and its annual growth rate

Figure 14.3 Information processing equipment as a share of the net capital stock (1925–93) in the United States and investment in communications in Japan.
Sources: Sichel (1997); Ministry of Posts and Telecommunications.

However, if we start from a more realistic situation where there is no unification of such networks, we may have some difficulties in reaching optimality. For example, as Katz and Shapiro (1985), and Matutes and Regibeau (1988) show, if there are costs for each firm to adjust its product to make it compatible, a firm may not choose to supply compatible products, since the benefit of increased demand may leak to other firms just because of network externality itself. In such a situation, a firm will deliberately supply a product which is incompatible with the standard product. In addition, in a period of rapid innovation, it may be quite hard for a firm to make a correct forecast of what kind of specification will be the standard in the future. Thus, in some cases, network externality may delay the propagation of new technology.

Adjustment costs at the macroeconomic level

We turn now to the effects of adjustment costs at the macroeconomic level. First, we shall discuss the aggregate effect of adjustment costs at the microeconomic level. In the present industrial revolution, the production or customization of computer software, and the education of staff in information systems departments, may be major sources of microeconomic-level adjustment costs, as Bresnahan and Greenstein (1996) insist. From the macroeconomic point of view, these kinds of costs may be regarded as the costs of developing complementary inputs for new technology. Based on this idea, Helpman and Trajtenberg (1994, 1996) show the general equilibrium model with R&D activities and imperfect competition in the markets of intermediate inputs. Their model shows very interesting characteristics in the trajectory between equilibria; we have to wait before accelerating in the growth of production, since, at the first stage of innovation (they call it a 'time to sow'), a larger proportion of productive resources must be devoted to R&D activities. In fact, the model suggests that there is a possibility of an economic downturn during this trajectory. On the other hand, the benefits of this innovation will be realized and the growth rate accelerated in the second stage. For our discussion of price mechanisms in the following section, we should note that the relative prices of labour and capital, and the relative wages of skilled and unskilled labour play important roles in the reallocation of such productive resources.

Another source of adjustment cost at the macroeconomic level is the cost of reallocation of productive resources. A firm that introduces new technology improves efficiency in production. As a result, compensation to productive resources employed by the firm will be improved by increasing marginal productivity. In a neoclassical general equilibrium model, capital and labour will move from other firms seeking these excess returns, and in the end, arrive at another equilibrium with no excess returns. However, in reality, a cost has to be paid to reallocate productive resources, since they were originally specified to comply with a certain method of production. In the literature of irreversibility of investment', Abel and Eberly (1995, 1996) illustrates the effects of the cost of reallocation of capital equipment. Their main result is that, even if there is an excess return of investment in some industry, it may persist for some time, since it may be optimal for some investors to do nothing because of the existence of such costs. Aghion and Howitt (1992), and Cabarello and Hammour (1994) also show that the costs of reallocation may enhance the effects of the 'creative destruction' we saw above.

Human capital is, of course, another important source of productive resources. We shall review the impact of IT on the compensation to human capital before we proceed to consider the effects of the costs of reallocation. A representative analysis is carried out in Krueger (1993). Krueger insists that the wage premium of computer users is about 10 per cent of the average wage. However, a series of analyses by Goldin and Katz (1996), Entorf and Guellec (1997), and DiNardo and Pischke (1997) point out that there might be an error in the regression specification; Krueger's result only shows that most computer users are high-ranking officers in their firms.[15] On the other hand, Kremer and Maskin (1996), and Agénor and Aizenman (1997) find empirically that the wage premium of skill in more articulate econometric models.[16,17] We also have a positive correlation between IT investment and the average level of skill in labour, which is shown by Wolff (1996), Doms (1997) and Motohashi (1996) for most developed countries. Therefore, we may conclude that IT investment is one of the sources of the wage premium of skilled labour via the increasing demand for skilled labour, as Lichtenberg (1993) suggests.

If such a premium exists, skilled labour moves to firms and industries where it will be better compensated. We may discuss the effects of the costs of reallocation by applying the above-mentioned 'irreversibility of investment' models. In a labour market, however, people react 'endogenously' to such a change in relative wages. They decide how much to invest in training for a required skill by comparing its costs and benefits. Such effects of human capital investment may be analyzed by using the two-sector growth model by Uzawa (1996), for example. Alternatively, using the simpler models of Grossman and Helpman (1991, ch. 3), or Cabarello and Hammour (1994), with a Leontief production function, we can show that if the cost of moving capital or skill retraining increases, the effect of IT investment decreases, since the supply of skilled labour decreases.

Information as an input for production

Information itself plays two different major roles in IT innovation. The first is as shown above: information as technology alone, or as embodied in some kinds of capital equipment or intermediate inputs. The second role is as the object of investment or consumption. For example, a firm buys market research data for more efficient marketing. People also consume the kinds of information presented by the internet or satellite communication. In the last part of this chapter, we shall discuss briefly the implications of the second role.

Almost all kinds of information have in common the characteristics of externalities such as non-excludability and non-rivalry. Standard microeconomics suggests that there may be excess demand in such a market, because suppliers are not optimally compensated as a result of the existence of externalities. Innovations in IT may make the situation better, since it may make it feasible for suppliers to exclude free-riders or to collect its fee at a lower cost. In addition, there may be even an excess supply of information, since the costs of delivery and storage of information will be decreased rapidly. We may also suspect that increasing returns to scale operate in the information delivery industries such as market research.

In addition to these stereotyped arguments, we would like to discuss whether the innovations of IT affect the asymmetry of information,[18] or the formation of expectations of future events, because this question has very important implication for financial markets where market participants consume the second type of information when deciding their transactions. With the introduction of IT, it is much easier and cheaper to collect information on the developments of markets – for example, the data on historical price. It is unclear, on the other hand, whether innovations in IT make it easier to access or produce information concerning the credit risks of other participants. Even when they have the same information, we have little idea whether or not they develop similar expectations. Considering the importance of this area of discussion, we hope that there will be future developments in both theoretical and empirical studies.

The impact of IT on the price mechanism and implications for monetary policy

In this last section we shall discuss the implications for monetary policy of innovations in IT. As we saw above, innovations in IT can have many and various effects on our economy, therefore we should check whether such effects will change the optimal way monetary policy is conduced. Because we do not yet have a literature on such a specific line of argument, our analysis here will be a patchwork of various theoretical models. However, we hope that this will be a starting point for future discussions by those who have an interest in this area.

Our strategy here is to focus on the price mechanism. As we discussed in preceding sections, innovations in IT will affect prices in various ways. Because of differences in marginal productivities between firms, and the effects of quality changes and substitution, the relative prices of productive resources, goods and services related to TFP growth are changed. These changes in relative prices should be regarded as desirable, since they play the role of signposts that enable firms and households to make optimal decisions. Under the standard framework of the Phillips curve or the NAIRU, effects of innovations in IT can be regarded as a 'supply shock', which will bring about a fall in the general price level or inflation rate and a rise in GDP growth.

These developments of the price mechanism have several very important implications for conducting monetary policy. As we saw in the second section above, mismeasurement of the price index related to innovations in IT has been detected almost everywhere. One of the most serious effects on monetary policy is the possibility of damaging credibility in central banks. As for 'supply shocks', standard discussion will guide us to the conclusion that we need not make any accommodation at all. However, it might be necessary to re-examine the optimal way of conducting monetary policy if the changes in relative prices have a simultaneous influence on the general price level. This is because, if uncertainty exists with regard to the general price level, efficiency may also be lost, since we can not observe the changes in relative prices accurately. Or, if nominal rigidities exist in some part of the economy, even perfectly foreseen fluctuations in the general price level will make the economy deviate from optimality. We shall discuss these issues below.

Mismeasurement of the price index and monetary policy

Concerning the way in which monetary policy is conducted, confidence has been the key concept following the seminal work by Kydland and Prescott (1977). In order to run the economy efficiently, they argue that it is of the utmost importance for central banks to increase confidence in monetary policy, since doing so will stabilize the expectations of inflation on the part of investors and consumers. Monetary Policy Targeting has been suggested as one of the practical ways to enhance such credibility. Taylor emphasizes that such policy is definitely different from policy rules, in the sense that monetary policy targeting should be regarded as a system of policy or a policy commitment. More concretely, while it is sought strictly for the achievement of an ultimate target of money supply alone under a rule of money supply, we do not in principle have any operational or medium target under a system of monetary policy targeting. There are two kinds of opinion as to which economic indicator should be better as a target. For example, Mishkin (1997) supports inflation targeting, since the price index is better for accuracy and frequency; he also suggests that it might be easier to reach a consensus on the target rate. On the other hand, Taylor (1985) and Hall and Mankiw (1997), for example, support nominal GDP targeting, since inflation targeting may have a 'deflationary' bias; they also insist that 'supply shocks' can be accommodated automatically under nominal GDP targeting.

Before we can judge which target is better suited to conditions of innovation in IT, we should, of course, take into consideration mismeasurement of the price index. If such mismeasurement exists, inflation targeting policy may not be feasible, since it may be difficult for both the central bank and private agents to judge whether such targets are being achieved successfully. Also, as with nominal GDP targeting, it may be difficult to set the optimal level of such a target, since we may not be able to review accurately the performance of inflation and real GDP.

For the purposes of this argument, we need to examine the characteristics of measurement errors caused by innovations in IT. For example, even if such measurement error exists, when the value of such error is stationary in a time series, it may not cause us too much trouble. The reason is that both central bankers and private agents can estimate the true rate of inflation by taking into consideration the average rate of errors. We should note, however, that such stationary errors may bring difficulties when they are large, since a wide target range has to be set. Alternatively, there may be a time lag before we have an accurate estimate of such errors. Either of these possibilities may damage confidence in a monetary policy targeting. But it is when such errors are non-stationary in a time series that more serious problems arise. With the errors of such characteristics, it may be almost impossible for us even to estimate the inflation rate, or, needless to say, to judge whether or not the target has been achieved.

Although examining the characteristics of the measurement errors of a price index is a very important task, there have been very few theoretical or empirical studies undertaken around this issue. The reason is, of course, that such errors cannot be observed directly from economic statistics. From the analysis of the effects of the hedonic approach by Shiratsuka (1995) and a number of empirical studies on quality adjustment quoted by Boskin (1996), we may suspect that measurement errors resulting from quality changes and substitution effects are volatile in a time series. Although Gordon (1992) shows that such errors may disappear at the time of revision of price indexes, we might say that five or ten years are relatively long lags for us when considering price changes caused by rapid innovation in IT. Thus we have discovered another serious problem in the mismeasurement of price indexes. When we take into consideration the fact that measurement errors of price indexes themselves are difficult to reduce, it may be feasible to change the method of constructing inflation indexes for the purpose of conducting efficient monetary policy.

Supply shocks and monetary policy

The Phillips curve/NAIRU.   It may be accepted that the standard framework for discussing the effects of innovation on the macroeconomy is the Phillips curve or the NAIRU. Under such a framework, the effects of innovation in IT can be regarded as 'supply shocks', which bring about a higher growth rate of GDP and a lower rate of unemployment without raising the rate of inflation. We can regard this change as the curve will shift to the left in the Phillips curve, or a fall of the NAIRU in some cases.

The recent macroeconomic situation of the USA at least coincides a with the result discussed above. Stiglitz (1997), Gordon (1997) and Lown and Rich (1997) emphasize that the NAIRU in the USA has fallen greatly from a rate of about 7 per cent in the 1980s to the around 5 percent at the end of the 1990s (Figure 14.4).[19] In the case of Japan, many academic economists are negative even about its existence.[20] The reason is argued to be that the expected rate of inflation has been insensitive to changes in the actual rate of inflation, and thus acceleration of inflation has not occurred since the oil price shock of 1973.

With regard to the reason for the fall in the NAIRU in the USA, Stiglitz (1997) and Gordon (1997) point out the possibility that improvements in productivity brought about by innovations in IT acted as 'supply shocks', in addition to a decreased mark-up caused by global competition in major products, and a higher elasticity of labour supply. With labour markets, if such innovations in IT bring about excess demand for skilled labour, this may cause an upward pressure on the NAIRU, as Blanchard and Katz (1997) suggest. We have, however, counter-evidence in the empirical study by Tootel (1994) which shows that there are scarcely any segments of the labour market in which such a mismatch of skilled labour is serious.

Thus, if we discuss the effects of innovations in IT under the framework of the Phillips curve or the NAIRU, we are led to conclude that such supply shocks should be regarded as a desirable change, and that monetary policy should not accommodate them at all. However, we should be careful about the possibility of incurring the costs of falling prices of some goods and services. This line of argument might be relevant to Japan where near-zero inflation can be observed. In the following sections, I shall review the discussions concerning the relationship between relative price and general price levels, and the costs of falling prices. I shall then re-examine the appropriateness of the 'supply shocks' comments made above.

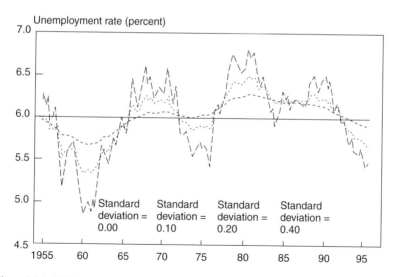

Figure 14.4   NAIRU for chain-weighted GDP deflator
Source: Gordon (1997).

Relative prices and the general price level. In the first half of this chapter we have seen the evidence for and the mechanisms by which the relative prices of goods and services related to innovations in IT have been decreased (see, for example, (Figure 14.5). Although it may sound natural to consider that this fall in relative prices bears some relationship to the general price level, it appears that academic economists have not reached a conclusion on what kinds of influences relative prices and the general price level have on each other. Nor do we understand in which direction causality exists.

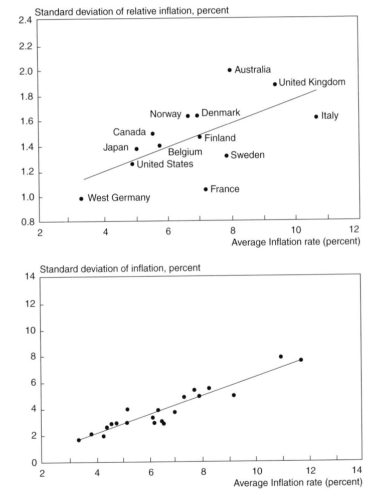

Figure 14.5 Inflation and volatility of relative prices/inflation, 1960–92.
Source: Hess and Morris (1996).

Some of the empirical studies – for example, one of the earliest ones by Vinning and Elwertowski (1976), and later studies by Parks (1978), Domberger (1987), and Ball and Mankiw (1992), report that they found a positive correlation between them. Moreover, Taylor (1981), and Hess and Morris (1996) show that such a positive correlation was identified in many of OECD countries in which inflation rates were higher see (Figure 14.8). As for the reasons for this positive correlation, we have a variety of hypotheses, most of which we see in the list by Fischer (1981) (see Table 14.4). For example, Mussa (1977), and Ball and Mankiw (1992) emphasize a combination of 'menu cost' and distortion of the distribution of shocks. Taylor (1981) and Plosser (1997) suggest that the endogenous action of monetary policy in the face of relative price change is the reason for changes in general price level. According to this hypothesis, even when relative price change itself has nothing to do with general price level, the general price level is changed by monetary policy. Domberger (1987), and Debelle and Lamont (1997) are negative towards macroeconomic reasons because they observe such a positive correlation even in their cross-sectional settings. Because we have not reached a conclusion on the reason for such a positive correlation, I, of course, am not able to say anything on the direction of causality. We should also note that some empirical results suggest that this correlation is weaker when the rate of inflation is very low. We can observe this characteristic in Japan (see Figure 14.6).

Even in such an ambiguous situation, there is at least one important implication for our discussion here. That is to say, we might at least imagine

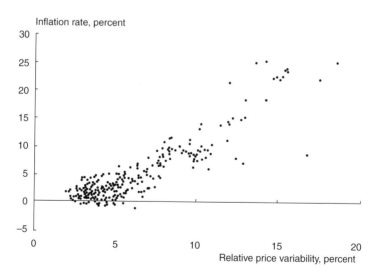

Figure 14.6   Inflation and volatility of relative prices in Japan (1971:2–1997:III)

424

Table 14.4 Hypotheses for the relation between relative price change and inflation

Approach	Exogenous factors	Function of inflation associated with relative price variability	Welfare implications
1. Market clearing with imperfect information	Policy disturbances	Unanticipated inflation or deflation	Misperceived aggregate disturbances produce resource misallocations
2. Menu costs	Inflation rate	Inflation or deflation	Inflation or deflation creates resource misallocations and generates unnecessary transaction costs
3. Asymmetric price response	Relative disturbances	Either inflation rate or inflation in excess of base rate	Price inflexibility feeds to resource misallocations: there is too little relative price variability
4. Relative shocks same as aggregate shocks	Real disturbances	Deviations of inflation from underlying rate in either direction depending on type of shock	Relative prices should vary for efficient allocation
5. Allocative effects of macro policy	Changes in policy	Changes in inflation rate	Given the changes in policy, relative prices should vary for efficient allocation
6. Endogenous policy	Real disturbances	Same as 3	Policy may offset welfare loss associated with relative shocks by making appropriate price adjustments possible

Source: Fischer (1981).

the possibility that downward forces are working simultaneously on the general price level, since we have some evidence of falling relative prices of goods and services in IT. Although this possibility may be a big 'if', I suppose that it deserves careful consideration, since a falling general price level has some important effects, as will be shown below.

The cost of falling prices – noise in respect of the observation of relative prices. In order to examine the cost of falling prices, it may be useful to start by reversing the arguments concerning rising prices. Cost of holding the money will be 'negative' in a situation of falling prices. In addition, Aiyagari (1990) and Wolman (1997) point out that this kind of cost will be negligible in the near future, since the means of transaction will be interest-bearing. Distortionary effects from a nominally fixed tax will also benefit tax-payers. Then the rest of the arguments consists of a problem concerning the informational function of a price. In other words, when the rate of change in the general price level becomes volatile, it becomes quite difficult to observe relative price changes accurately, and therefore difficult for economic agents to make optimal decisions. In such a situation, it is also problematic to allocate inter-temporal investment and consumption, since it is difficult for firms and households to observe inter-temporal relative prices (or the real discount rate), as Fischer (1993) shows. Although this line of argument generally refers to a period of high inflation, the argument may also be true when inflation is low, or during a period of deflation. As Hess and Morris (1996) show, if the linear relationship between volatility and the level of inflation rate is true, the ratio of the volatility to the level is constant regardless of the rate of inflation.

As for the relationship between innovations in IT and noise to observation of relative prices, we are able to present two important points. First, innovations in IT comprise several opposing forces. It is often argued that such innovations in IT make it easier to collect information on prices in general. On the other hand, it is quite difficult to measure prices accurately because of the mismeasurement of prices or price indexes.[21] If imperfect competition is one of the characteristics of the market in conditions of innovation, we may doubt whether fluctuations in mark-up ratios constitute another source of this noise.[22]

Second, it is important to note that when we discuss the price changed resulting from innovations in IT, we have to reverse the causality applicable to the cost of fluctuations in the general price level. We might assume implicitly that the accurate observation of changes in relative prices is prevented by exogenous changes in the general price level. On the other hand, in the argument concerning innovations in IT, by assuming that changes in the general price level occur simultaneously with changes in relative prices related to such innovations, the accurate observation of changes in the general price level are in turn prevented by relative price changes. Although our argument here appears to be contradictory, it may be worth examining if we add one more assumption that each firm or household is not able to observe relative price changes other than those of a few products with which it is familiar.

The cost of falling prices – nominal rigidity. Thus we have examined the reversed arguments concerning the costs of inflation. However, we have, another important argument which has no counterpart in the argument about inflation: it is the cost of nominal rigidity. A recent study by Blinder (1997) shows the evidence of nominal rigidities, and insists that the effects depend on factors such as co-ordination failures, imperfect competition, and implicit contracts. With nominal rigidities in some prices, as discussed in Aiyagari (1990) or Bernanke and Mishkin (1996), a fall in the general price level causes a substantial cost to the economy because of the inefficiency of the allocation of resources. For example, Akerlof *et al.* (1996) show, using their simulation model assuming rigidity in nominal wages, that the unemployment rate will be increased by 2.6 per cent when the inflation rate goes down from 3 per cent to 0 per cent. Moreover, Fuhrer (1994) and Freedman and Kuttner (1996) suggest that we should be very careful about the cost of disinflation when nominal rigidities exist in some prices.

As a matter of course, it should be noted that some academic economists present arguments against the existence of nominal rigidity. For example, in a comment in Akerlof *et al.* (1996), Gordon insists that the 'Lucas critique' is valid for their result; he argues that their empirical result of nominal rigidity shows only that a fall in nominal wages has been rare in the years of relatively high inflation. It is often suggested that workers may accept a fall in nominal wages during a period of lower inflation. As for Japan, most empirical studies, including those by Sachs (1979) and Gordon (1982) suggest that nominal wages have been more flexible than in other industrialized countries. Ueda and Kimura (1997) analyse empirically the mechanism of such flexibility by decomposing the wage into its component parts; they show that total compensation is very flexible, since it is adjusted by overtime compensation and bonuses.[23]

Thus the existence of nominal rigidity is still ambiguous, especially in a period of low inflation. At this moment, all we can point to is the possibility that, if the general price level falls because of a decrease in the prices of services related to computers and communications, *and if* nominal rigidity exists in some areas, such as in the wages of unskilled labour, a substantial cost may be incurred to the economy.

We may now summarize the two hypotheses discussed above. In general, if macroeconomic changes resulting from innovations in IT can be regarded as 'supply shocks' in a framework of the Phillips curve or the NAIRU, it may be optimal for monetary policy not to accommodate such shocks. On the other hand, if the changes in relative prices resulting from innovations in IT exhibit a correlation with the general price level, and if there exists a volatile general price level or nominal rigidities, a fall in the general price level may incur a substantial cost to the economy because of the inefficiencies in allocation.[24] In such a situation, accommodation by monetary policy might be better in the sense of optimality.[25] Thus, it should be our task in the future to examine empirically and explain theoretically the existence of pressures induced by relative price changes, and the conditions around the optimality of monetary policy under volatile inflation and/or nominal rigidity.

End notes

We have tried to present a comprehensive list of issues for discussion. Our final and most important goal is discussing and understanding the optimal ways of conducting monetary policy under the changing economic performance through innovation in IT. Although the effects of the innovation can be regarded as favourable 'supply shocks', we should also note the following possibilities which might be brought about by the innovation itself. First, the measurement error of economic statistics may incur some damage to the credibility of monetary policy, because such errors may make the accurate observation of economic performance quite difficult. Second, a fall in the general price level may cause a loss of efficiency, if there exists some correlation between relative price and general price levels, *and if* there exists nominal rigidity.

As will be clear from the discussion in this chapter, existing theoretical models and empirical studies have interesting implications, but with a limited coverage. In order to understand our changing economy and maintain its efficiency, we should tackle the tasks of further investigation one by one.

Notes

1. Some empirical studies, including Morrison and Berndt (1991) and Morrison (1997) show that increasing returns to scale can be observed at the firm level. If these findings are correct, the most important problems may lie at the aggregate level.
2. Brynjofsson (1993) and Sichel (1997) categorize the hypotheses for the IT paradox as follows: (i) mismanagement (there exists some overinvestment in IT); (ii) redistribution (investment in IT will bring about social costs and private profits); (iii) learning (we are in a learning situation with IT); (iv) a small share of computer stock in total capital stock (the share of computers in capital stock is still very small); (v) mismeasurement (we cannot observe the effects due to mismeasurements in statistics). It should be noted that (i), (ii), and (iii) are related to the adjustment costs of introducing new technologies; and (iv) and (v) can be categorized as the hypothesis of measurement errors in economic statistics.
3. Goldfinger (1997) quotes Gordon's findings that the share of economic values in the USA with accurate measurements fell from 50 per cent in 1947 to 30 per cent in 1990.

4. We should note that mismeasurement of value added in service industries brings about a serious problem for estimating GDP. The reason is that, in service industries, the share of value added to gross product is much larger than in manufacturing, since most of the inputs to service industries consist of labour.

5. Although the hedonic approach was introduced to estimate the price index of computers in both the USA and Japan, its coverage has been limited so far.

6. On the other hand, Mokyr (1997) suggests that the propagation of computers may be much harder than those of key technologies of past revolutions, since computers constitute the only technology in which a human interface is deeply involved.

7. David (1990) shows the importance of the structural change of a firm. Since a steam engine was very large and expensive, an ordinary firm installed only one engine and used its power for many purposes; the power generated by an engine being transmitted through shafts and belts to all parts to the factory. In order to ensure the efficient transmission of power, a factory was in general built vertically. But in an electrified firm, motors were installed for each part of the factory. By this dispersion of power generation, factories with a horizontal structure were made feasible, which dramatically decreased the costs of construction.

8. For example, Ramey and Shapiro (1997) simulate the development of the macroeconomy in the period of reallocation of capital caused by a demand shock under the assumption of irreversibility of investment.

9. The simplest way to apply their model to our discussion on the effects of new technology is to regard 'G' (infrastructure built by government expenditure) as new technologies.

10. At the microeconomic level as well, empirical results are mixed. Some studies, including Morrison (1997), suggest the existence of increasing return to scale at a firm level. On the other hand, most of the arguments of the Real Business Cycle school are based on the assumption of decreasing returns to scale at the firm level.

11. We should note that whether we should use gross product or value added for calculating TFP remains a difficult question to answer. For example, if we consider this question in relation to measurement errors in economic statistics, both alternatives have problems of quality adjustment; with gross product, there may be the problem in aggregation; and with value added, we may have the problem in estimating capital and labour inputs.

12. Cabarello and Jaffe (1993) also report that the number of patent registrations per cost of R&D activities has been decreasing in the USA. Although it this is a very interesting finding indeed, we should check the relationship between the contents of a patent and its fruits before we can conclude that the productivity of R&D activity has been decreasing.

13. Aghion and Howitt (1992) insist, however, on the possibility that the acceleration of innovation may harm incentives for R&D. The reason for this is that a potential entrant may expect that he/she will not be able to dominate the market for a long period because of the acceleration of innovation itself.

14. Concerning the cleansing effect that has been also discussed in the literature of creative destruction, some empirical studies deny its existence. See, for example, Cabarello and Hammour (1994).

15. For example, DiNardo and Pischke (1997) report that they found the wage premium of telephone users to be 9–14 per cent of the average wage under the same framework as Krueger (1993).

16. Agénor and Aizenman (1997) point out that, other than skill-biased innovation, the reasons for such a discrepancy in relative wages are the existence of an efficient wage for skilled labour, and downward pressure on the wage of unskilled labour through increased competition in unskilled-labor-intensive industries.
17. It should be noted that the 'skills' are rather well defined in the USA in the data by the Department of Labour, or the Census Bureau.
18. It should be noted that the asymmetry of information is a relevant concept only in a situation where one person has correct information but the other does not. It may also be important for us to consider the situation in which all the agents do not have correct information.
19. At the same time, we should note that some academic economists including Chang (1997) deny the usefulness of NAIRU, since the macroeconomics structure underlying the NAIRU should always be changing depending on the kinds of shocks affecting the economy.
20. On the other hand, some empirical studies exist showing that the NAIRU went up in the 1990s in Japan. See, for example, Nishizaki (1997).
21. In such a situation, suppliers may not want to change their prices frequently, because the benefits of price changes are also ambiguous for them.
22. Baba (1997) shows that, when the fluctuation in mark-up is considered, the cost of inflation in Japan increased by nearly 1 per cent of GDP in the years from 1974 to 1992.
23. At the same time, they show that the hourly wage is less flexible. Based on these results, if overtime compensation and bonuses reach zero because of a long-lasting depression, employment may be more flexible.
24. We may add another source from the 'Fisher relation'. If the expected rate of inflation falls to a very low level, monetary policy may not be able to stimulate the economy. The reason for this is that the real interest rate cannot be set low enough, even if the central bank sets the nominal interest rate at zero.
25. In discussing the optimality of monetary policy, of course, we should also take into consideration the effects of the changes in expected rate of inflation.

References

Abel, A. and Eberly, J. (1995) 'The Effects of Irreversibility and Uncertainty on Capital Accumulation', NBER Working Paper No. 5363.

Abel, A. and Eberly, J. (1996) 'Optimal Investment with Costly Reversibility', *Review of Economic Studies*, vol. 63, pp. 581–93.

Abramovitz, M. and David, P. (1996) 'Convergence and Deferred Catch-up: Productivity Leadership and the Waning of American Exceptionalism', in R. Landau, T. Taylor and G. Wright (eds), *The Mosaic of Economic Growth* (Palo Alto, Calif.: Stanford University Press), pp. 21–62.

Agénor, P. R. and Aizenman, J. (1997) 'Technological Change, Relative Wages, and Unemployment', *European Economic Review*, vol. 41, pp. 187–205.

Aghion, P. and Howitt, P. (1992) 'A Model of Growth through Creative Destructión', *Econometrica*, vol. 60 no. 2, pp. 323–51.

Aiyagari, R. (1990) 'Deflating the Case for Zero Inflation', *Quarterly Review*, Federal Reserve Bank of Minneapolis, pp. 2–11.

Aiyagari, R. (1994) 'On the Contribution of Technology Shocks to Business Cycles', *Quarterly Review*, Federal Reserve Bank of Minneapolis (Winter), pp. 22–34.

Akerlof, G., Dickens, W. and Perry, G. (1996) 'The Macroeconomics of Low Inflation', *Brookings Papers on Economic Activity*, vol. 1, pp. 1–76.

Baba, N. (1997) 'Markup Pricing and Monetary Policy: A Reexamination of the Effectiveness of Monetary Policy under Imperfect Competition', IMES Discussion Paper Series No. 97-E-2, Bank of Japan.

Baily, M. and Gordon, R. (1988) 'The Productivity Slowdown, Measurement Issues, and the Explosion of Computer Power', *Brookings Papers on Economic Activity*, vol. 2, pp. 347–431.

Ball, L. and Mankiw, G. (1992) 'Relative-Price Changes as Aggregate Supply Shocks', NBER Working Paper No. 4168.

Barro, R. (1990) 'Government Spending in a Simple Model of Endogenous Growth', *Journal of Political Economy*, vol. 98, no. 2, pp. s103–s125.

Basu, S. and Fernald, J. (1997a) 'Returns to Scale in U.S. Production: Estimates and Implications', *Journal of Political Economy*, vol. 105, no. 2, pp. 249–83.

Basu, S. and Fernald, J. (1997b) 'Aggregate Productivity and Aggregate Technology', International Finance Discussion Papers, Board of Governors of the Federal. Reserve System, No. 593.

Bernanke, B. and Mishkin, F. (1996) 'Inflation Targeting: A New Framework for Monetary Policy', NBER Working Paper No. 5893.

Berndt, R. and Griliches, Z. (1993) 'Price Indexes for Microcomputers: An Explanatory Study', in M. Foss, M. Manser and A. Young (eds) *Price Measurements and Their Uses*, BER Studies in Income and Wealth, vol. 57, pp. 63–95.

Blanchard, O. and Katz, L. (1997) 'What We Know and Do Not Know about the Natural Rate of Unemployment', *Journal of Economic Perspectives*, vol. 11, no. 1, pp. 3–10.

Blinder, A. (1997) 'On Sticky Prices: Academic Theories Meet the Real World', in Gregory Mankiw (ed.), *Monetary Policy* (University of Chicago Press).

Boskin, M. (1996) 'Toward a More Accurate Measure of the Cost of Living: Final Report to the Senate Finance Committee from the Advisory Commission to Study the Consumer Price Index', U.S. Congress.

Bresnahan, T. and Trajtenberg, M. (1995) 'General Purpose Technologies "Engines of Growth"?', *Journal of Econometrics*, vol. 65, pp. 83–108.

Bresnahan, T. and Greenstein, S. (1996) 'Technical Progress and Co-Invention in Computing and in the Uses of Computers', *Brookings Papers on Microeconomics*, pp. 1–83.

Brown, K. and Greenstein, S. (1995) 'How Much Better is Bigger, Faster, and Cheaper? Buyer Benefits from Innovation in Mainframe Computers in the 1980's', NBER Working Paper No. 5138.

Brynjofsson, E. (1993) 'The Productivity Paradox of Information Technology', *Communications of the Association for Computing Machinery* (December), pp. 66–77.

Burnside, C. (1996) 'Production Function Regressions, Return to Scale, and Externalities', *Journal of Monetary Economics*, vol. 37, pp. 177–201.

Cabarello, R. and Lyons, R. (1992) 'External Effects in U.S. Procyclical Productivity', *Journal of Monetary Economics*, vol. 29, pp. 209–26.

Cabarello, R. and Jaffe, A. (1993) 'How High are the Giants' Shoulders: An Empirical Assessment of Knowledge Spillovers and Creative Destruction in a Model of Economic Growth', *NBER Macroeconomic Annual*, pp. 15–74.

Cabarello, R. and Hammour, M. (1994) 'The Cleansing Effect of Recessions', *American Economic Review*, vol. 84, no. 5, pp. 1350–68.

Chang, R. (1997) 'Is Low Unemployment Inflationary?', *Economic Review*, Federal Reserve Bank of Atlanta (First Quarter), pp. 4–13.

Crafts, N. (1996) 'The First Industrial Revolution: A Guided Tour for Growth Economists', *AEA Papers and Proceedings*, vol. 86, no. 2; pp. 197–201.

David, P. (1990) 'The Dynamo and the Computer: An Historical Perspective on the Modern Productivity Paradox', *AEA Papers and Proceedings*, vol. 80, no. 2, pp. 355–61.

David, P. (1994) 'Positive Feedbacks and Research Productivity in Science: Reopening Another Black Box', in O. Grandstrand (ed.), *Economics of Technology* (Amsterdam: Elsevier Science), pp. 65–89.

Darby, M. (1992) 'Causes of Declining Growth', Paper presented at the International Symposium held by the Federal Bank of Kansas City.

Debelle, G. and Lamont, O. (1997) 'Relative Price Variability and Inflation: Evidence from U.S. Cities', *Journal of Political Economy*, vol. 105, no. 11, pp. 132–52.

Devine, W. (1983) 'From Shafts to Wires: Historical Perspectives on Electrification', *Journal of Economic History*, vol. 43, no. 2.

Diewert, E. and Fox, K. (1997) 'Can Measurement Error Explain the Productivity Paradox', Mimeo, University of New South Wales.

DiNardo, J. and Pischke, J. S. (1997) 'The Returns to Computer Use Revised: Have Pencils Changed the Wage Structure too?', *Quarterly Journal of Economics* (February), pp. 291–303.

Domberger, S. (1987) 'Relative Price Variability and Inflation: A Disaggregated Analysis', *Journal of Political Economy*, vol. 95, no. 3, pp. 547–66.

Doms, M., Dunne, T. and Troske, K. (1997) 'Workers, Wages, and Technology', *Quarterly Journal of Economics* (February), pp. 253–90.

Dosi, G. (1981) 'Technical Change, Industrial Transformation, and Public Policies: The Case of the Semi-Conductor Industry', European Research Centre, University of Sussex.

Dulburger, R. (1993) 'Sources of Price Decline in Computer Processors: Selected Electronic Components', in M. Foss, M. Manser and A. Young (eds), *Price Measurements and Their Uses, NBER Studies in Income and Wealth*, vol. 57, pp. 103–24.

Eaton, J. and Kortum, S. (1996) 'Trade in Ideas: Patenting and Productivity in the OECD', *Journal of International Economics*, vol. 40, pp. 251–78.

Entorf, H. and Guellec, M. (1997) 'New Technologies, Wages and Worker Selection', CEPR Discussion Paper No. 1761.

Farrel, J. and Saloner, G. (1986) 'Standardization and Variety', *Economic Letters*, vol. 20, pp. 71–4.

Farrel, J. and Shapiro, C. (1988) 'Dynamic Competition with Switching Costs', *Rand Journal of Economics*, vol. 19, no. 1, pp. 123–37.

Fischer, S. (1981) 'Relative Shocks, Relative Price Variability', and Inflation', *Brookings Papers on Economic Activity*, vol. 2, pp. 381–441.

Fischer, S. (1993) 'The Role of Macroeconomic Factors in Growth', NBER Working Paper No. 4565.

Friedman, B. and Kuttner, K. (1996) 'A Price Target for U.S. Monetary Policy?: Lessons from the Experience with Money Growth Targets', *Brookings Papers on Economic Activity*, vol. 1, pp. 77–146.

Freeman, C. and Soete, L. (1997) *The Economics of Industrial Revolution*, 3rd edn (Cambridge, MA: MIT Press).

Fuhrer, J. (1994) 'Goals, Guidelines, and Constraints Facing Monetary Policymakers: An Overview', *New England Economic Review* (September/October), pp. 3–15.

Fukuda, S. (1997) 'Kibono keizaiseito kaheikeizainiokeru keizaiseichou' (Increasing Return to Scale and Growth of Monetary Economy) in K. Asako and M. Ohtaki (eds). *Gendai Makuro Keizaigaku* (Modern Macroeconomic Dynamics) (University of Tokyo Press).

Goldfinger, C. (1997) 'Understanding and Measuring the Intangible Economy: Current Status and Suggestions for Further Research', Paper presented at the 23rd Conference of the Centre for International Research on Economic Tendency Surveys, Helsinki.

Goldin, C. and Katz, L. (1996) 'Technology, Skill, and the Wage Structure: Insights from the Past', *AEA Papers and Proceedings*, vol. 86, no. 2, pp. 252–67.

Gordon, R. (1982) 'Why US Wage and Employment Behavior Differs from that in Britain and Japan', *Economic Journal*, vol. 92.

Gordon, R. (1990) *The Measurement of Durable Goods Prices* (University of Chicago Press).

Gordon, R. (1992) 'Measuring the Aggregate Price Level: Implications for Economic Performance and Policy', CEPR Discussion Paper No. 663.

Gordon, R. (1997) 'The Time-Varying NAIRU and its Implications for Economic Policy', *Journal of Economic Perspectives*, vol. 11, no. 1, pp. 3–10.

Gordon, R. and Griliches Z. (1997) 'Quality Change and New Products', *AEA Papers and Proceedings*, vol. 87, no. 2, pp. 84–98.

Greenstein, S., Lizardo, M. and Spiller, P. (1997) 'The Evolution of Advanced Large scale Information Infrastructure in the United States', NBER Working Paper No. 5929.

Greenwood, J., Hercowitz, Z. and Krusell, P. (1997) 'Long-Run Implications of Investment-Specific Technological Change', *American Economic Review*, vol. 87, no. 3, pp. 342–62.

Griliches, Z. (1994) 'Productivity, R&D, and the Data Constraint', *American Economic Review*, vol. 84, no. 1, pp. 1–23.

Grossman, G. and Helpman, E. (1991) *Innovation and Growth* (Cambridge, MA: MIT Press).

Hall, R. (1988) 'The Relation between Price and Marginal Cost in U.S. Industry', *Journal of Political Economy*, vol. 96, pp. 921–47.

Hall, R. and Mankiw, G. (1997) 'Nominal Income Targeting', in G. Mankiw (ed.), *Monetary Policy* (University of Chicago Press).

Helpman, E. and Trajtenberg, M. (1994) 'A Time to Sow and A Time to Reap: Growth Based on General Purpose Technologies', NBER Working Paper No. 4854.

Helpman, E. and Trajtenberg, M. (1996) 'Diffusion of General Purpose Technologies', NBER Working Paper No. 5773.

Hess, G. and Morris, C. (1996) 'The Long-Run Costs of Moderate Inflation', *Federal Reserve Bank of Kansas City Economic Review*, vol. 81, no. 2, pp. 71–88.

Jaffe, A. and Trajtenberg, M. (1996) 'Flows of Knowledge from Universities and Federal Labs: Modeling the Flow of Patent Citations over Time and across Institutional and Geographic Boundaries', NBER Working Paper No. 5712.

Jorgenson, D. W., F. Gollop and B. Fraument (1987) *Productivity and U.S. Economic Growth* (Cambridge, MA: Harvard University Press).

Katz, M. and Shapiro, C. (1985) 'Network Externalities, Competition and Compatibility', *American Economic Review*, vol. 75, no. 3, pp. 424–40.

Kitamura, Y. (1997) 'Conceptualization ni kansuru keizaisi oyobi keizairiron karano tenbou' (A Survey on Conceptualization in the Fields of Economic History and Economics), Mimeo, Bank of Japan.

Klemperer, P. (1987a) 'The Competitiveness of Markets with Switching Costs', *Rand Journal of Economics*, vol. 18, no. 1, pp. 138–50.

Klemperer, P. (1987b) 'Competition when Consumers Have Switching Costs: An Overview with Applications to Industrial Organization, Macroeconomics, and International Trade', *Review of Economic Studies*, vol. 62, pp. 515–39.

Klenow, P. (1996) 'Industry Innovation: Where and Why?', *Carnegie–Rochester Conference Series on Public Policy*, vol. 44, pp. 125–50.

Kozicki, S. (1997) 'The Productivity Growth Slowdown: Diverging Trends in the Manufacturing and Service Sectors', Federal Reserve Bank of Kansas City, *Economic Review* (First Quarter), pp. 31–46.

Kremer, M. and Maskin, E. (1996) 'Wage Inequality and Segregation by Skill', NBER Working Paper No. 5718.

Krueger, A. (1993) 'How Computers Have Changed the Wage Structure: Evidence from Microdata, 1984–1989', *Quarterly Journal of Economics* (February), pp. 33–60.

Kydland, F. and Prescott, E. (1977) 'Rules Rather than Discretion: The Inconsistency of Optimal Plans', *Journal of Political Economy*, vol. 85, pp. 473–91.

Lichtenberg, F. (1993) 'The Output Contribution of Computer Equipment and Personnel: A Firm-Level Analysis', NBER Working Paper No. 4540.

Lown, G. and Rich, R. (1997) 'Is there an Inflation Puzzle?', Federal Reserve Bank of New York Research Paper No. 9723.

Matutes, C. and Regibeau, P. (1988) 'Mix and Match: Product Compatibility without Network Externalities', *Rand Journal of Economics*, vol. 19, no. 2, pp. 221–34.

Meltzer, A. (1997) 'Investment and GDP are Understated', unpublished.

Milgrom, P. and Roberts, J. (1990) 'The Economics of Modern Manufacturing: Technology, Strategy and Organization', *American Economic Review*, vol. 80, no. 3, pp. 511–28.

Mishkin, F. (1997) 'Strategies for Controlling Inflation', NBER Working Paper No. 6122.

Mizoguchi, T. (1996) 'Zyouhousangyouno hattento mienikui zyouhouseisan souryouno henka' (Evolution of Information Service Industry and Quantity Change in Intangible Information), in *Keizaitoukeini Miru Kigyouzouhoukano Kouzu* (Information and Economy), Fujitsu Institute for Corporate Management, pp. 111–29.

Mokyr, J. (1997) 'Are We Living in the Middle of an Industrial Revolution?', Federal Reserve Bank of Kansas City, *Economic Review*, vol. 82, no. 2, pp. 31–43.

Morrison, C. and Berndt, E. (1991) 'Assessing the Productivity of Information Technology Equipment in U.S. Manufacturing Industries', NBER Working Paper No. 3582.

Morrison, C. (1997) 'Assessing the Productivity of Information Technology Equipment in U.S. Manufacturing Industries', *Review of Economics and Statistics*, pp. 471–81.

Motohashi, K. (1996) 'ICT Diffusion and its Economic Impact in OECD Countries', in *Science Technology Industry*, Special Issue on Technology, Productivity, and Employment (OECD), no. 18, pp. 13–45.

Muniagurria, M. (1995) 'Growth and Research and Development', *Journal of Economic Dynamics and Control*, vol. 15, pp. 207–35.

Mussa, M. (1977) 'The Welfare Cost of Inflation and the Role of Money as a Unit of Account', *Journal of Money, Credit and Banking* (May), pp. 276–86.

Nakamura, L. (1977) 'Is the U.S. Economy Really Growing too Slowly? Maybe We're Measuring Growth Wrong', Federal Reserve Bank of Philadelphia, *Business Review* (March/April), pp. 3–14.

Nishizaki, F. (1997) 'The NAIRU in Japan: Measurement and its Implications', Economics Department Working Papers No. 173 (OECD).

Nordhaus, W. (1972) 'The Recent Productivity Slowdown', *Brookings Papers on Economic Activity*, vol. 3, pp. 493–536.

Nordhaus, W. (1997) 'Traditional Productivity Estimates are Asleep at the Technological Switch', *Economic Journal*, vol. 107, pp. 1548–59.

Parks, R. (1978) 'Inflation and Relative Price Variability', *Journal of Political Economy*, vol. 86, no. 1, pp. 79–95.

Plosser, C. (1997) 'Global Glut, Deflation and Other Nonsense', Paper presented at the Economic Outlook Seminar, December, Rochester, N.Y.

Ramey, V. and Shapiro, M. (1997) 'Costly Capital Reallocation and the Effects of Government Spending', Paper presented at Carnegie–Rochester Public Policy Conference, Rochester, N.Y., April 18–19.

Romer, P. (1988) 'Increasing Returns and Long-Run Growth', *Journal of Political Economy*, vol. 94, no. 5, pp. 1002–37.

Rosenberg, N. (1996) 'Uncertainty and Technological Change', in R. Landau, T. Taylor and G. Wright (eds), *The Mosaic of Economic Growth* (Palo Alto, Calif.: Stanford University Press), pp. 334–53.

Sachs, J. (1979) 'Wages, Profits and Macroeconomic Adjustment: A Comparative Study', Brookings Paper on Economic Activity, no. 2.

Schumpeter, J. A. (1934) *The Theory of Economic Development* (Cambridge, MA: Harvard University Press).

Shiratsuka, S. (1995) 'Zyo'yosha kakkuno hendouto hinsitsuhenka' (Variation of Automobile Prices and the Effect of Quality Changes), *Kin'yu Kenkyu*, vol. 14, no. 3, pp. 77–120.

Sichel, D. (1997) '*The Computer Revolution–An Economic Perspective*' (Washington DC: The Brookings Institution).

Slifman, L. and Corrado, C. (1996) 'Decomposition of Productivity and Unit Costs', Board of Governors of the Federal Reserve System.

Stein, J. (1997) 'Waves of Creative Destruction: Firm-Specific Learning-by-Doing and the Dynamics of Innovation', *Review of Economic Studies*, vol. 64, pp. 265–88.

Stewert, T. (1997) *Intellectual Capital* (New York: Doubleday Books).

Stiglitz, J. (1997) 'Reflections on the Natural Rate Hypothesis', *Journal of Economic Perspectives*, vol. 11, no. 1, pp. 3–10.

Taylor, J. (1981) 'On the Relation between the Variability of Inflation and the Average Inflation Rate', Carnegie–Rochester Conference Series on Public Policy, no. 15, pp. 57–86.

Taylor, J. (1985) 'What Would Nominal GNP Targeting do to the Business Cycle?', Carnegie–Rochester Conference Series on Public Policy, no. 22, pp. 61–84.

Tootel, G. (1994) 'Restructuring, the NAIRU, and the Phillips Curve', *New England Economic Review*, Federal Reserve Bank of Boston (September/October), pp. 31–44.

Ueda, K. and Kimura, T. (1997) 'Downward Nominal Wage Rigidity in Japan: Is Price Stability Costly?', Mimeo, Research and Statistics Department, Bank of Japan.

Ueawa, H. (1966) 'Optimal Growth in a Two Sector Model of Capital Accumulation', *Review of Economic Studies*, vol. 31, pp. 1–24.

Van Ark, B. and Pilat, D. (1993) 'Productivity Levels in Germany, Japan, and the United States: Differences and Causes', Brookings Paper on Microeconomics, no. 2, pp. 1–48.

Vinning, D. and Elwertowski, T. (1976) 'The Relationship between Relative Prices and General Price Level', *American Economic Review*, vol. 66, no. 4, pp. 699–708.

Wynne, M. and Sigalla, F. (1996) 'A Survey of Measurement Biases in Price Indexes', *Journal of Economic Surveys*, vol. 10, no. 1, pp. 55–89.

Wolff, E. (1996) 'Technology and the Demand for Skills', in *Science Technology Industry*, Technology, Productivity, and Employment, Special Issue (OECD), no. 18, pp. 95–123.

Wolman, A. (1997) 'Zero Inflation and the Friedman Rule: A Welfare Comparison', *Economic Quarterly*, Federal Reserve Bank of Richmond, vol. 83, no. 4, pp. 1–21.

Index